TEJANO LEGACY

TEJANO LEGACY

Rancheros and Settlers in South Texas, 1734–1900

ARMANDO C. ALONZO

University of New Mexico Press
Albuquerque

To my loving and supportive wife, Angelita

 3rd paperbound printing, 2000

Map 1 provided courtesy of Alfonso Ramírez of Edinburg, Texas.

Library of Congress
Cataloging-in-Publication Data

Alonzo, Armando C.
Tejano legacy : rancheros and settlers in south Texas,
1734–1900 / Armando Alonzo. — 1st ed.
p. cm.
Includes bibliographical references and index.
ISBN 0–8263–1866–5 (cloth). —
ISBN 0–8263–1897–5 (paper)
1. Lower Rio Grande Valley (Tex.)—History.
2. Frontier and pioneer life—Texas—Lower Rio Grande Valley.
3. Ranchers—Texas—Lower Rio Grande Valley—History.
4. Mexicans—Texas—Lower Rio Grande Valley—History.
5. Land tenure—Texas—Lower Rio Grande Valley—History.
6. Lower Rio Grande Valley (Tex.)—Ethnic relations.
I. Title.
F392.R5A46 1998
976.4′4—dc21 97–34454 CIP

CONTENTS

MAPS

TABLES

ACKNOWLEDGMENTS

In the process of researching and writing this book, I received assistance from numerous persons and institutions. Professors George I. Juergens, Silvia Arrom, John Bodnar, and Maurice G. Baxter of my dissertation committee at Indiana University directed my initial research and offered advice that proved invaluable in expanding my original study of Tejano land tenure in Hidalgo County, Texas to this book-length project. At Southwest Texas State University, Dr. Jaime Chahin provided timely support to help me complete the data entry phase of my research and Professor Charles Johnson assisted in the computer analysis of the data bases that I utilized here.

Since 1991 Texas A & M University has provided me research support that facilitated travel to local archives and courthouses in south Texas. These trips allowed me to enlarge the study to cover the entire Lower Río Grande Valley region. In the College of Liberal Arts, I want to thank Dean Woodrow Jones Jr. and Professors Larry D. Hill and Julia Kirk Blackwelder for their continued confidence in my scholarship.

A number of scholars offered suggestions that led to improvements in the manuscript. Dean Gilberto M. Hinojosa of the University of the Incarnate Word, San Antonio, Texas recommended a regional approach to the study of Tejano history and helped clarify historical questions that arose during the writing. Professor Emilio Zamora of the University of Houston, and my colleagues Professors Maria Cristina García, Albert S. Broussard, Henry C. Schmidt, Daniel E. Bornstein, Walter D. Kamphoefner, Carol L. Higham, and Marco Portales also read different chapters of the manuscript, and I thank them for their helpful critiques and suggestions. Professors David J. Weber and

Robert Jackson also read early versions of some chapters in the summer of 1994, when I attended an NEH seminar directed by Professor Weber.

Through the years, I received encouragement and support from family and friends. My aunt Celia Herrera of Edinburg, Texas, has always been there with a warm and genuine heart and unwavering support. Professor Hugh Miller of Edinburg has been a constant source of encouragement and a steady advisor. I also want to thank Antonio Balderas Jr. of Houston, Severo Reyna of Hereford, Texas, Joe Meredith and Mary and John Wolford of Bloomington, Indiana, Ann Todd Baum and Dale Baum of College Station, Sylvia and Lloyd Navarro of San Antonio, Juan M. Campos, M.D. and Lauro Guerra, M.D. of McAllen, and Alonso López of Edinburg. I want to thank my mother, Consuelo C. Alonzo, who instilled in me the value of education and my sister, Elizabeth A. Haskins for her interest and support in my work.

I also thank those individuals in the Lower Valley who assisted my research. María Concepción and María del Carmen Garza of Edinburg gave me several interviews as did Erasmo García, who died in March 1997. Al Ramirez of Edinburg provided me with the colonial map and photos of the Vela family. George Gause, Director of Special Collections at University of Texas at Pan American and David Mycue of the Hidalgo County Historical Museum assisted my research with local history materials.

My editors at the University of New Mexico Press, especially Dr. David V. Holtby, who never had any reservations about my research and the copyeditor, Dr. Floyce Alexander, who did a superb job to enhance the quality of the manuscript.

My wife, Angelita, provided considerable assistance in my writing, offering editing suggestions and raising questions that resulted in a much better manuscript. Lourdes, Marisa, and Ariel Victoria have added much socially and emotionally to my life during the years of research and writing to remind me that I am also a parent.

INTRODUCTION

THE PLACE AND THE PEOPLE

There is a continuing legacy for the Tejano—the descendants of the Spanish and Mexican settlers—of the Lower Río Grande Valley of Texas: deep historical roots, town and rural traditions, and an enduring culture and identity. For generations of settlers, adaptation to a harsh environment and adjustment to a changing society became the cornerstone of their existence. Beginning with the entry of Spanish stockraisers in the 1730s and 1740s, the pasturelands of the region have served as the main attraction for permanent settlement and for subsequent development of all of the natural resources of the region: its salt deposits; its waterways; its diverse fauna and flora, especially its abundant wildlife; and its native people.[1]

The early *pobladores*, or settlers, instinctively knew and appreciated the value of the desolate plains that became their home in the middle of the eighteenth century. Consider the observations reported in 1757 by two of the frontier captains who led the first settlers to the new lands along the Río Grande. When asked about the uses of the land, Carlos Cantú, the captain at Reynosa, answered that "all the land in this Colony [of Nuevo Santander] is very appropriate for the breeding and maintenance of small and large livestock, and . . . within the limit of this town there are several ranches of these kinds of livestock already established in which much growth and good progress are being experienced in breeding livestock; for all the land that pertains to this settlement for this purpose he believes without doubt as being one of the best and, also, with regard to general health, its climate is very appropriate." A few days earlier,

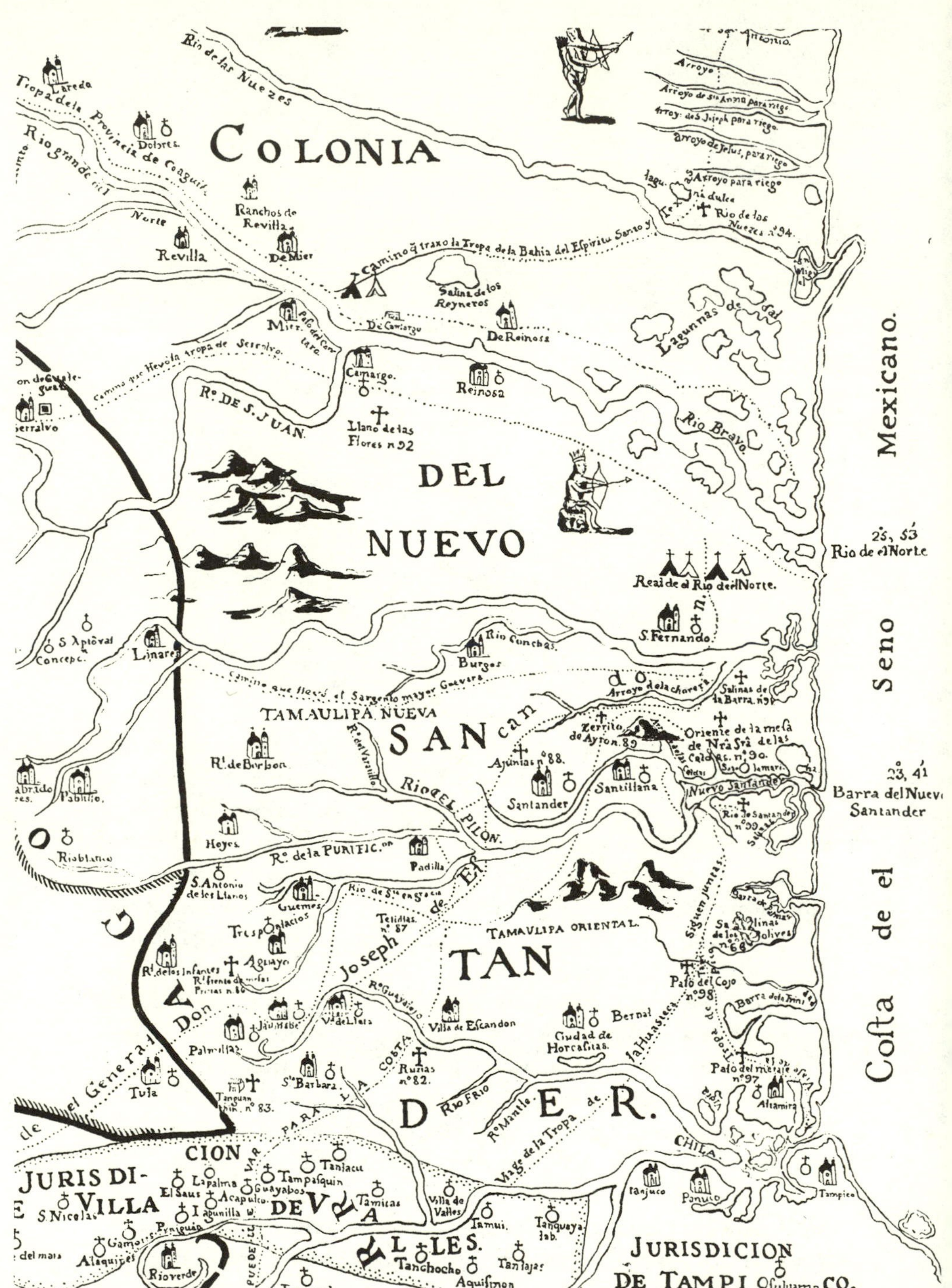

Rio de las Nuezes
Laredo
Tropa de la Provincia de Coaguila
Dolores
COLONIA
Ranchos de Revilla
Revilla
De Mier
Norte
Arroyo
Arroyo de Sn. Anto. para riego
Arroy. de S. Joseph para riego
Arroyo de Jesus, para riego
Arroyo para riego
Rio de los Nuezes n. 94
Camino q. traxo la Tropa de la Bahia del Espiritu Santo y
Salina de los Reyneros
De Camargo
De Reinosa
Lagunnas de Sal
Camargo
Reinosa
Ro. DE S. JUAN
Llano de las Flores n. 92
Rio Bravo
Mexicano.
DEL
NUEVO
25, 53
Rio de el Norte
Real de el Rio del Norte
S. Fernando
Seno
Linares
Rio Conchas
Burgos
Arroyo de la chorera
Salinas de la Barra n. 91
TAMAULIPA NUEVA
SAN
Zerrito de Ayton. 89
Oriente de la mesa de Nra. Sra. de las Caldas n. 90
R. de Borbon
Ajunias n. 88
Santander
Santillana
Nuevo Santander
23, 41
Barra del Nuev
Santander
Rio del Pilon
Rio de Santander n. 99
Pablillo
Hoyos
Ro. de la PURIFIC.on
Padilla
Rioblanco
S. Antonio de los Llanos
Rio de Sta. engracia
Guemes
Tres Palacios
Telidias n. 87
TAMAULIPA ORIENTAL
Rl. de los Infantes
Aguayo
Joseph
TAN
Paso del Cojo n. 98
de
Ro. Guayalejo
Villa de Escandon
Bernal
Ciudad de Horcasitas
la Huasteca
Colta
Don
Palmillas
Ruinas n. 82
Paso del metate n. 97
Tula
Sta. Barbara
el General
COSTA
RIO FRIO
D
E
R.
Altamira
Ro. Mante
Viage de la Tropa de
CHILA
CION
JURIS DI-
VILLA
La palma
Tanlacu
Tampasquin
Guayabos
El Saus
Acapulco
Tamicas
S. Nicolas
DE V
Villa de Valles
Tamui
Tanquaya lab.
Tanjuco
Panuco
Tampico
Gamotes
Alaquines
Rioverde
LES.
Tanchocho
Tanlajas
Aquismon
JURISDICION
DE TAMPICO
Ofuluama
Tancoyol

Captain Blas María de la Garza Falcón, at Camargo, had given a similarly optimistic appraisal of the utility of the lands in the Lower Valley for stock-raising. He also informed the royal inspectors of the colony that "seventeen ranches and *estancias* [or stock farms] have been established by the *vecinos* [citizens] of this town." After listing them and giving their locations in relation to the town, the captain concluded: "In all of these ranches the *vecinos* who have founded them and several others who have joined them maintain their small and large livestock, for which they care with much dedication."[2] More than a century later, Don Juan N. Cavazos, a Tejano *ranchero* and grandson of José Narciso Cavazos, the original grantee of the San Juan de Carricitos grant, in writing his last will and testament at his ranch in Cameron County, Texas, emphasized the value of the land. He advised his wife, who was to serve as guardian of their two minor sons, "that should the need arise to obtain funds for the care and maintenance of these children, the livestock could be sold but that the land was not to be sold except in the case of dire urgency."[3] These statements and others included in this history touch upon one theme that is central to Tejano history—the importance of land or space to the settlers' way of life and identity.

This is a history of the Lower Valley of Texas from its Spanish colonial roots to 1900. It examines the creation of frontier communities during the Spanish and early Mexican period and the persistence of those communities following the United States' occupation of the Lower Valley during the Mexican–American War. The history of Spanish expansion into Nuevo Santander, of which the Lower Valley is a part, represents a frontier experience, but with the passing generations, the settlers developed a sense of place that made the region Hispanic. This study focuses on the continuities and changes that occurred in one specific region of what is presently a larger geographic and political unit, namely Texas. Whereas the Spanish and the Mexicans always recognized Texas as a smaller territory occupying the space from San Antonio to the Louisiana border, Anglo-American westward expansion finally gave the state its present boundaries. Until the war with Mexico in 1846, the region from the Nueces River to the Río Grande had been considered a part of the *gobierno*, or government, of Nuevo Santander (1747) and later Tamaulipas (1824).[4]

Few places in the United States have retained to the present time the influences of Spain and its successor government, Mexico, as strongly as the Lower Valley of Texas, which includes the lands from Corpus Christi to Brownsville and upriver to Del Rio.[5] By the mid-eighteenth century, Spanish *pobladores* had founded five towns along the Lower Valley: Camargo, Reynosa, Mier, Revilla, and Laredo. A sixth town, Matamoros, developed from a ranching community, in 1770, to become the hub of social, economic, and political life

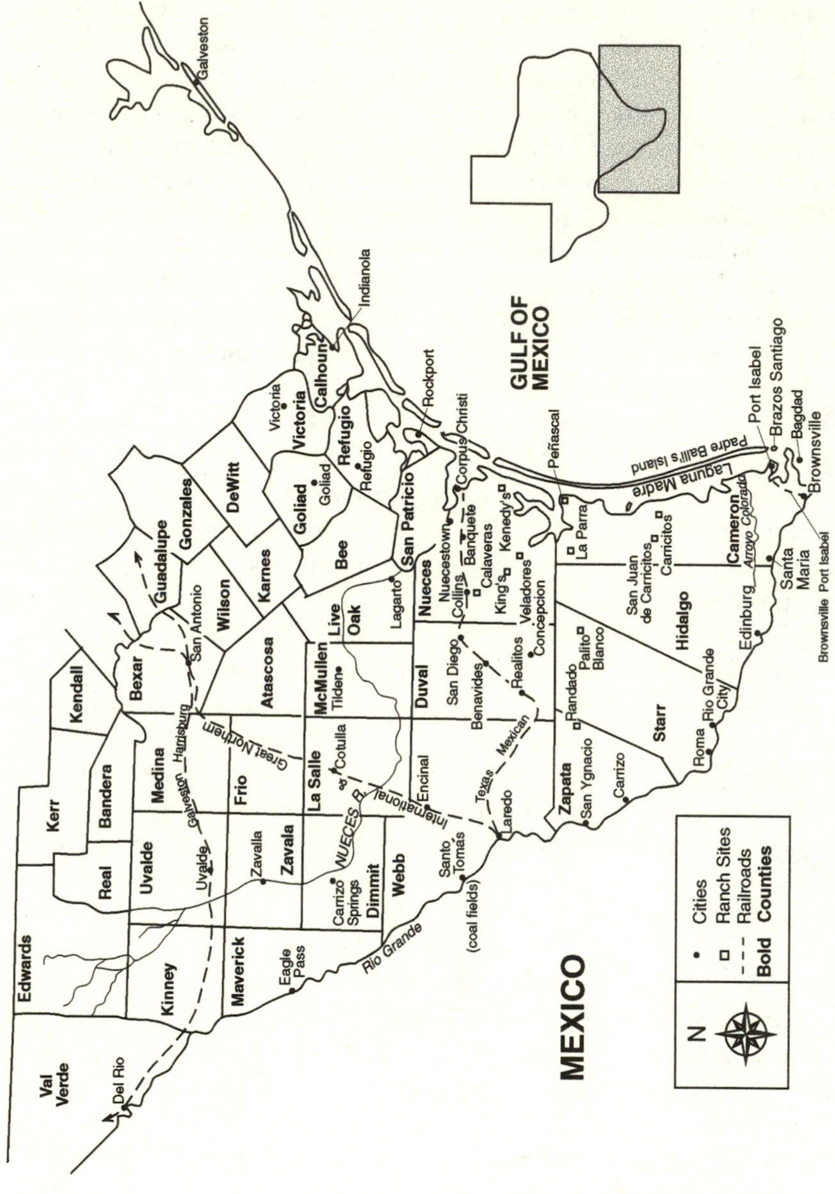
Galveston
Indianola
GULF OF MEXICO
MEXICO
Val Verde
Edwards
Kerr
Kendall
Bandera
Real
Bexar
Guadalupe
Gonzales
DeWitt
Victoria
Calhoun
Refugio
Goliad
Bee
San Patricio
Wilson
Karnes
Atascosa
Medina
Uvalde
Kinney
Maverick
Zavala
Frio
La Salle
McMullen
Live Oak
Nueces
Duval
Webb
Dimmit
Zapata
Starr
Hidalgo
Cameron
Del Rio
Eagle Pass
Uvalde
Zavalla
Carrizo Springs
Cotulla
Tilden
Lagarto
San Antonio
Victoria
Goliad
Refugio
Rockport
Corpus Christi
Nuecestown
Collins
Banquete
Calaveras
King's
Kenedy's
Veladores
Concepcion
San Diego
Benavides
Realitos
Encinal
Laredo
Santo Tomás
(coal fields)
San Ygnacio
Carrizo
Randado
Palito Blanco
La Parra
Peñascal
San Juan de Carricitos
Carricitos
Roma
Rio Grande City
Edinburg
Santa Maria
Brownsville
Bagdad
Brazos Santiago
Port Isabel
Padre Balli's Island
Laguna Madre
Arroyo Colorado
Brownsville Port Isabel
Rio Grande
NUECES R.
Galveston Harrisburg
Great Northern
International
Texas Mexican
N
Cities
Ranch Sites
Railroads
Bold Counties

for the region in the 1820s. These towns, in turn, provided the settlers who eventually colonized the lands in the Lower Valley. These settlers were an experienced and heterogeneous mix of peoples who traced their origins to older frontier districts of New Spain that had been occupied in the sixteenth and seventeenth centuries. They came to the new lands along the lower reach of the Río Grande to utilize the abundant grasslands and other resources in hopes of improving their lives. In the process of staking their claim to the land, the settlers became dominant over nomadic Coahuiltecan natives. Officials, military men, and missionaries also arrived in the new frontier to advance the imperial desire to occupy and protect the Gulf Coast region from foreign intruders, originally the French and then the English, as well as to Christianize the Indians.[6]

Following Mexican independence (after 1821), Tamaulipas, the successor government to Nuevo Santander, suffered from a turnover in its leadership, reflecting the political chaos present in the new republic. Still, the original settlers persisted, adjusting to the changes in politics and in the economic order. By 1800 the colony was much more populous and wealthier than its neighbor Texas and the much older New Mexico. By virtue of their location on the frontier, the settlers after 1820 were constantly affected by the influx of new immigrants from Europe and the United States, and by a variety of ideas, political movements, and economic activities.[7]

The annexation of the northern half of Tamaulipas by Texas in 1848 led to the founding of new towns populated mostly by Mexicans along the Lower Valley. A resilient, independent, and practical people, the *mejicanos*, or Tejanos as they later called themselves, gradually adjusted to the incorporation of the Lower Valley into the society and economy of the United States, in spite of the adversity Tejanos encountered as newcomers arrived in the region and attempted to displace them from the land and society.[8]

ANGLO MYTH AND TEJANO HISTORY

My purpose in this book is to offer a more balanced account of the history of Tejanos in the Lower Valley. Until recently, social scientists have generally neglected the Tejanos' important contributions in ranching, farming, and town settlement as well as their rich social life. Other writers have distorted the Tejano experience in the post-1848 period. One aspect of this problem is the tendency to see conflict as the central theme of Tejano history.[9] This view disregards the evidence of substantial Tejano–Anglo accommodation in social, economic, and political affairs after annexation. It is true that economic competition for the natural resources of the region and subsequent Tejano–Anglo conflict disrupted life and fostered ethnic divisions and violence, but one constant feature of society in the Lower Valley was its ability to overcome confusion and ethnic or racial strife.

For a variety of reasons, historians have downplayed the Tejano contribution to the settlement of the Lower Valley and the formation of this distinctive frontier community. In some accounts Tejanos had so little to do with the development of the region that they seem to be a people without a history. In essence, later Anglo arrivals have appropriated the history of the pioneer effort for themselves. With new beginnings in a place they imagined not so much as romantic but as different, the Anglo settlers saw the lands in the Lower Valley as a frontier instead of a settled place occupied by *mejicanos.* For some newcomers from the United States, the history of the region starts with the founding of the ranches of Richard King and Mifflin Kenedy in the 1850s.[10] For other new residents, the arrival of the St. Louis, Brownsville, Mexico Railway Company in the Lower Valley in 1904, or alternatively, the date of their migration marks the start of the region's history. As a result, the Anglo pioneer memory is selective in its interpretation of facts and of history. In this way, a Tejano way of life that rooted itself in the Lower Valley during the founding of Nuevo Santander is summarily dismissed. Take, for instance, what an Anglo writer, whose parents moved to south Texas at the turn of the twentieth century, recalled: "One can imagine the loneliness and heartache when [my mother] Molly Truitt left her family and friends to make a new home in that rough unsettled country down on [the] Mexican border." Adding more details to this view, she wrote that "when the family moved there [to the Lower Valley] in 1902 there was nothing but cactus, mesquite and an occasional band of Mexican *bandidos* on this land. This section of the country [south Texas] was so isolated from the rest of the world that between Sinton and Brownsville, a distance of 160 miles, there was neither a village nor a postoffice." Adding an element of mystery and romance to the origins of the region, the author quoted an anonymous writer who had previously said: "Prior to the coming of the railroad in 1904, the Lower Rio Grande Valley was virtually '*terra incognita*,' and fully ninety-five per cent of the population were Latins."[11]

A variation of Anglo mythic history of Texas is complicated by a depiction of the Lower Valley region as unoccupied or vacant, or, at best, a "no-man's-land." A recent writer, reminiscing about her struggle as a woman farmer and rancher in Hebbronville, Texas, in the twentieth century, summarized the area's history as "a no-man's land—where a sheriff seldom lived out his term—from the time of the Texas War for Independence until well after the Civil War." While conceding that "most of the [south Texas] area consisted of big grants" and "almost all of the grantees were Spanish," she noted that Anglo desire for that land led to turmoil. "Renegades from both sides of the border drifted into the sparsely settled area and tried to survive by any means necessary. There was practically no law and order. And . . . many of the old Spanish families fled."[12] The main problem with this myth is that writers fail to see the inherent contradiction of a "no-man's-land" existing in a place previously occupied by Spanish and Mexican settlers. They also equate momentary flight from the land as complete abandonment, though the two are not identical.

Some Texas historians have also built the theme of Anglo success and superiority as a logical progression of the myth of the "no-man's-land." Grounded in their ideas of settlement, progress, and race, the Anglo interpretation of history disregards the contributions of Tejanos and Mexican immigrants to the development of the region. J. Lee and Lillian Stambaugh, in their standard history of the Lower Valley, note that ranching was an important industry since Spanish settlement, but they prefer to focus on the heroic Richard King and the Texas Rangers who battled the hated Mexicans. "Since there were no examples which [the Anglo newcomers] might follow," they argue, "it was necessary that they develop this new country by experimentation." With rare exceptions, recent histories of stockraising in Texas repeat the Stambaugh thesis.[13]

The classic Anglo view of the early twentieth-century history of the Lower Valley is a simple restatement of the early "pioneer" thesis: "After the first trainload [of Anglo settlers], others followed. A veritable procession marched down the Valley, cleared away the brush, watered the fields, and settled down to a profitable farming."[14] Having inherited the ideology of Manifest Destiny, Anglo settlers saw themselves as a superior people who had wrested the land from unworthy Mexican stewards.

Naturally, Tejanos took exception to this "Anglo-pioneer" interpretation of the history of the Lower Valley. Recipients of a rich oral tradition, Tejanos have their own perspective of the role they played in the development of the region. Their view differs significantly from the "Anglo-pioneer" interpretation. First, they assert that much of the history of development was a result of Tejano efforts because new arrivals from the United States and Europe were a small minority up to the early part of the twentieth century.[15] Second, Tejanos disagree with Anglos on the critical question of how displacement from the land occurred. Tejanos continue to see land loss as a result of wholesale Anglo thievery accomplished through various means, such as lawsuits, intimidation, and violence, including the use of the Texas Rangers and other law-enforcement officers. A common view of the Anglo theft of Tejano lands is the version recounted by Catarino Lerma, a landowner in Cameron County, who asserted that "a man that [*sic*] could not rob could not be in society. When these people

[Richard King and his family] got enough [land,] they put up laws against stealing. King took the land and [Robert] Kleberg [King's son-in-law] settled it. Martin Hinajosa [*sic*] [a Tejano *ranchero*,] used to question him [Kleberg] about the existence of Mexican heirs [to land grants claimed by King]."[16]

Tejanos also offer a variation of this idea of Anglo confiscation of their property, claiming that Anglo attacks forced *rancheros* from their land and resulted in subsequent Anglo occupation. Leo J. Leo, a former schoolteacher, storekeeper, and well-known politician, resided nearly all of his life in La Joya, a small settlement located near the Río Grande in Hidalgo County. A descendant of European and Mexican background, he recounted the following oral tradition of what happened to the land belonging to his mother's family, the Elizondos and the Garcías. "Through my mother's side, she came from Camargo. . . . Her ancestors were given land grants [in south Texas] which my ancestors possessed but later found themselves without after the wars between Mexico and the United States and the war for Texas Independence before [that]. They went back to Mexico to live and abandoned their land. Then when they wanted to get it back, it was too late. Some of the land was sold at whatever price they could get for it because they had abandoned the land." Leo also asserted that during the turbulent 1830s Mexicans had been forcefully dispossessed by Anglo outlaws. "There were many stories being told by the old people about the ways the Mexican families who lived around Encino, Rachel, [and vicinity] were literally forced out of their homes which were burned, and they had to leave their land because they were thrown out by people who were operating outside of the law. . . . Most were fugitives from the United States."[17]

The use of fencing to acquire land illegally is an oft-repeated Tejano story of one way they lost their landholdings. For example, old-time *vaqueros* and their descendants informed an interviewer writing a social history of the Kenedy ranch that in the 1860s or 1870s "there were many small ranches belonging to Mexicans, but then the Americans came in and drove the Mexicans out and took over the ranches . . . [and] after that [the Americans] fenced the ranches—it was the [Americans who] fenced some land that wasn't theirs." To the present day, old Tejano *rancheros*, recalling the effects of illegal fencing, voice the popular refrain *con el alambre vino la hambre* (with barbed wire fencing came hunger).[18] Such Tejano memories of dispossession are important because that is how they remember the past and thus interpret the present. Perhaps the Tejano interpretation persists with special force because as they lost their lands, they also lost ground in the social, economic, and political arena.[19] At the same time, this interpretation—like the Anglo-settler one—needs to be scrutinized and revised.

Obviously, the story of Tejano–Anglo competition for the lands in the

Lower Valley of Texas and the resultant subordination to Anglo newcomers is a complex one that demands careful study. The corollary argument, made by Arnoldo De León and others, that the Tejano experience was particularly harsh vis-à-vis other *mejicanos* in the Southwest also merits analysis. In the material that follows, I have assessed these theses because they go directly to a major historiographical problem in the literature of the Southwest.

Most historians agree that land loss among the *mejicanos* in the Southwest after 1848 resulted in their reduction to second-class citizens. Whereas land tenure in California and New Mexico has been studied in depth, the literature on Texas is much more general. Examining social, economic, political, and environmental factors in both northern and southern California, Leonard Pitt postulated the "decline" thesis of the *californios.* While the Hispanic settlers in northern California quickly suffered losses to Anglo newcomers following the gold rush of 1849, *californios* in southern California declined more gradually; but they too were dispossessed by the 1870s and 1880s.[20] Victor Westphall and Roxanne Dunbar Ortiz have studied land-grant adjudication in New Mexico, and both have concluded that the adjudicatory agencies were greatly unfair to Hispanic claimants, who became minority landholders prior to 1900 even in the region of northern New Mexico, where the tradition of community land grants was most prominent.[21] The earliest view of Tejano land tenure in south Texas is found in Carey McWilliams's seminal *North from Mexico.* He asserts that Tejano settlers persisted as landholders and made a transition to the new farm economy of the twentieth century.[22] Rodolfo Acuña sees the usurpation of Tejano-owned lands in the Lower Valley as a quick, outright dispossession by shyster Anglo merchants and lawyers that resulted in the colonization of Tejanos.[23] David Weber and David Montejano describe the erosion of Tejano landholdings as resulting from complex causes, but following McWilliams's "persistence" thesis, they assert that some Tejanos survived in border enclaves past 1900.[24] Recently, geographer Terry Jordan addressed the origins and development of the cattle-ranching frontiers of North America. While he now recognizes the contributions of Nuevo Santander ranchers and credits their descendants with bringing cattle ranching to the lower Texas Gulf Coast, from Victoria to the Lower Valley, his portrayal of *rancheros* in the Lower Valley is problematic. He asserts that although "the aristocratic cattle estate survives [in south Texas] to the present day," there was "a decline in ranching in the [Nueces] Strip between 1810 and 1870, caused by Indian attacks and, later, the long period of Anglo–Mexican skirmish and warfare, which rendered the area a no-man's land."[25] Despite the centrality of landholding and ranching economy to all of these theses regarding south Texas, no quantitative study of Tejano land tenure, including the ranching economy, has ever been attempted.

This history is a reconstruction of the Tejano historical experience, and it is based on their oral and written traditions. Much of the written record remains not only in the "official" documents located in courthouses and other governmental agencies, but also in the hands of the Tejanos themselves, and in a wide array of forms. Most of their writings are only now appearing in print, but they are of uneven quality. I attempt, therefore, to place the Tejano story at the center of this history, a history that shows that Tejanos in the Lower Valley of Texas have persevered and prevailed, establishing a regional homeland, much like northern New Mexico.[26] With the decline of the Indians in the eighteenth century, Tejanos asserted control over a large territory and brought it into production as ranching lands. Their history was a long struggle to survive and adapt in a frontier environment, but they succeeded time and again in spite of setbacks. And in the process they identified with their place. To them, the land has always possessed meaningful cultural and economic values. It is their home, a special place.[27]

This history of the Lower Valley spans a considerable time—nearly two centuries—for two reasons. First, the century or so of Spanish–Mexican rule (from the 1730s to 1848) saw the formation of a ranching and commercial society, one that built on continuities to the colonial heritage as well as adapting to new challenges in settling new lands, discovering opportunities in ranching and trade, and experiencing conflict with Indians and Anglos. Second, social and economic patterns established in that century persisted, to a large degree, into the early American period (1848–1900). Yet adaptation to new conditions with the change in sovereignty reflected the ongoing dynamics by which Hispanic settlers forged an identity distinctive from their previous colonial history. Consequently, beginning Tejano history with the year 1836 or 1848—as many have done—is arbitrary and falls short of understanding the origins of the settlers in the Lower Valley of Texas, a unique historical region of the Southwest.

The key factor that made possible Tejano continuity in the Lower Valley was the ability of the original landholders, their descendants, and the new settlers from Mexico, with whom they readily mixed, to persist in spite of the changes in sovereignty and other adversities. Between 1750 and 1848, large numbers of settlers received land grants from Spain and Mexico in the territory from the Río Grande to the Nueces River. Those lands were eventually the subject of conflicting national claims. In the period from 1836 to 1848, that frontier was disputed by Texas—and later the United States—and Mexico. Despite the Texas republic's claim of jurisdiction over the Río Grande border after 1836, she did not effectively control the region until 1848, as a result of the Treaty of Guadalupe Hidalgo, which concluded the war with Mexico.[28]

The early years of American rule resulted in the consolidation of U.S. authority in the Lower Valley, with the creation of county governments and land-grant adjudication by the state of Texas.[29] In 1848, Texas created four large counties in the region: Webb, Starr, Cameron, and Nueces. Further divisions created Hidalgo County out of Cameron County lands (1852), Zapata County out of Starr County lands (1858), and Duval County out of Nueces County territory (1876).[30] No other counties were organized in the Lower Valley region until the early 1900s, when drastic changes resulting from extensive Anglo farm and town settlement necessitated a redrawing of the political map.[31]

This history consists of two parts. The first part, chapters 1 and 2, focuses on the Spanish–Mexican experience of settlers in the Lower Valley. My objective is to outline the basic features of colonization, landholding, and the social and economic life of the settlers. In the second part, chapters 3 to 8, which is the Tejano period, I examine the nature of the society and of land-grant adjudication, as well as landholding and the ranching economy. Because one of my main concerns is to address the issue of Tejano land tenure, I provide substantial quantitative data for Tejano landholding and ranching in Hidalgo County as well as data for the entire region. Chapter 9 compares Hispanic land tenure in the Southwest United States. My conclusions are discussed in the epilogue.

My research, based on qualitative and quantitative data, shows that Tejanos in the Lower Valley participated in an expanding commercial ranching economy and that they maintained control of their lands in much of the region until the 1880s. Shaped by their colonial experience, Tejanos were a resilient, pragmatic, and largely self-directed people. They adapted to the grasslands and struggled against Indians and newcomers from the United States. After 1848, they gradually adjusted to the incorporation of the newly annexed territory into the society and economy of the United States. Land loss among Tejanos was a complex process involving social, economic, and political factors, and it was only in the last quarter of the nineteenth century that drastic changes accelerated land loss. Still, Tejanos played a leading role in the commercialization of ranching and participated in other economic activities, assisting in the growth of the national economy; they held onto their lands and utilized them as best they could to the very end of the century, forging a distinctive identity and heritage that newcomers could not dissolve.

I offer an interpretation that revises much of the recent literature on Tejanos in the Lower Valley. First, the significance of the early Spanish–Mexican period is that it cemented the basic social and economic elements that shaped much of the fabric of Tejano life after 1848. A basically fluid, patriarchical society in which very few people were wealthy promoted the rise of a *ranchero* class whose members were resolute, hardworking, and pragmatic in outlook. Skilled workers also did well, but the unskilled hardly improved their lives. This period left a permanent imprint on the Lower Valley, making it Hispanic at its foundation, and conditioned the society to accept innovation. Second, the early American period (1848–1900) represented a gradual transition to a new order in which new ideas in education, politics, and economics affected Tejano society and made adjustment necessary. Periods of accommodation, competition, and conflict marked ethnic relations. At times, the hostile attitudes and actions of Anglos became overt and pronounced, straining relations that led to violence; for the most part, however, Tejanos and Anglos needed each other in order to develop the region. The remarkable growth of trade, commerce, and the livestock industry is indicative of this adaptation. Except for a few Anglo enclaves, Tejano stockraisers remained in the majority numerically. Until very late in the nineteenth century, *rancheros* were, in fact, dominant stockraisers in south Texas and they contributed to the growth of the national economy. The evidence also shows a growing and diverse Tejano workforce in the towns of the region, a development that was involved in the rapid changes ushering in the modernization of Texas at the end of the nineteenth century. In short, after 1848 continuity and change characterized the Tejano experience in the Lower Valley. Tejano history in the Lower Valley is thus a story of a frontier as well as of a place.

Whereas Hispanic settlers were quickly relegated to a minority in other parts of the borderlands, except New Mexico, Tejanos constituted a majority of the population in the Lower Valley region. The population rose from about ten thousand in 1850 to nearly ninety thousand by 1900.[32] About 85 percent of the region's inhabitants in 1900 were Tejano. The sheer size of the Tejano population and its importance in the economy contributed to making the Lower Valley the most vibrant Tejano region of the state.

It is true that by 1900 hundreds of Tejanos lost ground to Anglo competitors, unscrupulous individuals, poor markets, lenders, and a harsh environment. By then, only elite *rancheros* and smaller landholders who had not succumbed to the vagaries of the weather and/or the marketplace stood a chance of continuing in the tradition of landholding and stockraising. It is also true that the shift to irrigated farming in the delta lands of the Lower Valley in the early twentieth century as well as the effects of the Great Depression further reduced Tejano landholding.

To the present time, however, Tejanos remain a viable community in the Lower Valley. The number of *rancheros* who own large tracts of land is drastically down from the late nineteenth century, when much displacement from the land had already occurred. Yet the legacy is visible in the continuing participation of today's Tejanos in the social, economic, and political life of the region. While some of their descendants have stayed on the land, many others are comfortable in the small towns and bustling urban centers of the region. The successful transition of many Tejano descendants can be illustrated by the experience of Filemón Vela, a U.S. federal judge in Brownsville, Texas. Judge Vela is a fourth-generation descendant of Don Macedonio Vela of Hidalgo County, one of the most energetic *rancheros* who made a lasting contribution to the ranching economy in the second half of the nineteenth century.[33] Having weathered the rigors of frontier life and persisted through the chaos and conflict that resulted from the various shifts in sovereignty, the Tejanos proved to be a strong, resilient, adaptable, pragmatic, and successful people.

SOURCES

Much of the documentation for this history comes from official records. For the colonial period, I relied on official reports and traveler accounts, land-grant documents, and the papers of Anglo lawyers involved in land-grant adjudication. The sources for the quantitative material on landholding and the ranching economy in the post-1848 period comes from the records of the Texas General Land Office, county tax rolls, brand records and bills of sale of livestock, and federal manuscript censuses of population and agriculture. My principal data bases consist of the tax rolls for Hidalgo County for the period 1852–1900, and the manuscript census of population for Hidalgo County for the years 1860, 1870, 1880, and 1900. The size of these two data bases and the limitations of the data are discussed in Appendix 2.

My portrait of the settlers comes from a variety of sources, some of which are only now being published as genealogies, memoirs, and folk histories; and they are of uneven quality. Thus, I combed genealogies of the Vela family of Reynosa, the Benavides of Revilla, and other pioneer settlers of the Lower Valley. I also consulted census materials, wills and testaments, and other court proceedings of the nineteenth and early twentieth centuries to help me gain a deeper understanding of the social life of the Tejanos. In addition, I have utilized a small set of interviews with *rancheros* and their descendants to supplement the literature on border culture.

CHAPTER ONE

SPANIARDS, INDIANS, AND THE INHOSPITABLE SENO MEXICANO

The Spanish conquest of much of present-day Mexico was a dynamic process that proceeded with varying speeds and in various directions, continuing for generations and reaching particular regions at different times and sometimes because of different motives. After the conquest of the Aztec empire in 1521, small Spanish armies rapidly pushed across much of Middle America, defeating the once proud natives of old cultures in southern and southeastern Mexico. Within twenty years, strong Indian forces had also been crushed in the west and northwest along the Pacific Coast. After the discovery of silver at Zacatecas in 1546, the Spanish marched north through the land of the Chichimeca, searching for the elusive gold and silver lodes that they believed were surely there. By the end of the sixteenth century the northern prong of the frontier had reached into New Mexico (1598), and by the end of the seventeenth century Spanish soldiers and missionaries had made their way to eastern Texas from the older frontiers of Coahuila and Nuevo León.[1] Moving along the latter route to occupy Texas, conquistadores and settlers skirted a vast and inhospitable territory, the Seno Mexicano or the Mexican Gulf Coast.

Despite two centuries of conquest and frontier movement, the Seno Mexicano or Gulf Coast north of Tampico and extending into Texas remained unsettled until the mid-eighteenth century, when the colony of Nuevo Santander was organized to include present-day south Texas (the Trans-Nueces region) and the Mexican state of Tamaulipas.[2] Ultimately, the historical origins of a Spanish society and ranching economy in south Texas are intertwined with the eventual settlement of the Seno Mexicano and the earlier colonial heritage of the *primeros pobladores* or conquistadores, as the first families of northern New Spain called themselves.[3]

EARLY CONQUESTS AND SETTLEMENTS IN THE SENO MEXICANO

The first efforts of the Spanish, in the sixteenth and seventeenth and even in the early eighteenth centuries, to subjugate the natives of the Seno Mexicano and found new towns produced few positive results for the Catholic church and the state. In spite of exploratory *entradas*, or penetrations, by Spanish armies and missionaries into the coastal fringes of the Seno Mexicano, especially at the Río Pánuco, the Spanish could count as a success only the founding of the Villa de San Luis de Tampico in 1560. Tampico long remained a small enclave of Spanish and *mestizo* ranchers whose livelihood was based on raising *ganado mayor* in the surrounding pasturelands.[4] Also, between 1617 and 1627, a Dominican missionary, Fray Juan Bautista Mollinedo, founded missions at Tula, Palmillas, and Jaumave in the southwestern corner of the Seno Mexicano, some of which did not survive because royal protection was not always forthcoming. Spanish settlers who moved into that frontier zone found themselves in a similarly tenuous situation.[5] Within the jurisdiction of the *alcaldía mayor* of Río Blanco in southernmost Nuevo León, in a valley called San Antonio de los Llanos, Nuevo Leonese stockmen founded sheep *haciendas* around 1667. Their enterprises suffered heavy losses to Indian raids, but the *hacendados* persisted. Their entry occurred concurrently with the first Franciscan missionary activities in that district.[6]

The natives also proved to be particularly independent and resistant to Spanish conquest in the Sierra Gorda, a rugged mountain enclave just east of the fertile Bajío. Missionaries entered the district periodically, in the sixteenth and seventeenth centuries, to convert and to teach the Indians to work like the Spanish. All of these efforts failed, and one historian asserts that the natives of the Sierra Gorda "were the most autonomous of Mexicans during the colonial era." As late as 1704, Viceroy Francisco Fernández de la Cueva proposed a program of pacification. After a series of brutal wars against the Indians there, the viceroy was able to conclude a peace treaty with them in 1715. The natives promised not to molest the Spanish settlements nearby as long as they were allowed complete freedom in the Sierra Gorda. In the 1720s, the renewed settlement of Spanish settlers, who were to serve as their own militia, produced minimal success.

In 1744 Franciscans again tried their hand with the natives in the Sierra Gorda, setting up missions and preventing the estate owners from making the Indians into seasonal workers. Then, in 1748, Colonel José de Escandón led a large military force into the district, destroying the remaining elements of native opposition to the Spanish. Many of the captives were sentenced to labor in the Querétaro *obrajes.* As a result of these actions, hundreds of natives remained at the new missions, where their numbers declined due to exposure to epidemic diseases.

In the late eighteenth century, secularization and continued estate development in the Sierra Gorda, which was affected by the transformation of the Bajío into a major farming zone, produced more conflict in the form of land disputes. Faced with inadequate resolution of these disputes by the courts and the indifference of officials, the natives responded with rioting and, with the start of the Hidalgo Revolt, joined the insurrection. They supported other rebels, shielded insurgents, and held an area of north central Mexico from royalist hands until 1816.[7]

There were also at least two other Spanish attempts, in 1718 and 1727, to establish silver mining and ranching operations, respectively, in the unconquered territory at a place called El Malichen, perhaps a mesa in present-day San Carlos, Tamaulipas. Both failed. According to Don Benito Antonio de Castañeda, the *capitán* and *alcalde mayor* of Pánuco and Tampico, the first effort failed "because of the desertion of some troops and because the tribes to be found as we moved further in speak a distinct language than that of the expedition's interpreters." The second try succumbed to a familiar weakness: the Spaniards' inability to deal with numerous unknown bands of Indians.[8]

Due to the threats against Florida posed by the presence of the English in Jamaica and the growing problem of Indian incursions on the northern frontier that hindered the Spanish ranchers who were occupying new lands, Spain opted in 1747 to occupy the Seno Mexicano region. This was to be accomplished primarily by pacifying the natives of the Seno Mexicano and settling the region with frontiersmen from the surrounding provinces of New Spain.[9]

BOUNDARIES, GEOGRAPHY, AND CLIMATE OF THE SENO MEXICANO

The Seno Mexicano stretched in the form of an arc from the Pánuco River near Tampico, along the coast to the southern limits of Texas, which at first was the San Antonio River. In 1805 a royal *cédula,* or decree, established the boundary between the *gobiernos* of Texas and Nuevo Santander as the Nueces River. On the southwest it was bordered by the older frontier jurisdictions of Tampico, Charcas, and Valles, and on the west by the provinces of Nuevo León and Coahuila (see Map 1).[10]

Most of the lands of this region are within the Gulf coastal plain, with the southwestern part straddling the Sierra Madre Oriental and some peaks reaching an elevation of 3,300 m. In this high mountain district, Tula is located in a *bolsón* on the Mesa Central. South of the Río Grande, a series of volcanic ranges, dissected by the Soto la Marina River and the Río de las Conchas, rise in the Sierra Madre and flow through fertile valleys, carving deep canyons before emerging on a floodplain and entering the Gulf Coast. The coast is flat with barrier islands or peninsulas, behind which are found saline *lagunas*, or lagoons, of changing size. South of Soto la Marina is a smaller floodplain that is backed first by a range of hills and by the difficult Sierra de Tamaulipas (known in the colonial era as Tamaulipa Vieja or Tamaulipa Oriental), whose peaks reach 1,550 m. To the southwest of this sierra is the valley of Las Rucias or the Guayalejo River, which flows from its source in the Sierra Madre to join the Pánuco in its delta just above Tampico. The lower reaches of the Guayalejo is also called the Tamesí River. The Sierra de Tamaulipa Nueva or Tamaulipa Occidental is today's barren Sierra de San Carlos, located in the north central part of the present state of Tamaulipas. Its mountains rise to 1,800 m.[11]

North of the Río Grande, vast semiarid plains dominate the landscape. Originally, these plains were described by the Spanish as grasslands particularly appropriate for stockraising. One early name for the region from the Río Grande to the Nueces was the *Sabana Grande*, or large savannah. Another name given to this district is the *Llanos de los Mesteños*, in reference to the large numbers of wild horses and cattle found there since the colonial period. The first scientist to observe and document the natural landscape on both sides of the Río Grande Valley, from Laredo to Matamoros, was Jean L. Berlandier in the 1820s and 1830s. Berlandier's description of the searing plains in the region from the Frio River to the Río Grande may have led to naming the plains the *Brazada*, a word closely linked to burning embers or hot coals, or *brazas*. Shortly after leaving the Frio River, he wrote that "after two days of suffocating heat . . . [t]he ground burned the feet of the best-shod person. . . . The earth heats so much that after sundown in these regions the best-shod individual cannot walk continuously for more than an hour." As Berlandier approached the Río Grande near Laredo, he noted that "the terrain consists of vast plains, often half-seared, where there are few trees and little water. That portion of the route does not resemble either the temperate zone or the torrid zone of the New World." Some of the lands were said to be *salitres*, considered essential for supplying sodium to animals, and the settlers looked for lands that had *aguajes*, or watering sources—springs, lakes, or ponds. However, low brush shrubs and trees, particularly mesquite, were found in many localities even during the colonial period. These brushy lands are classified as the Tamaulipan thorn brush and contain mesquite, huisache, and anacahuite, interspersed with opuntia and organ cactus, yucca, and various grasses. It is believed that these "mesquite prairies" became much less pronounced with the passing of time and were replaced by "mesquite brush," but the exact cause of this aereal (or aerial) diffusion onto the plains is not clear. In a district appropriately called Encino, about seventy-five miles from the Río Grande, the Spaniards and Mexicans found clusters of live oaks called *mota*, which they often named and which appear in their surveys as landmarks. By the time Anglo ranchers entered the region in the second half of the nineteenth century, *motas*, which they corrupted to *mottes*, had become so numerous that it was impossible to name them.[12]

The middle course of the Río Grande, which runs from the El Paso Valley to the present area of Falcón Dam, forms a narrow alluvial valley below the twin towns of Eagle Pass and Piedras Negras and widens considerably within the Gulf Coast plain.[13] This wider lower valley or delta of the river can be seen downriver from Camargo and present-day Rio Grande City, Texas. A range of low, mostly eroded hills crosses this district from southwest to northeast on the western side of south Texas.[14]

The Nueces River has a much narrower valley, riparian vegetation, and small, wooded canyons at its source in the upper northwest corner of south Texas. This canyon area, with various springs and smaller tributaries of the Nueces River, became the home of roaming Apaches and Comanches in the eighteenth century and remained unsettled until after 1850.

The coastal part of south Texas is much like that below the Río Grande, with one long barrier island today called Padre Island extending from near the mouth of the river toward Corpus Christi Bay. The lagoon that separates the mainland from the island in south Texas is known as the Laguna Madre, and the various bays that empty into it are a valuable source of animal and fish life. Sandy soils with prairie grasses, live oak clusters, and much wildlife abound along the coastal lands, and inland this area is known as the Eolian Plain. The Spaniards and Mexicans often referred to this district as La Costa. In the nineteenth century, travelers and others called it the Wild Horse Desert.[15]

The new colony possessed a variety of water sources of varying quality, but water was usually not available in sufficient quantity for farming purposes, and at times droughts occurred. The southwest region of the Sierra de Tamaulipa Vieja received the greatest amount of rainfall, up to 1,400 mm annually. North of that range, rainfall decreased to less than an average of 500 mm per year in the Río Grande Valley.[16] Escandón reported in 1747 that only the coastal region between the San Fernando River and the Río Grande contained "frequent lakes and ponds" of fresh water.[17] Excessive rains produced floods along the valleys and lowlands. Fortunately, the new towns in the northern part of the province were all located adjacent to the Río Grande or one of its tributaries, so that plenty of drinkable water was usually available.[18]

While the river lands and surrounding grassy plains were fertile, only thirteen rivers traversed the colony, and not all of them carried sufficient water for the irrigation of significant areas of cropland. Smaller valleys and plains that were susceptible to irrigation works were utilized, with the settlers and Indians building *acequias.* Also, a few of the rivers had very broad floodplains, which could not be farmed because "great floods sweep off everything."[19]

The colony has only four major river basins. The Río Grande's main tributaries are on the Mexican side of the river and provide more than half of the discharge into the river's basin. Whereas in the upper section of the Río Grande (above El Paso) the main discharge is in the spring, in the lower portion it occurs in late summer and early fall. South of the Río Grande are three other important drainage basins: the Conchos-San Fernando, Soto la Marina, and the Río Tamesí.[20]

Of special value to the Spanish settlers of Coahuila, Nuevo León, and, later, Nuevo Santander were the salt deposits on the coast of the colony at Altamira, Presas (now Aldama), Tampico, near San Fernando, and on the north side of the Río Grande at La Sal Vieja and Sal del Rey, two lakes of salt rock. Since about the 1680s these latter two deposits had been exploited by the older provinces in annual visits to the lakes. The people of the Lower Valley made use of the salt lakes, mining the salt and trading it along the frontier for other goods. In 1795, Félix de Calleja, a Spanish military officer, said that these valley salines, compared to the others, were "not only better but very special. Their beds are solid masses of coagulated salt that the rains do not liquify. Blocks are taken out as from a quarry, and salt has been known to coagulate to a depth of two varas."[21] After the war with Mexico, Anglo settlers desired, primarily for the purpose of commercial exploitation, the lands on which these lakes—especially the larger of the two, Sal del Rey—were located. This lake and coastal deposits were tapped commercially during the American Civil War period, but the records disclosing production levels have not been located.[22]

THE CLIMATE OF NUEVO SANTANDER AND OTHER BARRIERS TO SETTLEMENT

Northeastern Mexico and south Texas belong climatically to the Tamaulipas subhumid lowlands, a transition zone between the subtropical southeastern United States and the tropics of the Gulf and Caribbean coasts of Middle America. Consequently, nearly all of the province suffered from an oppressive hot climate that made summers seem almost endless.[23] Contemporaries noted that long periods of hot and humid weather prevailed in settlements such as Reynosa, which was nearest the Gulf Coast. Further inland, at Camargo, Mier, Revilla, Dolores, and Laredo, the climate was "hot and dry and the winter was very cold and dry." Thus, the royal engineer Agustín López de la Cámara Alta, who assisted Don José Tienda de Cuervo in his inspection of the new colony of Nuevo Santander in 1757, remarked that because of these extremes in climate the "people are healthy" and "become robust." Still, drought periodically struck the land. In summertime the "extreme heat of the months of June, July, and part of August, when the suns are burning hot and the wind from the southeast blows strongly everyday, passing over the endless salt lagoons and picking up an infinitude of invisible nitrate particles, burn[ed] all of the planted crops." When their lives were not put in danger from the overflows of the Río Grande, Reynosa's settlers were especially susceptible "from July to September to an epidemic of fevers." Although these fevers were not fatal, they were nevertheless bothersome.[24]

Respite from the heat came in the last days of the summer, but especially during the fall and winter, when cold fronts from the north, or *nortes*—what are now called "blue northers"—periodically blew into the region, abruptly lowering temperatures sometimes to near freezing and below and bringing much-needed rainfall. Field Marshal Juan Fernando de Palacio, who visited all of the towns of Nuevo Santander in 1767 to demarcate town and mission boundaries and to allot private land grants to the settlers, has left a good description of these swift and destructive north winds: "We left the said *villa* [of San Fernando] for this one [Burgos] on the 27th of [September]; and though it is not more than sixteen leagues distance, we did not arrive until the 3rd of this month [October] on account of having been detained in camp by a horrible tempest of a furious north wind, that placed us in consternation, leaving us isolated between [the Río Grande and the Río San Fernando], without food and in impassable roads."[25] Hurricanes were capable of causing great damage from their strong winds and heavy downpours, but their rains were also beneficial. Snows were limited to the high elevations of the mountain ranges of the region and on rare occasions fell on the lower elevations of the northern plains when severe winter storms raced southward. Only towns and rural districts located in the higher elevations of the colony generally benefited from a drier and healthier climate.[26]

There were other barriers to settlement besides the oppressive heat, especially in the lands north of the Río Grande. Although he had not traveled in that country, Cámara Alta depicted the Trans-Nueces as a wilderness. He was informed by the *pobladores* and the captain of Camargo, Blas María de la Garza

Falcón, who knew the country well, of the impracticality of founding settlements there. Their observations revealed, he wrote, that "all the land is broken and full of briars and brambles and being limitless in this condition one is unable to go across it on account of its denseness, breeding an infinity of wild animals, such as leopards, tigers, bears, wildcats and other kinds of animals." And, the *visitador* added, "water . . . is not to be found, except for two small wells, and it is very bad to drink."[27]

While Cámara Alta assumed these statements to be factual with regard to the quality of the lands, others knew better because of firsthand observation. Among the latter were travelers like the royal engineer and captain Nicolás de Lafora, who, upon traversing the semiarid plains north of Laredo, found the lands rough and partly timbered but rich in grasslands. On his return to northern New Spain from the Marquis de Rubí's inspection tour of the frontier *presidios* in Texas in 1767, Lafora noted that, on crossing the Río Frío where it joins the Nueces, the country had "some small hills, covered with grass, cactus and some hardwoods," and past the place of Saint Joseph, on the edge of the Nueces River, there were several ponds. The inspectors then came upon "a *cañada* [small vale] called del Prieto, through which ran a small creek that was impractical to cross during the rainy season." Continuing in a southwesterly direction toward the outskirts of Laredo, they crossed several creeks, and at "the arroyo del Pato, where the road [from Laredo] divides to go to San Antonio de Béjar, there was no other particularity in this day's journey other than the prodigious multitude of rattlesnakes which breed in these lands." In their final day's travel to reach Laredo, they passed "hills and more hills covered with much grass, plenty of cactus and mesquites."[28]

MOTIVES FOR HISPANIC SETTLEMENT IN THE NEW COLONY

Perhaps the settlers' depressing statements about the land beyond the Río Grande were partly self-serving, for in 1753 the missionary Juan Baustista García Suárez, who had been in Camargo since early 1750, remarked that "according to current opinion the land that lies between the Río Grande and the Nueces is even better [than here]." In fact, in 1753 five families petitioned José de Escandón, the founder of the colony, for two hundred *sitios* and a corresponding number of *cabellerías* on the north side of the Río Grande. They promised to bring in an additional fifteen families to Camargo. Escandón acceded to their request, but gave them only one hundred *sitios* of land. A few years later, in 1761, Escandón reported that settlers of that town "have already settled all the opposite bank of the Río Grande del Norte, within the limits of the land granted them, and the country as far as the Nueces has become so desirable, that most of the settlers aspire to it because of its size and good pasture."[29] In 1766, Blas María de la Garza Falcón founded the first ranch settlement in the Nueces Valley, Santa Petronila, when he received a five-league grant. Other settlers followed; many, indeed, were *vecinos* from Camargo.[30]

From the settlers' standpoint, occupying new lands in the frontier meant more opportunities, greater security, and even freedom from taxes. In many cases these motives for migration were certainly more real to them than the lofty desire of a distant monarch for imperial consolidation of an untamed and exposed territorial claim along the Seno Mexicano. Thus, for example, the extensive plains provided ideal pasture, which ranchers from the more settled northern frontiers coveted as their herds increased, good grazing land eroded from overuse, springs and other water resources went dry, and competition pushed them out of the few well-watered valleys of arid Coahuila and Nuevo León. Others came because the nomadic Indians in the isolated and rugged northern frontier were too great a match for them and the few soldiers stationed in distant *presidios.* To still other settlers, moving to this new frontier meant escaping the payment of taxes to the king. Cámara Alta noted, for instance, that the settlers of Camargo "had come from Nuevo León in order not to pay to the king that which his loyal servants are entitled to do so." Thus, "they have been leaving [Nuevo León], selling their *haciendas* there, everyday more so, for not wanting to contribute [their share of the taxes]."[31]

INDIANS OF THE SENO MEXICANO

The Spanish *pobladores* who occupied this new province also had to contend with the presence of thousands of unsettled Indians. Who were these Indians of the Seno Mexicano? Except for the Huaxtecs of the Tampico area and the Olives and Pisones, who lived north of the Huaxteca and may have been descendants of Chichimecs, nearly all of the Indians were culturally related to each other and are identified by anthropologists as Coahuiltecan. The Chichimec Indians, who occupied the middle and lower drainage of the Río Grande in pre-European times, used the river for drinking and occasional fishing. The lower drainage portion of the river had an abundance of North American fish, especially cats, suckers, and sunfish.[32] At first contact with the Spanish, there were evidently hundreds of individual *rancherías,* or bands, of Coahuiltecans. They are considered an extension of the nomadic desert cultures of northern Middle America and are classified as members of the Sioux-Hokan language group.[33] Unfortunately, the ethnohistory of these tribes cannot be accurately reconstructed due to the lack of written data and other difficulties, particularly the constant movement of tribes by Spaniards who often engaged in slaving expeditions. These had occurred in the southern zone since the time of Cortés, circa 1523, were renewed under Luis de Carbajal in 1581, and were continued for a considerable time by Spanish settlers from Nuevo León. These Indians had individual differences, including speech, and lived in relatively small bands. They led a simple existence as hunters, gatherers, and fishermen. Indigenous animal and plant life was diverse and the Indians utilized much of it for food and medicines as well as for fashioning weapons and clothing. They wore little clothing and were primitive in their material possessions. Their social organizations and customs were also simplistic and typical of similar societies of nomadic hunters and gatherers.[34]

In the mid-eighteenth century, when Escandón embarked on his colonization project of Nuevo Santander, the Spanish reported that their relations with the Indians varied on account of the different character or disposition of the tribes, which was apparently influenced by their earlier contact with the conquistadores and *pobladores.* On the one hand, those bands living in the delta of the Río Grande were generally docile and willing to settle in the missions and work for themselves and the Spanish.[35] In the early years of settlement, the frontier captains from Laredo and other downriver settlements informed officials that Indians on the Río Grande frontier, including the Lipan Apaches who were about thirty or forty leagues north of Laredo, "maintained themselves in peace."[36] On the other hand, nomadic Indians who had taken refuge in the southern sierras of the Tamaulipa range in the early eighteenth century, were a troublesome problem for the settlers in that area. The latter tribes were more belligerent because they had long been persecuted by the Spanish in the older districts of the northern frontier, and, therefore, they distrusted Spanish rule.[37] Peter Gerhard notes that while a few Indians remained in the missions, after 1762 most withdrew to the Sierra de Tamaulipa Vieja or fled northward to join Apaches.[38] Later, in about 1773, the more well-known Apaches, pressed by westward-moving Anglo frontiersmen, harassed the Spanish and *mestizo* pioneers who migrated to the northern reaches of the Seno Mexicano in the present-day area of southwestern Texas as well as Nuevo León and Coahuila. Even at the end of the colonial period, winning control of these lands had not been fully achieved.[39] In fact, sporadic Indian depredations remained a vexing problem in the area above Laredo and northern Mexico until the last quarter of the nineteenth century.[40] By then, however, the Seno Mexicano had been settled by hardy settlers for several generations.

CHAPTER TWO

HACIA LA FRONTERA

The Origins of Spanish and Mexican Society in Present-Day South Texas, 1730s–1848

The Spanish bureaucracy in New Spain considered a number of proposals before deliberately choosing a colonizer for the conquest and settlement of the Seno Mexicano. The first two proposals for the conquest of the Seno Mexicano were made in 1736: one by Narciso Barquín de Montecuesta, former *corregidor*, or municipal officer, of Santiago de los Valles near Tampico, who proposed colonization of the southern part of the unsettled territory; and the other by Joseph Antonio Fernández de Jáuregui y Urrutia, governor of Nuevo León, who proposed to lead settlers from his province to the northern part of the Seno Mexicano.[1] Two years later, Antonio Ladrón de Guevara also submitted a proposal to the viceroy in Mexico City.

Born in Castilla la Vieja, Spain, in 1705, Guevara arrived in Mexico City in the late 1720s, and by 1730 he had relocated to Nuevo León. A learned and intrepid man, Guevara held several minor political and military offices in Nuevo León before initiating explorations of the Seno Mexicano on his own in 1734 and 1735. Guevara's contemporaries said that he was often seen in the company of nomadic frontier Indians and that he prided himself as their defender. His proposal was similar to that of Fernández de Jáuregui y Urrutia, except for the former's plan to institute *congregas*, or native communities, as the long-dissolved *congregaciones* were called in Nuevo León. Under a *congregación* system, the Spanish would supervise the Indians who would perform personal services for them. In return, it was expected that the Spanish were to instruct the natives in the Christian faith and provide for the physical needs of the natives. He also recommended that a subsidy be given to settlers wishing to colonize the new lands, and he requested that the crown provide the necessary tools for the construction of churches, houses, and *presidios*.[2] As subsequent events showed, Guevara's determined efforts to be named colonizer made him a leading contender.

Aware that his rivals had made similar proposals, Guevara decided to travel to Spain in 1738, where he again presented his proposal. On July 10, 1739, the royal court in Spain ruled in favor of Guevara but still stipulated that the viceroy in New Spain consider all of the possibilities in deciding what was best in the pacification and occupation of the new territories. He was also granted authority to name the best qualified person to carry out the conquest of the Seno Mexicano.[3]

On his return to New Spain, Guevara collected two parties of three Indians each in the frontiers of the Seno Mexicano and Nuevo León, to whom he issued titles of captain and took to Mexico City to demonstrate the Indians' reconciliation with the Spanish and their acceptance of peace. By doing so, Guevara's main idea was to present them as evidence of his success in the pacification efforts of the frontier. While at the viceregal court, he made a number of suggestions regarding the northern frontier and demanded that he be named governor and captain general of the colonization project. Disgusted with Guevara's antics, the viceregal authorities denied his request, took the Indians' titles away, and gave them three hundred pesos to return to their homes. When the Spanish court was informed of this, it issued a *cédula* dated January 13, 1743, ordering that the viceroy return to the Indian caciques the titles that Guevara had given to them. More importantly, it also demanded that Guevara be prohibited from involving himself in pacification of the Indians and that the petitioner not be allowed to intervene in viceregal affairs.[4]

The time required for these clarifications between the Spanish court and the viceroyalty in Mexico resulted in a considerable delay in the selection of the colonizer. During the deliberations of Guevara's proposal, Juan Rodríguez de Albuerne, the marquis of Altamira and as *auditor general de guerra* an influential member of the Mexico City viceregal *junta*, or council, strongly condemned the idea of reinstituting the dreaded *congregaciones*. This method of subjecting Indians to imperial rule was so reminiscent of the way in which the *encomienda* system had resulted in the abuse of the natives that *congregaciones* were now deemed to constitute an unwise policy. Aware that Guevara had used them in Nuevo León and had been unscrupulous and immoral in his dealings with the Indians—allegedly because he fathered children with Indian women everywhere he went and asserted his power in the frontier, according to the charges made by the marquis—the council refused to choose Guevara. In effect, the marquis' maneuvering delayed the selection, thwarting Guevara's chances of being named to lead the *entrada*. According to Viceroy Francisco de

Güemes y Horcasitas, count of Revillagigedo, it was the marquis who advised him "to commit and place in charge" José de Escandón to conduct the *entrada* into the Seno Mexicano. Finally, on August 21, 1746, the council recommended to the viceroy Escandón, a proven military commander in the Sierra Gorda. The marquis advised the *junta* to consult Escandón, who accepted the offer to lead the colonization venture into the Seno Mexicano. On September 3, 1746, the *junta* officially recommended Escandón to the viceroy, who accepted the recommendation because he believed that pacification would be of "utility to the service of God, of the king and of the public . . . " Viceroy Güemes y Horcasitas then proceeded to name Escandón "my lieutenant-general . . . " The viceroy later explained that he had given Escandón that title and authority "not only to distinguish him from the rest of the governors, *alcalde mayores* and justices who cooperated with the *entrada*, but also to pay him for the work and expenses in the pacification, and also to encourage him for all of the new activities which presented themselves during the time demanded by the *entrada*."

Escandón received detailed instructions on how to achieve the pacification of the Seno Mexicano. Exploration of the country was to be followed up by its subjugation. The latter required him to place the Indians in missions and to recruit Spanish settlers to found new towns in the region. In effect, Escandón was to be military leader, colonizer, and administrator of the enterprise.[5]

Born in 1700 at Soto La Marina on the northern coast of Spain, Escandón, at the age of fifteen, chose a military career. Shortly thereafter he went to Mérida, Yucatan, where he served as a cadet in a cavalry company. In Mérida, in 1718, he helped the governor repel English pirates who were occupying the island of Tris, which is now called Isla del Carmen. In 1721, he transferred to the militia force at Querétaro, where he quickly rose through the ranks, suppressing three Indian uprisings in that region between 1727 and 1734. By 1740 he had become a colonel in the militia regiment of Querétaro, and at the death of the commander, Escandón was made lieutenant captain general of the Sierra Gorda frontier, with jurisdiction over its *presidios* and missions. According to Fray Vicente de Santa María, his biographer and a family friend, Escandón made three *entradas* into the Sierra Gorda "at his own cost and accompanied by troops and people under his command." During this four-year period (1743–46), he developed a pacification program in which he eliminated the protectors who were exploiting the Indians, reestablished old missions, and founded new ones in the Sierra Gorda district, actions which proved to be effective,[6] according to Fray Santa María.

Besides being a capable and fair-minded military leader and administrator, Escandón was a merchant in Querétaro, where he owned a textile mill. It is likely that the crown's preference for the participation of private capital in imperial projects, such as the colonization of the Seno Mexicano, made the choice of Escandón a good one because he had the needed financial resources to carry out the enterprise.[7]

Upon receiving word of his appointment in September 1746, Escandón immediately made plans for the inspection of the territory he was authorized to conquer and settle. His extensive planning required several months, for he had to coordinate the procurement of supplies, the recruitment of volunteers, and the cooperation of provincial governors. Escandón's exploration plan into the Seno Mexicano called for the use of seven military forces, traveling different routes, to cross the entire territory.[8]

At the beginning of January 1747, Escandón left Querétaro, gathering several contingents of soldiers along the way. His own force, the largest of all seven troops, consisted of 150 soldiers, several missionaries and servants. The other six troops consisted of one from the Huasteca, one from Tampico, one from Monclova, Coahuila, one from Texas, and two from Nuevo León. In all, the expedition totaled 765 soldiers. Escandón's plans called for each of the expeditionary forces to explore the area that it traveled, to map and record the topography, and to learn the character of the Indians, who were not to be antagonized. It was agreed that all of the captains of the troops were to submit written reports to Escandón at a designated point near the mouth of the Río Grande.[9]

On February 24, 1747, Escandón arrived at the Río Grande, about twelve leagues from the mouth of the river, which he proceeded to explore. Except for the captain of the Texas troops, who had arrived farther upriver and sent his report to him, all of the captains conferred with Escandón at the designated rendezvous before they returned to their homes. All of the captains reported that the territory they had crossed had fertile lands for both irrigation and ranching, except for Captain Miguel de la Garza Falcón of the Coahuilan troops, who had moved along the north bank of the Río Grande. De la Garza Falcón reported that the land was arid with little grass and no timber, and therefore unfit for settlement. This gloomy appraisal of the north-bank frontier may have reflected the fact that it was midwinter, when one or two cold spells could easily stunt the growth of the grasses and turn them dry. Having concluded the consultations with the various leaders of the expeditions, Escandón returned to his home to write his report to the Mexico City *junta.*[10]

On October 26, 1747, Escandón completed his report of the *entrada* and his plans for the colonization project, sending the report to the *fiscal,* or royal attorney, at Mexico City. Initially, Escandón planned fourteen sites for settlement, two in the present area of Texas's Gulf Coast and twelve in what is today the border state of Tamaulipas. The frontier was to be settled with people from neighboring provinces, who were to be given generous land grants and special exemptions from taxes for a period of ten years. Not wanting to establish *presidios,* Escandón called for experienced frontiersmen who could defend themselves. He expected to settle 436 families, whom he was to relocate in new settlements. He anticipated a one-time expense of 115,000 pesos, and thereafter 29,000 pesos for the administration of the new colony. The royal attorney forwarded Escandón's report to the viceroy, who called a meeting to discuss the colonization plan.

After several days of meetings, on May 13, 1748, the *junta* approved the project, agreed to make 115,000 pesos available, and placed Escandón in charge of the colonization expedition. On June 1, 1748, the viceregal authorities designated Escandón as governor, captain general, and personal representative of the viceroy in the new territory, which at the suggestion of the marquis of Altamira was formally named Nuevo Santander in honor of the colonizer's birthplace. On October 23, 1748, one and a half years after the *entrada,* the king approved the recommendations of Escandón and the Mexico City *junta.* For his services, the king knighted Escandón and named him count of the Sierra Gorda.[11]

Back at Querétaro, in June 1748, Escandón began to make all of the necessary preparations for settlement of the new territory. Supplies of all kinds, especially seed, farming implements, guns, and munitions, were obtained. Requests for settlers went out to the governors whose provinces bordered the Seno Mexicano, requesting settlers. Escandón wanted farmers, ranchers, and men with building skills as well as mariners to develop fishing and coastal trade. Settlers were to receive from one hundred to two hundred pesos as assistance in moving, and preference was to be given to the men who had come with Escandón in his *entrada* of 1747. By December 1748 the different colonizing parties were ready to enter the Seno Mexicano.[12]

On December 25, 1748, Escandón founded the first *villa,* or town, in the plains of Las Rucias, christened Santa María de Llera. As he did in all of the other settlements, Escandón formally dedicated the townsite, selected sites for church and civic buildings, and vested civil and military power in a captain that he left in place. This investiture of authority in an officer attested to the semimilitary character of the colony and that practice would characterize the government of Nuevo Santander until Mexican independence. Besides the captain, eleven soldiers and forty-four families took up residence at Llera. It was expected that the soldiers would marry into the local families, augmenting the number of colonists. After he founded a number of other settlements in the southern and central parts of the colony, Escandón traveled north to the Río Grande.[13]

In the Lower Río Grande, Escandón founded six settlements, four on the south bank of the Río Grande and two on the north bank of the river. The first of the *villas del norte*, as the Río Grande towns were called, was Nuestra Señora de Santa Ana de Camargo, founded by Escandón on March 5, 1749, at the juncture of the San Juan River and the Río Grande. The settlers for this town came from Cerralvo, Nuevo León, and were under the command of Captain Blas María de la Garza Falcón, one of Escandón's most trusted collaborators in the *entrada* of 1747. The settlement consisted of forty families and a few soldiers. These frontier colonists brought with them large numbers of livestock, including thirteen thousand sheep. Twelve leagues downriver, settlers under Captain Carlos Cantú from Nuevo León awaited Escandón, who on March 14, 1749, christened a civil settlement with the name of Nuestra Señora de Guadalupe de Reynosa. According to historian Carlos E. Castañeda, Cantú had visited the area earlier and he had become familiar with the local Indian language. Unfortunately, the captain failed to locate the site that he had previously found as most appropriate for the new settlement. Consequently, the settlers suffered from recurring rises in the Río Grande and no solution was obtained until they moved to a new site forty years later. These recruits listed their homes as being Cadereyta, El Pilón, Sabinas, and Pesquería Grande. To help them adjust to their new homes, humble settlers at Camargo and Reynosa received a subsidy of one hundred pesos per family and donations of grains and other foodstuffs. Those who were not poor settled "without cost" to the government.

Two additional sites were settled upriver from Camargo, on the south side of the Río Grande. At a site called Los Moros, near the juncture of the Salado River and the Río Grande, a prominent rancher, Don Vicente Guerra, who had earlier brought forty families from Nuevo León, founded the villa de San Ignacio de Loyola de Revilla on October 10, 1750. He had been a soldier under the command of Captain Blas de la Garza Falcón at the Presidio de San Francisco de Coahuila in the mid-1740s. It is likely that Guerra knew of the Escandón *entrada* through his commander, and he was familiar with the new lands because of his ranching activities in the area. Three years later, at a site downriver from Revilla, a settlement called Lugar de Mier (1753) was established by José Florencio Chapa, who brought thirty-eight families from Cerralvo, Nuevo León, in addition to nineteen families who were already living on ranches in the vicinity. The latter settlers were experienced *pobladores* who provided a wealth of knowledge about the resources of the area to the newly arrived colonists.[14]

The last of the Río Grande settlements were made on the north bank of the river, as a small number of *rancheros* and *hacendados* moved their herds of livestock into unclaimed pasturelands. One of these enterprising stockmen was Don José Vásquez Borrego from Monclova, Coahuila, who as early as August 3,

1750, had established a ranch settlement known as Nuestra Señora de los Dolores on the north bank of the Río Grande, at a point ten leagues downstream from present-day Laredo. Vásquez Borrego obtained from Escandón rights to approximately 329,000 acres in present-day Webb and Zapata counties, Texas, as a site for stockraising. The owner's nephew, Don Bartolomé Borrego, was the administrator of the *hacienda*, as the owner and his family remained resident in Coahuila. He also developed two other ranching centers downriver from Dolores, namely Corralitos and Hacienda de San Ygnacio. Corralitos was administered by José Fernando Vidaurri, Vásquez Borrego's grandson, and San Ygnacio was placed in the charge of José Fernando, the youngest son of the *hacendado*.

Of the three sites, the *hacienda* of Dolores was the principal settlement on the north bank of the river. In 1757, Dolores had thirty families totaling 111 inhabitants, all of whom were the *hacendado*'s "servants," including "12 men who were "fully equipped with arms and horses, all uniformed, to serve as a guard of his Hacienda, and to serve him in every other thing required to be done." Vásquez Borrego's herds numbered 3,000 cattle, 3,400 horses and 2,650 mules and donkeys. Dolores also gained a measure of importance because it was located on an easy-to-cross ford in the river. Crossing the river at this ford, appropriately called Paso de Dolores, soldiers, missionaries, and settlers followed the road from Coahuila and Nuevo León to Texas. Until the founding of Laredo, Dolores served as the most direct route to Texas from Coahuila.[15]

The last civil settlement founded on the north bank of the Río Grande was the Villa de San Agustín de Laredo. In this case, too, a rancher pioneered the settlement. In search of pastures for his expanding herds of cattle, horses, sheep, and goats, Tomás Sánchez de la Barrera y Gallardo, a native of Nuevo León, had driven his herds across the river at a well-known ford called Paso de Jacinto de León. When Escandón arrived on an inspection tour of the river *villas* in 1754, Sánchez went to see him at Revilla to ask permission to establish a town at his ranch and to bring in more settlers. Escandón agreed to the settlement proposal, but asked Sánchez to explore first sites other than his ranch in the upper reaches of the Nueces River Valley. Sánchez accepted that condition, but found the Apaches in the valley unwilling to accept Spanish settlement. In the meantime, Escandón had returned to his rural estate near Tampico, leaving word with Vásquez Borrego, whom he designated frontier captain, that Sánchez could proceed with his original proposal to convert his ranch into a town settlement. Sánchez offered to bring in twelve Spanish families, who owned herds and other property, at his cost. Asserting that the lands were not suitable for farming, he promised that the settlers would dedicate themselves to raising livestock so that they could trade for food and clothing. He asked for fifteen *sitios* of land for himself and somewhat less land for the other settlers who had joined his enterprise. He also agreed to place a canoe at the disposal of those who wished to cross the Río Grande. On May 15, 1755, Sánchez took four families, his wagons, and livestock from Dolores to Paso de Jacinto de León, selecting an area of elevated land overlooking the river for the townsite of Laredo. It was there that Vásquez Borrego then proceeded to name Sánchez as founder of the new town, allowing him to establish his ranch on the property between the "Arroyo del Pato and Arroyo Salado, in whatever part he deemed most convenient, so that he not be prejudiced by anyone nor the peace disturbed . . . " Vásquez Borrego also encouraged the growth of the settlement by adjudicating to Sánchez "the wild cattle, the unclaimed horses, fish and all other resources that were to be found in said place so that no one could interfere or impede with those resources . . . " Of the river *villas*, Laredo had the humblest origin, growing slowly in comparison to the other river settlements because of its proximity to Apache warriors, its arid climate and isolated lands.[16]

Coming from a similar frontier background, the town founders, or *capitánes*, provided the leadership essential to guide the growth of the settlements. Blas María de la Garza Falcón was the fifth generation of Garzas to have lived in New Spain. The family was founded by Captain Marcos Alonso Garza y del Arcón, a native of Lepe, Huelva, Spain. He arrived in New Spain in 1550, moving to Durango, where he was a miner. By 1603, he had entered Nuevo León, where he owned the *estancia*, or stock farm, of San Fernando, in the jurisdiction of Monterrey. One of his grandsons, Sergeant Major Blas de la Garza Falcón, became a leading settler in the province. The latter also owned an *estancia* named San Francisco. In 1653, de la Garza Falcón prided himself in having a very large family and other accomplishments: "I have eleven married sons and daughters who live of their own account, with their homes, of whom there are more than thirty-six grandchildren, who increase the growth of this city and kingdom, and five maidens." He also noted that he had often led and furnished armies to fight the nomadic Indians. The third generation were all military men and in the fourth two of the de la Garza Falcones were governors of Coahuila and Texas in the 1720s and 1730s. By 1740 Captain Miguel de la Garza Falcón, as commander of Presidio Santa Rosa, had granted over 300,000 acres to two brothers along the Sabinas River in the Santa Rosa Valley. By granting land to each other and through other purchases, the de la Garza Falcónes had amassed about 457,160 acres of mostly ranching lands. Their vast holdings consisted of a *hacienda* on each side of the river, but they were eventually displaced by the Sánchez Navarros, one of the most powerful of the *latifundista* families of the Spanish New World. Their displacement perhaps contributed to their migration to the Lower Río Grande Valley. Blas María de la Garza Falcón III was born in 1712 near Monterrey, married in Boca de Leónes, Nuevo León, and since 1734 had served as captain at Cerralvo, which was and is located at the edge of the Río Grande frontier, southwest of the new town of Mier. His three children were born in Cerralvo.[17]

Similarly, Captain Vicente Guerra was a fifth-generation American at the time of the founding of the colony of Nuevo Santander. His family originated in the seventeenth century in the town of Montañas de Castilla, Spain. According to family tradition, the founder of this family was Antonio Guerra Cañamar, who first settled in Mexico City before moving to the northern frontier. A settler of Nuevo León, he declared in 1607 that he was a soldier who had "served his majesty since he has been able to bear arms." By the end of the seventeenth century, Guerra Cañamar held a Spanish land grant in the vicinity of present-day Laredo as well as two other small grants near the Río Salado in Nuevo León. Vicente Guerra was one of five children of Juan Guerra Cañamar, who in 1718 was a *vecino* of Cerralvo. The latter was a captain who had engaged in stockraising and mining in that vicinity. He was married to a sister of Captain Blas María de la Garza Falcón.[18]

Prior to recruiting and leading settlers to Nuevo Santander, Carlos Cantú was a prosperous *hacendado* in the valley of San Mateo del Pilón, where corn and sugar cane grew abundantly. He was a son of a frontier soldier also named Carlos Cantú. The Pilón Valley, a major livestock-producing area, had suffered irreversible losses due to Indian raids in the early decades of the eighteenth century. The Cantús were pioneer settlers, arriving in 1596 in the mining district of Ramos in the northern frontier; Ramos is located east of Zacatecas and about eighty miles southwest of Matehuala, an old *real de minas* northeast of San Luis Potosí. There were three brothers, possibly of Italian descent: Fray Lorenzo, Jerónimo, and Jusepe or José. They entered Nuevo León in the early seventeenth century, evidently as part of the contingent of *pobladores* who followed the new governor, Martín de Zavala. Soon they helped to revitalize the impoverished and isolated *reino*, or kingdom. Fray Lorenzo Cantú served as a missionary in Matehuala in 1626, and later founded the mission of San José del Río Blanco, known today as the town of Zaragoza, Nuevo León. The other two brothers worked their way north to Monterrey. Both Lorenzo and Jerónimo were evidently the great uncles of Sergeant Major Carlos Cantú, a son of José Cantú and María de Treviño, the latter a granddaughter of Marcos Alonso Garza y del Arcón. In 1683, Sergeant Major Carlos Cantú asserted that he had "served for more than fifteen years" in the service of the king and "in more than twenty expeditions that have gone out against the Indians in rebellion." The sergeant major also went to Texas with General Alonso de León, his brother-in-law, to search for the French in the expedition of 1686. He was also the grandson of Captain Alonso de Treviño, who arrived in Nuevo León in 1603, where the latter played a key role in the pacification of the Nuevo Leonese frontier and assisted with its economic growth. The Treviños introduced large numbers of cattle, sheep, and horses, as well as farming implements and stones and equipment for a flour mill. Like the other families whose brief histories are noted here, several generations of Cantús held military offices. They were also major landholders in the vicinity of Cadereyta and in the Pilón Valley, where the sergeant major was one of the founders of the town of Montemorelos in 1701. He also participated in the founding of General Terán, Nuevo León (1730), which is located northeast of Monterrey in a district called la Mota Valley.[19] The sergeant major is also credited with establishing the first sugar mill, or *trapiche*, in Nuevo León in 1692. In the last quarter of the eighteenth century, some of the Cantús were still holding land in those Nuevo Leonese districts while others were selling out and moving to older towns in the northeast frontier.[20]

After a thorough inspection of nearly all of the *villas* of Nuevo Santander in 1755, Escandón, convinced that the colonization of Nuevo Santander was complete, wrote a report on the status of his province in which he noted the successes and trials of the settlers. From 1749 to 1751 a drought, which affected all of New Spain, had plagued the colonists and the settled Indians. Escandón wrote that there were "three sterile years" in which the settlers had to receive corn from the crown in order to subsist. The viceroy reported that the colonizer "had obtained corn in the surrounding districts buying this grain at very high prices, up to 10,000 pesos" and that this was done annually "until Divine Providence in the following years facilitated them with this foodstuff that is so natural to this kingdom." Escandón added that the drought was followed by heavy rains that produced disease, with malaria striking both the Spanish and the Indians. The resulting floods also ruined homes, irrigation works, and crops, so that in some settlements not enough food was produced to allow them to live. To subsist, during these years the colonists traded salt, livestock, and meat with the older communities on the frontier for corn and other foodstuffs. Escandón had also opened a port at Soto la Marina, but a sandbar made the site unsuitable for the entry of large sea vessels. Smaller sea crafts brought in farm implements and other supplies, exporting tallow, salt, meat and hides. He added a chart to the report, showing that between December 25, 1748, and October 13, 1755, he had established twenty-three settlements, consisting of one city; seventeen *villas*; two *poblaciones*, or settlements; one *lugar*, or place; and two *reales de minas*, or mining camps. As of 1755, the population totaled 1,481 families, or 6,383 persons, including 144 families of officials and soldiers. There were also 2,837 Indians living in missions administered by Franciscan missionaries. Declaring that some Indians still posed a problem, Escandón felt that a small military force would be needed for a short time until the settlers were able to protect themselves. At that point, he projected that the king's sole expense would be the salaries of the missionaries. Already, however, there was praise for the work Escandón had done in colonizing this frontier, and the viceregal officials expressed high expectations for the continued development of the colony. In his report to the incoming viceroy of New Spain, Viceroy Francisco de Güemes y Horcasitas, wrote that for Escandon's colony "favorable results should be forthcoming due to the fertility of the soil and other conveniences which promise the development of this new enterprise materially and spiritually."[21]

Escandón also reported why he had not given individual land titles to the colonists who held the lands in common. He acknowledged that some settlers were calling for the breakup of the common lands into individual property. Escandón resisted these pressures, citing three reasons why during the early stage of colonization common lands were more advantageous than individual properties: (1) it would be disruptive to have settlers arguing over preferred sites; (2) new and better settlers were still arriving, which made it wise to allow everyone to enjoy common lands, pastures, fields, and irrigation works rather than having them monopolized by a few; and (3) he was unable to occupy himself with the task of making the allotments due to his many duties, and no one else was qualified to carry out the task with integrity and fairness. While the colony was, in fact, still in its infancy, and while demographic growth of the colony supports Escandón's second argument, the third argument is open to question. His reluctance to assign the important task of dividing the land apparently reflected his bias for preferring *peninsulares* instead of *criollos* and others of mixed ancestry. For on another occasion Escandón submitted to the viceroy the names of local *vecinos* "of the lowest social class" to serve as officials for the towns and leaders of the troops, lamenting they were the only ones available to choose from, although he promised that "I am correcting this situation as time permits." Still, the settlers' calls for individual land grants and other events brought the issue to a head in 1766, when the viceroy recalled Escandón to Mexico City.[22]

Two developments precipitated Escandón's recall: (1) some of the settlers and missionaries had leveled charges of maladministration against the governor; and (2) the viceroy wanted to consult with Escandón about the necessity for implementation of the partition of common lands. Escandón, who for more than two years had been urging the central government to conduct an official visitation of the colony, took advantage of the opportunity to recommend the immediate division of the common landholdings. Viceroy Carlos Francisco de Croix responded to both pressures, creating in 1767 a commission, known as the General Visit of the Royal Commission to the Colony of Nuevo Santander, to carry out the division of the lands and to investigate the charges against the governor by his opponents, who were evidently envious of Escandón's success. Field Marshal Juan Fernando de Palacios was appointed to head the commission and was also designated interim governor of Nuevo Santander. Other officials named to assist him included José de Osorio y Llamas, secretary of the Royal Council and Palacio's special assistant. The objectives of the royal commission were to appoint surveyors to review the common landholdings and to survey municipal jurisdictions; to arrange for the granting of land to individual settlers and missions; and to make certain that all transactions were duly recorded so that both settlers and the missions would have proper title to their lands.[23]

THE FIRST ASSIGNMENT OF INDIVIDUAL LANDS IN THE RÍO GRANDE *VILLAS*

In May 1767, the royal commissioners arrived in Laredo. As in each of the towns they had previously visited, the officials proceeded to make a division or partition of the common lands to individual colonists and the missions and granting *ejidos*, or common land, to the town. A variety of land grants intended for specific purposes were made in each of the town settlements. Some of the lands were designated for irrigation. These were called *caballerías*, which consisted of 177 acres. Larger tracts were allotted for pasturage. *Sitios de ganado mayor* were designated for raising cattle or horses, and *sitios de ganado menor* for raising sheep and goats. A *sitio* measured 4,428 acres of land. Each settler was to receive a tract of land within the limits of a town. From the outset of Spanish colonization, however, land was not distributed equally nor to every settler. The basis for determining how much land a colonist received was merit and seniority. Merit was defined as civilian, military, or community service. Seniority referred to the length of time each settler's family had been on the frontier. Settlers with more than six years residence were called primitive settlers. Next came old settlers, those who had lived in the town for a period of six years and not less than two. The last category was the recent settlers, those who had arrived within the last two years. The primitive settlers, their sons, and heirs received two leagues (8,856 acres) of pastureland and twelve *caballerías* (1,500 acres) of land for planting crops. For his service, the captain of the *villa* received twice as much land as the primitive *poblador*. Settlers in the second category were entitled to receive two leagues of pastureland, but only six *caballerías*. The recent settlers obtained two leagues of land for grazing.[24]

The procedure followed by the commissioners in awarding land grants to the settlers can be illustrated by examining the report or proceedings of the *Auto de la visita general* of Reynosa, which was the name given to this event. On the morning of August 23, 1767, after mass had been heard by the inhabitants of the town, the royal officials ordered the settlers to convene, informing them that they were to select two among them to serve as surveyors, along with Don Santiago Longoria and Don Joseph Bernardo Gómez, citizens of Camargo, whom the crown had appointed as its surveyors. The commissioners informed the surveyors that their duty was "to execute said distribution [of lands] in conformity with the instructions which shall be given to them, with attention to the particular circumstances of the lands, the Town and its inhabitants." The officials then instructed the surveyors, who were called "land experts," to "classif[y] the lands in reference to those that are irrigable and those that are temporarily irrigable and suitable for cultivation, grazing, pasturage, commons, and those suitable for the Town, for the purpose of giving them an equitable distribution, that all may share in the good and the bad, and to select those best adapted to the Mission." As instructed, the citizens then elected Don Joseph María Ballí and Don Joseph Antonio Velasco as their surveyors.

The settlers also selected Don Juan Antonio Ballí and Don Joseph Matías Tijerina as their attorneys. In their petition to the king's representatives, Ballí and Tijerina requested that the settlers be given the bulk of the grants on lands on the south side of the Río Grande because of the dense woods on the north side and the danger of hostile "pagan Indians." Requesting that the officials be generous in their awards of land, the petitioners noted "the deficiency of water which these lands suffer for cultivation, and so as to extend [the grants] in such a way as to encourage the growth of our stock, which we possess in small numbers for our maintenance."

On the following day (August 24, 1767), the surveyors agreed to measure the six leagues of the town, which was to remain at its original site despite a history of suffering from repeated overflows from the river. On the evening of that day, Gómez and Velasco marked the west and east boundaries of the town, while Longoria and Ballí first surveyed the south line from the center of the town, returned to the town, and then surveyed the north line crossing the Río Grande.

Two days later, on August 26, 1767, Ballí and Velasco declared that they had "carefully examined the lands set apart and marked out for this Town" and advocated for the disposition of lands in a way that favored the townfolks. They requested that the lands to be apportioned to the settlers should be judged on the basis of their aridity and sterility because of the "rains which are rare in this country, and [because the settlers] have no other privileges or watering places except the Río Grande del Norte." They also informed the crown's officials that the lands west of the town were most appropriate and best adapted to the mission because it was there that Indians were congregated and those lands were nearer the town.[25] Escandón had selected a site for the mission in 1750, but according to the missionary priest, as late as 1752 the Indians came and went because there was no mission. Father Agustín Fragoso explained this fact to his superiors, saying that the sites selected for the town as well as the mission were too close to the river and impracticable for settlement due to the river's rampaging waters during times of flooding.[26] The mission existed in 1757, for Cámara Alta recorded that it was located "one league from the town in the desert on somewhat elevated ground from the river, but that, when the river left its course, it is an unsafe place because it is there that the river runs most swift." This was the same place Escandón had favored for the relocation of the town because it was adjacent, but the settlers objected and the *visitador* Tienda de Cuervo concurred with them that "it did not remedy the situation because that site is more unhealthy than the one they currently have due to the fact that the elevated lands of the mission are surrounded by marshy waters." It was these so-called poor lands that the Indians received, although later observers reported them to be good and fertile.[27] As to the town commons, the town's surveyors declared that the lands situated in its vicinity were best for pastures and grazing land. They also asserted that the remainder of the lands should be awarded to private landholders.[28]

On August 27, 1767, the royal officials concurred with the petition of the town's land experts, ordered the surveys to be conducted, and directed each of the ninety-two citizens to receive his or her portion of land. These grants were called *porciones*. The surveys of these tracts allowed for frontage on the river so that livestock could have easy access to a watering place. Gómez and Velasco began the surveys on August 29, 1767, and continued into the next day. They marked a total of eighty tracts for individual settlers. Of this total, thirty-seven *porciones* were surveyed on the south side of the Río Grande and the balance on the north side of the river.

Any "registered" settler could have petitioned the crown for land, but a few were left out for various reasons. For example, the commissioners noted that "there are a few [settlers] who are wanting to complete the number registered, but there may be three or four who are without merit." It is unclear why some persons were not qualified to be given land, but the officials took seriously the requirement that a person wishing to receive land must be a *vecino*, or resident-citizen. The report of the Reynosa *visita* explained the facts in several cases, including that of "Bernardo Ynojosa, the Sergeant of this squadron [of soldiers who] took his [land grant] in the Town of Camargo, where he has improvements; Joseph Felis Barrera and Joseph Jasso, Original Colonists of this place [Reynosa] presented themselves and renounced their [grants], the first because he has his family in the Nuevo Reyno de León and refused to subject himself to the conditions imposed [on new settlers], and the latter appears to be disposed to remove to the Town of Camargo."[29]

Working rapidly from town to town, the commissioners completed their *visita* at summer's end, returning in the fall to Mexico City to present their report to Viceroy de Croix.[30] In his 1771 report to the incoming viceroy, Croix summarized the work of the *visitador* Palacios and his assistant Osorio y Llamas. He gave them credit for resolving the proceedings against Escandón, for reforming the troops into one *compañía volante,* or "flying squadron," consisting of 110 men and 3 officials, and for eliminating the subsidies (*sínodos*) of the local priests. These changes, he said, produced a savings of twenty thousand pesos annually. Equally important, the work of the commission resulted in the establishment of private, individual landownership throughout the colony. The commissioners awarded at this time land grants to more than one thousand *pobladores* of New Santander.[31] With this foundation, the colony would prosper as the ranching economy expanded.

LAND GRANTS IN PRESENT-DAY SOUTH TEXAS: A CASE STUDY OF HIDALGO COUNTY

Under Spain and Mexico, citizens who settled in the frontier received land grants that made for three types of settlement patterns. Here, I have selected Hidalgo County as a case history since all three patterns can be found there. The *porciones* along the Río Grande were the first lands awarded the settlers. Beyond the town settlements, the land grants were never called *porciones,* but *mercedes de tierras,* which usually contained at least two or more *sitios,* or leagues of land. Grants of two, three, or four *sitios*—intermediate-size *mercedes*—predominated during the Spanish and Mexican periods. The largest land grants, consisting of five or more leagues, were also awarded to common settlers, but favorites of the king or other crown officials often received these large grants. Such grants were intended to support *hacienda*-type ranching enterprises involving *ganado mayor,* although few genuine *haciendas* developed during the Spanish—Mexican periods.[32] Based on these classifications, the various Spanish and Mexican land grants in Hidalgo County can be grouped into the following kinds of land distributions: forty-three *porciones* out of the jurisdiction of Reynosa, twelve intermediate grants, and fourteen large land grants.

Porciones were rectangular in shape and measured nine-thirteenths of a mile of river frontage or width and eleven to fourteen miles deep (length). In a few exceptions, these grants were not riverine, but located back from the river because other settlers already occupied river *porciones.* A *porción* varied in area from about 4,200 acres to about 6,200 acres. The larger *porciones* were awarded to settlers whose lands were of poor quality because they were rocky, sandy, hilly, and/or covered with dense woods, or *montes.* By being awarded these larger tracts, each settler received lands of equal value. Each *porción* allowed the settlers adequate land for grazing and access to water for livestock. Settlers were required to take possession of their property within two months after allotment and to start stockraising. They were prohibited from selling the land to undesirable persons, and were also required to defend the settlement. If any of these conditions were not fulfilled, the land grant would revert to the king. The settlers were required to reside in the towns, in keeping with Spanish civic tradition and because of the need for security, but the men or their ranch help migrated back and forth to herd their livestock on the ranches established on the *porciones.*[33]

POPULATION GROWTH IN THE NUEVO SANTANDER AND THE RÍO GRANDE *VILLAS,* 1749–1821

During the late colonial and early Mexican period, the colony recorded a phenomenal population growth. Tienda del Cuervo's inspection of the colony in 1757 found a population of 8,993. Succeeding censuses reported the continuing growth of settlers. The census of 1782 listed a total of 21,991 persons. Six years later, in 1788, the population had grown to 26,618. According to Calleja's report, the population of Nuevo Santander province in 1794 stood at about 31,000 Spanish and *mestizo* settlers and about 3,500 Christian and Gentile Indians.[34] The 1800 census report enumerated 34,455 persons, increasing to 56,937 in 1810. In the very early years of the nineteenth century, Nuevo Santander surpassed the much older province of Nuevo México, whose population stood at 35,000 in 1815, and the kingdom of Nuevo León, whose inhabitants numbered 43,739 in 1810.[35] Between 1810 and 1821, notwithstanding the disruptions caused by the war of independence, the colony's population continued to grow sharply, reaching 67,434 persons at the time of independence.[36] This growth typified the sharply rising population trends in the late colonial period reported for other regions of Spanish and Portuguese America for which reliable information is available.[37]

The *villas del norte* reflected the overall demographic growth experienced by the colony, as the towns doubled and tripled in size during this period. In the

Table 2.1 Population of the Río Grande *Villas* in Selected Years[a]

Villa	1749	1757	1770	1794	1828–29
Reynosa	279	290	440[b]	1,191	4,060
Camargo	531	678	1,008	1,174	2,587
Mier	166	274	655	973	2,831
Revilla	336	357	230[b]	1,079	3,167
Laredo	167	208	NA[c]	636	2,041
Matamoros					10,000[d]
Total	1,479	1,807	2,333	5,053	24,686
% increase		22%	29%	117%	389%

Sources: Alejandro Prieto, *Historia, geografía y estadística del estado de Tamaulipas* (Mexico City, 1873), 190, 194; *Visita a la Colonia del Nuevo Santander, hecha por el Licenciado Don Lino Nepomuceno Gómez el año de 1770* (Mexico City, 1942), 56, 59, 60, 61; "Nuevo Santander in 1795: A Provincial Inspection by Felix de Calleja," 475, n. 27; Jean Louis Berlandier, *Journey to Mexico during the Years 1826–1834*, trans. Sheila M. Ohlendorf, Josette M. Bigelow, and Mary M. Standifer, 2 vols. (Austin, 1980), 1:262 and 2:426, 428, 430, 431, 434.

[a] Excludes Indians in missions and presidial soldiers.

[b] Children were not enumerated.

[c] Not available. However, in 1767, Nicolás de Lafora credited Laredo with 70 *vecinos*. Nicolás de Lafora, *Relación del viaje que hizo a los presidios internos situados en la frontera de la America Septentrional perteneciente al Rey de España* (Mexico City, 1939), 229.

[d] This is Berlandier's figure, provided to him by a municipal official. Also, see Eliseo Paredes Manzano, *Homenaje a los fundadores de la heroíca, leal e invicta Matamoros en el sesquicentario de su nombre* (H. Matamoros, Tamaulipas, Mexico, 1976), 58, 66, who gives the population of Matamoros as 2,320 persons in 1820 and 3,933 in 1826.

initial years of their founding, the small Spanish towns in the Lower Río Grande region grew slowly, but the rate of population growth quickened around the 1770s, when the second strong wave of territorial expansion began to move toward the Nueces River Valley. As noted in Table 2.1, the total population of the five *villas* in 1749 was 1,479, with Camargo the largest single settlement with 531 people. After their founding, the towns continued to grow and attract new residents. For instance, Cámara Alta reported that in 1757 there were in Camargo 95 families, with a total of 679 persons. He was of the opinion that this town would become very populated "because of the increase in wealth experienced by the *vecinos* [who] were always attracting those who served them."[38] By 1770 there were at least 3,000 inhabitants in the towns of the Lower Río Grande. This estimate is based on the census figure of 2,333 because children were not enumerated in both Reynosa and Revilla and no count was given for Laredo. However, the inspection of Laredo in 1767 reported a count of 429 persons. By 1794 the population of the five towns had increased to 5,053, a 117 percent growth since 1770. At this time one-sixth of the entire population of the colony lived in the five *villas* on the Río Grande. By 1821 the valley towns had increased their share of the colony's population to nearly 21 percent, or 13,956 persons out of a total of 67,434.

During the period from 1770 to the 1820s, a natural rise in the population and migration fueled the increase in the number of town settlers in the Lower Valley. The relative absence of severe Indian attacks apparently allowed for an increase in population at the same time that new settlers were being attracted to the frontier. Two factors that stimulated migration included the continuing expansion of the ranching economy and the opening of a port at Matamoros in 1820. The latter, in particular, attracted new settlers to the river towns as commerce became a more significant economic activity.[39]

The war of independence and the resultant economic recession, however, slowed down population growth in some of the towns of the region. Laredo, a strong royalist base, saw a smaller rise in its population during the period from 1789 to 1819, a rate of only 2.3 percent annually, when compared to the thirty-year period prior to 1789. By 1819 the town's growth had come to a halt and turned into a small loss in 1823.

At the end of the war of independence, recovery of the ranching economy encouraged additional settlers to settle in Laredo. This development, in turn, combined with high birthrates to fuel the town's growth, as reflected in the rise of the population from 1,402 in 1823 to 2,041 in 1828.[40]

Nearly all of the initial population of Nuevo Santander originated in the adjacent provinces of the new colony. Nuevo León and Coahuila contributed at least half of the household heads, or about three hundred families, and most of these participated in the founding of the Lower Valley towns. San Luis Potosí, with eighty-five household heads, contributed the third largest contingent, and Vera Cruz or the Huasteca was fourth with fifty-five. Huastecan settlers as well as others from nearby provinces settled in the southern part of the province. As a result of this population movement, some of the older frontier towns lamented the loss of *vecinos.* Historian Israel Cavazos Garza has noted that "of a bit more than 3,000 inhabitants that [Monterrey] had in 1753 the number had declined to under one thousand" as a result of the colonization of Nuevo Santander.[41]

Because of the growth in the ranching economy and perhaps from a desire for independence from the authorities, many *vecinos* of the towns actually lived in dispersed ranching settlements. Of the town of Mier, Cámara Alta in 1757 noted that "in its environs there are some *rancherías* belonging to the settlers, who [take] advantage of the land, being watered by various *arroyos* . . . which makes the land fertile for the breeding of all kinds of livestock, especially those lands with access to the water of the Río del Norte." In a final observation, he reiterated that "the *jacales* of this town are dispersed as is shown on the map . . . and that it has a *plaza* that is demarcated, which is not occupied . . . " This was also the case in Revilla, where Cámara Alta observed that "there are very few *jacales* in the town, most of the settlers are dispersed in the hill . . . there are various *rancherías* of the *vecinos*, where they live to care for their livestock." He also explained that "since for many leagues around these environs there were no Indians to harass them, [the settlers] live in security and with complete carelessness in the countryside."[42] As time went on, however, more settlers constructed homes in the towns.

According to Palacios and Osorio y Llamas, in 1767, housing construction in the towns along the Río Grande varied from place to place, but not many improvements had been made since the arrival of the first settlers. Of Camargo, they remarked that "it has very good houses made of standard rubble work, some large adobe *jacales*, with grass roofs and others with standard roofs." Dolores, Mier, and Revilla were in the same unhappy condition. Obviously, in some towns the settlers had made material improvements while in others they continued to live as poor country people.[43]

In 1795, Calleja again condemned the persistence of dispersed ranching settlements and poor housing throughout the colony. He reported that nearly everywhere the poor inhabitants continued to dwell in *jacales*. As late as 1815, Laredo *jacales*, for example, were valued as low as five pesos, while other stone structures with walls had a value of twelve hundred and fourteen hundred pesos.[44]

In the beginning of the new settlements, Escandón had wisely prohibited the settlers from dispersing to the countryside, in order to foster town development as a way of ensuring the survival of the colonization project and to prevent the loss of lives and herds to Indian attackers. This prohibition tended to encourage the growth of community and gave the settlers a common history. From the earliest stages of settlement, however, settlers actually occupied new lands beyond the limits of the towns.[45] Consequently, in addition to town settlements, the founding of *ranchos* in the outlying districts quickly characterized Spanish settlement patterns. The awarding of land grants in 1767 further encouraged the dispersal of the population, limiting the physical growth and improvement of the towns.

SOCIAL CHARACTERISTICS OF THE SPANISH SETTLERS

Historically, social class was not an important feature of the society. Most of the early pioneers were common folk or *paisanos* who seized the opportunity presented by the founding of a new colony to improve their human condition. For some of them, the harshness of living in older districts where they suffered from hunger, Indian depredations, mistreatment, or abuse by government officials and by their landlords served as motives to move in hopes of finding personal and economic security.[46] Since the settlements were close to each other, in time nearly everyone was related to everyone else by blood or marriage, usually in the third or fourth degree. Church dispensations to marry a relative were not uncommon and dated to the beginning of Spanish society in the northern frontier.[47] Moreover, the lack of rich mines in the Coahuila-Nuevo León frontier and the late settlement of Nuevo Santander meant that few wealthy persons were attracted to this corner of New Spain, restricting the rise of an elite society similar to what had happened in the older and wealthier mining districts.[48] Since the settlers, servants, and other hired workers resided on the land and worked together, the tendency was for the society to be fluid and generally egalitarian. In effect, frontier conditions fostered a sense of social equality among the colonists, despite some differences in wealth and status.[49]

Still, the social structure was stratified with three distinct layers. Large landholders, high governmental officials, and merchants were at the apex of society. *Rancheros*, administrators, and artisans made up the middle group, while servants and Indians were at the bottom. There was a degree of conflict in this complex society, mostly as a result of the mistreatment of peons, in spite of regulations prohibiting abuses and allowing for the punishment of offenders, who were usually the masters. Without social histories of the various towns, it is impossible to determine the extent of this problem. However, very few areas of Nuevo Santander and later Tamaulipas had peons. For example, in 1839 Don Manuel Payno, a high-ranking official in the treasury, wrote a brief account of the character, manners, and industry of the people in the Matamoros area and noted that there were servants but no peons who were indebted as they were in the rest of the country. Of course, power struggles, as well as other types of clashes, existed among governmental, church, military, and private citizens.[50]

Beyond the towns, *rancheros* were dominant. In 1794, Calleja enumerated only seventeen *haciendas*, as compared to 437 ranches, in all of Nuevo Santander. Thus, the basic unit of social organization was the *rancho*, or ranch settlement, where several families built their houses in the general vicinity to maintain a sense of community and to provide for mutual protection.[51] The predominance of *ranchos* restricted the rise of a more class-oriented society, but did not prevent the rise of a limited number of *latifundios* in the new colony and the continuation of a few that predated Escandón's colonization.

The few who were moderately well off tended to remain in the older urban sites of New Spain or in the new towns of the colony, sending administrators to manage their rural estates and servants to care for their livestock. This, of course, was a longstanding practice among the *hacendados* of Nuevo León as well as the rest of Latin America. In the selection of administrators, preference was given to sons or other relatives.[52] Blas María de la Garza Falcón, for example, placed his son, José Antonio, as majordomo of Rancho Santa Petronila, and as early as 1750, the captain's household included sixteen servants who undoubtedly worked on his Camargo rancho called Carnestolendas, located on the north side of the Río Grande.[53] Reports indicate that Nicolás de los Santos Coy employed over one hundred men to work on his *ranchos* (one was on the north and the other on the south side of the river) in the vicinity of present-day Río Grande City, Texas, in the early 1750s. While he resided in Camargo in the early years of its founding, he evidently later returned to Cerralvo, where he died in about 1767 and was buried. It is likely that he left a majordomo in charge of his *ranchos*, for when he died he left a considerable number of small and large livestock and he claimed no land anywhere else other than houses and *solares* in both Saltillo and Cerralvo, where he had been a resident. In fact, both his wife and a sole daughter received *porciones* in Camargo in 1767, and evidently the ranching operations on those lands continued.[54]

While our knowledge of the *pobladores*' daily life is sketchy, community life revolved around the towns and *ranchos* of the region. Isolated from New Spain's main centers of government and commerce and largely responsible for their own defense, patriarchy became the basis of social and economic life in Nuevo Santander. Américo Paredes, who has studied the region's folklore and music, asserts that patriarchs held the reins of power in the *ranchos*, making decisions concerning planting, *rodeos*, or roundups as well as decisions affecting family matters. Groups of elders thus made decisions on actions that called for community projects, such as building ditches and dams, and opening up the levees along the Río Grande in time of floods.[55]

As noted above, military men also exercised authority and their actions affected the colony's townspeople. Calleja, however, argued that the colony had seen its greatest development when it was under Escandón's tight military administration, but had declined when the half-*cabildos* were organized following the Palacios and Osorio y Llamas visit (1767) and the subsequent erosion of military preparedness.[56] There is some evidence to support Calleja's assertion, although, except for the study of Laredo by historian Gilberto M. Hinojosa, competition and conflict among the different authorities in the towns have not been studied. For example, in Laredo Tomás Sánchez, whose power base in the town government, or *cabildo*, was eroded by newcomer settlers from Revilla in the late 1760s, used his military authority to remove opponents from office. Also, when the new settlers removed the town records across the river to the south side, where they held their lands, Sánchez appealed to the governor for assistance and the latter sided with the *capitán.*

Observers who recorded their views about the character of the settlers found much to dislike, although others presented more positive impressions. While Escandón esteemed colonists who genuinely appreciated him, other official inspectors were not so kind in their assessments of the settlers. One of the first to write down his views was Cámara Alta in 1757. Of the Reynosa settlers, he noted that "many of them had become rich," from the trade in salt and stockraising, but "he who is not [rich] is . . . lazy, which in the extreme they are." Of the Camargo settlers, the *visitador* merely remarked that they too were well off, in fact, better off than in Nuevo León because their herds had increased dramatically. In Revilla, the settlers too had done well from the salt trade and stockraising so that their profits "were worth two or three seasons of planting," precluding them from applying themselves to farming, which was very difficult to do on account of the dry, hot weather. He did not, however, revile the settlers of Revilla as he had those of Reynosa.[57] Félix de Calleja, a professional military man who became viceroy in 1813, hardly knew the *pobladores* in Nuevo Santander, but this did not prevent him from making harsh observations about them. He said that "in character and customs, the people are lazy, dissipated, with relative luxury in their dress, arms, and horses, pusillanimous, captious, and sarcastic murmurs, all stemming from the fact that the population of this province was formed from among the vagabonds and malefactors of the others." However, in another observation, he faulted the colony's lack of development on the prevalent pastoral, migratory nature of the settlers. This, he explained, "hampers industry, ruins good customs, and makes the people lazy with all the attendant accidents and vices as well as an untidy air." In still another observation, he moved away from criticizing the settlers' character to blaming the failure of development on external factors such as a lack of markets, roads, and ports, which he urged the government to sponsor.[58]

Favorable views and perceptions of the settlers can be found. In a florid description of the northeastern provinces, Ramos Arizpe found the settlers to be brave and hardworking people who sought "to reap the benefit . . . of prosperity by means of agriculture."[59] In the early 1830s, the abolitionist Benjamin Lundy made several sojourns to both Nuevo León and Tamaulipas, spending more time in the latter state. His appraisal of the people's social, religious, and political mores was both positive and optimistic:

> The moral character of the people (every thing considered) will not suffer in comparison with that of the inhabitants, generally of our southwestern States. It is, indeed, far above the standard in many southern parts of the

> northern Union. Such degrading exhibitions of drunkenness, profanity, and impiety, are never witnessed, among the native Mexicans, here. . . . If we do not meet with as many instances of exalted piety and philanthropy, as in some other civilized communities, neither do we perceive the corrupting giant vices so extensively exercising their debasing influence. Many of the inhabitants are polite and genteel.

Still, he noted that "there is, among all classes, a want of industry and enterprise. Many creditable exceptions, however, must be made to this general remark." Finding them to be simple in tastes, fond of amusements, and convivial, he remarked, "the natural disposition of these people is mild, and their demeanor unassuming." Perhaps not fully understanding the importance of race because he was an abolitionist who wanted to find a refuge for Black Americans and mulattoes, he thought that the settlers were not prejudiced toward each other on account of the racial intermixture of the population. Finally, he judged them as being republican in sentiment and fair in the conduct of their legal proceedings.[60]

Besides observers' perceptions, insight into the character of the Spanish and Mexicans can be gained by examining individual and group behavior in varying situations. Especially in a time of need, cooperation among settlers, soldiers, and missionaries served to unite the settlements. Indian uprisings had traditionally led to soldier-civilian campaigns. Other occasions that were not as critical called the settlers to a common cause. For example, the twelve families from Camargo and Reynosa who moved in 1774 to the new lands near the mouth of the Río Grande all built their first houses at the ranch site of their leader, Captain Ignacio Anastacio de Ayala. Captain Ayala offered to accommodate them so that they would "benefit from its geographical location and for the necessity of defending themselves against the Indians."[61] Due to recurrent floods in Reynosa, the townspeople made repeated requests for permission to relocate the townsite to safer ground, with the last petition having been made in 1799. The officials did not respond. However, a great midsummer storm in 1802, which completely destroyed the frontier town of Azanza in Nuevo León and caused considerable damage downriver, including Reynosa, prompted the settlers in the latter town to act quickly to restore their well-being. Don Juan Ignacio Ramón of the military squadron of Punta de Lampazos reported, among other details of the destruction, to the militia commander of Nuevo León that "in the town of Reynosa, all of the citizens evacuated the town on rafts made with the doors and lumber of their houses, besides completely abandoning that location, and forming a settlement of *jacales* in the Hacienda of San Antonio." Located five leagues east of the town, the *hacienda* belonged to José Francisco Ballí, who asked the authorities compensation and other privileges for the loss of his lands, which he had incurred "in order to protect and free those citizens from the risks in which they found themselves."[62] As a consequence of this storm, the relocation of Reynosa took place in 1803, bringing to an end the bureaucratic impasse that for so long had precluded the settlers from moving to a new and safer site. In the following year, Ballí too was rewarded with a new grant north of the Río Grande.[63]

While survival and adaptation to their new lands necessitated a spirit of neighborly cooperation, disputes arose among the settlers from a variety of sources. For example, unfriendly lawsuits, or *pleitos*, were part of the Hispanic cultural legacy these *pobladores* brought to the Río Grande settlements. Already in 1779, José Fernando Vidaurri, grandson of Vásquez Borrego, and his administrator of Hacienda de Corralitos, was engaged in litigation with the *hacendado*'s two sons, Fernando and Macario Borrego, over Viduarri's alleged "rights to a portion of lands [consisting of] *sitios* and *caballerías* that he has possessed and made a claim for which the Privativo de Ventas y Composiciones [has] authorized the survey."[64]

Disputes were not always over such high stakes as land and water rights. For instance, Señora María Miguela Estrada complained to the town justice at Palafox, a new *villa* upriver from Laredo, that one Don León Montesuma had sold a horse belonging to her. The justice promptly informed the latter of the complaint and wrote the *alcalde* of Laredo for help in resolving the issue. In another case, José Rafael Enríquez, Palafox's town justice, asked the help of Rafael López de Orepesa, a citizen of Laredo, in recovering four or five boat loads of wood, which he claimed the "Indian Marcelo with four others have taken." Enríquez advised de Orepesa to seek out Laredo's chief justice, explain the facts, and obtain an "order that the same persons who removed [the wood] from [Palafox] will deliver it to the home of Don Victorino Dovalina, with the approval of the justice."[65] Despite conflicts among the *pobladores*, the settlers as a whole possessed enduring qualities that fostered the development of the colony.[66]

Nuevo Santander's population included various racial and ethnic groups resembling the pattern found in much of the northern frontier of New Spain. Among them were *españoles*, or Spanish, who were either Spanish or American-born of Spanish descent; another equally large category consisted of *mestizos*, or mixed-bloods of Spanish-Indian descent; another group included smaller numbers of blacks and mulattoes, principally in the southern coastal areas of Nuevo Santander bordering on the Huasteca region. Persons of African-Indian ancestry were also known as *zambos*. Christianized Indians were considered Gentiles, who had their own legal and social status. Generally, they were settled in nearby missions and counted separately in the censuses. According to the census of

1788, *españoles* constituted the most numerous of the population groups, but they were greatly outnumbered by the total of all ethnic and racial groups. In that year, there were 5,220 Spanish, 4,744 Indians, 3,428 *lobos* (a mixture of Indian and mulatto), 3,047 *mestizos*, 2,942 mulattoes, 2,761 *castas*, or castes (a category including all persons not of Spanish or Indian descent), and 1,372 Negroes. In 1810, the colony's population counted 14,639 Spanish, 28,825 *castas*, and 13,251 Indians. Nuevo Santander consisted of heterogeneous peoples, although culturally the Spanish element was predominant.[67] The *villas* of the north had a mix of peoples similar to the colony's, except for the low numbers of Negroes, probably because there were no mines and but one or two *haciendas* in the region.[68]

Even after racial identification was outlawed, following Mexican independence, an unofficial draft of the Laredo census for 1835 classified the heads of household according to racial and ethnic background.[69] However, the legal formalisms that had established and sanctioned racial distinctions among the inhabitants were no longer acceptable. In fact, the Spanish legacy of *mestizaje* continues to this day in the American Southwest.

Still, the question remains: were racial and ethnic distinctions in the late colonial and Mexican period significant? Most scholars assert that race and ethnicity often became blurred in the periphery of New Spain, and that the frontier had a way of lessening the importance of color. This was especially true if a person experienced upward economic mobility or attained the social characteristics of the more dominant and preferred racial groups in society, which in New Spain meant the Spanish or *criollo*. *Mestizos* and even mulattoes who achieved wealth and prominence sought to pass themselves off as Spanish. Without further study, it is, however, difficult to document individual cases of this sort, or the degree to which it occurs.[70]

One aspect of Spanish society that persisted was the use of the title of *don* and *doña*. Employed with discretion, such titles designated high-born status reflecting wealth, power, or authority in the *villas* of Nuevo Santander. However, persons who used such titles definitely had to be Spanish in origin (except for Tlascaltecans who also used the title in the northern frontier). In 1835, for instance, only 20 percent of the Spanish in Laredo, usually the largest landowners, held such titles.[71]

SPANISH–INDIAN RELATIONS IN THE FRONTIERS OF NUEVO SANTANDER: A LEGACY OF WAR

The so-called *indios bárbaros* were a major concern that dated to the time of the early *entradas* into these vast, semidesert regions. While some groups had been subdued through warfare or mission life, many others had not. Throughout the eighteenth century, viceregal authorities, provincial governors, and military commanders in the field were well aware of the Indian menace to the settlements in the northeastern frontier of New Spain, including Texas, Nuevo León, and Nuevo Santander. According to Calleja, during Escandón's tenure the colony faced hardly no severe Indian problems, except for intermittent and short-lived attacks in the Sierra Gorda district. Calleja attributed the colonizer's success to the swiftness with which he used military force. This is how he summarized Escandón's approach to dealing with the Indians:

> He treated the Indians as required; he watched things very closely; none challenged his efforts. His interest was the same as that of the residents and troops. . . . The enterprises were prompt and opportune and his successes corresponded. Enemies, spied upon and pursued by all, had no security in any part, succumbing slowly and becoming reduced to the missions after much effort in which they and the troops had different successes.

Escandón's years of frontier experience must have paid off, for the colony in general enjoyed peace and prosperity during his tenure of office. When this peaceful and prosperous period ended in the 1780s, Calleja, a military man who was a product of the eighteenth-century world, blamed the change in policy that emphasized peace over warfare for the resumption of Indian raids.[72] The astute and capable second count of Revillagigedo, Don Juan Vicente de Güemes Pacheco de Padilla y Horcasitas, viceroy of New Spain (1789–1794), defined that policy, saying that "it is necessary to accommodate oneself to the character and manner of making war to the savages, with whom as a general rule, peace is always preferable, it being necessary to make war on them only to punish them, for their failure to keep the peace which they have made, and then again granting it to them."[73] Still, military preparedness was of necessity a priority on that frontier, and several important military inspections of the *presidios* during the eighteenth century had resulted in a general reorganization of Spain's defensive system in the borderlands. Among the most important changes were the creation of the intendencies to govern the vast frontier provinces, relocation of some *presidios* and the augmenting of their forces, and a greater dependence on provincial militias.[74]

Toward the final years of Spain's reign, the viceroys continued their vigilance over Indian raids and possible foreign threats in the northeastern frontier provinces, expending considerable resources in their attempts to protect the settlers. In 1798, Nuevo León counted one *compañía volante* with one hundred men, while Nuevo Santander had three such units, each consisting of seventy-five soldiers and officers.[75] In addition to these regular forces, extensive provincial militias were also available. These forces were part of the command of Lieutenant Colonel Calleja, military commander of the intendancy of San Luis Potosí. Officially, the provincial militia forces of Nuevo Santander totaled 2,358 men, and those of Nuevo León numbered 1,156 men. All of the militia were cavalry and dragoons. These numbers represented by far the largest militia forces in all the *gobiernos* of New Spain, attesting to the dangers presented by being exposed to Indians on the frontier.[76] Calleja, who urged a more aggressive campaign toward the Indians, doubted, however, the ability of the militia forces, but he held on to a lingering hope that the troops could be instructed, armed, and "inspir[ed] . . . with military and patriotic ideas which they will need."[77] In spite of the presence of these regular troops and the availability of a large number of militias (including twenty-six independent units alone in Nuevo Santander and sixteen units in Nuevo León, the Tenth Brigade), the last viceroys of New Spain continued to counsel caution against the Indians and other enemies who might attack the kingdom by landing on the "*mar norte*" or Gulf Coast.[78]

A brief history of Indian attacks in Nuevo León and Nuevo Santander during this period reveals that these activities were largely intermittent skirmishes. In 1800, Viceroy Miguel José de Azanza reported that there were no Indian hostilities in Nuevo León and in Nuevo Santander, due to a peace treaty with the Lipan Apaches.[79] The next viceroy, Félix Berenguer de Marquina, however, noted in 1803 the return of Indian hostilities to both provinces, but especially to Nuevo Santander, where Indians in the Sierra Tamaulipeca "had been punished opportunately, and at present can be found in perfect tranquility." Reflecting the sentiment of frontier settlers, the viceroy expressed considerable fear of the Lipans, who were also then at peace but whom he did not trust because of the "bad faith that characterizes that nation." They were at peace, he thought, not because of a change in their character, but because a *viruelas*, or smallpox, epidemic had struck them and reduced their number. Consequently, they had taken refuge in the frontier of Nuevo León, across the Salado River, on account of the fear of the Comanches, their bitter enemy.[80] Perhaps because of the worsening conditions on the frontier, by 1803 the regular cavalry troops of Nuevo Santander had risen to 370 men.[81] In addition, the militia forces were still available to defend the frontier not only against Indians, but also against the Americans pushing into Texas, a new concern. Still, in 1807 the commanding officer in Texas, Don Nemesio Salcedo decried the lack of discipline among the militia of both colonies, who "though much more agile and intelligent in the use of the horse . . . [,]in order to unite them in unison it has been indispensible to reorganize them again on account of the many old veterans, the ill, and those married and with large families . . . "[82] This state of affairs was a bad omen for frontier settlers, for following its independence Mexico would hardly improve on this military arrangement.[83]

THE DECLINE OF THE INDIANS IN NUEVO SANTANDER

At the start of the conquest of the Aztecs, there may have been as many as 190,000 Indians in the territory that became Nuevo Santander, but most of the colonial period saw a rapid deterioration in their numbers. Prior to Escandón's colonization, it is impossible to document the ethnohistory of this area and to understand the dynamics of Indian migrations and settlements. In broad terms, the Tampico area represented the northernmost reach of the Huaxtecans. Beyond the Purificación and Soto la Marina rivers lived the Chichimecs, perhaps the ancestors of the Olives and Pisones tribes. North of the Chichimecs were the *rancherías* of the nomadic hunter-gatherers Coahuiltecans. These latter two groups were often the targets of slaving expeditions, especially in the late sixteenth century, which resulted in their movement from their Seno Mexicano homelands to adjacent Spanish frontier zones, such as Nuevo León and Saltillo. In the seventeenth century, some Indians were in missions in the south and central areas, and others were free Indians competing with Spanish and *mestizo* stockmen and herders.

By the middle of the eighteenth century, Peter Gerhard estimates that fifteen thousand Indians remained in this immense and hostile territory, of whom one-third had been reduced and the rest were still living unreduced. During Escandón's governorship (1748–1767) some Indians were congregated in missions, while others fled to the Sierra de Tamaulipa Vieja region or northward to join Apache warriors.[84] By the end of the colonial period, the Indian population was practically wiped out, with only about two thousand remaining in settlements and another thirteen hundred still in the wild. As occurred in most other parts of the New World, however, the Indians rebounded following this long period of population loss. Fernando Navarro y Noriega's statistical reports cite a figure of 13,251 Indians for the colony in 1810.

Contact with the Spanish rapidly brought about the decline of the Indian population. Fighting Indians began with the conquest of Cortés, but more importantly it figured in the experience of the settlers and *presidio* soldiers who had lived in Nuevo León and Coahuila, where their more recent history (since the start of the eighteenth century) was a story of generalized warfare against raiding bands and rebellious Indians. Since the 1570s, however, the Spanish and Indians had fought bitter, drawn-out wars in the northeastern frontier. This was the period known as the time of the *guerra viva.*[85] But other motives could justify a war against the Indians. For example, because many Indians would not accept settlement in missions, Spanish frontier officials often dealt sternly with Indian raiders. In 1780, Governor Manuel Ignacio de Escandón, the colonizer's son and the second count of the Sierra Gorda, decided on a military campaign to put down Indian unrest in the mountainous country of central and southern Nuevo Santander, the perennial trouble spots of the colony. But the Spanish had very little success, although many Indians and settlers perished in the war.[86] In addition to Indian losses due to voluntary migration, and more particularly the slave hunts that resulted in the formation of *congregas,* some Indians in the coastal areas of the Seno Mexicano were recruited by missionaries from San Antonio, according to the Marqués de Rubí.[87] Epidemics also took a toll. Gerhard has identified the following epidemics: the plague of 1684, *matlazáhuatl,* or typhus of circa 1740, smallpox in 1748 and 1777, and again in 1792.[88] In short, as had occurred throughout the New World, disease, warfare, enslavement, recruitment by missionaries, and other causes depleted the bulk of Indians, regardless of whether they were nomadic or settled, peaceful or belligerent.

The dramatic impact of Spanish contact with the Indians can be seen in the rapid drop in the population of Indians living in missions in the new colony. In 1755, 4,300 Indians resided in twenty-one missions. Two years later the number had dropped to 3,473. When the Franciscans from the Colegio de Guadalupe of Zacatecas, who were at odds with Escandón from the beginning of the colonization project, left Nuevo Santander in 1766, the number of Indians in the missions declined again. The priest Lino N. Gómez, who made an official visit to all of the missions in Nuevo Santander in 1770, found missions at Camargo, Mier, Revilla, and Reynosa. The number of Indian families ranged from a low of twenty-six at Mier to a high of ninety-seven at Reynosa.[89] He listed Camargo as having 246 Indians, Mier 101 Garzas, Revilla 25 Garzas and Malaguecos, and Reynosa 222 Comecrudos, Tejones, and Pintos.

In 1772, Governor Manuel Ignacio de Escandón noted that there were only nine missions in the colony, two of which were located on the Río Grande. This report indicates that two missions had ceased to exist within two years after Father Gómez' visit. The two remaining missions on the Río Grande were San Joaquín del Monte and San Agustín. The first was under the jurisdiction of Reynosa and the second under Camargo's jurisdiction. According to Escandón, San Joaquín had a tribe of "*indios pintos y tejones*" ("spotted and racoon-like Indians") augmented sometimes by 275 "*indios comecrudo*" ("Indians who eat raw"). Mier had no congregation of Indians, but two "nations" regularly came there. At Revilla about forty Indian families would come and go as they pleased. On the outskirts of Laredo, in the *despoblado,* or unpopulated lands, Escandón reported that numerous Borrado Indians devoted themselves to stealing livestock and, on occasion, killing people. Lipan Apache Indians participated in these raids.[90]

The mission Indians were a pastoral people whose lives improved very little while under the guidance of the missionaries. According to Father Gómez, all of the missions had fertile and abundant lands, but their material success was limited to some farming and sheepraising. Gómez recommended better care of the missions and better use of the land. Governor Manuel Ignacio de Escandón found that the Mission San Joaquín del Monte had no irrigation system, due to the high banks and rapid flow of the river, but the Indians grew corn and other crops along the meadows and hollows of the river. Mission San Agustín at one time had had up to 500 Indians of "many nations," but the number was now reduced to 249 Indians, who were all Christians. The governor reported that the Indians were skilled in carpentry, masonry, and other occupations. They also farmed the humid valleys, raising corn and vegetables, but their lands were more appropriate for stockraising.[91]

The Indian population in Nuevo Santander continued to fall during the late colonial period. In 1793, Revilla Gigedo reported a total of 3,791 for the entire colony in missions. Of that total, the Lower Valley had 1,328 Indians. According to Calleja, in 1795, 1,434 Christian Indians and 2,190 Gentile Indians lived in the colony of Nuevo Santander. Calleja also reported that 2,030 warriors who were considered to be their enemies lived north of the Río Grande in Spanish Texas. Another 420 warriors lived in the southern part of the colony in the Sierra de Tamaulipa region.[92] Ramos Arizpe asserted that in 1810 fewer than 1,000 Indians inhabited the region, some nomadic and others settled in six missions. His claim is reasonably correct. A statistical study, made in 1813, of the *curatos,* or parishes, and missions of New Spain listed seven missions in the colony: Croix, Forlón, Guadalupe, San José de Palmas, Palmitos, Prétil, San Roque de Llera, and San Vicente. None of these missions were located on or near the Río Grande, although the missions of Mier and Camargo were still in existence in 1816. Unfortunately, the number of mission residents is not given. A significant number of Indians must have either died or mixed with the Spanish population. Others evidently migrated away to impede settlers in adjacent frontier communities. At least one historian, Jesús Franco Carrasco, is of the opinion that the mission program failed because the Indians were too few and of such low cultural development and the missionaries not especially capable or qualified that the mission program failed. He argues that the hunter-gatherer

Indians of the region easily found comfort in returning to their roaming ways in the Tamaulipan brush country.[93]

Lack of detailed studies of the social structure of the *villas* in the late Spanish and Mexican periods makes it difficult to know to what degree the settled Indians were acculturated and absorbed by the more dominant Spanish and *mestizo* town settlers. Still, a few Indians persisted in the settlements. In Laredo there are records of marriages of several Indian couples in 1792 and of at least one other couple in 1811.[94] Also, in the 1830s Berlandier noted that Indians were still living in missions and some were married to Mexicans in the towns along the Río Grande.[95] Some Hispanicization had obviously taken place among the surviving Indians. For example, in 1832 "auxiliary citizens and Indians of the 'Garza nation' " of the town of Mier petitioned the state government for redress of a longstanding dispute with the local *alcalde* over the rental of their lands.[96] As noted above, however, much of the *mestizaje*, or race mixture, that did occur had already taken place in the older frontier areas of New Spain.

ADDITIONAL LAND GRANTS IN SOUTH TEXAS, 1774–1848

After the formal adjudication of the *porciones* along the Río Grande, unoccupied lands north and east of the Río Grande towns attracted the attention of the growing population of new *pobladores* whose herds were multiplying at a rapid pace. As noted in Table 2.1, the population of the Río Grande *villas* rose from 1,807 in 1757 to more than 5,000 in 1794. As a consequence of this increase, Spanish officials granted extensive tracts for stockraising to the citizens of Camargo and Reynosa. These colonists founded new *ranchos* that accounted for rapid territorial expansion and for a large part of the rise in the number of livestock. The first of these large territorial expansions occurred in 1774. In that year, thirteen families—twelve from Camargo and one from Reynosa—named Captain Don Ignacio Anastacio de Ayala of Camargo as their representative to arrange the purchase of a huge acreage east of Reynosa and south of the Río Grande. This tract, which consisted of 113 *sitios*, or square leagues of land, was part of a much larger grant that belonged to the estate of Don Antonio de Urizar, a Mexico City merchant. The buyers immediately occupied and stocked their land, although its legal division into thirteen separate ranches did not take place until late 1784. The site selected by Captain Ayala lay at the easternmost part of the tract, near the mouth of the Río Grande, and with his permission the thirteen families made their home at his ranch, San Juan de los Esteros, for mutual protection. Within a short time, the

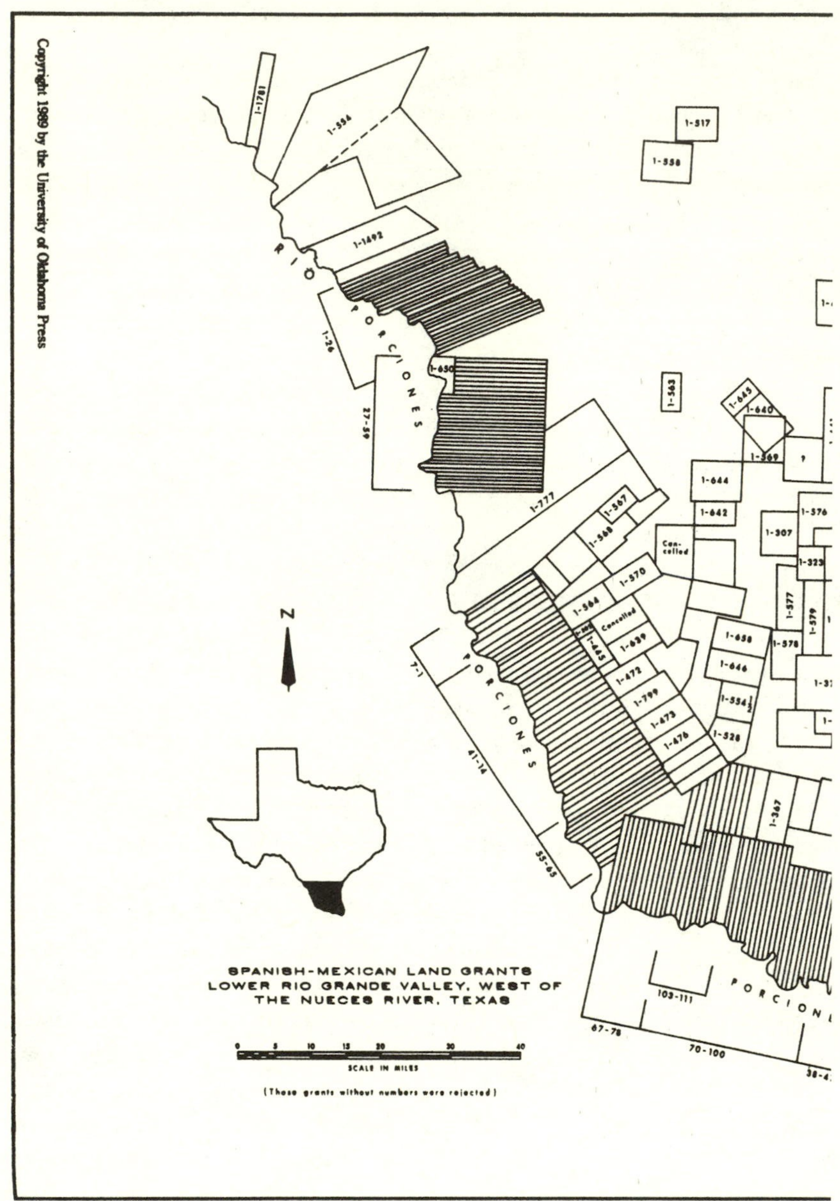

Reproduced courtesy of the University of Oklahoma Press from Warren A. Beck and Ynez D. Haase, Historical Atlas of the American West.

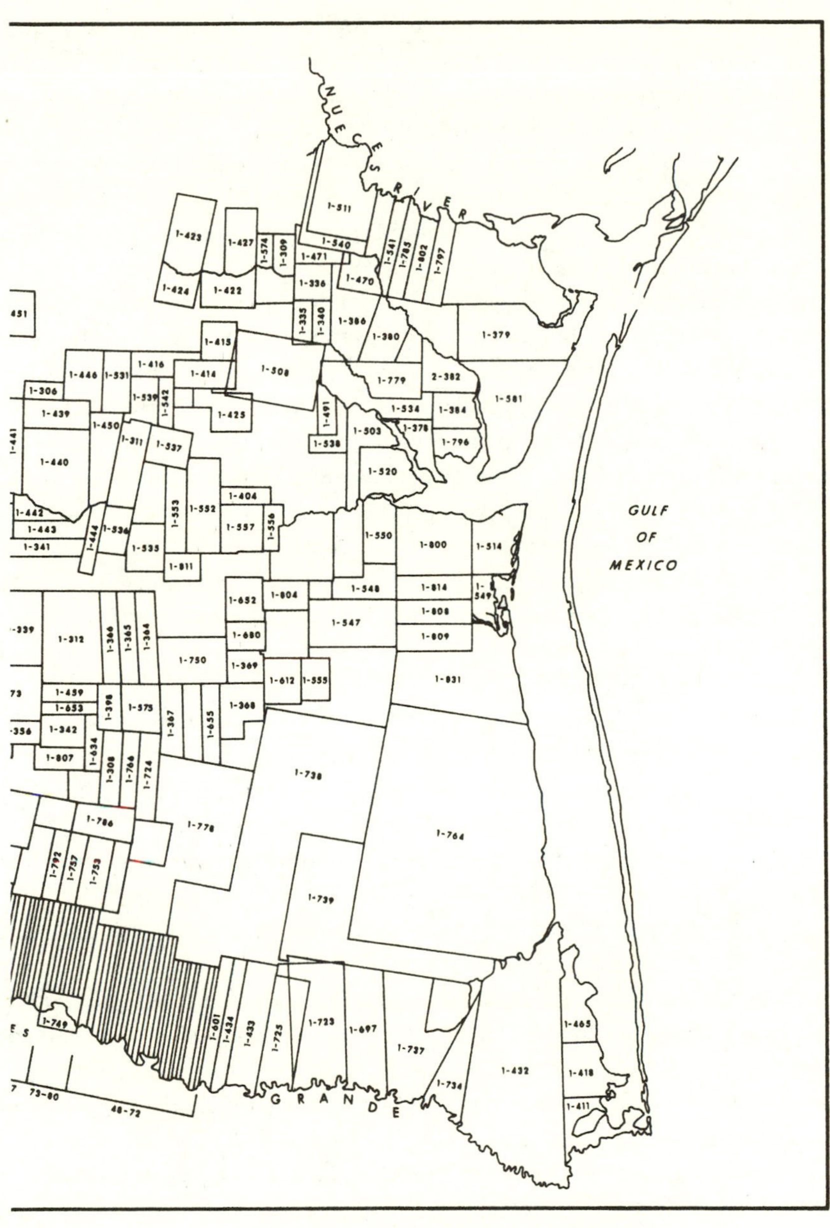
NUECES RIVER
GULF OF MEXICO
GRANDE

site became known as Congregación del Refugio, growing rapidly to the status of a town. Renamed Matamoros after Mexico achieved independence, the town experienced a boom in the 1820s, when it became the major port of entry for commerce to all of the river towns.[97]

A corollary to this territorial expansion took place on the north bank of the Río Grande. Coveting more pasturelands for their growing herds of sheep and cattle, the leading *pobladores* at Reynosa petitioned the courts in 1777 for large tracts of land east of the *porciones* (see Map 2). The captain and chief justice at Reynosa, Juan José Hinojosa, and his son-in-law, José María de Ballí, were among the first *vecinos* to seek new grants. In 1778 Hinojosa received the Llano Grande grant, containing twenty-five leagues with about fifteen miles of river frontage. Ballí was granted an adjoining tract known as La Feria, containing about twelve and a half leagues of land. Both of these grants were but a day's ride from Reynosa. After the death of her father and husband, Rosa María Hinojosa de Ballí applied in her own name to the crown for lands north of Llano Grande and La Feria. In 1794 she received the San Salvador del Tule Grant, which she apparently intended for her son, Juan José Ballí, to whom she transferred the title. The San Salvador del Tule comprised seventy-two leagues of land. In the same proceedings, she obtained an adjoining grant for her brother, Vicente Hinojosa. His grant, known as Las Mesteñas, consisted of thirty-five leagues. Shortly afterward, Vicente Hinojosa conveyed by sale the eastern half of his grant to his sister, who had evidently paid for the surveys and necessary improvements on the grant. It became known as the Ojo de Agua grant.[98] Before the eighteenth century came to an end, a large number of tracts north of the Río Grande had been granted to leading residents of Reynosa and the other river towns.

Spanish grants continued to be made in the area until about 1820, although many were in fact settled much earlier in the late eighteenth century and early 1800s. Obtaining title to land often proved to be a rather long, bureaucratic procedure that was often stretched out by delays, competing bids, and the competency of the petitioner's agents. Typically, settlers would select vacant lands away from the known grants before making a public declaration, or *denuncio*, for it. Take the case of the Espíritu Santo grant in present-day Cameron County, acquired by Don José Salvador de la Garza of Camargo. A son-in-law of the founder of Camargo, de la Garza owned Porción 77 in that town, but he sought additional grazing land. By 1770 he was holding the land, although he did not apply for the grant until 1772. Due to the negligence of his agents, however, Spain did not grant title until 1781, following the public sale of the land in 1779.[99]

Legal documents illustrate the lengthy procedure for obtaining a Spanish land grant. In 1804, three brothers, Francisco, Julián, and Alejandro Farías, *vecinos* of Camargo, initiated the process for obtaining a land grant for each of them. Appearing before the local notary, Captain Manuel María de Ampudia, an officer in the royal navy and the *intendente corregidor* of the colony, their agent, J. Ygnacio de Alustiza, obtained the official's approval of the *denuncio* made on October 20, 1804. The *denuncio* was for four leagues of pastureland for "cattle . . . at a place called San Ramón on the other [north] side of the Río Grande . . . " The official also ordered that the government should proceed to survey and make an appraisal of the lands. This report was then sent to Lt. Col. Manuel de Iturbe e Iraeta, the governor, who in turn dispatched another order on November 23, 1804, to Captain José de Goseascochea, commanding officer at Camargo. As the town's chief justice, de Goseascochea was then commanded to carry out the surveys and appraisals of the requested lands.[100]

The local captain appointed Antonio Margil Cano, surveyor, and José Simón Villarreal, as an "expert in lands." As a preliminary to conducting the surveys, the official cited the adjoining landowners to appear so that their boundary lines were respected. The surveyor first marked off the four leagues of land requested by Julián, then Alejandro's, and finally those of Francisco. This local phase of the procedure, however, was not complete until a report of the surveys, *vista de ojos*, or actual visual examination of the land, and maps were made. All of this necessary information eventually reached the intendency authorities in San Luis Potosí.

On September 7, 1808, the auction of the lands petitioned for by the Farías took place at the capital of the intendency. Each of the four league grants brought a bid of 48 pesos. All told, one Francisco Sandoval, a local agent of de Alustiza, paid 154 pesos and three-quarters of a bit, the value of the purchase price plus fees. This payment was then made in Mexico City on October 20, 1808. With the completion of these steps, the papers of the sale were sent back to San Luis Potosí, where they were deposited on January 16, 1809. The authorities there directed that the titles be issued and that the agent for the Farías be so informed, so that he could deposit the cost of the title papers. Finally, on January 24, 1809, the titles were issued. These authorities then proceeded to inform the colony's governor at San Carlos, Nuevo Santander. On March 22, 1809, the latter official mandated that the Farías be placed in possession of the land by the local authorities. In the case of Francisco, he was to "plant willows and [other] trees on the boundary and limits of the land . . . and shall within one year after possession, occupy and cultivate his lands."

The local chief justice of Camargo, who was still Captain de Goseascochea, finally gave possession to Francisco Farías on May 1, 1809, nearly four and one-half years after the Farías had initiated the process. The captain further stipulated that the grantee was allotted four months in which to build corner monuments of stone and mortar to mark his land grant. When the Bourland Commission, which was created by the Texas legislature in 1850 to examine Spanish and Mexican titles to land grants in the Lower Valley, received claims to the land grants in the Trans-Nueces in 1851, the heirs of Francisco, represented by one Máximo Farías, probably a son, made the claim. Testimony presented indicated that the grant was, in fact, first occupied in 1809, the date of possession.

In some cases *rancheros* made considerable improvements before title to a land grant was formally awarded. These usually consisted of wells, water tanks, corrals, some type of housing either for themselves or for their servants, and the movement of livestock to the ranch site. For example, the Bourland Commission noted that J. J. Treviño's Mexican grant, Agostadero del Gato (1833), located on the southeastern corner of Hidalgo County, merited validation by the state because "witnesses prove[d] the occupation, cultivation and pasturage of [the land grant] for many years prior to March 2, 1836."[101]

Occasionally lands had been petitioned earlier in the Spanish period, but for one reason or another title had not been secured by the applicant, so that his title papers, or *escritura*, ultimately came from Mexico. A few documents bear this out in particular petitions for lands. Enrique Villarreal, a native of Matamoros and a Spanish military officer, first grazed cattle in 1810 on a site called Rincón del Oso, which circled the shores of Corpus Christi Bay. In a later petition for the same grant of land, he claimed that he had lost his title papers in 1812, in a flood of the Río Grande and Salado rivers at Revilla, now known as Guerrero. He also noted that it was at Revilla where he had acquired the cattle to stock his Rincón del Oso ranch. According to a contemporary witness who knew Villarreal, the captain grazed cattle on the Oso Creek, for which purpose he built one small and one large corral. He also had servants, two *vaqueros*, and a *jacal*. It is believed that Captain Villarreal also had a fort and a ranch village on the bay. In 1817 and 1818 Indian raiders drove the captain from the grant. About 1818 Villarreal relocated to the Lower Valley, leasing grazing land from the owners of the middle one-third of the Espíritu Santo grant at a site called Rancho Paso Viejo, north of the Arroyo Colorado. In all probability Villarreal's herds remained at that location until about 1831. In April 1831, at Matamoros, he again petitioned the state of Tamaulipas for ten *sitios* of land for stockraising. Villarreal offered a stockraiser's traditional litany of the reasons for his request:

> I own one thousand head of branded cattle, herds of horses, and small stock consisting of goats and sheep. Also, it is public knowledge that I do not have any land proper for grazing cattle and horses. For the same

reason I have searched for vacant and uncultivated land belonging to the State [of Tamaulipas].

He added that use of the land would contribute to the settlement and security of the frontier. On November 16, 1831, the governor approved the grant, ordering the officials at Camargo to grant title and place Villarreal in possession of the land.[102] Thus, in this case two titles were evidently issued to the same grantee and on the same land by two governments.

After Mexico gained its independence in 1821, new ranches continued to be established. These *ranchos* were founded along the Río Grande, and especially in the plains east and north of Reynosa toward the Nueces River Valley. The French-born naturalist, Jean L. Berlandier, who in the 1820s made his home in Matamoros and was a member of official Mexican scientific expeditions to Texas and large parts of the Mexican republic, noted in his diary that the plains from Reynosa to Matamoros were "covered with dense forests, where everyday a large number of ranches [were] established."[103] This growth represented the second major wave of territorial expansion in the northern half of the old province of Nuevo Santander.

Population growth influenced the expansion of the frontier. As noted in Table 2.1, the number of people in the *villas* of the Río Grande increased from 5,053 in 1794 to 13,956 in 1823, and to 24,686 in 1828–29. In a span of thirty-five years (1794–1829), the populace of the towns had increased 389 percent. The state's population also continued to grow rapidly. By 1840 it had 106,748 people.

Some of these settlers moved into new territory as a result of the state of Tamaulipas distributing land grants prior to the outbreak of the Texas Revolt in 1835, and their movement into the Trans-Nueces continued after the end of the conflict. The impetus for this colonization effort paralleled developments in neighboring Coahuila and Texas—principally Texas, where Stephen F. Austin and other *empresarios*, or contractors, had introduced hundreds of new settlers in the 1820s and early 1830s. Strong Mexican fears that not only Texas but the rest of its northern frontier would be overrun by Anglo frontiersmen set in motion diverse colonization plans, although the efforts were for the most part not well conceived nor well executed. Tamaulipas nonetheless pushed the frontier northward. Primarily used for stockraising, Tamaulipan land grants north of the Río Grande varied in size from two to twelve leagues, with most of them having four to six leagues of land.[104]

Once the grants had been made by the Spanish and Mexican authorities along the Río Grande and northward to the Nueces River, land transfers among the settlers unfolded as they had in the older frontiers of northern New Spain. A few generalizations can be advanced about land transactions. Much of

Table 2.2 Intermediate and Large Land Grants Issued under Spain and Mexico in Hidalgo County, Texas

Grantee	Name of Grant	Date Granted	Size of Grant
J. J. Hinojosa	Llano Grande	May 29, 1790	25.5 leagues
J. J. Ballí	San Salvador del Tule	1794	ca. 72 leagues
Vicente de Hinojosa	Las Mesteñas	1794	35 leagues
Manuel Gómez	Santa Anita	1798	15 leagues
Lino Cavazos	La Blanca	May 19, 1834	5 leagues
J. J. Treviño	Agostadero del Gato	Apr. 16, 1833	5 leagues
Benigno Leal	Santa Ana	Apr. 16, 1834	2 leagues
Máximo Domínguez	Agostadero de los Torritos	May 19, 1834	2 leagues
Segundo Flores	Los Guajes	by Mexico, unknown date	2.5 leagues
Nicolasa Salinas	Los Magueyes	by Mexico, unknown date	2.5 leagues
José A. Morales	El Venadito	Sept. 15, 1835	5 leagues
Alejandro Farías	San José	1829	4.5 leagues
Julián Farías	San Román	Oct. 20, 1804	5 leagues
Guadalupe Sánchez	La Rucia	Nov. 23, 1835	5 leagues
Juan Garza Díaz	Vargas	Mar. 25, 1835	4 leagues
Pedro García	El Perdido	Mar. 25, 1836	4 leagues
Gil Zárate	La Blanca	Nov. 25, 1835	5 leagues
Pilar Zárate de Bayarena	La Alameda	1835	3 leagues
Juan Manuel & Luciano Chapa	La Encantada	1832	9 leagues
Ramón Cavazos Guerra	Loma Blanca	Dec. 19, 1831	5 leagues
Antonio Elizondo	El Lucero	Nov. 25, 1835	3 leagues
Esteban Martínez	La Noria de Tío Ayala	unknown date	4 leagues
José Antonio Leal de León	San Antonio del Encinal	1833	6 leagues
Antonio García	El Tule	Mar. 23, 1836	more than 2 leagues
Teodoro Garza	El Alazan	July 3, 1834	3 leagues
Irineo Gómez	Las Barrosas	Jan. 28, 1833	5 leagues
Ramón Garza	El Paisano	by Mexico, unknown date	2.5 leagues

Source: Texas General Land Office, *Bourland and Miller Commission Report* (Austin, 1851), n.p.

the lands (as well as other properties) did not really change hands, but was inherited. Some lands were presented as gifts during the life of the landholder, usually during the marriage of a son or daughter. There were, of course, many sales of land, often to relatives, and the prices varied from period to period and from place to place. Rarely did lands revert to the crown or its successor government, Mexico, because there were no heirs or because of failure to fulfill the legal requirements necessary to obtain possession. Among the latter were, for instance, the inability to remain on the land the required five years or the lack of material improvements. The following cases show how these land-tenure elements concerning lands in present-day south Texas operated.

A few settlers forfeited their lands—lands that were sometimes granted to new petitioners. Such was the case, for example, of certain grazing lands located up the river, near the *presidio* of San Juan Bautista de Río Grande del Norte, in what are now Maverick, Dimmit, and Webb counties, Texas. In 1765, Antonio de Rivas, a Spaniard who had been residing for twenty-five years in San Juan Bautista, petitioned for vacant lands "on the other side of the Río Grande, notwithstanding the frequent dangers resulting from the frontier Indians [which are] still continuing." He asserted that he had "a large family and some stock, without owning any property in which to maintain said stock." As was customary, the chief justice of the *presidio* was ordered by the provincial governor to ascertain if there were any neighbors on the lands requested by the petitioner. The testimony of five witnesses revealed that the lands sought by de Rivas had been "settled by Don Joseph Dias de Oropeza, a traveling merchant, who possessed the same about one year and eight months more or less; that he took his stock out of them, that the lands have remained vacant and abandoned for seven or eight years." In view of the collaborative testimony of all five witnesses, the local captain concluded that the law requiring four years of occupation of the lands for a grantee to obtain domain and possession had not been complied with. Thus, he found no reason to prevent the award of the land grant to de Rivas, who received the twenty-five *sitios* of land for his livestock—twenty for cattle and horses and five for sheep and goats.[105]

Some landholders speculated on land, acquiring a variety of tracts which they then left to their descendants and others. Take the case of José Francisco Guerra Chapa of Reynosa. In 1831, Guerra Chapa received a Mexican grant called Loma Blanca, in present-day Brooks County. Prior to his death in 1853, he had acquired eight Reynosa *porciones*, although the circumstances surrounding his acquisitions are unknown at this time. According to his sons, Bartolomé Treviño, who had obtained Porción 97 in the jurisdiction of Camargo on the north side of the river in 1767, purchased four other *porciones* in the same vicinity.[106]

Much property also changed ownership upon the death of one or both of the parents. This property tended to remain within the family, although transactions involving gifts and sales to heirs and others were common. In the early years of the new colony, the settlers repeatedly continued to take trips to the other provincial towns in Nuevo León, or they would send an agent, to sell lands belonging to them by previous purchase or inheritance. For example, on July 18, 1783, Vicente García Guerra of Revilla sold a part of a *labor* and pastureland, located in the Hacienda Estazuela adjacent to the city of Monterrey, with the corresponding water rights to Blas José de la Garza Sepúlveda of Monterrey for fifty pesos. García Guerra explained that the sale involved property that he had inherited from his parents.[107] In the above-cited case of Francisco Guerra Chapa, his wife and adult living children, and the children of a deceased daughter, inherited his properties. Of the eight *porciones*, he gave four to his wife and one each to his three living children. He left the eighth *porción* to the three children of his deceased daughter.[108]

With the opening of new lands on the frontier, some *agostaderos*, or pasturelands, were soon placed on the market to take advantage of the expanding ranching economy. Consider the case of the cleric, José Lorenzo Báez Treviño of Camargo, who in 1759 bought the *agostaderos* of Zacate, San Antonio, and San Simón in the jurisdiction of Camargo, Nuevo Santander, for four thousand pesos. The quantity of land is not noted in the record of the sale, so it is difficult to say how many *sitios* Báez Treviño actually acquired.[109] Settlers and absentee landlords also used land located in Nuevo Santander as a guaranty for loans and mortgages. For example, in 1779 Juan José Dávila, *alcalde* and *capitán* of Linares, Nuevo León, pledged as collateral several tracts of land, including eighteen *cabellerías* in the "New Colony" of Nuevo Santander.[110] In 1781, Captain Juan José Gómez de Castro of Monterrey used as collateral for a loan the Báez Treviño pasturelands. He valued the property at "more than 5,200 pesos, on account of its qualities."[111]

While the price of land appreciated in the eighteenth and nineteenth centuries, the cost of a *sitio* of land was not too expensive. In 1841, Jesús Treviño of Guerrero declared that for 700 pesos he had purchased 183/4 *sitios* from the heirs of Don Atancio Borrego in the lands of San Ygnacio. In explaining the purchase, he noted that he had received 110 pesos from "my nephew Blas María Gutiérrez and my son-in-law, Don Vicente Gutiérrez" and that they "were vested with title to that part of the 183/4 *sitios* which was to be their share in community according to the price and terms with which we agreed upon." Such a practice of pooling their monies to buy land was not uncommon. Seven years later, Blas María Gutiérrez sold to Blas María Uribe "a *derecho* of pasture land for large livestock acquired by purchase by his deceased uncle, Don Jesús

Treviño in the *hacienda* of San Ygnacio, consisting of 21/2 *sitios*." The sale price was one hundred pesos. In this type of land sale, the seller typically required half of the price as down payment and the other half in installments. A *sitio* was now worth forty pesos, slightly more than the earlier purchase price of nearly thirty-six pesos.[112]

As long as stockraising represented a viable activity, land in the Lower Río Grande Valley appreciated in value. Take the case of a grant of five leagues of land made to José Antonio García Garza of Mier. He paid 50 pesos to the Tamaulipas government, in 1836, for the entire tract called El Rendado or Randado, later the headquarters for a major Tejano ranch. Ten years later (1846), the grantee sold three of the five leagues to Victoriano García and José María Barrera for 180 pesos. According to the vender, the latter purchaser was also the owner of the remaining two leagues on account of an "agreement with said Barrera," who had evidently contributed some of the money to acquire the original land grant. Thus, in 1846, a *sitio* of land was worth 60 pesos, six times more than the 10 pesos which the buyers had paid in the initial purchase in 1836.[113] For unknown reasons, some sales yielded a high price per league of land. Las Comitas, a Mexican grant that had been occupied since 1812, is a good illustration. According to evidence presented before the Bourland Commission (1851), shortly after the end of the war with Mexico on February 22, 1849, Frederick Bedinghaus and Sabas de la Garza bought the three-league grant for 800 pesos. Located in the center of present-day Starr County, it may have been an abundance of grasslands or a good water source that made the grant more valuable.[114]

CONCLUSION

The arrival of Spanish and *mestizo* settlers in the Lower Río Grande Valley and the rest of the colony in the mid-eighteenth century laid the foundation for the growth of an adaptive and successful Hispanic society. Change was not very rapid or noticeable in this distant *gobierno*, but it did occur. The early years of settlement were a time of peace and growth under the steady guidance of Escandón and his military captains. Although missionary endeavors were not very fruitful, the church had tried to do its duty. The demarcation of town and mission boundaries and the allotment of private lands in 1767 marked the first stage of maturity in the new settlements. The beginning of ranching and trade endeavors occupied the populace, who were required not only to settle the lands but also to defend them from the Indians and foreign interlopers. As sporadic Indian disturbances increased in the 1770s, vigilance on the frontier became a greater concern for both the settlers and soldiers. Overall, their efforts paid off, not withstanding the criticisms of high-ranking military or governmental officials. Outside Laredo, most of the *rancheros* and townspeople in the Lower Valley were not beset by woes that resulted from the raids of the "Indians of the north." By the mid-nineteenth century, the communities founded by Escandón had survived difficult times, maturing into small towns—towns that were defensive against outside threats and yet open to new economic opportunities. In short, the settlers had wrested the land from the Indians, and the Hispanic society had taken root largely in an agrarian setting but within the confines of a town culture.

There were, of course, other developments that helped to solidify the Hispanic presence in the new lands north of the Río Grande. The society of the colony and, in particular along the Lower Valley, was not classless, but differences in wealth, status, and race were not very significant. The fact that hundreds of heads of households received land grants meant that initially a large degree of social and economic egalitarianism prevailed among the settlers. This is why the residents of the Lower Valley identified so strongly with a *ranchero* society, rather than with a *hacendado* or wealthy merchant class.

Viable population growth in the *villas del norte* had encouraged a steady territorial expansion northward, and land grants had facilitated ranching activities over a large expanse of grasslands. By the third generation these frontier settlers had reached the Nueces River Valley. As before, the settlers engaged in lively land transfers that were part and parcel of the basis of land tenure whose legacy had its origin in the older colonial and peninsular past.

The basic Hispanic social characteristics that formed the core of the settlers' way of life gradually took root as they adapted to frontier conditions, as generations of Spanish and *mestizo* citizens had done in much of the borderlands region. These *pobladores* were a tough and resilient people who tended to work together in spite of the conflicts that arose among them. Gradually, a sense of community or town culture emerged that gave the various sectors of the population a common Hispanic destiny and identity. Belligerent Indians were not allowed, of course, to become part of the evolving Hispanic society; most of them would perish from one calamity or another. Escandón was lucky that he had recruited frontiersmen and women—many of whom were related to each other—who not only sought new opportunities but had the experience necessary to survive the natural and human elements that made life difficult. Their economic life tested their values and attitudes as they struggled to stay on the land.

CHAPTER THREE

EARLY ECONOMIC LIFE IN THE LOWER RÍO GRANDE FRONTIER, 1730s–1848

Origins of Commerce, Ranching, and Farming Enterprises

While the settlement of an exposed frontier and the Christianization of Indians were lofty goals of Spain's imperial policy in the Seno Mexicano, the success of the enterprise was significantly dependent on the ability of the settlers to make a decent life for themselves. Historians long have had an interest in the economic history of the colony, and especially in the Lower Río Grande Valley, but the focus has always been on the international commerce that was centered in Matamoros (1820s–1848) and, later, the Matamoros-Brownsville complex (1848–1880s). Histories of the ranching economy are general in nature. While much more study is necessary, what follows is an attempt to systematize this regional economic history, for the Lower Valley played a key role in the colony's, and later Tamaulipas's, development.

Under Spanish and Mexican rule, ranching and commerce became the principal economic activities of the settlers, especially in the Lower Río Grande Valley. While the towns served as centers of local government and trade, stockraising developed in the surrounding territory, especially in the north bank area. Of the two key enterprises, stockraising easily became the more popular occupation of the Hispanic settlers, who not only took advantage of the benefits provided by the virgin plains but also utilized a long history of ranching to develop stockraising. At the same time, the Spanish engaged in farming, but largely as an ancillary economic activity relying on other provinces to obtain the necessary foodstuffs. These activities provided opportunities for internal trade, while foreign trade suffered as a consequence of the effects of Spanish mercantilism. With the opening of a port at Matamoros

(1820) and the arrival of European and American merchants in the 1820s and 1830s, however, the economy of the Río Grande made an important transition from one based largely on ranching and trade to international commerce.

THE ORIGINS OF TRADE AND THE TRANSITION TO INTERNATIONAL COMMERCE

In the years spanning Spanish rule, the colonists engaged in the intercolonial trade network of New Spain, except for the sporadic contacts made with other European sea traders who evaded the laws and introduced contraband goods. While livestock and its by-products constituted the bulk of the goods traded in the interior or internal trade, the inhabitants also sold or bartered other "products of the country," such as hides, salt, corn, and sugarcane, with the latter often in the form of *piloncillo.* The commerce in salt was the most rewarding and an easy way to become wealthy by the standards of the day. In the Lower Valley, the residents of Reynosa, Camargo, and Revilla controlled the trading of salt that came from Sal del Rey and La Sal Vieja. As early as 1755, Cámara Alta reported that some of the settlers of Reynosa were rich on account of the trade in salt, "which they have traded and in which many trade." The citizens of Camargo, too, were "very rich" primarily because of the large numbers of livestock, which they traded in the outlying frontier districts, and because "they collect salt for their use and for sale, . . . though not many want to depend on it." Cámara Alta was informed that the salt mines or "*salinas* on the north side of the Río Grande were known since over eighty years (since the 1680s) and that it was from there that all of Nuevo León and Coahuila were provided, and that the settlers came in groups, meeting at Cerralvo in order to come by way of the Río Grande and the Nueces." He added that the *vecinos* of Revilla engaged in the same enterprises as those of Camargo and they too were well off.[1]

By 1755 there was a sufficient amount of trade and commerce in the towns to warrant the *alcabala* or sales tax, but it was not immediately imposed, probably because of Escandón's earlier promise of no taxes for ten years. This policy changed, however, in 1767, when the *visitador* and interim governor, Field Marshal Juan Fernando de Palacio, charged with implementing administrative reforms in the colony, ordered that the tax be collected in the colony, because he believed that it would not prejudice the settlers and, at the same time, would serve to bring in revenue to the crown. The *alcabala* tax, which varied from 2 to 6 percent throughout New Spain during the Spanish period, was set at 4 percent in Nuevo Santander. The Mexican historian Juan Fidel Zorrilla notes that some settlers protested its collection, argues that it was a burden, but he offers no proof.[2] In 1795, Calleja fixed the value of the four thousand loads of salt extracted by the inhabitants of the province at twenty thousand pesos, after subtracting twelve reales paid to the royal treasury for mining the salt. Initially, the settlers could gather the salt without a fee, but the crown imposed a fee that private contractors collected at the site of the salt mine. For example, many years after the authorities began its collection, an old Tejano named Pacífico Ochoa, of the Ojo de Agua settlement in Hidalgo County, recalled that the first administrator at Sal del Rey was Jesús de la Garza, who "lived there and collected payment on account of [*sic*] the Government from all persons who went there." When Mexico became independent, the same practice continued. Ochoa identified the *ranchero* Antonio Cantú Sánchez of Reynosa as the administrator [who] "was taking care of [Sal del Rey], collected payment for the salt, and paid the products to the government, and [he was] so employed until the American invasion up to 1846."[3]

Fish were another important resource that entered the trade network of the *villas* of the Río Grande. Camargo sold fish that were abundant in two smaller rivers flowing into the Río Grande. As early as 1757, the inspectors who came with the Tienda de Cuervo Commission noted that at Laredo there were "very large perch" in the Río Grande.[4] Actually, fish were abundant throughout the colony into the early nineteenth century. According to Ramos Arizpe, the "rivers furnish a great many fish of all kinds and, in the ports of the coast, abound bacalao, mullet, seabass, and shrimp."[5]

During the Spanish period, the coastal and sea trade were negligible, except for some of the years during the wars of independence, when the violence disrupted the customary channels of trade between Spain and New Spain. Mercantilistic policies nearly always favored the port of Veracruz, and even though officials examined the possibility of opening other facilities along the long coast of the Seno Mexicano, they discovered severe limitations due to the presence of barrier islands and shallow, unprotected bays. Still, since Escandón's *entrada* of 1747 and the much later visit of Félix de Calleja in 1794–95, the necessity of opening inland routes and seaports was deemed urgent. In the end, only land trade routes to the surrounding provinces were developed and maintained.[6] Escandón, however, had long operated two *goletas*, or two-sail boats, using a point called the port of Santander, north of the Soto la Marina River. The colonizer reported in 1755 that he used his *goleta* to convey "[goods] which he himself made annually of purchases of a considerable amount of small livestock on account of sales that he had outside of the province and also of a vast number of mules, which are obtained from the hacienda de Dolores and Villa de Camargo." No improvements were made to the port, and beginning with the visit of Captain Tienda de Cuervo and Cámara Alta in 1757, Escandón's use of the port and projected improvements were forbidden as a result of the opposition of those high-ranking officials. In spite of these restrictions, however, his *goletas* remained in use, exporting tallow, hides, wool, and salt. The boats brought into the colony textiles from the ports of Altamira and Veracruz. There was also a sea trade with Altamira involving open boats that carried fruit and cotton textiles to the colony. Political pressure was brought to bear, first in 1763 and then again in 1773, to prohibit the development of the port and to restrict all sea trade to only Escandón's vessels. In 1795, Calleja confirmed the continuing operation of a boat belonging to the count, but characterized the goods introduced from Veracruz as "extremely few."[7]

Further south of the *villas del norte*, Tampico, soon to become second to Veracruz in importance as a port, came into use in 1814 due to the disruptions caused by Father Hidalgo's Revolt. Whenever the violence flared up in central New Spain, Tampico gained more trade.[8] On November 9, 1820, the Spanish Cortes officially sanctioned the opening of several new ports on both coasts of New Spain, including Matagorda in Texas, and Tampico, Soto la Marina, and Matamoros, all in Nuevo Santander. It was, of course, too late for an immediate impact on the colony since by this time Spain was barely holding on to its wealthiest New World possession.[9] In sum, the effect of Spanish policy severely limited the growth of internal and external trade so that much of the northeastern frontier provinces became dependent on merchants from the larger urban commercial centers such as Saltillo, Zacatecas, and Mexico City. Consequently, consumers paid dearly for goods that they ultimately received, many necessities were lacking, and opportunities for exports by sea were highly limited.[10]

The 1820s brought a new wave of prosperity to the ports of Matamoros, Soto la Marina, and Tampico. Of these, the port of Matamoros had the most direct effect on the towns in the Lower Valley. While most of the Lower Valley merchants were located in Matamoros, the impact of foreign trade was noticeable all along the river *villas* and even further inland, in expanding commercial centers like Monterrey and Saltillo, as manufactured goods, mainly textiles, made their way to distant markets. In fact, merchants at Matamoros who were engaged in the Mexican trade, as it became known, supplied four of Mexico's largest fairs. These fairs, like Saltillo's, which took place every September, were held for several days to allow agricultural producers, consumers, and wholesale merchants to sell and barter their goods.[11]

There are few descriptions of the Mexican trade in northeast Mexico. One of the best comes from Reuben M. Potter, an American, who operated out of Matamoros. In September 1828, he took a cargo of goods to sell in Monterrey and Saltillo. Six or eight fully armed muleteers led thirty to forty pack mules, which carried the freight of a merchant. Normally they traveled fifteen to twenty miles a day. At nightfall the muleteers unloaded the bales and boxes of goods and made a protective wall in case of attack by bandits or Indians. The caravan first stopped at the Monterrey fair and then made its way to Saltillo, where the fair lasted another week. At the latter place, the merchants made sales of two to three hundred dollars a day, mostly at retail. According to Potter, there were "such a number of merchants" at Saltillo, that, on returning, he and about a dozen foreign merchants, mostly French, carried "sixty or seventy thousand dollars in specie."[12] Frontier merchants, like the Englishman John Linn of Victoria, also ventured into the Mexican market at the Río Grande with an eye to reaping quick profits because the demand for consumer goods was high. Competing with these merchants were Texas colonists, who occasionally introduced contraband goods along the border to make money quickly.[13]

The Mexican trade quickly proved lucrative enough to entice merchants and others to the region. By the late 1820s, if not earlier, some merchants in Matamoros operated large businesses, usually in partnerships. Such was the case of Francis Stillman of Connecticut and Daniel Willard Smith, the United States consul at Matamoros, both of whom entered the Mexican trade in 1828. By 1832 there were three hundred foreign residents in Matamoros, many of whom were merchants. Despite the disruptions in trade caused by political upheavals along the Río Grande, merchants handled large sums of goods. In 1848, J. P. Schatzell, the U.S. consul at Matamoros, testified that his annual business ranged from 200 to 250,000 dollars. Charles Stillman, son of Francis Stillman who had died in 1838, conducted a 75,000- to 80,000-dollar business.[14]

While statistics for this trade are incomplete, nearly all of the trade was through New Orleans, mostly on U.S. ships. In the 1820s, the tonnage of imports varied from a high of 1,440 tons in 1827 to a low of 620 tons in 1828. The value of imports and exports rose from 399,937 pesos in 1825 to 843,068 pesos in 1827.[15] There are few statistics of the income generated by this trade to the port of Matamoros, but it must have risen as trade increased, notwithstanding the growing contraband that entered Mexico without paying duties. According to one student of the region, in 1826 the Matamoros customhouse reported earning 51,000 pesos. A 25 percent duty on imports encouraged smuggling and hampered the operations of the port. With the end of the Veracruz monopoly, Tampico and Matamoros became the second and third most important ports of entry on the Gulf Coast. During this time, San Luis Potosí, located inland from the coast, became the hub of trade in the northeast, receiving most of its goods through Tampico and Soto la Marina. Matamoros supplied the markets of Monterrey and Saltillo, as well as surrounding frontier towns.[16]

The volume and value of the trade through Matamoros and other Tamaulipan ports varied widely in the period from the 1830s to the 1840s. The growing importance of these Gulf ports was confirmed by the national government in 1837, when Matamoros, Santa Ana de Tamaulipas (Tampico), and Veracruz were designated as first-class maritime customhouses. Data for the years 1833–46 indicate that the tonnage of goods flowing through Matamoros into Mexico ranged from a low of about one thousand to a high of four thousand tons. The value of the imported goods is difficult to measure accurately because of extensive smuggling, but it reportedly reached several million dollars.[17] Moreover, on account of the changes in the volume and value of trade, the port revenues collected at Matamoros varied widely from year to year. The port received slightly over 900,000 pesos in revenues in 1831–32, dropping to a low of 234,096 pesos in 1836–37, rising to a bit more than 300,000 pesos in 1841 and dropping under that in 1842 and 1843, the last two years for which figures are currently available.[18] While the corruption of officials may explain some of the decline in collections, there were other factors, especially the contraband trade that bypassed the port. Again, the relative insecurity of the frontier affected the movement of commerce along the lower Río Grande. In sum, the Mexican trade passing through Matamoros (as well as most other Mexican ports) rose sharply in the 1820s and early 1830s, but contracted with the political problems in Texas in the mid-1830s and U.S. and Mexican conflict in the mid-1840s.[19]

During the troubles in Texas, threats to close the port of Matamoros in 1835 quickly elicited a response from the Tamaulipan legislature. In a petition to the national legislature, they argued that not only did the fourteen thousand citizens of Matamoros benefit from the port, but also all of the northern states of Mexico that were tributary to the Río Grande trade. Closing the port, they asserted, would destroy all the economic gains and the growth in the population of Matamoros, which had occurred in such a short time.[20] Shortly afterward, in 1836, the governor of Nuevo León informed the inhabitants of the frontier that the Mexican president had decreed that during the war "with the rebels in Texas the introduction of foodstuffs through the port of Matamoros would be allowed."[21] Unfortunately, escalating problems in rebellious Texas and the eventual coming of the war with Mexico affected border trade. As a consequence, the early economic arrangements that had been worked out between Anglo and European merchants and Mexican *rancheros* and *comerciantes* in the far northern frontier were breached twice prior to annexation of the Trans-Nueces. What is interesting to observe, however, is the resiliency with which buyers and sellers on the Río Grande frontier managed always to resume border trade.[22]

The existence of a state-of-war mentality in Texas, especially since the success of the 1835 revolt, subjected Mexican—Anglo trade relations to abrupt change. The revolt itself brought normal frontier trade to a halt. Mexico's international trade suffered one of its lowest marks in 1837, due to the effects of the war in Texas and internal Mexican political struggles. These problems, however, did not stop all trade; for some time, the Mexicans traded illegally in Texas. With the revival of trade on the frontier with Mexico, the Republic of Texas officially opened, on June 13, 1838, the border to those residing on the Río Grande so that they could trade at San Antonio and other designated points in Texas. Risking their lives due to the presence of marauding bands, Mexican traders, some of whom were murdered by roving bandits, conducted a brisk trade in livestock and edibles like flour and beans.[23]

Trade with the Texans was not one-sided. Mexicans who came to trade also brought specie to buy American-made cloth and other consumer items. An unknown author evidently familiar with trade in the Lower Valley reported that "during the last six years of active or threatened war between Texas and Mexico, the traders from the Northern provinces of Mexico, without any adequate protection against the Indians, have made their way to San Antonio and Corpus Christi, and brought with them on an average $300,000 annually in gold and silver, for the purchase of goods."[24]

During this time (1820s–1840s), imports tended to be higher in value than exports. Mexicans purchased mostly European consumer goods, with U.S. goods gradually being substituted as time passed. Mexican specie, particularly silver, paid for almost all of the imports.[25] The exports from Matamoros are more difficult to specify. In the 1830s, Tamaulipas exported coined silver, mules, hides, horns, wool, cotton, and sugar, but not much of the latter two products.[26]

The growth of the Río Grande trade stimulated rapid changes in population and economic activity in the Lower Río Grande Valley region. By 1829 the towns on the Río Grande had a total population of about 24,686. Matamoros, the primary beneficiary of the Río Grande trade, due to its location near the seaports of Port Isabel and Brazos Santiago, grew from 500–600 persons in 1821 to 7,000 in 1829. By 1837 it more than doubled its population to 16,372. The growth and prosperity of Matamoros was directly linked to the expanding commercial activities that attracted immigrant merchants and Mexican workers to import, sell, and distribute goods. Soon harbors, customhouses, and warehouses were erected to handle the new business that flowed to the port of Matamoros and its trade region.[27] In addition, trade stimulated improvements in transportation, particularly the use of steamboats. In response to a 1824 federal decree to build up commerce on the Río Grande, the government granted a concession to John Davis Bradburn and Stephen M. Staples to operate a steamship, which evidently went up the river, but little else is known about this venture.[28] Beginning in 1835, at least one steamboat operated from the mouth of the river to Matamoros.[29]

THE DEVELOPMENT AND PERSISTENCE OF A RANCHING ECONOMY IN THE TRANS-NUECES, 1730S–1848

During most of the century in which Spain and Mexico held dominion over the Trans-Nueces country, ranching made swift progress, with a number of factors facilitating its growth. The foundation for a ranching industry rested on the introduction of large herds of cattle, horses, mules, sheep, and goats during the initial years of settlement of Nuevo Santander. A number of *hacendados* from the surrounding frontier provinces had established stockraising enterprises as early as 1734, in the vicinity of Mier, and in the mid-1740s at Revilla. Because of the widespread availability of pastures, the herds multiplied rapidly and new ranches were founded as population pressure increased and the herds expanded. Fortunately for the colonists, the amount of territory available for exploitation was vast and populated by eighty different bands of nomadic Coahuiltecan Indian tribes, many of whom were docile and wanted to settle in missions adjacent to the *villas*. Lack of valuable silver mines, ports, and industries compelled the majority of the people to make their living by farming, ranching, or trading in livestock and other natural products, such as salt, fish, and deerskins, that could be found on the frontier.[30] But more than any other resource, the grasslands of Nuevo Santander constituted the basis for the burgeoning ranching activities of its settlers.

By 1757 the hot and arid plains of Nuevo Santander contained more than eighty-five thousand head of cattle, horses, and mules or large livestock and nearly a third of a million head of sheep and goats, and the numbers of livestock continued to increase rapidly. The *vecinos* of the river towns, the wealthiest region of Nuevo Santander, owned 25 percent of the large stock and 40 percent of the sheep and goats, or small stock. In addition, stockmen from older frontiers of New Spain seasonally pastured 914,000 sheep on the southern plains of Nuevo Santander nine months out of the year, as earlier sheepraisers had done in Nuevo León since the second decade of the seventeenth century. Many shepherds were employed in this yearly migration of sheep that had started before Escandón's settlement of the region. One source states that the Tula district in 1620, barely three years after the missionaries had founded a mission there, accommodated 200,000 sheep, a figure that rose to one-half million by 1685.[31] Both wealthy private owners, usually from outside the province, and several missionary orders, particularly the Jesuits and Carmelites, owned the migratory herds. Provincial officials considered their activities useful because they employed local settlers and because their shepherds assisted in repelling Indian incursions on the towns.[32]

The expansion of stockraising was even more apparent in 1795, when the number of all kinds of livestock (excluding migratory flocks) totaled 799,874—a remarkable 210 percent increase since 1768. These herds consisted of 92,198 mares, 37,501 horses, 28,800 mules, 8,621 donkeys, 111,777 cattle, and 530,711 sheep and goats. As Calleja noted in 1795, the land was "suitable for all types of planting," but "[the country] is even better suited to the production of all species of livestock."[33]

Although it is difficult to measure the value and profitability of stockraising, ranching was the primary economic activity in the entire colony. Whereas in the early colonial period Nuevo Santander ranchers traded mainly with the older, more populous provinces to the south as far as Mexico, in the late colonial period the trade in livestock was mainly with the provinces surrounding Nuevo Santander: Nuevo León and Coahuila to the west and Texas to the north. The profitable livestock trade engaged in by the ranchers of Nuevo Santander included cattle, horses, beef, mutton, tallow, and hides. These products were the basis of the barter commerce through which the settlers obtained the consumer goods from other places in the kingdom, mainly Veracruz.[34] Cowboys, shepherds, and muleteers conducted the trade through well-worn routes to the neighboring provinces.

During the colonial and Tamaulipan period, ranching, like most other significant economic activities, developed its own practices, which were often regulated by decrees and state laws. In Nuevo Santander livestock grazed in open rangeland in common pastures, although ranch and *hacienda* lands were subdivided and held in fee simple title. This situation soon gave rise to a number of stockraising practices including identifying, collecting, and making a division of stock collected in *corridas*, or roundups, by the property owners. Cattle, for instance, were collected in a "great rustic corral built of branches, to which cattle were conducted by fenced trails called *mangas* constructed for this purpose." *Vaqueros* herded the stock by shouting and blowing special horns made for this purpose. Authorization of the town *alcalde* was necessary to hold a roundup, and it was forbidden in "time of drought and in time of the rainy season." At the end of the *corrida*, the stockraisers divided the stock on the basis of the pastures from which they came and the characteristics of the stock in relation to their ownership. Where the origin of the stock or its owner could not be determined, the unclaimed stock was divided among the stockmen in proportion to the number of breeding stock owned by each of them and with respect to the total stock rounded up. Officials also enacted ordinances and posted regulations concerning migratory herds, which were moved from place to place and especially during the winter, when they were pastured in different lands. In sum, the laws pertained to the use of the lands, the movement of stock from one site to another, and payment to the church of tithes derived from the sales of livestock and wool. Juan Fidel Zorrilla, who has made a study of the state legislation of Tamaulipas, has concluded that "this use of the land [for ranching] with time became written in the laws and the [uses] were mandatory for all stockmen with sanctions imposed on those who did not attend to the picturesque roundups . . . "[35]

There is evidence that offers some indication of the value of the ranching industry as compared to other economic endeavors. Félix de Calleja's official inspection of the colony in 1794 summarized the annual sale of livestock as follows: 7,500 mature mules at 20 pesos sold outside the province, 1,000 horses at 10 pesos, 2,000 cattle at 7 pesos, 20,000 sheep at 14 reales, and 18,000 goats at 6 reales. In addition, he tabulated 8,000 deer skins at 6 reales, and 6,800 bundles of wool at 20 reales. Overall, agricultural production based on livestock and wild animals accounted for slightly more than 250,000 pesos, considerably more than the 64,000 pesos produced from silver, copper, and lead mining.[36]

Still, Calleja was highly critical of the condition of the livestock industry, arguing that *rancheros* were careless in their management of the land and lacked knowledge to breed animals in sufficient numbers despite the large herds of brood mares. In the same breath, however, he asserted that "lack of development of this area [of animal husbandry] results largely from a lack of markets." A fairly recent newcomer to New Spain, it is possible that he did not have reliable facts on ranching practices and internal markets. He also noted that the ranchers' products could be taken to the port of Veracruz, the most important in New Spain, but that the costs of registering and transhipping their livestock would be too expensive and the profits small because of the overflow of goods to that port. He argued for the opening of either the ports of Tampico or Santander to facilitate trade in livestock. He also urged that mules be sold in Cuba, where they would command a price triple the forty pesos presently obtained in distant markets, with the further advantage that sellers could return with Cuban goods to sell in the province.[37]

In fact, stock from Nuevo Santander sometimes made its way to very distant places. When a drought in 1775 afflicted New Mexico and the horse stock was badly decimated, the governor of that province requested from the crown a gift of fifteen hundred horses to save the province. The viceroy quickly approved the request and ordered the commandant inspector of the *presidios*, Hugo O'Conor, to buy and ship the horses to Santa Fe as quickly as possible. Despite the viceroy's quick response, a year passed before the horses had been purchased in Nuevo León and Nuevo Santander and driven to New Mexico. There is also the interesting case of the purchase of 915 mules and horses in Camargo by two citizens of Louisiana in 1801. These animals were driven across Texas to New Orleans.[38]

A more favorable description of the livestock industry of Nuevo Santander came from José Miguel Ramos Arizpe, in his 1812 report to the Spanish Cortes on the Provincias Internas, although his report is not complete as to all kinds of livestock. He spoke glowingly about ranching in Nuevo Santander and the other provinces that he represented, claiming that

> being better suited to the raising of horses and mules, Nuevo Santander has taken a great lead in that field. It regularly raises sixteen thousand head of mules a year and a like number of horses. As the mares of this species serve to augment and reproduce the breed, there is an excess of eight thousand horses annually for profit. Also the province breeds much large and small game, the most profitable being that of the deer and jaguar because of their hides. Its plains are very suitable for the raising of sheep and goats, and in the northern part along the Río Grande, these are extensively raised.

Of wool, he noted "two abundant harvests a year are made. . . . It is exported to the factories of the exterior provinces, from where it returns in hats, cloths, baizes, braids, thin light serges, blankets etc."[39]

In the final two decades of Spanish rule, ranching was still important to the stockraisers of Nuevo Santander, in spite of the inconveniences resulting from the wars of independence and Indian raids in the northern part of the province. During this time, Texas, in particular, suffered recurrent shortages of horses, mules, and beef cattle. Nuevo Santander ranchers, usually from Laredo, and others in Coahuila, the natural marketplace of Spanish Texans, supplied the needed stock.[40]

Prices paid for livestock remained stable in most cases, although some stock was worth more than previously reported by Calleja. At Laredo, for example, tamed horses and stallions were valued at ten pesos each. Mules with harnesses were priced at thirty-five pesos, while unbroken mules were sold for only fifteen pesos. Donkeys were worth eighteen pesos. Mares sold for three pesos and colts for four pesos. The price of cattle also varied but remained steady. Cows sold for seven pesos, and heifers and two-year-old bulls were worth six pesos. Lambs sold for half a peso, but sheep were worth four pesos.[41]

A look at the wills of several *pobladores* who lived through those confused times attests to the persistence of a ranching economy. Don José Domingo

González of Laredo declared, in 1819, that "Don J. Jesús Sánchez of this *villa* owes me 610 lambs, 100 goats and 400 sheep which I gave him on a lease in December of 1813 to be paid at the customary rate, excepting the sheep during the first year . . . " González listed other debtors with whom he had made contracts or leases involving livestock:

> Vicente Botello owes me 147 pesos as part of the principal of the stock which I leased to him and he lost. . . . Juan Esteban de los Santos, of the Pueblo of Tlascala, owes me 50 pesos the value of 100 lambs which I leased to him. . . . José María González of Palafox and resident of the villa owes me 88 pesos on account of stock which I leased to him.

Several persons owed González money for sales of stock, including "Don Gregorio Vela of Mier [who] owes me 80 pesos which he agreed to pay for mules . . . [, and] Pedro González formerly of Palafox owes me a riding horse. I request that he be charged 10 pesos or have it return[ed] to me."[42]

After Mexico's independence, ranching continued to take place along and north of the Río Grande. Some districts had seen a marked increase in stock-raising. For example, Matamoros had twenty-eight *ranchos* in 1814, a figure twice the number of those in existence shortly after its founding as a ranch settlement in 1770. By 1826 its population totaled 3,993 persons, of whom only 72 were involved in trade or crafts. There were 1,097 tracts of land within its jurisdiction, and the *rancheros* had 25,319 horses, 7,623 cattle, and 27,082 sheep and goats. By 1837 its population had risen to 16,372 and there were seventy-three *ranchos* in its district. According to one report, in 1835 the river towns had 3 million head of livestock on their tax rolls, although it is not clear how this statistic was obtained.[43] Most of the stock belonged to Mexican ranchers in the territory between the Río Grande and the Nueces River, territory under the jurisdiction of the old river *villas*. Thus, in less than three generations ranching had spread through a considerable expanse of what is now south Texas. Still, a number of severe problems hampered and temporarily disrupted the ranching economy during this time.

The persisting conflict between Anglos and Mexicans over the Texas—Mexico boundary was the most disruptive factor that adversely affected ranching, but droughts, disease, Indian raids, and thefts of stock were also serious problems. Sporadic military threats, which occasionally led to skirmishes and battles, intensified the conflict between the two groups and heightened their biased perceptions of one another. The raiding of herds by both sides in this conflict only served to exacerbate the already bad feelings—an omen that did not bode well for future Anglo—Tejano relationships in the Trans-Nueces region.[44]

Beset by these problems, some aspects of livestock production dropped by the late 1830s. For example, an official statistical report of 1837 claimed that the state of Tamaulipas had 107,506 horses, 218,438 cattle, 3,604 donkeys, and only 180,170 head of sheep and goats. Obviously, the number of sheep and goats had declined considerably from the colonial and early Mexican period, while horses had declined about 25 percent since 1795. The number of cattle, however, doubled, although the reasons for this development are unclear.[45]

The 1830s and 1840s saw the development of a trade in livestock between the Lower Valley and Texas as well as New Orleans, orienting the region northward for the first time in its history. The naturalist Jean L. Berlandier, who based his observations on his travels and residency in Matamoros in the 1820s and 1830s, reported that mules and horses were the only stock sold outside the state of Tamaulipas. Of cattle and beeves, he remarked that "their *casco* (head) was very soft, a defect which made them depreciated so that their owners sold them in the United States of America."[46] Also, in 1824 Francisco de Arrillaga, the minister of Hacienda, addressed a memorial to Mexico's legislature in which he called for a tax on the export of Mexican stock because "livestock of great value is taken out of our frontiers to Louisiana, and so that the stockraisers and this commerce not be prejudiced, there ought to be imposed [a tax] of one peso per head taken out by land or by sea." It is not clear whether his reference was to Texas livestock and/or to other stock from adjacent Mexican states, such as Tamaulipas. However, Governor José Rafael Gonzales of Coahuila and Texas reported in 1824 that the citizens of Tamaulipas had introduced "many horses and mules" to New Orleans since 1822 because beginning with that year they had been allowed to trade by land with Anglo Americans.[47] In the early 1830s, Benjamin Lundy, the well-known American abolitionist, saw *rancheros* herding large numbers of livestock in Nuevo León and Tamaulipas. In an 1835 circular written to promote colonization of a land grant he had received from the state of Tamaulipas, he noted that "mules are bought up and driven to the other Mexican States, and to Louisiana, Mississippi, &c." It is likely that this stock was from the Lower Valley because he spent most of his time in the town of Matamoros. While there, Lundy learned that livestock prices were very cheap. He reported that breeding mares sold for two to five dollars, good saddle horses for eight to twelve dollars, cows with calves for five to ten dollars, and "large well broken working oxen at from fifteen to twenty dollars per pair."[48]

Contemporary promotional literature intended to attract U.S. colonists to Texas also acknowledged the Matamoros—Texas livestock trade connection. An early guide to Texas, written in 1835 on behalf of the Galveston Bay and Texas Land Company, informed prospective settlers that "good jacks can be purchased in the neighborhood of the Río Grande for about $20, and good unbroken mares, which are equally as valuable as broken ones, can be had at two to five dollars per head, and driven into Texas at an expense, including all risks, estimated at about 50 per cent on the first cost . . . "[49] The same land company put out a second guide called the *1840 Emigrants Guide to Texas*. This time, the author reported that Mexican *rancheros* at Matamoros sold livestock, particularly horses, mules, and cattle to Texans at a "considerable profit."[50]

Edward Dougherty, an early settler, prominent lawyer, and judge in the Lower Valley, wrote in 1867 that stock from the Río Grande Valley was sold in St. Louis prior to the 1830s. He claimed that the old residents had so informed him and that these trips to St. Louis involved taking horses, mares, and mules. Unfortunately, Dougherty does not indicate whether Tejano or Anglo Texans drove the stock north or whether they were shipped by boat to New Orleans and then to St. Louis. He added that wool was also sold for three cents a pound at that time (prior to the 1830s), and that by 1848 the abundant stock of the area was relatively inexpensive. Locally, sheep sold for fifty cents each, and mares and stock cattle for three dollars each.[51] Until other reliable sources can be obtained regarding this livestock trade, the validity of Dougherty's assertion cannot be ascertained, but if true this early commerce in stock to American markets outside Texas was a precursor to the more famous and well-known drives of the post–Civil War period.

There is considerable evidence, however, that by the late 1840s, and especially the 1850s, Texas livestock, which included animals imported from Mexico as well as from south Texas, reached new markets in Missouri and elsewhere in the Midwest.[52] General Zachary Taylor's troops at Corpus Christi also bought livestock, especially mules and horses from Mexican smugglers and traders, for eight to eleven dollars per head.[53] However, a military historian who studied the Mexican-American War found that good saddle horses sold for twenty or thirty dollars.[54]

EXAMPLES OF LARGE PRIVATELY OWNED LIVESTOCK HERDS IN THE COLONIAL AND MEXICAN PERIOD

During the colonial period some settlers owned vast herds of livestock. Escandón's Hacienda de San Juan, located near Soto la Marina, covered seventy square leagues of land. In 1757 its labor force consisted of ten families of servants classified as *gente de razón*, five families of shepherds, and nine single shepherds, totaling fifty-seven persons. The *hacienda* had 545 horses, 118 mules, 25 burros, 1,800 cattle, and 20,900 sheep. At Dolores, Tienda de Cuervo reported that Captain Vásquez Borrego had twenty-three families working at his *hacienda.* The ranch had 400 horses, 1,600 mules, 3,000 mares, and 3,000 cattle.[55] Ten years later, in 1767, the interim governor, Juan Fernando de Palacios, reported to the viceroy that the yearly production of mules at Dolores averaged 500 to 700, whose number and quality "no other stockman of New Spain could match."[56] These are but two examples of the wealthier *hacendados* who invested large sums of capital in large-scale stockraising in the colony. Although such *haciendas* were atypical of the pattern of land tenure that developed in Nuevo Santander, Mexican historian Juan Fidel Zorrilla notes that Escandón had permitted them in the early phase of colonization and that, in some cases, others had been established earlier in border areas of the older frontier provinces—areas later incorporated in the boundaries of the *gobierno* of Nuevo Santander.[57]

Economic opportunities in this new colony fostered the rise of self-made men who became well known in their own times because of their success in mining, commerce, and/or ranching. One such person was Don Nicolás de los Santos Coy. Originally a native of Coahuila, where he still had a home, he had also lived at Cerralvo. He was an "original settler" at Camargo, where he engaged in ranching on the north bank of the Río Grande. According to de los Santos Coy, neither he nor his wife had brought any capital into their marriage. Yet, in 1762, he owned four teams of oxen, 297 mares with their stallions, 58 mature mules, 59 mature *machos,* 55 two-year-old mules, 46 young mules to be branded, and 46 *machitos* (male mules), as well as 34 tamed mules, *de recua* (of the muletrain); nine *tiros* (teams of horses); 8 donkeys, 88 colts and fillies, 76 tamed horses, 56 breeding cows and 13 *anejas,* 9 adult bulls, 18 small ones, and 41 steers and heifers. In addition, he had 1,537 breeding sheep, 2,129 *primales* (one-year-old lambs); 2,438 goats, 405 lambs, and 123 *chivatos* (goats less than one year old).[58] His mixed ranching activities were representative of the tradition that had arrived by way of the older northeastern frontier settlements of New Spain. From these kinds and numbers of livestock, we can only surmise that de los Santos Coy's stockraising activities were diversified and included breeding stock as well as producing small stock for meat and sheep for wool. It is also likely that he engaged in the muleteering business or rented his mules to a muleteer *de recua,* in view of the ages and kinds of mule stock that he owned. His team of horses were also evidently used for business purposes. The presence of oxen indicates that he also farmed some land. His workforce must have included ranch administrators and/or *caporales,* cowboys, herders, and muleteers, as well as related farm and ranch workers, such as blacksmiths, wheelwrights, and others.

One of the most successful *rancheros,* among those whose lands were on the north bank of the Río Grande, was José Narciso Cavazos. In 1790, he established his claim to a large tract of land granted to him in 1792. This grant is known as the San Juan de Carricitos, and it contained 106.5 *sitios* of land for large livestock, about 470,000 acres. Cavazos, a native of the Pilón Valley, migrated to Reynosa after the original founding. According to the *visita general* of 1767, in which he was granted a *porción* on the north side of the Río Grande, he qualified as an "old settler." He married twice and had eleven children and a foster child. At the time of his first marriage, Cavazos had a small herd consisting of twenty-five mares, two donkeys, nine tame horses, fourteen cows, six little bulls, and one yoke of oxen. He also claimed rights to twelve hours of water for his lands in the Pilón Valley. His wife brought to the marriage twenty-five mares and a stallion and two cows with their calves. By combining these two herds, Cavazos raised considerable *ganado mayor* so that, upon the death of his wife, he gave to each of his first five children three hundred cattle and an unspecified number of horse stock as their share of the maternal inheritance. Like others who came from Nuevo León, Cavazos was familiar with mixed ranching, though it appears that his preference was for the raising of large livestock. At the time of his second marriage, the Reynosa *poblador* claimed ownership of a sizable herd: fourteen jacks and jennets, two hundred mares, twenty-nine tamed horses, eight stud-jacks, thirty-four jennets, two jacks, fourteen hundred goats and sheep, and twelve hundred cattle. It is likely that some of his herd came from the foundation stock he had raised in Nuevo León, but much of it increased in the new colony. According to the testimony presented to the Bourland Commission (1851–52), Cavazos introduced nine hundred head of small and large stock when he first occupied the San Juan de Carricitos grant. It is this stock that evidently multiplied in very rapid fashion. In 1807, Cavazos claimed ownership of sixty-four hundred sheep, two hundred mares in *manadas* of twenty-five each and one stallion per *manada*, thirteen jacks, and four donkeys as well as "all of this species which may be found in my camp outfits." Of his cattle, he noted that "it is impossible to ascertain the exact number as they are running on the range in abundant numbers something like five thousand and for this reason they are not branded or marked." He also claimed another fifty or more mules, which were branded and marked, and an unknown number of sheep and cattle that were also marked. The old *ranchero* also owned some mules, which he said were in use by muleteers, but he gave no number.[59]

While we do not know many details about how Narciso Cavazos conducted his various ranching and marketing activities, he was obviously quite successful in increasing and diversifying his stock. By the time of his occupation of San Juan de Carricitos, he had considerable experience as a rancher, and it was there that he engaged in stockraising on a very large scale. The fact that he had entered and occupied virgin grasslands in a more favorable zone than de los

Santos Coy probably also explains part of the reason for Cavazos's impressive success as a *ranchero*. The ranching tradition of Cavazos would be carried into the nineteenth century by his descendants as well as by newcomers, as new *ranchos* were carved out of the huge grant.

The inventory records of a *hacienda* in present-day Hidalgo County sheds additional light on the raising of livestock during the colonial era. Don Manuel Gómez, a native of Coahuila, received the Santa Anita grant in 1798. Gómez lived at Reynosa, where he was a merchant, rancher, and sergeant in the militia. When he died unexpectedly in 1803, an inventory was made in preparation for partition of his estate. According to the inventory concluded on March 19, 1803, Santa Anita's stock consisted of 12 horses, 24 pack mules, 23 mares, 28 mules, 10 jacks, 94 yearling colts, 5 stallions, and 190 mares. In addition, he owned 2,523 lambs, 1,010 grazing sheep, 481 young sheep, 46 goats, 21 breeding cows, 6 heifers, 9 bulls, and 4 working oxen. The entire stock was valued at 3,209 pesos.[60] The inventory reveals that most of the stock at Santa Anita was for breeding purposes, although sheep were raised for shearing and some agricultural produce or other "products of the country" were evidently transported by pack mule.

Late in the eighteenth century, Captain José María Ballí and his wife, Rosa María de Hinojosa de Ballí of Reynosa, operated a large livestock operation at Rancho de la Soledad de la Feria on the north side of the river in present-day Hidalgo County. The captain's will (1788) enumerated fifty *manadas* of mares (or one thousand head of mares and stallions), thirty-five donkeys, one hundred horses, ten or twelve other donkeys, and two hundred branded cattle. The ranch itself consisted of three *jacales*, four corrals, a fenced irrigated field, and the pasturelands of the ranch. He said he owned some "other animals" in addition to two thousand sheep that were leased. Ten years later, his wife's will listed similar livestock, except that she also claimed two hundred mules as well as a group of twenty tamed mules in an *atajo*, or team. She also noted that she had a stock farm of two hundred cattle on Padre Island. It is likely that this was part of the seminal herd that her son, Padre Nicolás Ballí, owned. In 1800, he claimed to have placed one thousand branded cattle in the island, for which he had filed a land-grant claim.[61]

MATERIAL WEALTH OF RANCHEROS IN THE LOWER VALLEY: A SAMPLE OF WILLS AND TESTAMENTS OF THE SPANISH PERIOD

The relative prosperity of *pobladores* engaged in stockraising, most of whom were not wealthy, can be seen in the kinds and amounts of property owned by settlers. Oakah L. Jones, Jr., in his study of wills and testaments of Laredo, found that most residents owned few material possessions other than land and livestock. The people he describes were generally small *rancheros* who lived in *jacales* and whose principal items were valued for their everyday utility. For example, in 1771 Don Nicolás de Campos's will included 990 livestock of all kinds, a *jacal* or house with a roof of straw, a shotgun with its case, a sword, some silk stockings, a short undergarment, cloth trousers, a white undercoat, two large trunks with their keys, two pairs of scissors for shearing sheep, two large books and another of medium size, and two religious pictures. Doña María Nicolasa Uriburu distributed her sheep and goats to her daughters and other designated persons, and left a large trunk to one of her daughters and a medium-size trunk to another daughter. Her other possessions included a bed, two copper kettles, six plates, a dress of blue silk, one blouse, and her *jacal*.[62]

In 1811, José María Elizondo, a soldier of the militia company of Laredo, listed as his property a stone house of one room, 200 head of cattle, 3,100 head of sheep and goats, and other livestock. In the same year, Don Yldefonso García described his inheritance from his father-in-law as a small house worth 150 pesos and 139 head of livestock, of which 100 were sheep. Another *vecino* from Laredo, Faustino Ramírez, who died in 1815, left an estate valued at 767 pesos with debts of 308 pesos. His house consisted of one stone room and a surrounding mud wall valued at 150 pesos, and he had one *porción* of land estimated to be worth 50 pesos, as well as various kinds of livestock. He listed eight mules worth 25 pesos each, three work mules at 15 pesos apiece, one hundred goats at 4 reales a head, and four cows at 8 pesos each.[63] Don José Domingo González claimed a value of 793 pesos in assets, mostly livestock, and debts of 624 pesos and 6 reales. He did not give a value to his home, land, and uncounted livestock. These properties he merely described as "a *jacal* with a stone fence, [it being] made of wood with a grass roof, and a lot on which it is located . . . a rancho situated in the *paraje* de las Pintas and in whose *agostadero* and surrounding lands I have some ranching items and animals which carry the brand and mark which I use, [and] which because they are few I do not specify on account of not having certain knowledge of those that still remain."[64] Paredes Manzano found similar kinds of property and values in wills and testaments as well as censuses of Matamoros *rancheros*.[65]

There were, of course, some *ranchero* families who inherited land and stock in such quantities that provided them with moderate wealth. One or two examples will suffice here. In Matamoros, some of the wealthier *vecinos* merely claimed, as did the widow Doña Rosa María Treviño de Chapa, "several hundred head of cattle, horses, and small livestock," totaling 5,745 pesos in value.[66] In 1789, Doña María Gertrudes de la Garza of Camargo acknowledged that after her husband Don José Salvador de la Garza had died, an inventory had been made of his property, and "her property having been separated from his to the satisfaction of his heirs, the part belonging to them . . . was divided . . . in equal shares." In this case, the property consisted of livestock, 59 *sitios*, and 111/2 *caballerías* in the Espíritu Santo grant. Under Spanish custom and law, her share was one-half of the property.[67] Following the death of his wife, Antonia Longoria, Antonio Domínguez initiated in 1830 an extrajudicial procedure at Reynosa for the purpose of effecting a family partition of the inheritance. The lengthy document not only shows the careful steps involved in this procedure, because some of the children were minors whose rights were to be protected, but it also lists all of the property of the deceased woman. In addition to the standard description of her household and personal items, there is a long list of stock animals and real estate. The value of her estate totaled 6,639.72 pesos. Among the more valuable properties were her house and *solar* at Reynosa valued at 1,250 pesos, a share in another piece of property and a brand worth 150 pesos, 71/2 *sitios* of land in the *agostadero* of San Juanito located on the Santa Anita grant and valued at 300 pesos, and buildings at the *agostadero*, which consisted of two stone wells and other improvements valued at 350 pesos. In addition, she owned three *porciones* of land valued at 150 pesos.[68]

THE DETRIMENTAL EFFECTS OF INDIAN AND ANGLO RAIDS ON THE STOCKRAISING ECONOMY OF THE LOWER VALLEY, 1830S–1848

Comanche and Lipan Apache raids, which had affected the colony during the last years of Spanish rule, recurred in the 1830s. According to Calleja, in the late colonial period the Indians usually entered the frontier by way of several routes. Their preferred routes ran through the north or south side of La Punta de Lampazos, Nuevo León, and between Presidio del Río Grande and Laredo or between Laredo and Revilla. The Indians sometimes took another entry into the region of the Lower Río Grande "by Mier, Camargo, and Reynosa, but with difficulty, and only when their enterprises have turned against them." The official sentiment at the time was that the Indians raided almost at free will in Nuevo León, Coahuila, and Nuevo Santander, and then fled, if undetected, through any of several routes. But the Indians preferred, Calleja reported, to return to their Texas homes by traveling south of Laredo in order to evade the troops stationed there, usually crossing the Río Grande between Laredo and Revilla and into the northern plains of Nuevo Santander, a route that was "shorter, level, and supplied with water."[69]

When the troublesome Comanches and Lipans renewed their raiding in the mid-1830s, they ventured deeper into the delta of the Río Grande Valley. The unsettled conditions resulting from the struggle between Mexico and Texas, and then between Mexico and the United States, as to the true boundary between Texas and Mexico may have influenced these developments.[70] According to Berlandier, the Lipans were at this time located north of the *presidios*, or forts, on the Río Grande at Laredo and Presidio del Río Grande, but they roamed southeasterly toward the creek of San Fernando. Berlandier also noted that Lipans were often "in search of wild horses, which were not lacking, and which travellers and the inhabitants of the *ranchos* of that region (Trans-Nueces) go to buy from them. In these wilderness regions a large number of domestic horses frequently run away from the dwellings or leave travellers afoot on the road." At about the same time, the Comanches, whose home was in central and western Texas, also made their appearances in the outlying ranching districts of the Río Grande *villas*.[71]

The *ranchos* of Laredo, in particular, bore the brunt of the Indian raids. In his study of Laredo, Hinojosa noted that not only were many ranches in the Laredo district depopulated, but livestock herds sharply declined due to the Indian raids. In the winter of 1835–1836, the Indian raids in Laredo resulted in twenty-four deaths and the loss of 1,000 livestock. Sheep declined from 6,500 in 1833 to 5,800 in 1835, reaching a low mark of 1,500 sheep in late 1837. Similarly, horses declined from 2,400 in 1833 to 548 in 1835, and only 100 in late 1837. According to Hinojosa, the Indians were still raiding Laredo in 1846 and again in the late 1850s, although he does not indicate what damage they caused.[72]

In 1836 and 1837 the southward-moving Comanches and Lipan Apaches made their presence felt for the first time in the delta of the Lower Valley, where for a considerable time, the *rancheros* had prospered because the local Indians were few and generally at peace. According to the *alcalde*, or mayor, of Matamoros, the Comanches appeared in large numbers around the ranches on the coast in the jurisdiction of Matamoros, on April 14, 1836, killing a rancher and his servant and stealing horses. The Indians were pursued, but not located by a detachment of soldiers. On May 4, 1836, large numbers of Indian tribes were sighted close to Mier, Camargo, and at Revilla, which was renamed Guerrero after Mexican independence. The commandant general on the frontier requested aid from the governor, who, in turn, asked the citizens to respond, but they did not. On August 5, 1836, the citizens of Matamoros complained that the Indians had committed still more murders and destruction without being opposed by the Mexican army stationed in their city. The Matamoros newspaper reported in September that Lipan Apaches had come to the north side of the Arroyo Colorado. Indian threats and raids also alarmed the *vecinos* of

Reynosa, whose *alcalde* also appealed to the governor to assist in repelling the Indian invaders; according to him, Indians had appeared near Reynosa at Las Cuevas on February 24, 1837. The *vecinos* pursued the Indians, but failed to locate them. Four days later, five hundred Comanches approached Camargo and Reynosa, destroying property in the area and slaughtering nine hundred head of livestock. The citizens counterattacked and killed several Indians, while suffering eight wounded. The Indians then roamed upriver and attacked Guerrero, capturing several persons. Lack of arms, ammunition, and horses precluded further pursuit.[73]

For some time, the Indians did not relent in their raids on the Lower Valley. The *alcalde* of Matamoros wrote to the governor that on March 1–2, 1837, two hundred Indians raided ranches outside the jurisdiction of Matamoros, on the north side of the Río Grande. The Indians had killed five men and driven off a large number of horses, which had been recovered from Texans and Indians the previous year. One hundred head of cattle were also wantonly killed. The *alcalde* appealed to the local military commander, but lack of horses prevented him from pursuing the enemy. In July 1837 an even larger force, reportedly one thousand Comanches, came within a few leagues of the city of Matamoros, attacked the military outposts, killed a colonel, carried off large numbers of horses and mules, and burned several *ranchos*. According to the U.S. consul in Matamoros, D. W. Smith, the Indians attacked every full moon and "have compelled the greater part of the frontier inhabitants to abandon their stock farms and remove on [*sic*] the south side of the Río Grande." Fearing that the Indians would return to the river towns, the commandant general, in October 1837, detached several battalions of troops from Matamoros to the frontier towns. In November 1837, several hundred soldiers were sent to the Nueces River because of reports that Indians were harassing the settlers there. Because of inadequate records, it is not known what success they experienced. According to historian David Vigness, the Indians continued to mount raids in subsequent years, although not with the same severity as their earlier forays into the Lower Valley.[74] He offers, however, no evidence to show the extent of these raids.

After these raids, the Indians reverted to their traditional strategy of hit-and-run attacks conducted by small groups of Indians, except for a concerted drive they made in 1844. One of the bloodiest and costliest attacks on the Lower Valley occurred on October 7, 1844, when four hundred Comanches destroyed two ranches in the vicinity of Guerrero. The Comanches defeated the town's local auxiliary force, which included a contingent of Carrizo Indians. The Comanches killed seventy persons, including twenty-two who died from fires set to their dwellings. Quickly alerted, the military forces reacted in an attempt to locate the enemy and rescue more than sixty settlers who had been captured. On October 15, 1844, one of the commanders surprised the Indians and, in a vicious attack, rescued fifty-nine captives at the cost of ten dead and forty-one wounded. (Among the dead were ten children killed by the Indians, who, in turn, suffered ten casualties.) The Indians then dispersed in small bands, which was their customary strategy. A second skirmish, evidently with a band of raiders, occurred on the twenty-fifth of the month, south of the Río Grande. Heavily pursued by troops from Béjar and all of the northeastern states, the final battle took place on the Arroyo of San Pedro in Texas, on October 25, 1844, resulting in the defeat of the Comanches.[75]

Accustomed to fighting Indians, the pioneer settlers of the Lower Valley faced a new threat when Anglos attempted to wrest control of the land and herds from them. After the Texas Revolt, Anglos saw the Río Grande frontier as a no-man's-land and Mexicans as their bitter enemy. In the 1830s and 1840s, they openly raided *ranchero* herds on both sides of the river. More than the Indians, Anglo raiders dealt a severe blow to the livestock herds owned by the *rancheros* in the Trans-Nueces region from about 1836 to 1860. Beginning in the 1830s, Anglo Texan "cowboys" systematically stole livestock from the ranches of the Mexicans who lived in the vicinity of the Arroyo Colorado, the Nueces and the San Antonio rivers, sometimes penetrating across the Río Grande into Mexico. Seeking retaliation against the hated Mexicans, the cowboys justified their actions on the grounds that retreating Mexicans had taken property from Texans during the Texas Revolution. In 1839, Dr. James Starr reported that he saw twelve miles from La Grange, Texas, "a Company of Texas Cowboys" who had stolen hundreds of horses, mules, and cattle from the inhabitants of Chihuahua (Dr. Starr probably meant Tamaulipas). In addition, Texan army commanders often sent detachments south of the Nueces to gather cattle needed to feed their troops. After the fighting ended, veterans of the Texas Revolt not only stole from the "enemy," but also from peaceful settlers. Coming together in small bands, one historian says, "[cowboy] activities gave rise to the saying that to become a cowman, a fellow needed only a rope, a branding iron, and the nerve to use them." "Cattle hunts" or gathering cattle became a bona fide occupation. Working by moonlight, the cowboys herded several hundred wild cattle, driving the herd two or three days until it was worn out. By then the cattle were tame and easy to manage.[76]

No one knows how many cattle and horses were gathered by these cowboys, but "cattle hunts" were commonplace. Many observers noted the presence of immense herds of "wild" and "Spanish cattle" in the plains, thickets, and waterways which undoubtedly made the hunts easy. Moreover, the involvement of Anglo and Mexican ruffians made it more difficult to contain cattle rustling. Hiding and disposing of stolen herds was easy. As one historian wrote, "the captured cattle were used to start new herds or to replace *beeves* that had been marketed in Louisiana."[77]

While some histories assert that all of the Mexican cattle were rounded up by the cowboys by 1840, this was not the case. For example, a Mexican War veteran who settled in Nueces County, Captain N. Gussett, informed James Cox, compiler of the *Historical and Biographical Record of the Cattle Industry and the Cattlemen of Texas and Adjacent Territory,* that in 1852, with less than 500 dollars, he employed "Spaniards [Mexicans] to assist him in rounding-up and branding wild Spanish cattle, a commodity at that time in abundance. His first year's work resulted in 5,000 head [being collected], of which less than 1,000 were fit for ranch purposes. The others he disposed of, and with the proceeds went to Kentucky and bought fifty-four head of Durham bulls and turned them loose on the range," developing from this stock his cattle herd.[78]

The Mexican-American War led to a repetition of the cattle stealing that had taken place after the Texas Revolution. As *rancheros* fled to the river towns, they left their stock behind. Anglo cowpunchers renewed the hunt for cattle. Even tame unbranded cattle, the so-called mavericks, were rounded up. With so many unbranded cattle on the prairies, cowmen did not think of hunting mavericks on public land as stealing. Only later, when unbranded cattle became scarce and ownership easy to determine, was mavericking frowned upon as a form of rustling. As prices increased for beef, Anglo cowboys drove the cattle to the coast or to New Orleans to make a quick fortune.[79]

The impact of Indian and Anglo raids on the herds of Mexican *rancheros* in the Lower Valley proved to be devastating. Whereas the assessment rolls of the river towns in the mid-1830s recorded 3 million head of livestock, statistical evidence and contemporary observations confirm that a sharp decline in numbers took place thereafter.[80] Berlandier remarked on this development in his second trip to the river towns in 1834. Of Camargo, whose jurisdiction went to the Nueces River, the southern boundary of Texas, he wrote that "in other times there were several hundred thousand animals of all kinds in the jurisdiction of Camargo . . . whereas now all the herds together number scarcely twenty-five thousand head."[81] Moreover, it appears that ranching was neglected in the early 1840s. According to both Mexican and Anglo military reports, *rancheros* often left their homes in the towns along the Río Grande to join Mexican forces defending the frontier.[82]

THE GRADUAL DEVELOPMENT OF A FARMING ECONOMY

Because the plains of Nuevo Santander were semiarid, farming received significantly less attention than stockraising, except in well-watered valleys. Consequently, farming was of secondary importance to the *rancheros.* In effect, farmers had limited success, with much of it occurring only in years when the rainfall was sufficient. Since the 1750s the settlers in the *villas del norte* had tried to build irrigation ditches near the river, but their work proved futile because either drought precluded irrigation or excessive rainfalls led to flooding and the destruction of their works. Irrigation works remained incomplete and were later abandoned on the recommendation of colonial officials. The high banks of the Río Grande also precluded gravity irrigation.[83]

In spite of all the natural and technological limitations, *rancheros* cultivated a variety of crops for local consumption as well as trade with neighboring districts. Settlers used *chalanes,* small flat-bottomed boats, to carry the produce from place to place along the Río Grande. The colony also exported a hot pepper known as *chiltipiquín,* and some localities in central and southern Nuevo Santander produced sugar cane and cotton. Aridity made the cultivation of wheat impossible, and the production of important foodstuffs, such as corn, usually never satisfied the needs of the river *villas.* Consequently, *rancheros* in the Río Grande region sold or traded livestock, meat, salt, and hides for grains and other foodstuffs grown at more favorable locations in the interior of Nuevo Santander, Nuevo León, Coahuila, and even at San Antonio and La Bahía in Texas, where irrigation was moderately successful and the climate more temperate.[84] In 1778 Father Agustín de Morfí made an inspection of Presidio del Río Grande, Coahuila, whose jurisdiction included one town and four missions with more than twelve hundred persons. This gave him an opportunity to discuss the trade network that connected these remote provinces of New Spain. He wrote that the "crops that are usually grown are chile, beans, and corn, with such an abundance, there remain[ed] an excess for the provisions of the immediate presidios even including San Vicente, and for much of the Colonia [of New Santander], Nuevo Reyno de León, and some settlements of the Province [of Coahuila]."[85]

Some *rancheros* were also *labradores,* or farmers. In the 1830s farming gained a measure of respectability with the cultivation of cotton along the delta of the Río Grande. Leroy Graf, in his economic history of the Lower Valley, notes that there was one gin in Reynosa in the 1830s.[86] However, farming was difficult due to the lack of a workable technology to convey water from the river to the adjacent high ground to irrigate cropland, although Berlandier recommended the use of pumps during his residence in the Lower Valley in the 1820s and 1830s. As a result, farmers depended on dry farming or *de temporal* techniques, planting their seed in the fertile, low-lying *ancones*, or hollows, of the river. They usually planted corn, beans, vegetables, and melons for local use.[87] Unfortunately, virtually no specific descriptions of Lower Valley farms exist. However, in a claim against the United States for indemnification for property allegedly taken without payment by the U.S. Army under General Zachary Taylor, representatives of a Mr. Miguel Salinas claimed that Salinas had purchased a tract of land out of the Espíritu Santo Grant in 1835 and developed a *hacienda*. He asserted that he grew sugarcane, corn, beans, and vegetables, and that he owned machinery for grinding sugarcane. The author of the memorial also claimed that the *hacienda* had four thousand fruit trees, but no mention was made of what kind. The annual farm production was valued at 20,000 dollars.[88]

The crops grown in the Lower Valley in the 1830s were the same ones harvested throughout the state of Tamaulipas. According to official statistics, in 1837 the inhabitants of the state sowed 3,800 fanegas of seed on 13,551 hectares. This netted 95,735 fanegas of corn and beans. The *piloncillo* sold for 55,759 pesos, and all other crop production totaled 152,000 pesos. The total value of agriculture was given as 494,864 pesos.[89]

The cultivation of corn, cotton, and sugar continued to receive attention in the 1840s and 1850s. Although not extensively grown, the products of these crops were described as "wonderful" by soldiers stationed in the Lower Valley during the Mexican-American War. In 1843, *La Gaceta del Gobierno* of Tamaulipas published a list of eighty-eight cotton growers from El Estero, El Taguachal, El Soliceño and El Longoreño, *ranchos* in the jurisdiction of Matamoros. They expected to produce twenty-five hundred bales of cotton. In 1847, an early American traveler, Dr. Frederick A. Wislizenus, reported seeing on his approach to Matamoros "sugar and cotton plantations among [the settlements] but chaparral always in the background."[90]

THE DAWNING OF A NEW ERA: THE TRANSFER OF THE LOWER VALLEY LANDS TO THE UNITED STATES, 1848

The United States' victory over its neighbor, Mexico, resulted in a change in sovereignty for the northern half of Tamaulipas. At the conclusion of the treaty negotiations, the state government of Tamaulipas informed Mexico City that it regretted its loss of four thousand square leagues of land—land that included the valuable river valleys of the Río Grande and the Nueces. The state governor, Francisco Vital Fernández also feared the loss of control of navigation in the Río Grande. He was especially aggrieved by the loss of extensive herds estimated to include 2 million head of livestock valued at 1 million pesos. To compensate stockraisers for these losses, governor Vital Fernández asked that 2 million pesos of the amount paid to Mexico under the treaty be given to Tamaulipas to build schools, improve navigation, and establish a fund whose interest would be used to assist ranchers.[91] The governor was certainly aware that thousands of Mexicans would also choose to relocate to the north side of the Río Grande. The state's population had continued to increase since independence until reaching 106,624 persons in 1850.[92] Migration of Mexicans to the left or north side of the river evidently started as soon as the treaty was concluded, if not earlier. Although Don Jesús C. Cárdenas, the state governor, characterized the *mejicano* immigrants as "*ladrones de ganado y sirvientes fraudulentes*" [cattle thieves and deceitful servants], most were honest people who chose to cast their luck across the river in Texas. In fact, the U.S. census of 1850 enumerated 8,541 persons in the Lower Valley, of which a substantial majority were of Mexican descent.[93]

In 1848 economic developments temporarily took second place to the unfolding of political events. The conclusion of the war with Mexico made the Río Grande the boundary between the United States and Mexico. As a result, Mexicans living, working, and owning property on the north bank of the Río Grande were now split off from the jurisdiction of the old river *villas*. The entire northern section of Tamaulipas was now annexed to the United States, becoming part of Texas. By treaty, the Mexicans in the annexed territory, which soon became known popularly as the Lower Río Grande Valley, were to be protected in their persons and in their property. Whether, in fact, these protections would be honored was a matter of conjecture.[94] Indeed, Mexicans were apprehensive about their new status as citizens of the United States, a country whose people had twice inflicted war on their homeland.[95] Still, Mexicans must have known that some adjustments had to be made if they were to persist in the Lower Valley, as several generations of *pobladores* before them had done.

CONCLUSION

While the economic history of the lands in the Seno Mexicano predates the founding of the Escandón settlements, the towns organized by Escandón and a few others that were founded later contained the bulk of population which shaped the economic life of the colony and then of the state. Although the climate was harsh and rainfall uneven in most locations, much of the lands consisted of grasslands that attracted well-established stockraisers such as the del Garza Falcón, the Vásquez Borrego, and others. Many more settlers came in search of free land, and some became prolific *rancheros* like Nicolás de los Santos Coy and José Narciso Cavazos. The ranching economy's initial markets were the older mining districts located south and west of the colony, but in the 1820s and 1830s markets in Texas and Louisiana attracted the attention of Mexican stockmen along the Río Grande. The growth of the herds also promoted the territorial expansion of Nuevo Santander and Tamaulipas, with land grants extending to the Nueces by the 1820s. The most serious limitations on the ranching economy were the decline of the mining economy in New Spain, a key marketplace for livestock and its by-products, and the disruptive inroads made by raiding Indians and, later, Anglo cowboys. The *rancheros* had a stubborn tenacity, and their resiliency in the midst of distant and turbulent frontiers helped them to endure. Adaptation to change was essential for survival in this part of the New World.

While ranching remained a dominant economic activity of most of the settlers, a few tried their luck with farming and others chose to make a living by engaging in the regional trade network of the river towns, and later commerce expanded to distant world markets through the port of Matamoros. Farming was always a precarious economic activity; few areas contained adequate and/or easily accessible water resources. Still, corn, sugar cane, and, later, cotton were produced for sale. Early dependence on the salt trade and the livestock trade might have retarded the development of farming enterprises, but other problems hampered farming. In the Lower Valley, the most severe was the lack of irrigation works to ensure a consistent supply of water to the *rancheros*' fields. Consequently, the inhabitants remained dependent on imported foodstuffs until this problem was resolved in the early twentieth century, with the development of intensive irrigation projects on the delta of the Río Grande. Trade and commerce were originally tied to the colonial markets that favored larger commercial centers of the northern frontier and the seaport of Veracruz. However, the wars of independence initiated by Father Hidalgo brought havoc to the traditional ways of marketing goods in New Spain. Tampico, Soto la Marina—Escandón's old port—and Matamoros benefited from this turmoil. Eventually, Matamoros became a legitimate port of entry for foreign goods as well as for exports. As the hub of the so-called Mexican trade on the Río Grande, it grew rapidly into an urban center. While most wealth flowed to the merchant class, muleteers, teamsters, artisans, laborers, and others benefited from the expansion of international commerce. The Lower Valley region played a role in the unfolding drama that contributed to the growth of a vibrant economy, whose reach extended deep into Mexico. After the war with

Mexico, some settlers and merchants opted to relocate to the north side of the new international boundary, in search of better economic opportunities. In short, the foundation for what was to come in the land north of the Río Grande had been well rooted in the old *villas* of the valley. Stockraising, trade and commerce, and to a lesser extent, farming were all essential economic activities that continued and thrived in the new lands that became a part of Texas in 1848.

CHAPTER FOUR

THE MAKING OF A TEJANO HOMELAND IN SOUTH TEXAS, 1848–1900

Population Growth, Adaptation, and Conflict

Ever since the appearance of the so-called Mexican problem in the American Southwest during the 1920s, both native and foreign-born Mexicans in the United States have been the subject of considerable study by social scientists. Much of their focus has centered on the group's social customs, family organization, and its assimilation into American life. The older literature depicted Mexicans generally as a largely ahistorical people or as a people with a deficient culture and social organization.[1] In the 1960s Chicano historians and sociologists discredited much of that scholarship as shortsighted and based on impressionistic research and outdated models.[2] Still other researchers saw Mexicans in the United States as a colonized people marginalized by the new settlers from the United States and Europe.[3] Some Chicano scholars have countered by asserting that Mexican Americans were historical actors who shaped their lives and identities in spite of the barriers presented by the dominant Anglo society.[4] The current literature emphasizes the importance of the diversity of the Mexican American experience and the group's adaptation to changing forces.[5] One recent study of the Mexican Americans and the Catholic church, for instance, shows the adaptive strategies of the settlers as a new hierarchy took control of the church activities in the American Southwest after 1848.[6] Despite the new historiography, the myth that Tejanos have no history to speak of is commonly resurrected in the general literature and periodicals, including major newspapers. Equally alarming is the persistence in scholarly literature of the notion that they are a colonized society. Others have tended to see the Tejano as either a landed class or a peon class.[7] Yet De León and Stewart have demonstrated that, in fact, the Tejano workforce consisted of a sizable number of artisans, clerks, and shopkeepers.[8]

While I agree that in the second half of the nineteenth century Tejano society was diverse and not monolithic, important questions remain unanswered regarding this large and important ethnic group. My purpose here is to examine anew Tejano social history to understand the forces that shaped Tejanos and the ways that they, in turn, influenced new settlers as the region underwent development. Specifically, how did *rancheros* and other Tejanos in south Texas adapt to a changing society, one that was gradually becoming incorporated into the culture and economy of the United States? What was the rate of population growth for the region and for its towns, and what were the sources of that growth? In view of the previous century of landholding, who among the Tejanos remained on the land and who stayed in the region? What characteristics of their family structure and folkways stand out as unique or as different from Anglos? What tensions existed in the Tejano community? What was the nature of Hispanic–Anglo relations, and how significant was conflict to the overall history of interethnic relations in south Texas?

REGIONAL POPULATION GROWTH, 1850–1900

From 1850 to 1900 south Texas experienced rapid population growth. In 1853 an anonymous writer in *De Bow's Journal*, a highly respected authority out of New Orleans, engaged in wishful thinking more than analysis when he matter-of-factly wrote that "the Mexican and aborigines [of Texas] are reduced to a cypher, and will soon disappear."[9] Contrary to such uninformed Anglo views that were repeated by others, the number of Tejanos in the state rose sharply, especially in south Texas. As noted in Table 4.1, the population of the region's core counties of Cameron, Hidalgo, Starr, Zapata, Webb, Duval, and Nueces grew nearly ninefold from slightly over 9,000 in 1850 to 79,925 inhabitants in 1900, with the largest gains occurring from 1860 to 1880. About 85 percent of the total population in south Texas consisted of Tejanos who were native and foreign born.[10]

The most impressive decennial gains in the population of south Texas occurred in the 1860s and 1870s, when the rate of growth was 45.6 percent and 50 percent, respectively. The expansion of commercial ranching and the development of trade with Mexico accounted for this first phase of rapid population growth. It is possible that the totals even underestimate real growth, since entire ranches could have been missed or *rancheros* and *vaqueros* out trailing livestock might have escaped the count—some trail drives lasted up to three

Table 4.1 Population of Counties in South Texas, by Decade, 1860–1900

County	1860	1870	1880	1890	1900
Cameron	6,028	10,999	14,959	14,424	16,095
Hidalgo	1,182	2,387	4,347	6,534	6,837
Starr	2,406	4,154	8,304	10,749	11,469
Zapata	1,248	1,285	3,636	3,562	4,760
Webb	1,397	2,615	5,273	14,842	21,851
Encinal[a]	43	427	1,902	2,744	
Duval		1,083	5,732	7,598	8,483
Nueces	2,906	3,975	7,673	8,093	10,430
Total	15,210	26,925	51,826	68,546	79,925
Decennial change in %		45.5	50.0	25.9	14.2

Source: *1972 Texas Almanac,* 157–60.

[a] Encinal County was formed from lands in Webb County, but it was never officially organized. In effect, its population was drawn from Webb County, and it was again added to the latter county in 1900.

months.[11] Also, some people were not always willing to be counted by census enumerators. The 1880s, with an increase of only 25.9 percent, represented a bit over one-half the previous ten years' rate of increase. The smallest rate of growth in the region's population came in the 1890s, when hard economic times in the rural and urban sectors resulted in a 14.2 percent increase.

That the growth of the population in south Texas was sharply related to the ranching economy can be seen in the characteristics of the rural workforce. I selected Hidalgo County to show this development. Table 4.2 reveals that the percentage of the total workforce who were farmers and stockraisers reached its apex in 1860, with about 43 percent claiming those occupations. As the ranching economy began to decline in the 1880s, the percentage of farmers and ranchers dropped to 20 percent in 1900. At the same time, unskilled laborers, many of whom worked in the agricultural industry or as domestics for farmers and ranchers, constituted a significant element in the workforce, averaging about 42 percent for the forty-year period. The only noticeable drop occurred in 1870, when 39 percent of the workforce were unskilled. This is probably related to the rapid expansion of ranching that occurred in the late 1860s, with the commencement of the boom era, attracting men to stockraising, farming, and ancillary jobs. The loss of jobs in the ranching sector toward the end of the century was partly offset by a small rise in the number of officials, professionals,

Table 4.2 Percentage of Working Population in Each Occupation, Hidalgo County, 1860, 1870, 1880, 1900

Occupation	1860	1870	1880	1900
	(N=357)	*(N=795)*	*(N=1,158)*	*(N=2,182)*
Public Service, Professional	1.0	2.0	2.0	2.6
Merchant, Clerk	1.0	[a]	2.0	2.6
Craft, Skilled	2.2	3.3	4.1	5.1
Semiskilled	.7	2.1	1.2	2.5
Farming, Stockraising	42.6	34.8	27.5	19.5
Shepherds, Herdsmen	—	18.0	2.6	11.2
Unskilled Labor	53.0	39.1	51.8	53.4
Other Agriculture (Skilled)	—	—	—	3.2

Sources: *U.S. Census of Population,* Hidalgo County, 1860, 1870, 1880, 1900.
[a] Less than 1 percent.

other white-collar workers, and skilled artisans from about 4 percent in 1860 to 10 percent in 1900.

Table 4.3 shows the comparative occupational distribution of Mexicans and Americans in 1880, the apex of the ranching boom. The data reveals the dominance of Mexicans in all categories, except for officials, teachers, and government workers who were mostly Anglos. Again, the role of Tejanos in the agricultural economy is clearly evident, with large numbers employed as farmers, ranchers, herders (cowboys), laborers, and artisans.

GROWTH OF THE TOWNS IN THE REGION

Towns, cities, and even *ranchos* in south Texas grew at varying rates, for the economy lacked uniformity in such a large territory and geographical advantages favored one town over another.[12] As commerce with Mexico increased and as ranching expanded through the grasslands of the region, towns began to increase in population and economic activity. Merchants, artisans, and laborers found new opportunities in urban communities, while ranchers, cowboys, shepherds, and other rural workers went to work on the farms and ranches of

Table 4.3 Occupational Distribution of Mexicans and Americans in Hidalgo County, Texas, 1880[a]

Occupation	Number of Workers		Percentage of Workforce
	Mexican	*American*	*Mexican*
Professional	2	2	—
Teachers	1	5	.90
Government	—	5	—
Merchants and Grocers	9	4	.76
Business (Other)	—	1	—
Clerks	—	—	—
Artisans	63	1	5.30
Farmers	174	21[b]	14.73
Stockraisers	115	—	9.74
Herders	143	—	12.11
Shepherds	30	—	2.54
Labor	568	5	48.09
Domestic Servants	67	—	5.67
Total	1,182	44	99.84%

Source: *U.S. Census of Population*, Hidalgo County, 1880.

[a] Excludes a small number of U.S. soldiers and state troops stationed at Hidalgo, the county seat.

[b] Five of these farmers were mulattoes.

the region to supply foodstuffs and livestock to local consumers, including the military, and distant marketplaces.[13] Military contracts for foodstuffs, beef, hay, corn, oats, livestock, charcoal, cord wood, lumber and shingles, and transportation services were an important source of income to settlers in the lower border country.[14] In addition, the U.S. government hired hundreds of persons to work at the various posts on the frontier. In one of the first reports on government spending in Texas, Col. J. K. F. Mansfield remarked that contracts, salaries, wages and other costs amounted to $990,957.10 in 1855 and $635,322.77 in 1856.[15] While Brownsville became the leading town of the region by virtue of its access to sea trade, the upriver towns of Santa María, Edinburg, Río Grande City, Roma, Zapata, and Laredo served the surrounding ranchers and became bases of operation for merchants. The latter bought livestock, skins, bones, wool, and agricultural produce, usually corn, cotton, and vegetables, and they imported Mexican livestock, silver, and other metals. These were the same merchants who supplied the local populace with imported foodstuffs and luxury items.[16] Exact figures for this commerce are hard to come by, but contemporary reports from authoritative observers, such as state legislator and merchant John L. Haynes of Río Grande City, claim that by the 1850s it amounted to several million dollars.[17]

Capitalizing on its favorable location to engage in the Mexican trade, Brownsville ranked as the most important town in south Texas, a rank that it relinquished temporarily to Laredo sometime in the early 1880s. In the first description of this new, "flourishing town" (January 1849), Helen Chapman, the wife of the quartermaster at Fort Brown, described its population "as motley as you can ever conceive—drawn together I believe from every nation on the globe. There are a large number of Mexicans, most of them from the laboring class." She noted that already some of the leading town merchants had erected brick warehouses and more were going up. She also said that "there are three or four good brick dwelling houses—more in process of erection—and great numbers of an inferior character." As for the Mexican trade, she remarked that "there are great quantities of goods in the place, and sometimes business will seem to be dull—then again American and Mexican traders will come from the interior, and the town will be completely swept of goods." Mrs. Chapman added that "an immense deal of smuggling" went on.[18] An early Protestant missionary, Melinda Rankin reported that in 1850 the Brownsville trade was worth 6 million dollars, and it was replacing its sister city, Matamoros, in importance.[19] By this time, Brownsville's population totaled about twenty-five hundred, although town boosters asserted that it numbered five thousand people "of all colors. . . . It is a right bustling, business place; every one [*sic*] seems to have something to do, and to be intent on doing it. Several two and three story brick houses are going up."[20]

Brownsville's occupational structure reflected its position as the leading urban and commercial center of the region as well as the differences between Tejano and Anglo employment. Tables 4.4 and 4.5 examine the data for male and female workers in 1880, a relatively good economic year and prior to the slump that affected the town following the entry of the international railroads into Laredo and the subsequent movement of the Mexican trade to the Corpus Christi–Laredo axis. Nearly one-half of all Tejano male workers, 49 percent, were employed as laborers, domestics, or other unskilled, as compared to only 8 percent of the Anglo males. On the other hand, Anglo males clearly dominated white-collar jobs in government, the professions, and business, with the exceptions of grocers and kindred businesses in which Tejanos were numerous. Interestingly, the artisans still played a key role in urban employment, and most of these were also Tejano as compared to Anglo, by a three-to-one ratio. Small numbers of Tejanos and Anglos were ranchers and cowboys, but rela-

Table 4.4 Occupational Structure of Mexican and American Males, Brownsville, 1880[a]

	Number of Workers		Percentage of Workforce	
	Mexican	*American*	*Mexican*	*American*
Professional	5	42	—	13
Governmental	9	25	1	8
Merchants	1	49	—	16
Grocers and Other Business[b]	92	10	10	3
Shopkeepers	4	20	—	6
Clerks	54	49	6	16
Artisans	287	86	30	27
Stockraisers	3	6	—	2
Herders	32	6	3	2
Labor	377	18	39	6
Domestic and Other Unskilled	101	6	10	2

Source: *U.S. Census of Population*, Cameron County, Texas, 1880.

[a] Excludes U.S. troops living at Fort Brown (280 persons) and 39 persons aboard a U.S. gunboat in the Río Grande. There were also 14 blacks and 1 mulatto. The blacks consisted of 1 coffeehouse keeper, 3 cooks, 1 porter, 1 watchman, 1 bootblack, and 7 domestic servants. The mulatto was also a servant.

[b] Includes hucksters.

tively speaking, they constituted a very small percentage of the male workforce in Brownsville.

The composition of the female workforce in Brownsville indicates again that there were some differences between the two population groups. Tejano women in the workforce outnumbered Anglo women by a ratio of five to one, and most of them were employed in low-paying work as domestics, washerwomen, laundresses, and hucksters. The skilled and better-paid Tejanas worked as dressmakers, and a handful were sewing-machine operators. In contrast, very few Anglo women performed unskilled work, but they were more likely than Tejanas to own stores or other businesses or to work as teachers. In short, while the numbers of Anglo women workers were small, it is obvious that for Tejanas in Brownsville employment outside the home was important.

After 1850, Brownsville, Port Isabel, which was located on the bay or Laguna Madre, and Santa María, which was located near the river on the border with Hidalgo County, remained the most important communities in Cameron County. Of these, Brownsville grew most rapidly due to its importance as a

Table 4.5 Occupational Structure of Mexican and American Females, Brownsville, 1880[a]

Occupation	Number of Workers		Percentage of Workforce	
	Mexican	*American*	*Mexican*	*American*
Teachers	—	8	—	17
Merchants	—	7	—	15
Business (Other)	1	3	—	7
Dressmaker	38	5	16	11
Domestic	58	5	24	11
Washer	45	6	24	13
Laundress	72	14	30	13
Huckster	21	—	9	—
Sewing-Machine Operator	5	—	2	—
Other	5	—	2	—
Total	245	46		

Source: *U.S. Census of Population*, Cameron County, Texas, 1880.

[a] Excludes 23 Catholic nuns, all but 3 foreign-born. They taught 31 children in Brownsville. There were also 2 black laundresses and 2 domestic servants. One mulatto servant also resided in Brownsville.

trade center and county seat. In 1880, the population of Brownsville reached six thousand, while that of Port Isabel numbered about five hundred, and Santa María had about two hundred persons.[21]

Annexation brought a measure of stability to Laredo, and by the mid-1850s Laredo and the new town of Eagle Pass, together, handled a half-million dollars in trade mostly with neighboring Mexico. Still, Laredo remained a small town for more than thirty years after the war with Mexico. It barely grew from 1,173 persons in 1850 to 1,306 in 1860, and 2,043 in 1870. As the ranching economy improved in the 1870s, the town experienced substantial growth. By 1880 Laredo contained 3,811 persons and observers described it as a wide-open, boisterous town. In addition to attracting Mexican immigrants, 357 Anglo and foreign-born, non-Hispanics lived in the town. Its best growth years came after the intercontinental railroads reached the town in the 1880s. The town's population soared to 11,319 in 1890 and consisted of a sizable enclave of American and European settlers and a more diverse workforce than ever before, including hundreds of Mexican immigrants attracted to work activities in the ranching industry, railroad shops, coal mining, and urban jobs. The 1890s brought slower growth, as Laredo reached a population of 13,429 settlers in 1900.[22]

The rest of the new towns along the Río Grande were smaller in size, but they also experienced growth due mainly to the expansion of ranching and commerce. Harry Love, commissioned by the U.S. Army to explore the Río Grande by boat in 1850, reported to William Chapman, the quartermaster in Brownsville, that the population of Roma was about five hundred and it had "several enterprising merchants." Río Grande City was described as a "new and flourishing place on the American side."[23] Another officer, Lt. Egbert Vielé, who had been stationed in 1850 at Fort McIntosh near Laredo, informed the Geographical Society of New York that Río Grande City "contains several good buildings and stores, facing a plaza, where a market is daily held in the open air."[24] A resident of Roma who was well versed on trade in the western part of the Lower Valley informed *De Bow's Journal*, in 1860, that regular river transportation from Roma to Brownsville would greatly benefit commerce in New Orleans. He reported that only one steamer had been on the upper part of the river in 1859 and made only three trips, so that "carts [were] continually in demand to bring up merchandise of our merchants here and all over Northern Mexico." He anticipated a rapid development in the export of hides, wool, lead, and specie for 1860 if a steamboat or boats were available.[25] Temporary disruptions caused by Cortina's activities in 1859 and the French intervention in Mexico in 1862–67 hampered normal trade patterns along the river towns. The Civil War years also saw a renewed involvement in "black-market activities." By 1870 both Starr County towns flourished with as many as thirty steamboats plying the river.[26] In 1880, the number of settlers in Río Grande City numbered 2,109, and there were 829 persons in Roma. The Texas commissioner of insurance and agriculture noted that the former had a "large trade with the surrounding country and Mexico." Roma's merchants also catered to the Mexican trade.[27]

The Mexican trade strongly influenced the physical development of both towns. To handle river traffic, each town had a steamboat landing and a large rectangular mall-type plaza. Commercial, residential, and institutional structures surrounded Roma's plaza, and a main street linked Río Grande City's plaza to the courthouse on the north side and the steamboat landing on the south side.[28] By 1893 Roma had about one thousand settlers and counted seventy-eight major buildings. These structures were largely of stone and brick construction, reflecting its recent commercial success.[29]

Besides these border towns, other communities in south Texas were founded shortly after 1848, and they too underwent development. While favored by its seaside location, Corpus Christi's fortune as a trading center prior to the early 1880s fluctuated wildly. This was due mainly to its lack of an adequate deep-water port and the premier position of San Antonio as the main interior port for the far western Mexican and Texan trade. Since its founding as a trading post by H. L. Kinney in 1838, Corpus Christi had enjoyed some trading with the Mexican frontier, but it never rivaled Brownsville, which maintained tight control of the northern Mexican trade. In late 1852 William Chapman, the former quartermaster at Brownsville, relocated to Corpus Christi, which he described as "a very quiet place with no dust and scarcely any Mexicans."[30] With a population of about one thousand in 1853, Corpus Christi was actually a hamlet of Anglo ranchers, farmers, merchants, seamen, and artisans, sprinkled with a few Tejano *rancheros* and herders. In 1854 steamships began regular runs to New Orleans. This encouraged local business and ranching interests, as Morgan Line steamers transported beef cattle to distant markets. By 1860 Corpus Christi had 1,200 residents, 374 of whom were foreign born. Of the native born, 485 were of Mexican descent. In 1870, the town's population stood at 3,500, reflecting steady growth.[31] By 1880 its population had increased to 4,000, and its trade had a value of 2 million dollars.[32] With the building of the Texas Mexican Railway from Corpus Christi to Laredo in 1881 and subsequent channel and port improvements, Corpus Christi entered a period of expansion, replacing Brownsville in the 1880s as the most important seaport in the region. In the year ending August 31, 1883, the total value of all imports and exports at Corpus Christi was 2,711,196 dollars, compared to 2,190,512 dollars at Brownsville.[33]

The ranching boom also gave impetus to the growth of new trading towns in the interior of the region, especially San Diego and Benavides, both located in the western area of Nueces County. In the 1870s this district became organized as Duval County. Tejanos, Anglos, and a few Europeans were attracted to these towns. The two towns, however, remained small because the natural regional gateway to the Mexican trade was through Brownsville and up the Río Grande. Of the two, San Diego, which catered to the local trade in livestock and wool, was the most active, with a population of about fifteen hundred to eighteen hundred in 1882.[34]

Upstream from Laredo and on the periphery of the core region, the towns of Eagle Pass and Del Río served as trade centers to nearby Mexico, but they too grew slowly, partly because they were subjected to sporadic Indian raids and because they were isolated from the more settled regions of the state. The valley of the Río Grande was narrow in that district so that while some Mexicans were engaged in farming, most of the lands in the surrounding countryside that were eventually organized after 1870, as Maverick, Val Verde, Dimmit, La Salle, and Uvalde counties, were devoted to cattle and, to a lesser extent, sheep raising. Consequently, Anglo, European, and Hispanic settlement there occurred slowly. The merchant class consisted of Europeans and a few Anglos. The artisans were nearly all *mejicanos*, as were most of the "cattle hunters," or *vaqueros*, and shepherds. A few Mexicans owned livestock, but nearly all of the ranchers were Anglos or Europeans. Consequently, these rural districts, excepting the new towns, were not so visibly Hispanic as the rest of south Texas.[35]

POPULATION GROWTH THROUGH MEXICAN IMMIGRATION AND HIGH BIRTHRATES AMONG HISPANICS

In the second half of the nineteenth century, population growth in south Texas derived from two sources: immigration, much of it from Mexico; and a natural increase. The importance of immigration in the region's growth is suggested by De León and Stewart, who assert that about 50 percent of the Mexicans in south Texas were foreign born during the years from 1850 to 1900. Census data for Hidalgo County illustrates this point. Out of 1,338 household heads, 883, or 66 percent of all household heads living in the county in 1900, were born in Mexico.[36]

Due to the limited nature of census data, there are no precise birthrates for any population group for the nineteenth century. However, De León and Stewart's survey of representative south Texas counties found that in 1900 the net reproduction rates of Mexican and Anglo women were nearly identical: 2.96 children for Mexicans and 2.85 for Anglos.[37] There are, of course, suggestive data based on individual family histories, supporting a general presumption that some Tejano families were indeed quite large. This is particularly true of Tejano landholders who enjoyed the benefits of prosperity during the ranching boom or who held on to the land for a considerable period, surviving the good and bad times. With access to better medical care, their children usually survived to adulthood. The 1850 Lower Valley census reported that Don Bartolo García, a key Hispanic patriarch-politician in Laredo, had eight children.[38] Tirza García, one of his daughters, married the French merchant and later rancher and politician Raymond Martin in 1870, and together they had ten children.[39] Don Cosme Martínez, founder of the town of Dolores on the Vásquez Borrego grant in 1859, married twice and had seven children.[40] One of his sons, Don Proceso Martínez, an early rancher and merchant in San Ygnacio, Zapata County, married the daughter of another well-known family, the Uribes, in 1869; and they had six children.[41] John Young, Jr., married Bertha Ballí in about 1884, and they had eight children. They lived at Delfina in northern Hidalgo County, where he was engaged in stockraising.[42] Guillermo Cano and his wife, Santos Fernández, had eight children; when Cano made his last will in 1906, he resided in Rancho Toluca in Hidalgo County. At the time of the probate of his will, all of his children survived except one daughter, who also had surviving heirs.[43] Of the Salvador Vela and Leonor Zamora children who married and had children in Hidalgo County, all of whom were *rancheros* or had married *rancheros*, the number of children ranged from three born to Cecilia, eight to Pedro and to Macedonio, eleven to Salvador, and eight to the daughter Natividad. Some of the children of this first post-1848 generation of *mejicano* stockmen also raised large families. Macedonio's son Ramón Vela, who became a leading rancher in southwest Hidalgo County in the late nineteenth and early twentieth centuries, had a total of twelve children from his three marriages, but only seven survived infancy and youth. Macedonio's two other sons, Jesús María and Macedonio II, each had nine children.[44]

In general, outside of the larger cities such as Brownsville, Laredo, Corpus Christi, and the Mexican border towns, medical care from trained physicians or surgeons was so difficult to obtain that poor settlers resorted to home remedies and folk healers, or *curanderos*. Counties without important urban centers, such as Hidalgo, usually depended on the services of one or two doctors, and maybe an additional one in prosperous years.[45] Some of the physicians who had originally been assigned to U.S. military posts stayed in the region once their tours were completed. Río Grande City, home to Fort Ringgold, usually obtained doctors in this way.[46] As had been done traditionally, settlers had recourse to Mexican physicians in the older river *villas* if they could afford the fees and transportation costs.

Lack of doctors in hinterland communities probably affected net reproduction and mortality rates among lower-income Mexican settlers, but there is no precise way of measuring these vital statistics. History has all but forgotten the crucial role of *parteras*, or midwives, in the delivery of newborns. Their story remains unchronicled today.

Some *curanderos* became well known and respected, such as Don Pedro Jaramillo of Falfurrias. Most healers, however, were viewed as quacks and harshly condemned by Anglo observers.[47]

In spite of all these limitations, the general health of the settlers was satisfactory. Only rarely did deadly diseases reach epidemic proportions. In the spring of 1849, cholera reached the Brownsville-Matamoros area and reportedly claimed the lives of one-third of the people of Brazos Santiago and one thousand persons in Matamoros.[48]

PERSISTENCE RATE OF SETTLERS: A BRIEF CASE STUDY OF HIDALGO COUNTY

Despite the large number of Mexican immigrants who established new homes in south Texas, much of the Hispanic population tended to remain in place.

Hidalgo County offers a good illustration. About a third of the population in the county persisted for several decades. The rate of persistence totaled about 11.6 percent from 1860 to 1870, increasing to 36 percent from 1870 to 1880, and remaining near that rate from 1880 to 1900, when it stood at 31 percent. The smaller rate of persistence in the 1860s is an anomaly and reflects the temporary movement of *rancheros* across the river during Cortina's 1859 uprising. The census enumerator emphatically noted every "vacant" dwelling in 1860, a number estimated at about 20 percent of the county's total.[49]

It is likely that those household heads who persisted were related to each other by blood or marriage. Individuals who owned land were particularly inclined to remain settled. One of the few studies of this aspect of rural societies in the United States, a study of a frontier community in Illinois, indicates that landholding and family connections were the key factors that conditioned persistence in the population.[50] Unfortunately, the data for Hidalgo County lack sufficient precision to be able to trace the degree of relationship among persisting landholders, but it appears to be a key factor. A study of vital statistics and church records would be necessary to establish the connection conclusively.

Some family histories, however, are indicative. Macedonio Vela of Rancho Laguna Seca, in Hidalgo County, had eight children, five sons and three daughters. All survived to adulthood except the first-born son. Of the three daughters, only one married, as did each of the sons. Eloisa Vela Chapa married twice. Her first marriage was to William Dougherty of Brownsville. They lived at their ranch, Jardín de Flores, near present-day Mission, Texas, along the Río Grande. He died in 1908, and the widow remarried in 1917, this time to a Mexican immigrant named Alfredo Flores. The first son, Ramón Vela Chapa (1859–1926), married Joaquina de la Vega, a daughter of a Spanish immigrant father and a Ballí on her mother's side. A leading stockraiser, Ramón Vela Chapa founded a twenty-thousand-acre ranch, Chihuahua, near the southwest corner of the county. Jesús María Vela Chapa, the second son, also married a de la Vega. He was part-owner of Laguna Seca with his father, and he owned another *rancho* at a site called Guadalupe as well as a home at Monte Cristo. The third son, Macedonio Vela Chapa II, married Teresa Cárdenas Chapa, a daughter of one of the principal owners of Rancho La Noria Cardeneña, a major stockraising district in central Hidalgo County. A *vaquero*, Macedonio II also owned livestock, but he did not acquire land. He died unexpectedly in a ranching accident in 1912. The youngest son, Alberto Vela Chapa, married Adela Chapa Montalvo, daughter of Félix Chapa and Augustina Montalvo, owners of El Rucio ranch. Alberto owned a ranch, Medanito, five miles south of Laguna Seca, where he farmed and raised cattle, polo horses, and sheep.[51] Other family histories indicate that this process of intermarriage with old

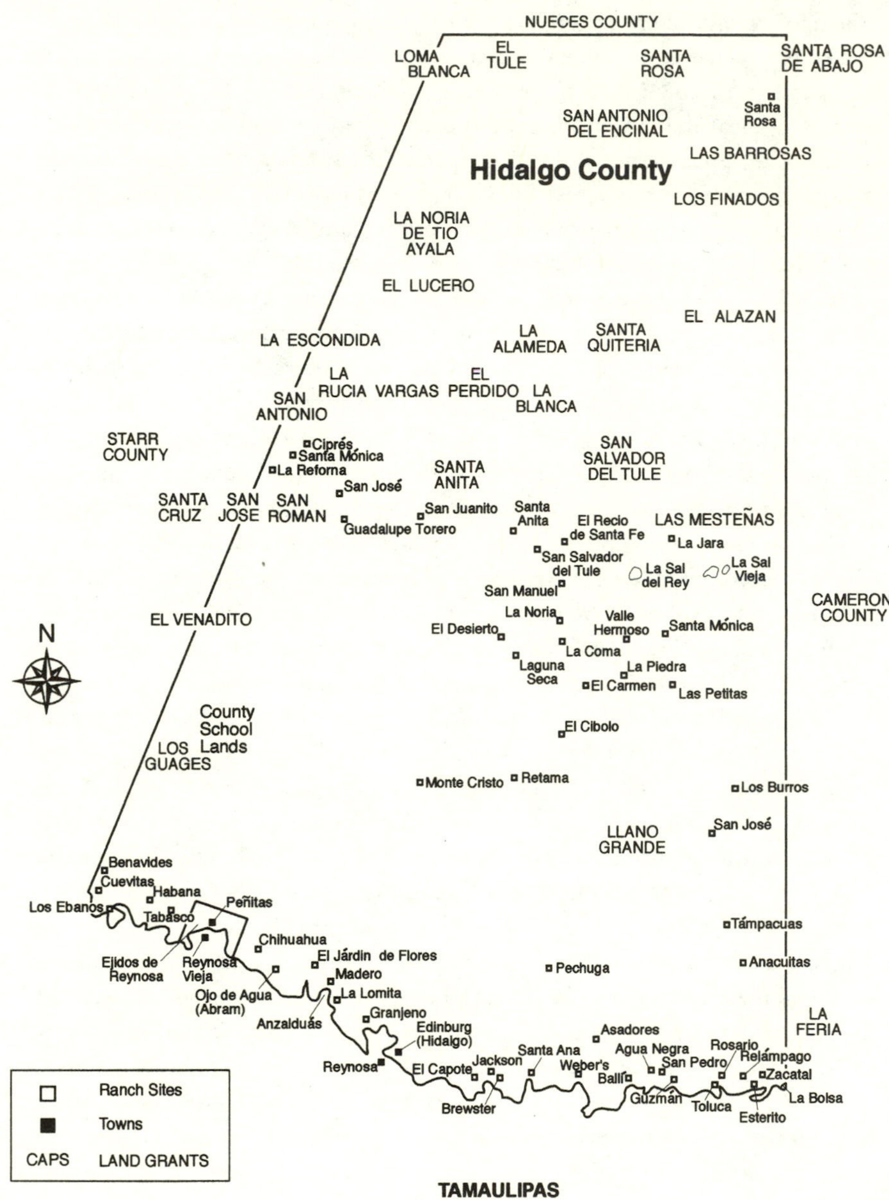
NUECES COUNTY
LOMA BLANCA
EL TULE
SANTA ROSA
SANTA ROSA DE ABAJO
Santa Rosa
SAN ANTONIO DEL ENCINAL
LAS BARROSAS
Hidalgo County
LOS FINADOS
LA NORIA DE TIO AYALA
EL LUCERO
EL ALAZAN
LA ESCONDIDA
LA ALAMEDA
SANTA QUITERIA
LA RUCIA
VARGAS
EL PERDIDO
LA BLANCA
SAN ANTONIO
STARR COUNTY
Ciprés
Santa Mónica
La Reforma
San José
SANTA ANITA
SAN SALVADOR DEL TULE
SANTA CRUZ
SAN JOSE
SAN ROMAN
Guadalupe
San Juanito
Torero
Santa Anita
El Recio de Santa Fe
LAS MESTEÑAS
La Jara
San Salvador del Tule
La Sal del Rey
La Sal Vieja
San Manuel
La Noria
El Desierto
Valle Hermoso
Santa Mónica
CAMERON COUNTY
EL VENADITO
N
La Coma
Laguna Seca
La Piedra
El Carmen
Las Petitas
County School Lands
El Cibolo
LOS GUAGES
Monte Cristo
Retama
Los Burros
San José
LLANO GRANDE
Benavides
Cuevitas
Habana
Los Ebanos
Tabasco
Peñitas
Támpacuas
Chihuahua
Ejidos de Reynosa
Reynosa Vieja
El Jardín de Flores
Madero
Pechuga
Anacuitas
Ojo de Agua (Abram)
La Lomita
Anzalduás
Granjeno
Edinburg (Hidalgo)
Asadores
LA FERIA
Reynosa
El Capote
Jackson
Santa Ana
Weber's
Agua Negra
Ballí
San Pedro
Rosario
Relámpago
Zacatal
Brewster
Guzmán
Toluca
Esterito
La Bolsa
Ranch Sites
Towns
CAPS LAND GRANTS
TAMAULIPAS

landholding families was not an isolated occurrence. Mexican immigrants who arrived earlier in the area appear to have benefited most from this social dynamic, for Tejano landholding was still widespread before 1885.

Persisting households also included persons who immigrated to south Texas soon after 1848, as well as descendants of landholding families who remained in the region or returned after the war with Mexico. Among the former, some became landowners or married into established landholding families, which helped to keep them on the land. The Salvador Vela family of Reynosa is a good example. Beginning with the coming of his son, Macedonio, in 1857 to Peñitas on the Río Grande, his other siblings followed him to Hidalgo County. All four sons acquired substantial ranches of their own, and the two daughters married into Tejano landholding families. This family persisted largely because they had a stake in the land, which they refused to surrender until hard times forced some of them to do so in the early twentieth century.[52]

Another good example can be found in the descendants of one Edward Dougherty, a New York-born serviceman of Irish descent who met his Mexican wife near Monterrey, Nuevo León, during the Mexican-American War. A lawyer, Dougherty first lived with María Marcela García in Río Grande City and then in Brownsville, where the 1850 census listed his household as consisting of his wife, a two-year-old child, and three boarders, two Americans and one German. The Doughertys settled permanently in Rudyville at Rancho Zacatal, in the southeast corner of Hidalgo County. They had three children: María Concepción, William, and James. The daughter first married the sheriff of Hidalgo County, Alexander Leo, son of a German trader of the same name who had lived in Brownsville at the same time as the Doughertys. When he died, she then married Mariano Treviño of Brownsville, who came from a Tejano *ranchero* family. Their daughter, María del Carmen Treviño, married José Julián Garza (1883–1970). The latter was a son of Esteban Garza (ca. 1803–1898), a major stockraiser in the region who had two *ranchos* in Cameron County and two in Hidalgo County. At the turn of the century, Rancho El Castillo, located near present-day Edinburg, became their headquarters. It was from there that the family moved into town about 1915 or 1916, and the *rancho* was finally sold around 1920 to Anglo newcomers. William and James, who played leading political roles in the county, both married locally. The Dougherty descendants still live in the region, mostly in the Lower Valley.[53]

Two other examples will suffice to illustrate the persistence of Tejano settlers on the land. Take the case of the Margarito Hinojosa family of Rancho Santa Mónica, in northwest Hidalgo County. This *ranchero* was the eldest son of José Lino Hinojosa (1836–1900), a resident of Río Grande City who purchased four thousand acres in 1881 from a descendant of Julián Farías, grantee of the San

Ramón grant. José Lino himself was an old settler in the region. According to the Hinojosa family history, his great-grandfather was José de Hinojosa, a land grantee at Camargo during the time of Escandón's settlement. Margarito Hinojosa (1862–1943) moved to the new property, cleared the brushland, and developed the first Hinojosa ranch. A brother, Fabián Hinojosa, the youngest of the family, developed a second ranch on the four-thousand-acre tract after serving in the Philippines in 1903–4. Their *ranchos* are today known as Santa Mónica and Ciprés, respectively. To the present day, their children operate the two ranches.[54] The Chapa family of San Manuel settled in Hidalgo County, in the early nineteenth century, with Don Manuel Chapa, who established a trading business in which he exchanged or sold hides and salt for groceries and dry goods. He bought a 640-acre tract, founded his *rancho*, and continued the business. At present (1994), seventy-three-year-old Joe E. Chapa, a fourth-generation descendant, runs the San Manuel Butane Co. store as well as a family ranch of 3,000 acres. Early arrival in the region and the eventual acquisition of land explains the persistence of settlers like the Hinojosas, Chapas, and others.[55]

SOUTH TEXAS: HISPANIC HOMELAND

Despite fifty years of settlement by newcomers from Europe and the United States, south Texas remained a virtual Mexican homeland until the 1910s and 1920s, when large numbers of midwestern and southern farmers, businessmen, and professionals migrated to the region with the inception of intensive irrigated farming. As noted above, about 85 percent of the population in south Texas were of Mexican descent in 1900, although Anglo observers generally considered the Mexicans to be even more dominant numerically. An 1878 memorial to the U.S. Congress urging the construction of a railroad from Galveston to south Texas for the defense of the coast claimed that the region was 90 percent Mexican.[56] In 1895, Colonel Anson Mills, United States Commissioner to the International Water and Boundary Commission, described the population of the Lower Valley in a letter to the U.S. secretary of state as "almost exclusively Mexican, perhaps not one in a hundred of any other race, Spanish being almost exclusively spoken, the habits, sympathies, and general character being entirely Mexican."[57] Other observers agreed with this general view. In assessing economic opportunities in southwestern Texas, the Merchant's Association of New York acknowledged, in 1901, the continuity of the region's *mejicano* character, saying that "nearly everyone speaks both English and Spanish, preferring the latter, as a large element of the old settlers and their descendants are of Mexican origin."[58]

Table 4.6 Number of Households in Hidalgo County, by Ethnicity, 1860–1900

	1860	1870	1880	1900
Mexican	239	503	840	1258
Anglo	14	24	18	29
European	—	8	7	6
Black	5	8	12	28
Blend	—	1	5	22

Source: *U.S. Census of Population*, Hidalgo County, 1850, 1860, 1870, 1880, and 1900.

In counties along the Río Grande, where the percentage of Mexican households was higher than the regional average, Hispanic culture remained dominant and even Hispanicized Anglo settlers. For instance, as noted in Table 4.6, the number of Mexican households in Hidalgo County rose sharply in the period from 1860 to 1900, from 239 to 1,258, a 500 percent increase. Fully 95 percent of all households were Hispanic in 1900. Emilia Schunior Ramírez, an educator of Hispanic and Anglo ancestry, wrote that "the majority of the [county's] pioneers . . . were Mexican." Such large absolute numbers of Mexican households in the region left a deep cultural imprint on the land. As Mrs. Ramírez noted, "up to the last quarter of the [nineteenth] century, there was little or no [Anglo] culture in [Hidalgo] county. As recently as 1915, there was hardly any difference in the way of life between the people on the Mexican side of the Río Grande and the native inhabitants of Hidalgo, Starr, and Cameron counties."[59] In Starr County intermarriage and business ties had Hispanicized the few Anglos who had settled there, some as early as the 1850s.[60] In Webb County, where Americans and Europeans households numbered thirty-two in 1860, ninety-two in 1870, and eighty-nine in 1880, a similar process occurred. The coming of the railroads to Laredo in the 1880s facilitated greater Anglo migration, as opportunities in trade, business, and industry increased. According to local tradition, Anglos and Europeans in Webb County acculturated to a significant degree without the clash of cultures, as in other parts of the Southwest.[61]

Cognizant of the overwhelming numbers of Mexicans in south Texas and their impact on the society and economy, leading Anglo residents had long urged greater American settlement. For example, both King and Kenedy had long supported Anglo migration to develop the region economically and socially, or, as the Galveston-Camargo railroad proponents openly declared, "populating this valuable section with Americans, who would soon outnumber the Mexicans that now control the vote of that district."[62] As this did not occur in much of the ranching country, proponents lamented that they had failed to see the region Americanized. In 1892, Kenedy wrote Robert J. Kleberg, King's son-in-law and successor at the King ranch, declaring that "for many years, Captain King and myself tried to Americanize that portion of the country . . . but we failed; it is very little more American in feeling today than it was in October 1848 when the Americans evacuated Matamoros and crossed over to this side."[63]

By 1900 only Brownsville, Corpus Christi, and, as noted above, Laredo contained an appreciable number of non-Hispanic households and individuals. As the first trade and commercial center of the region, Brownsville early on attracted significant numbers of Anglo and European settlers, most of whom worked in skilled, business, professional, and public service jobs. In fact, in contrast to the rest of south Texas, by 1850 Brownsville comprised a decidedly cosmopolitan social and economic milieu.[64] This process of development continued as the town grew in importance. By 1880 there were 316 Anglo and European household heads. Of this total, 160 household heads were Anglo, with 56 percent listing southern birthplaces as against 44 percent from the northern states or territories. The Europeans came mostly from Spain, the German states, Ireland, and France. In addition, 111 single persons of Anglo or European descent also resided in Brownsville. About one-third of these men and women came from Europe and the rest were from the United States.[65]

Due to early settlement by Anglos, Corpus Christi was the only town in the region whose majority population by the last quarter of the nineteenth century was non-Hispanic. It had a strong southern social milieu, one that began about midcentury with the arrival of Anglo newcomers.[66] Between 1880 and 1900, the population of Corpus Christi was about 60 percent Anglo, 30 percent Mexican, and 10 percent Black.[67]

Historian Gilberto M. Hinojosa concludes that from 1850 to 1870 Laredo's Anglo and European population never exceeded 4 percent.[68] However, as noted previously, their numbers increased after the railroads reached Laredo.

Whereas the key trade centers in south Texas enticed Anglos and European settlers, counties lacking substantial commercial development attracted few non-Hispanic households. As noted in Table 4.6, in Hidalgo County, where the ranching economy was dominant, such housesholds varied from decade to decade, but they never totaled more than one hundred in any of the decennial censuses from 1860 to 1900. In 1900 they barely constituted 5 percent of all households. The county's Anglo, Black, and "blend" households increased modestly between 1850 and 1900, but the remoteness of the area, the lack of free land, the limited economic development, and a surplus of Mexican labor precluded any large-scale Anglo settlement.[69] Blacks and "blends" increased through natural population growth rather than through new migration. Except for the few individuals singled out in this history, European immigrants hardly ever made their way to Hidalgo County.

TEJANO FAMILY VALUES AND STRUCTURE

The Tejano *ranchero* family cherished traditional values, such as love, honor, and respect for every family member. They were also united in purpose, egalitarian in their treatment of family members in matters of property rights, and fair in their dealings with each other and with outsiders.[70] Forms of address show the affection that Tejanos had for close and distant relatives. An uncle was often called *papa,* or father, and "cousins and other relatives were called *hermano y mi hermana.*"[71]

Tejano families were usually nuclear and headed by an adult male. In Laredo, where a Confederate calvary force under the command of Tejanos had operated in the Civil War years, Gilberto M. Hinojosa found that nuclear families among *mejicanos* ranged from 78 percent in 1850 to 55 percent in 1870.[72] This decrease was evidently related to the turbulence of the Civil War and to economic adjustments made after the war's conclusion. Although Hinojosa does not indicate what percentage of the families lived in single family dwellings, the more recent findings of De León and Stewart suggest that the Tejano family became more stable toward the end of the nineteenth century. By 1900 fully two-thirds (66 percent) of all Tejanos in south (as well as central and western) Texas lived in single family dwellings, and 93 percent of the families were nuclear. Also, a father headed a Tejano household nearly 90 percent of the time.[73] Unfortunately, they offer no explanation for the increased stability of the Tejano family, but it probably reflected the increasing impact of urbanization on the family structure. The importance of widespread male-headed families meant that interpersonal relations and other social matters were strongly affected by the thinking and behavior of fathers or patriarchs. Patriarchy was perhaps more important among Tejano landholders, for whom family networks were essential to maintaining continuity on the land.[74]

Some families were extended with a relative or unrelated person living in the same household. This was often the case with an elderly widowed parent and of unmarried brothers and sisters or some other relative. For instance, Emilia Schunior Ramírez notes that a *ranchero* family sometimes "included married brothers or sisters or children or even cousins, although each family unit had its own home."[75] Occasionally, one or both of the parents might live in the same household, but according to census data, not more than three generations were present at one time. Lieutenant Vielé's claim that "frequently five generations are to be seen in one house, all living in peace and unity" is thus not supported by census data.[76]

The only unrelated household members consisted of boarders, servants, and hired workers. Usually the boarders were adult males, apparently immigrants who were employed by the family or by someone in the community. Many of them were sojourners passing through the region on their way north. Servants ranged in age from youth to old age, and they too were present in the population merely for economic reasons. In some cases—a few, to be sure—hired workers were enumerated in the household of their employer, although they lived in separate quarters. Such was the case with *rancheros* engaged in commercial farming along the river who required the employment of farmers and farmworkers. In 1850, thirty-seven male laborers lived in the household of the Doña Rita Domínguez, a thirty-five year-old widow with three children and the owner of Rancho Rosario, located in the delta lands near Santa María. Similarly, stockraisers who owned extensive herds also hired a resident workforce consisting of *vaqueros* and sundry workers. Sometimes these workers are listed as living in the same household as the landholder.[77]

Tradition-minded Tejanos preferred marriage as a way to maintain order and stability in their society. As in the colonial past, some males signed nuptial contracts in which they promised to provide specific gifts to the wife-to-be. For example, in 1852, Sixto Domínguez, a resident of Hidalgo County who came from a prominent family of Reynosa that owned large tracts of land on the north side of the Río Grande, promised Salomé Vela the following: 4 yoke of oxen, 1 cart, 130 head of sheep and goats, 22 hogs, 3 cows and their calves, rights to 14 *sitios* in the Santa Anita grant, and rights and interests in 3 different *porciones* of land.[78] The marriage ceremony was often performed by a Catholic priest in the main *rancho*, or the ranch chapel if one existed. City and town residents usually used the Oblate chapels and churches. Under state law, weddings could be conducted by ministers of any religious faith and public officials.[79]

Wedding celebrations, or *bodas*, reflected the economic standing of the families involved. Whereas the more humble *mejicanos* held a simple dinner and maybe a dance with the participation of one or two musicians, the well-to-do marked the event with a gala celebration befitting their status. Among the latter, *bodas* became three-day festivities for the enjoyment and remembrance of the families of the marrying couple and their invited guests, most of whom were relatives. There was plenty to eat and drink, and musicians played well into the night. The wealthy usually hired an orchestra from one of the larger towns in the region, in place of the traditional *conjunto*.[80]

Remarriage, a practice with origins in medieval Spain, was not uncommon among *ranchero* widowers and widows. Juan Anaya, a *vecino* of Reynosa, dying from "mortal wounds inflicted on my person by the [*indios*] "*bárbaros*'" declared, in his will (1842), "to have been married and a widower" with two children from his first marriage and one from his second. When Martín Hinojosa del Toro, a moderately prosperous *ranchero* in Hidalgo County. died in 1892, his surviving widow noted that together they had four daughters, ranging in age from six to eighteen years, and that four other children, all of them adults with one daughter already deceased, had been born to her husband during his first marriage.[81] Following the death of his first wife who bore four children, *ranchero* Sabas Cavazos, who was a brother to Juan N. Cortina and lived in Brownsville, married a second time in 1850, at the age of forty. Among the more well-known widows who remarried was Doña Petra Vela de Vidal, whose second husband was steamboat captain and, later, rancher Mifflin Kenedy, but there were other women who remarried.[82] Fernando Uribe, a Zapata County rancher who died in 1877, first married Refugio Arispe and they had three children; and his second wife, Margarita Pérez, also bore him three children.[83] Some *rancheros* married more than twice. For instance, Ramón Vela Chapa (1859–1926), whose first wife had died in 1883 and his second in 1914, married for a third time in 1916.[84]

Even men who came from *ranchero* backgrounds but received a formal education and moved to the towns and cities of south Texas remarried. A good example is Don Mercurio Martínez (1876–1965), who was born in San Ygnacio in Zapata County and was a descendant of settlers who came with Escandón to the Lower Valley. Educated at St. Edward's College in Austin, in the 1890s, Don Mercurio was a talented musician, schoolteacher, public official, farmer and rancher, and political broker. In 1921, he moved to nearby Laredo, where he worked for a law firm in a number of capacities and as a public notary and political broker between Tejanos and Anglo officeholders and state and federal agencies. His first two wives died as well as his first child. In 1937, he married a third time.[85]

TEJANO CHILDREN AND THE ADOPTION OF CHILDREN

What we know presently about the Tejano parent-child relationship is sketchy. To try to understand this dynamic, much reliance must be placed on Hispanic oral tradition and the impressions of non-Hispanics who came into contact with *mejicanos* whose cultural traditions on family life were quite different from Anglo Protestants. Still, three observations can be made. First, it is evident that children were by and large treated lovingly, with indulgence, and not given too much responsibility. Better-off parents were indeed indulgent, providing their children with a variety of material goods and experiences, such as separate rooms, vacations, and other diversions. That this was the case among landholders is attested by oral and written histories of Tejanos that are now being published. Naturally, the dynamics involved varied from family to family.[86] Some childraising traditions remained strongly rooted. J. T. Canales, reported, for example, that because he was the eldest grandchild his early years were spent with his paternal grandparents, as was the custom.[87] Second, in the case of orphaned children, if a parent died—especially the mother—grandparents or an older brother assumed the responsibility of raising the children. Such was the case with the eight children of Pedro Vela Zamora, a brother of Macedonio Vela. When Pedro's wife died in 1868, his children were first raised in Camargo by the maternal grandparents, and later at El Desierto ranch, in Hidalgo County, by his widowed mother, who lived there with her eldest son, Rafael Vela Zamora. The unexpected death of Macedonio Vela II, the elder Macedonio's son, led to the children being raised by the mother and her oldest son, Filemón. His burden became permanent with the death of his mother seven years later.[88] Mercurio Martínez, who knew well the customs of the Lower Valley, asserted "that on the ranches on this frontier there were no orphans, for if a child were unfortunate enough to be deprived of both parents, it was at once taken into the home of any ranchman who arrived first [*sic*]."[89] It is impossible to ascertain how often this situation actually occurred, in view of the fact that Tejano families usually consisted of several generations and extended relatives were often present. These related persons usually helped to raise orphaned children, and in this way the Hispanic family remained intact. A third observation concerns the adoption of children. Tejanos placed great importance on having children partly because of the rural nature of their society, but also because the Catholic church had long sanctioned procreation. If no children were born to a family, adoption was a common solution.

Among Tejanos, adoptions of children who were often related to the adopting parents were sometimes formalized in law, but many were informal in nature. For instance, Victoria Ballí of Reynosa, a moderately wealthy *ranchera* who owned land in Hidalgo County, declared (1887) as her heir Cristóbal Leal Ballí, because "since his infancy we raised him and gave him our surname and for his [loyal?] services rendered to us as a true son." Later, she explained the familial ties to her adopted son, saying that "I name as my universal heir Cristóbal Leal, legitimate son of the late Cristóbal Leal Ballí [a brother of her deceased husband] and Rafaela Treviño."[90] Sotero Alvarez of Rancho Agua Negra, Hidalgo County, listed his wife, one nephew, two nieces, and "my adopted son,

Faustino Chapa," as his heirs.[91] Don Florencio Sáenz, the founder of Rancho Toluca (1880), married Sostenes Cano, a daughter of Antonio Cano, who for many years was a leading stockraiser in Hidalgo County. Having no children of their own, the couple adopted Sostenes' niece, Manuela. Later, Manuela Sáenz married a Spanish clerk who worked at the *ranchero*'s mercantile store, and they had eight children.[92] The Yturria family is another important Tejano family that continues today due to adoption. Francisco Yturria, the founder, married Felicitas Treviño, who came from a landholding family near Brownsville. They had no children of their own, adopting a boy and a girl.[93] Don Hipólito García, of Rancho Randado, and his wife, Andrea Montalvo, had one adopted daughter named Margarita García.[94] Descendants of these nineteenth-century families continue to live in *ranchos* and cities across the region and elsewhere.

The fact that adoptions were so accepted among Tejanos may have influenced Anglo newcomers who adopted Tejano children. In Cameron County there are numerous records of such adoptions: Guadalupe Dávila, a girl of eleven years, adopted by James L. and Jane Rudolph (1880); Leocaria Rivera Field, ten years old, by H. M. Field (1895); Tomasa González (or Garza), also ten, by D. Lively (1890); Victoria Flores, daughter of Antonio Flores, by Joseph and M. L. O'Shaughnessey, age of child and date not given; Thomas Richter, child of Petra Barbosa, by John H. A. Splitter (1887), as well as others too numerous to list here. Whereas Anglos tended to give practical reasons for adopting Tejano children, including giving them a home because they were orphans, or raising them to give them an opportunity for an education, Tejanos emphasized its social utility, including adopting children to have heirs, to legitimize an illegitimate child, or because a child's parents were both deceased.[95]

Anglos, too, informally adopted children. For example, J. P. Kelsey noted, in his memoirs, that one day a Mexican woman in Camargo brought an undernourshied child of two years to his wife. They raised her until the age of seven, when she died in Brownsville of yellow fever.[96]

Children were sometimes deserted by their parents or given away because they were unable to care for them. Consider the case of one Santiago Riojas of Hidalgo County, an eleven-year-old boy, for whom Edward Dougherty petitioned, in 1857, for an indenture of two years because his parents had deserted the child.[97] Also, in 1891 Jesús Treviño of Hidalgo County asserted:

> I am a single man, of advanced age and ill and for this reason unable to care for a daughter whom I have, and wanting to give her her well-being, I have thought it and think it convenient and totally voluntary that my daughter, Josefa Treviño, be and remain in the home of Mrs. Rita Ritchie . . . to whom I give [my daughter] and I leave as a daughter forever.

Treviño promised not to intervene in anything that followed, but he reserved his right "only to see her and greet her whenever I wish to do so."[98] These cases in which children were given away were not very common, but they were not unheard of and reflected the hardships that poor families endured. Those who resorted to this action probably did so out of compassion because they had no other alternatives to deal with family responsibilities that were too burdensome for them.

Giving away children who were subsequently adopted continued into the early twentieth century. In 1909, Pantaleón Cano Gonzáles applied to the county court at Edinburg to be appointed guardian of the estate of the minor Antonia García Cano. According to Cano González, the child, who was three years old, had resided at his home in the Cámpacuas ranch since she was eight days old because her mother had died when giving birth to the child. The natural father of the child, Tomás García, gave the child to Cano, who adopted her "as his own."[99]

Although few records exist, it is also evident that some children who were cared for or raised by a family were not adopted legally or even informally. Kelsey recalled the story of a foster parent named Cruz Tijerina, who worked as a clerk in his store. Tijerina and his wife had no children of their own, but they "raised and cared for more than twenty nephews, nieces, sisters, cousins and god-children."[100] At the turn of the century, the estate of Juan Garza Treviño was thrown into turmoil when one F. C. Rahlmann, an attorney, obtained an order naming him temporary administrator of the estate whose lands were located in Hidalgo County. Rahlmann procured a power of attorney from one Francisco Garza Treviño, who claimed to be a son of one of the daughters of Juan Garza Treviño, a well-to-do *ranchero* whose estate was conservatively estimated to be worth forty thousand dollars. Believing that an injustice was being perpetrated against them, the heirs immediately sought to defeat Rahlmann's appointment. According to them, Francisco Garza Treviño "was merely a boy raised by [us] without any adoption." The probate-court judge ruled in favor of the heirs and revoked Rahlmann's appointment.[101]

CONTINUITY OF *LO MEJICANO*

Tejanos enjoyed a variety of social-cultural activities that not only enriched their daily lives but deepened their ethnic identity. Some events were personal and enjoyed by family members; others were communal and shared by the community, which could be a *rancho*, a cluster of *ranchos*, usually called a *comunidad*, or community, or a town. Family celebrations usually brought together a large number of kinfolks. Esteban García, a well-to-do border *ranchero*, recalled that even at the turn of the century the ranching families were typically held together by "strong family ties, *visitas*, and family reunions."[102] Emilia Schunior Ramírez affirmed this view of the *ranchero* family, declaring that, indeed, "ties of friendship and of family were close. . . . Everyone knew everyone else, and though the means of communication and transportation were scarce, there was a feeling of kinship and unity among all the early settlers." She added that "home life was about the same in all the ranches."[103] Two Tejana sisters born at the turn of this century, María Concepción Garza Ramírez and María del Carmen Garza of Edinburg, nostalgically recalled with a smile those happy days when "*ranchero* families and friends were very united."[104] Baldomero Vela, Jr., a genealogist of the Lower Valley, wrote recently that "[our ancestors] visited frequently and helped each other through difficult times because of a deep sense of loyalty and pride in the family."[105] The fact that landholding families were interrelated in one way or another to each other meant that emotional and economic needs often served to foster enduring alliances.[106]

Besides the traditional family fiestas and reunions, other special cultural events, such as the New Year's ball, the playing of "music in the main plaza," the *paseo*, or promenade, *funciones*, or public dances, horse races, cockfights, bullfights, and patriotic days became occasions for whole *ranchos* and nearby towns to hold celebrations.[107] One of the first reports by an outsider or newcomer on music was provided by the Abbé Domenech, who spend a few years in the Lower Valley in the late 1850s. He remarked that the *rancheros* were "musically talented."[108] Actually, music, dance, and other literary traditions had old colonial origins in the frontier of New Spain, which, in turn, went back to Spain and other parts of the Old World. Self-taught musicians typically performed at family gatherings, and a local poet or guitarist wrote *corridos*, or ballads, to commemorate a hero or some other noteworthy event or person.[109] J. P. Kelsey recalled with fondness the Río Grande City band and orchestra of the late nineteenth century, both under the direction of an accomplished musician, Don Urbano Garza.[110] By the early 1890s Mercurio Martínez, who played the guitar and violin, and his brother Eudoxio, a guitar player, performed "in dances, weddings, fiestas, and all kinds of entertainments in San Ygnacio and other places." They were also hired to play for both U.S. and Mexican troops stationed along the border during the so-called Catarino Garza Revolution in 1892–93.[111]

Many of these social customs persisted well into the twentieth century. Erasmo García, whose early life was spent on the family's *rancho* in Starr County, remembers that *conjunto* music was ever-present in the first third of the twentieth century.[112] María Concepción Garza Ramírez and her sister María del Carmen Garza of Edinburg recall that their mother especially enjoyed holding *bailes*, or dances, on her birthday and New Year's Day. St. John's Day was also a special day, with the ranchers riding about in their finery. Public dances called *funciones*, held at someone's *rancho*, were also popular. Some *rancheros*, like Don Patricio González of Edinburg, had *plataformas*, or specific areas, designated as dancing grounds. He had one at his *rancho* and one in town, and he held *funciones* frequently. Not everyone liked the relaxed social mixing of all classes that occurred at such public dances. The Garza sisters also remember that their mother did not especially like the idea that a small fee was charged and that males had to buy *pan dulce*, or Mexican pastries, to give to those who danced with them.[113]

In the Tejano view of border society, the river was merely an "imaginary line" where they crossed the international border not only to visit family and to conduct business, but also to enjoy or take part in diverse public entertainment activities and other private events. Even the most isolated *rancheros* participated in the social and civic activities found in the towns and cities of the region. Long distances and rudimentary means of transportation did not prevent them from customarily making trips to the old river *villas* or to the new American border towns. For some of them, semiannual visits were a custom. Sometimes these journeys were made simply to buy provisions and other consumer goods not produced by the family or by local artisans. At other times, the trips were made to visit a doctor or relatives, or for business purposes, such as selling property, recording legal documents, serving on a jury, attending court, or delivering the "products of the country" to a local merchant.[114]

Throughout the nineteenth and early twentieth centuries, Mexicans living on both sides of the river celebrated traditional religious and secular days. There were several important religious holidays. For nine days prior to Christmas, the settlers staged *pastorelas*, or shepherds' plays. Mexicans did not have a Christmas tree; instead they placed a *nacimiento*, or nativity scene, in their homes, and carols were sung after Christmas until January 6, which was known as the Day of the Three Wise Kings. On that day, gifts were exchanged among family members.[115] The rural nature of the society also encouraged special religious celebrations, some which are rarely observed today. On May 3, the Feast of the Holy Cross, the settlers prayed for rain. Saint Isidore, patron saint of the farmers, was revered, especially during time of *secas*, or prolonged droughts. The Garza sisters remembered that during such times the "people would gather, lead a procession along paths around the fields until a spot was found and San Isidro was placed on an niche. When the rains finally came, the rosary was prayed in thanksgiving for nine days."[116] Esteban García recalled that in well-to-do baptisms part of the festivities involved throwing coins to the children.[117] The coming of age of daughters was also celebrated by these Hispanic settlers. As noted above, weddings sometimes lasting up to three days were lively and gay.[118]

Towns and *ranchos* also organized a variety of secular activities to break the monotony of the hard existence of the *pobladores* and to reaffirm their Mexican cultural identity. *Cinco de mayo*, or May 5, commemorating Tejano-born Ignacio Zaragoza's defeat of the French in 1862, was a patriotic day, given to speechmaking and eating. Some communities also held festivities on September 16, in honor of Father Hidalgo's call for independence. Public *plazas* were used for such fiestas, as well as for other civic and business purposes.[119] Emilia Schunior Ramírez recalled that *ferias*, or fairs, were also held in makeshift *plazas* in the *ranchos*, usually at the end of the harvest season, lasting up to two weeks and including concession stands, restaurants, *lotería*, or raffle games, and public dances.[120]

Despite the dissolution of Spanish rule in the borderlands and the disintegration of Mexican control over the region, religion remained important in the lives of the *mejicano* settlers of south Texas. While it is true that few Mexican clergy persisted anywhere in Texas in effectively serving Tejanos previous to the coming of the Oblates of Mary Immaculate or Oblates, a religious order of French missionary priests in the late 1840s, the settlers were not completely oblivious to their Catholic faith, as many outsiders often reported. The work of the new missionaries eventually stretched from Galveston to San Antonio to the border and occasionally into the Mexican river towns. The Oblates or country priests called the "cavalry on the cross" served both Tejano and European Catholics who settled in various districts of the region.[121] These circuit-riding priests on horseback imparted the basic doctrine of the church and officiated at religious services that celebrated the church's sacraments. As historian James Talmadge Moore notes, "mass was celebrated at an altar set up in the home where the missionary was staying. The custom was that someone, usually a small boy, would go from house to house ringing a little bell signaling the residents to come to where the priest was staying. Once the people were assembled and if it was morning, mass was celebrated; if it was evening, catechism, the rosary, hymns, and a homily followed."[122] Sister Enriqueta Vela, a descendant of *ranchero* Macedonio Vela, recalled that even in the early twentieth century "the priests came to the ranches once in a great while . . . and then only to administer the Sacraments."[123]

Churches, schools, and the first hospitals in the region were often under the direction of the Oblates or of several Catholic women religious communities that came to work among the Mexicans and Mexican Americans. Brownsville's first wooden chapel (1850) gave way to an imposing Gothic cathedral in 1859, the largest structure built by the Oblates. The Oblates also established permanent churches and residences at Roma (1853), Río Grande City (1880), and La Lomita (1899). They also built little chapels in scores of missions. By the mid-1850s Corpus Christi also had a Catholic church. As more priests arrived to serve Tejano Catholics in south Texas, new chapels and churches were built in the hinterland communities away from the river, beginning in the late 1860s and continuing into the 1880s.[124]

Catholic schools were soon founded to educate children in the larger towns and cities of the region, where the settlers could best support them. For the most part, these institutions benefited the well off and urban dwellers. The reasons for this are twofold: first, the Oblates' hierarchy decided to cast their fortune in the urban areas with the intention of serving English-speaking Catholics, both Anglos and Europeans, whom they perceived to be wealthier; and second, Catholic schools were dependent on tuition and boarding fees, which meant that large numbers of Tejano families were cut off from these opportunities.[125] For example, in Laredo the Ursuline Academy (1868) educated the children of Tejano, Mexican, and newcomer elites.[126]

In spite of their long and hard work with Tejanos, Oblate missionaries had ambivalent attitudes toward them. At times, they saw them as humble and sensitive, folklike people barely beyond the pale of savagery, and thus treated them with paternalism. At other times, they had much admiration and respect for the settlers' strong family values and religious fervor. Despite their shortcomings, Tejanos revered the *padres* on horseback because they had a genuine dedication to their work.[127]

Tejano Catholic material progress varied considerably from place to place. It reflected the economic condition and religious commitment of the individual landholders and the community-at-large. Some of their facilities and holy icons were simple and folklike, and others were more modest in construction and decoration. In the early years, settlers built temporary altars for masses, and simple, private homes or other buildings served as chapels. Gradually, thatched-roof and mud-plastered structures gave way to sturdy missions and church buildings constructed of lumber, stone, or brick. Also, a few Tejano families founded their own *capilla*, or chapel, such as the Vela's at Laguna Seca in about 1878, and Don Florencio Sáenz's St. Joseph's, a Gothic structure dedicated in 1899. Some were much older; for example, the chapel of San Rafael in Rancho Randado, in Zapata County, dated to about 1836.[128] As in previous generations, large profits from ranching were essential in order to construct and endow private chapels; only a few *rancheros* achieved that kind of economic wherewithal. Some of these out-of-the-way chapels have deteriorated with the passing years, as settlers moved to the new towns of the south Texas region, attracted by the irrigation projects in the early 1900s. Others are still in use today, such as that at Rancho Toluca, used by the descendants of the founders. Much more common than private chapels was the practice of keeping a home altar adorned with the family's treasured *bultos*, or wooden carvings of the saints and other Biblical figures and paintings on tin or wood called *retablos*. These elements of their religion's culture were largely the domain of devout women who were charged with passing the practices and its values to the younger generation.[129]

Rancheros in the countryside and in the towns founded *camposantos*, or cemeteries, for burying their families, friends, and workers. In contrast to Anglo family plots that excluded nearly everyone not related, Tejano cemeteries included early-day newcomers who intermarried, trusted friends, *compadres* of the landholders, and workers. The old ranch cemeteries, some of which are still in use today, vary in size, the types of monuments used, and their kinds of fencing. The more elaborate have wrought-iron fences or hurricane fences, family vaults, and stone monuments. Two good examples near Mercedes are the Hinojosa cemetery at Anacuitas (off north Texas Avenue and the north side of U.S. Expressway 83) and the Solis cemetery, on the border of Hidalgo and Cameron County and located on the road of the same name as the *camposanto*. The founding patriarch is usually buried in a vault at the center of the cemetery. The resting place of farm hands, *vaqueros*, servants, and their families is typically a corner of the cemetery. Their humble graves are marked with a simple stone or wood marker, and some are not identifiable today because of years of neglect and the effects of the elements. In many places, however, relatives continue to maintain the *camposantos* in a clean and orderly condition. On special days, such as All Souls' Day, Tejanos can still be seen clearing brush and other debris and planting shady native trees and favorite plants of the region.[130]

Some historians have argued that the Catholic church could have done more for Tejanos, especially in providing permanent churches and other facilities and in developing a native clergy. Certainly, the need to serve Catholics in the region grew as the size of the population increased, much of it due to the immigration of poor *mejicanos* in the latter years of the nineteenth century. Of an estimated sixty-five thousand persons in south Texas in the 1880s, Mexican Catholics comprised forty thousand. Anglo and European Catholics numbered about twenty-five hundred. By 1900 the number of Catholics had grown to sixty thousand. A new study shows that in the nineteenth century (and early twentieth century) more financial and human resources were sent to less populous Anglo Catholic dioceses in Texas, such as Galveston and Dallas, than to the diocese in south Texas. In effect, Tejano Catholics, who were often described as very poor and stingy, significantly contributed monies and other resources to build facilities and to support religious activities. That the commitment of the Catholic church to the communities in south Texas was far from complete is a logical conclusion, but this does not deprecate their honest efforts.[131]

In the second half of the nineteenth century, Protestant churches in south Texas made very little headway with Tejanos, probably because their approach to conversion dwelled on anti-papacy diatribes.[132] Melinda Rankin, a schoolteacher and Presbyterian missionary who arrived in Brownsville in 1852, strongly opposed the influence of the Catholic church on the Mexicans. She believed that its followers were "buried beneath the rubbish of papal error and superstition." She also asserted, however, that resistance to her work was due to the prejudices of many Anglos in Texas, whom she described as believing that "Mexicans were a people just fit to be exterminated from the Earth."[133] In the Brownsville area, the most active were the Methodists (1850), Presbyterians (1852), and the Society of Friends (ca. 1872), all of which founded congregations and schools.[134] In the 1870s and 1880s, Mexicans themselves founded Methodist missions in Corpus Christi and the San Diego areas.[135]

Of the Mexicans who converted, a few became active ministers, such as Angela Aguilar y Zúñiga and her husband, Luciano Mascorro. They worked for the Society of Friends in several locations in neighboring Tamaulipas, especially Matamoros, using Brownsville as a base.[136] Their efforts demanded a persistent dedication, courage, and religious zeal, qualities that few *mejicanos* on either side of the river understood and rarely supported because of their Catholic tradition. Consequently, Protestants gained few followers until very recent times (in the middle and late twentieth century).

TEJANO ADAPTATION OF AMERICAN POLITICS AND EDUCATION

The arrival of Anglos and Europeans in larger numbers after 1848 made for greater interaction than ever before between Tejanos and newcomers in social, economic, and political affairs. Whereas prior to the war with Mexico, social and economic matters cemented ties among the old and new residents of the Lower Valley, political and social institutions organized by Anglos and Europeans after the Treaty of Guadalupe Hidalgo gained importance in the everyday life of the emerging communities north of the Río Grande. Two key institutions that captured the attention of Tejanos were politics and education. The first appeared early, with the settlement of lawyers and others interested in politics, and soon the Lower Valley counted on a Democratic and a Republican party. Private groups mostly associated with religious organizations took the lead in the field of education, but public education eventually took root. Tejanos must have understood the necessity of participating in these new institutions to maintain a sense of presence in the changing society. For them, survival meant learning from the conquerer's ways of doing things lest they be excluded from the new order and pushed to the periphery of society. In time, Tejanos accepted some of the traditions introduced by the new settlers.[137]

Tejanos took politics seriously. Since annexation, Tejanos had declared their right to vote and participate in electoral politics. Shortly after the Civil War, when the citizenry of the region were required to indicate how they claimed citizenship in the state, Tejanos asserted their rights by giving a litany of reasons based on their long residency in Texas. Some asserted their claims by virtue of the fact of "the naturalization of [my] father by the annexation of Texas [in 1845]." Others based their rights of citizenship on an even longer period of residency in Texas, claiming that their "father was a citizen of Texas prior to annexation."[138]

Politics served to quickly acquaint *mejicanos* with the new order, and, in turn, helped to foster the building of Hispanic-Anglo alliances. Except for those few places where Hispanics were a small minority of the voters or where discrimination kept them from voting, they voted, aspired to, and won elections at the local and county level. In rural counties balloting often took place in the *rancheros*' homes or community schools. This allowed them to coalesce behind particular candidates, thereby diminishing some of the pressures of both the Democratic and the Republican parties to control them. While some Hispanic politicians were not bilingual or formally educated, others were and they served well. Still others participated in government by serving as election judges, as jury foremen and members, as road overseers, and on special commissions created by the commissioners' court. At the local and county levels, Tejanos largely governed their own activities in an orderly way.[139]

It is true, of course, that Tejanos rarely won election to a state office. One key factor for this was that their experience with legislation was limited on account of the half-*cabildo* used in the colonial period and the persistence of elite rule in the Lower Valley towns during the Mexican period. Other barriers limited the possibilities of being elected to such an office, including factionalism among Tejanos often based on class interests, limited English proficiency, a large number of immigrants among the population, and the overpowering experience of Anglo politicians.[140]

Tejanos did not always vote as an ethnic bloc, and they sometimes divided into two factions. For instance, in Laredo partisan politics in the 1850s and 1860s divided *mejicano* elites. The Benavides family allied itself with European merchants, and the de la Garza family with the smaller Anglo merchant class.[141] In any case, by working together to achieve common political objectives, Tejanos and Anglos slowly learned to accommodate each other's interest. Consequently, at different times in the various communities of the region, mutual respect replaced intergroup suspicion, distrust, and misunderstanding. These problems, to be sure, never completely went away. At times intergroup conflict existed in the political arena, but the most serious political fights were not really racial but factional in nature. The last twenty years of the nineteenth century were evidently much more volatile, and in some districts Tejanos lost substantial ground in officeholding, but they were not totally displaced until the early twentieth century, when new dynamics altered the political fabric of the region.[142]

Opportunities for joint Tejano-Anglo cooperation were limited to those who were directly involved in the political affairs. Leaders and officials represented the core of those who played a significant role in politics, much more than the casual voter. These activities occurred primarily at the local and county levels, where the Tejanos had considerable staying power. In some counties, they continued to hold a variety of offices up to the coming of significant numbers of midwestern and southern farmers and town settlers after 1905.[143] Moreover, Tejanos learned quickly to petition the state government with matters of importance to them. Thus, on various occasions they supported Anglo efforts to maintain the state ranger force in order to curb banditry, they urged the creation of a new county near Duval County, they opposed the disfranchisement of voters, and they sought help in establishing favorable boundaries among the several counties of the region.[144]

One special area in which Tejanos played a key role was law enforcement. In most towns and counties of south Texas, they sought to uphold the law. They chased after, arrested, and shot escaped prisoners or those who were suspected of crimes. In all of these ways, Tejanos acclimated themselves to the new political reality. They, of course, had familiarity with Spanish-Mexican law enforcement practices that were similar to American tradition, except for jury trials.[145]

If politics allowed Tejanos to participate in the political life of the United States, education was seen as essential for the future well-being of the first generation of their children who were growing up as citizens in a new country. With the passing years, Tejanos gave little thought to returning to the old country; instead, they focused on the reality of their presence in a new land. For that reason, education represented an important vehicle to help them make adjustments. While outside observers usually asserted that *mejicanos* in Texas were indifferent to education, the reality was that Tejanos supported the education of their children by enrolling them in a variety of institutions.[146] In fact, there is evidence of a Hispanic tradition in formal primary education in some of the old towns as early as the colonial period, such as Matamoros (1814) and Laredo (1822), but such schools were usually opened only intermittently and few students attended because their parents were required to pay the schoolmaster's salary.[147] Initially, individual proprietors, religious orders, and *rancheros* themselves founded the first schools. In most cases, few records have been preserved of these early private educational endeavors.

Most *ranchero* families aspired to providing at least a few school terms to their children. Thus, ranch schools were founded across the region in the second half of the nineteenth and early part of the twentieth centuries. One or two examples illustrate the Tejano support for these schools, in which the first teachers were from Mexico, followed by American male teachers, and finally by women teachers. In the last quarter of the nineteenth century, the Vela family founded a school at Rancho Laguna Seca. Also, Margarito Hinojosa of Rancho Santa Mónica allotted land for a school to be built on his property, for his children and surrounding families. He also provided room and board for the teachers who came to teach at the school, which was in existence from 1915 to 1933.[148]

After 1848, Brownsville, Laredo, Corpus Christi, and county governments in rural districts led the way in establishing the first public schools. For example, a learned Dane named Col. Charles G. T. de Lovenskiold served as the principal of the public school district in 1854, when Nueces County created five school districts with the same boundaries as its voting precincts. It is likely that the Corpus Christi school experienced some problems because de Lovenskiold's pay was irregular and meager—two hundred dollars for the period from January 1857 to August 1858.[149] Similarly, in 1856 Hidalgo County created three school districts, one for each of the election precincts, and held elections of school trustees. Within a few months, there were 215 children attending those schools.[150] Laredo counted about a dozen teachers and schools in the 1860s, but the schools evidently were not permanently opened due to lack of adequate funding.[151]

After the state constitutional convention of 1870, renewed efforts to provide public education for children led to the founding of community schools. Such was the case, for example, in Hidalgo County, which opened new community schools in the more populated communities along the delta of the river. Late that year, John McAllen wrote G. D. Kingsbury that "we are about to establish a school system [in this county]. We will be in want of a grate [*sic*] many teachers. All persons are compelled to send their children at least 4 months."[152] Upriver at Zapata, old-timers recalled that Antonio Barrera, a justice of the peace, and his wife, Rosa, conducted school for the town's children in the late nineteenth century.[153]

By the 1880s Brownsville had a first-rate public school system as well as several Catholic schools. Teaching Spanish-speaking children the English language was a pressing concern then, and remained a major methological issue for generations of teachers and administrators. In practice, some form of bilingual education was implemented to overcome this difficulty.[154]

The children of well-to-do *rancheros* and permanent town dwellers appear to have had the most success in education. This was partly due to the fact that families who had been in the region longer became increasingly aware of the importance of education. Also, those families with greater economic resources had advantages over the working class. Such families succeeded in sending their children to local schools, public and private, as well as to distant academies, business schools, colleges, and universities, mostly in the United States, but occasionally in Mexico.[155] The very poor and those who were merely sojourners evidently saw less of a need to educate their children, mainly because economic survival represented the most pressing issue for these families.

At the start of the twentieth century, public education in south Texas was still not fully mature, but it had undergone improvements, especially in urban areas. Eventually, it would surpass private education in terms of students, teachers, and resources. Yet Catholics continued to support parochial schools at the lower levels, and the larger cities, such as Laredo, Brownsville, and San Antonio, offered Catholic high school education to local as well as boarding students who came from well-to-do Tejano families.

RELATIONS BETWEEN TEJANOS AND NEWCOMERS FROM THE UNITED STATES AND EUROPE

The nature of relationships between Tejanos and Anglos seems to have depended on the character of the contact. Direct contact usually produced good, positive relations, but little or no contact resulted in distorted impressions that led to problems between the two groups. Conflict, regardless of its nature, also tended to intensify the distortion. Due to the scarcity of Tejano written sources, it is admittedly difficult to ascertain their views of Anglos, but the overall pattern of behavior indicates considerable tolerance and acceptance. At the same time, because Anglo and European views of Mexicans often appeared in print it is easier to assess their beliefs and actions. A complex set of mixed attitudes guided the conduct of Anglos toward Tejanos. Two general views predominated: (1) the *mejicano* had good qualities that made him an equal citizen; or (2) the *mejicano*'s character was such that he had bad qualities, so that he was basically inferior. Thus, on the one hand, whenever *mejicanos* and

Anglos worked together in an economic activity that fostered the material development of the region, such as stockraising or trade, the interaction was positive. This was the case because Anglos and Europeans were interested primarily in utilizing existing Tejano economic traditions and technologies in agriculture, transportation, and labor. Additionally, as in New Mexico, the need for Tejano assistance in defense of the frontier elicited positive responses from newcomers.[156] As noted above, cooperation in political affairs also produced a degree of Tejano-Anglo amity in spite of the fact that periods of intense conflict, such as the Cortina affair of 1859 and similar events, resulted in temporary setbacks and disruptions. Gradually, most newcomer Anglos accepted the realization that Tejanos were an integral part of the evolving society, even as that society was changing to one in which they controlled most of the economic and political resources. The ascendancy of the Anglos hardened the distinctions between the two groups, and it sanctioned the newcomers' view of themselves as first-class citizens while subordinating the poor Tejanos to an inferior position. This event, however, occurred late in the nineteenth century, when Tejano participation in the ranching economy had diminished considerably. On the other hand, fleeting moments of contact and a cursory knowledge of Tejanos generally facilitated the growth of negative impressions and attitudes. As noted below, prejudice and discrimination had longstanding roots in the earlier period of Spanish–Anglo confrontation.

All along the lower border, in places where Tejanos still held on to the land or owned property, relations between Tejanos and newcomers were generally amiable and were conducted in an atmosphere of fairness and equality. Perhaps this was so because landownership signified personal worth and a sense of belonging to a place, values that were intrinsic to citizenship, or because, as historian Sarah Deutsch argues, Anglo values connected sexuality and private property so that "manliness itself depended on landownership and dominion."[157] Thus, some histories of the region written by non-Hispanics are willing to concede that Mexican landholders were equal citizens because they too had tamed the harsh grasslands of the region. In any case, regardless of whatever values Anglos were willing to ascribe to Tejano landholders, the fact remained that much interaction was grounded on friendly relations.

There are many examples of *mejicano*–Anglo/European friendships that grew out of business and social relations. Juan Anaya of Reynosa noted in 1842 that he owed to "my compadre D[on] René Guyard a native of France and resident of this villa the amount noted in the account book [*sic*]." Guyard, who died a widower and without children, had left the lands known as El Capote, in Hidalgo County, "for the benefit of my godchild, María Yrene Anaya." He also bequeathed to María Yrene, Juan Anaya's daughter, all of the household items in his house, and he donated certain sums of money due him to Hilario Cantú because he was the "husband of my godchild." Among other dispositions, Guyard ordered that after his death seventy pesos were to be taken out of his business establishment to pay a debt that the deceased Don Juan Anaya owed to Don Jesús Cavazos. He also ordered the debts of Doña Ysabel Cavazos erased in compensation of her work for him. Finally, he named as his estate's *albaceas*, or executors, three Reynosa citizens.[158] Old-timers like Kelsey and William Neale likewise interacted with Tejanos and Mexicans with whom they became *compadres*.[159] Some friendships were born out of genuine appreciation of Hispanics. For example, the missionary Rankin, who had become ill in a trip to the Lower Valley, recounted that she was cared for by a Mexican grandmother. Her overall experiences with Mexicans convinced her "that they are a kind people, if treated with kindness. I can truly say I have never found firmer and better friends among any nation of people than I have among some of the Mexicans."[160]

In some cases, intermarriage also promoted friendly and longlasting bonds between *mejicanos* and newcomers from the United States and Europe. Several factors encouraged intermarriage. The initial lack of local Anglo and European women, and later their very small numbers, limited opportunities to find a spouse from one's own cultural or national background. Occasionally, newcomers returned home and married brides of their own nationality or ethnicity; this the merchant Charles Stillman did in 1849, but not many did so, for they saw the lower border as a wild place or frontier and not as a place for a "civilized woman."[161] Thus, for some of the newcomers, it was only natural that they chose local Hispanic women for partners. Other considerations made them attractive, such as the fact that many belonged to landholding or influential old families. These intermarriages were probably more calculated than natural. Places like Brownsville, which drew larger numbers of new Anglo and European male settlers because of its commercial enterprises, witnessed this development. In fact, this intermingling of the native settlers and newcomers from the United States and Europe had occurred earlier, across the river in Matamoros, with the beginning of the port business in the 1820s. Along the length of the river, the 1850 census listed numerous intermarriages involving Anglo and European men and local Hispanic women. Today, the legacy of these peoples can be seen in the continuity of numerous non-Hispanic surnames Hispanicized in pronunciation, whose forebears consider themselves Hispanic, such as Champion, Krause, Margot (now Margo), Volpe, and many others.[162]

Rural Hispanic enclaves such as Hidalgo, Starr, and Webb counties also had intermarriages, but they were few in number, probably because the new settlers from the United States and Europe were not numerous. In Hidalgo County, for instance, from 1852 to 1882, out of nearly five hundred marriages involving Tejanos eleven Anglo–Hispanic marriages occurred in which the woman was Hispanic. In the period 1883–88, only three out of nearly two hundred marriages involving Tejanos were between Anglos and Hispanic women. In neighboring Starr County, a number of prominent newcomers married into the established families, including Henry Clay Davis, the founder of Rancho Davis, later renamed Río Grande City, whose wife, Hilaria Garza, was the daughter of the landholder on whose land the townsite was laid out.[163] Needless to say, not all Anglo– and European–Hispanic marriages involved daughters of elite families, but the cases that are best known do indicate that newcomers selected brides from the more established Tejano settlers.

Tejano males seldom married outside their ethnic or nationality group. This was due mainly to the absolute predominance of Hispanics in the population. Still, racial prejudice in Anglo enclaves such as Corpus Christi, a place where most Tejano stockmen had been displaced from the land by the 1880s, strongly deterred intermarriage. Eventually, in the second generation, a few Tejanos married daughters of Anglo–Hispanic or European–Hispanic parentage, furthering the process of Hispanicization. (Marriages among the latter also took place, although it is difficult to say whether the Hispanic culture was preferred over the Anglo–European culture.)[164] Overall, slow rates of intermarriage between Mexicans and Anglos precluded the widespread assimilation of Tejanos.

Mexicans living along the border often enjoyed cordial business and political relations with Anglos. The former served as sureties for Anglo administrators and executors of Anglo-owned estates. For example, when L. H. Box swore to faithfully administer the estate of J. F. Fulton, who had been a merchant, two of the sureties on Box's eight-thousand-dollar bond were Tomás de la Garza and Luis Anaya. In 1873, Box also served as the administrator of the estate of J. M. J. Carvajal, a well-known border revolutionary, who owned land in Hidalgo County.[165] In his will of 1878, Cipriano Hinojosa named "Mr. Teodoro [Thaddeus M.] Rhodes as my only executor." Shortly after Hinojosa's death, Rhodes applied to the court and succeeded Hinojosa as guardian of the minor, Gregorio Cantú, who had inherited an estate worth about two thousand dollars, which Hinojosa had carefully administered for many years prior to his death.[166] Angela Chapa opted to have her brother's estate administered by Frank Philibert of Havanna ranch, a duty that demanded his attention from 1895 to 1903. On other occasions, Anglos and Tejanos served jointly as appraisers and auditors of estates, usually of *rancheros* and newcomers.[167] Judge J. T. Canales, whose paternal and maternal families owned *ranchos* on the borders of the King ranch, recalled that from the time of his youth his family were on friendly terms with Richard King and his wife, partly because landholders met to discuss fence lines and other issues relevant to the livestock industry. Later, as a lawyer in Brownsville, Canales assisted in clearing up titles to properties acquired by the Kings.[168] A King ranch *vaquero* credits the destruction of Peñascal, a rustlers' headquarters along the Gulf Coast, to a combined force of Tejano *rancheros* and Anglo Texans.[169]

Old Anglo and European settlers counted on the business with Mexicans from both sides of the river to make a living. Consider the case of Mr. N. Gussett, an early-day merchant and rancher in Nueces County, "one of the principal buyers of wool, hides, hair and bones brought from as far south as Saltillo. His [Corpus Christi] store, 'El Borrego,' was sought out by his many Mexican customers, and was the gathering place for vaqueros, traders, and many of the townsfolk."[170] Tejano wills and testaments attest to their frequent business contacts with Anglo and European traders, merchants, storekeepers, and professionals.

TEJANO–ANGLO CONFLICT: ITS SPORADIC NATURE AND SOURCES

Despite widespread friendly and cooperative relations between landholding Tejanos and Anglos in south Texas in social life, business, and politics, there were periods of intense conflict between the two groups. It is during these tense times that the common goal of peaceful coexistence broke down. Violence became rampant and its effects were detrimental for Tejano–Anglo relations. For example, the continuing boundary conflict and the subsequent war with Mexico resulted in raids and counterattacks by both Mexicans and Anglos in the Lower Valley, in the period from 1846 to 1848. For instance, at the start of the war with Mexico in 1846, border *rancheros* committed the ghastly murder of several men, women, and children who were leading a American supply train from Corpus Christi to the Lower Valley.[171] Other such times included Cortina's raids in the Lower Valley in 1859. What is often forgotten is that conflicts of this nature fanned hostility that was followed by vengeful attacks on peaceful Tejano citizens.

Occasionally, conflict appeared in the form of random episodes of violence against Mexicans. It is reported, for example, that the death in July 1877 of a twenty-one-year-old desperado named Lee Rabb, son of a wealthy rancher in Banquete, a district near Corpus Christi, led to reprisals that resulted in the death of forty Mexicans in that locality. According to one tradition, Rabb had become involved in a difficulty with some Mexicans who killed him. Incidents such as this were largely singular acts of crime and vengeance, whereas during the Mexican-American War and the bandit raids of the mid-1870s animosities reached a high pitch and a more generalized period of conflict ensued.[172] While interethnic conflict appears continuous, it is apparent that in general racial or ethnic tension and violence was more accurately episodic in nature. Accordingly, the allegations of "race wars" should be carefully weighed, for often they were more products of the minds of a few unhappy and frustrated individuals, not necessarily actual events. Both groups, however, saw the utility of maintaining peace for the common good.

It is impossible to ascertain the extent to which racism played a role in the Anglos' confrontation with Mexicans in south Texas. However, as historian Sarah Deutsch argues, racism figured prominently in Anglo–minority relations in the West.[173] The difficulty of understanding racism and its development in the new American Southwest lies in the fact that the bases for prejudicial beliefs and behavior have complex origins. Spanish–English colonial rivalry bred considerable antagonism toward Hispanics. Historians believe that the beliefs and attitudes that arose from that conflict were later transferred from Americans to Mexicans.[174] One way in which Anglo racism was manifested in the early and mid-nineteenth century lay in their adherence to the ideology of Manifest Destiny that justified U.S. expansion westward and at the cost of the older inhabitants. Not surprisingly, prospective Anglo settlers, such as Helen Chapman, the wife of the quartermaster in Matamoros and Fort Brown, commented that the origins of racism dated to the war with Mexico. She was also aware that Anglos in Texas saw Mexicans as people "in the way. They are an unsightly blot on a flourishing community. [Anglos] dislike the sight of them. The races do not harmonize and the weak and the helpless must give way." Mrs. Chapman reasoned that Mexicans were hated "more for their father's sins than their own."[175] The missionary Rankin similarly argued that "prejudice existed against the Mexicans, engendered during the late war."[176]

At times, Anglo prejudice toward Tejanos in south Texas was open, persistent, and insidious, but more often it was subtle in nature. Much of this prejudice was based on the *americanos*' ideology of superiority, their moral righteousness, and their arrogance. Southerners, in particular, brought with them attitudes and mores that affected the way they saw Mexicans in south Texas. In a way reminiscent of their treatment of Blacks, they condemned dark-skinned Tejanos to the bottom of society. For instance, in Corpus Christi, Anglos, who were dominant in numbers and economic power, rejected Hispanic influences. In some cases, Anglos sought to keep their distance from lower-class Mexicans, many of whom were dark-colored or Indian in physical appearance, setting up social and physical boundaries that later developed into patterns of segregation. Unfortunately, the designation of separate business districts, *plazas*, or town squares, schools, and residential districts institutionalized racism in a few south Texas communities.[177]

The complexity of Anglo thinking and behavior in south Texas that was based on racism can be illustrated with a few examples. One factor that affected racial thinking was the evidence of *mestizaje* among the people of the lower border. Emory, in his report to Congress of his survey of the Río Grande Valley, attributed the decadence of the military and the church to the intermarriage of "whites and Indians," whereas "throughout Mexico, where ever the white race has preserved its integrity, there will be found a race of people very superior in both mental and physical ability."[178] By these standards, those not clearly "white" did not fit the right classification of a race.

Anglo superiority also served to rationalize the "very common idea in Texas that it is no wrong to kill a Mexican." When Mexican bandits raided Nuecestown in 1875, Anglos retaliated by attacking innocent persons solely because they were Mexican. As a result of such clashes, Anglos' view of Mexicans, and vice versa, sank to lower levels. General Steele testified before the U.S. House of Representatives that "there is a considerable [Texan] element in the country bordering on the Nueces that think the killing of a Mexican no crime" and that "the [Mexican] thieves and cut-throats who have collected on the border think the killing of a Texan something to be proud of." Texas Senator Edward Dwyer agreed with this observation. He noted that "the taking of a Mexican's life by the white desperadoes was of so little importance in their eyes that they actually didn't count such a 'incident' in their list of killings, as the murders were styled by them."[179]

Other observers saw the Mexican character as flawed. Lieutenant Vielé said that Mexicans were peasants who "are, naturally, a good and innocent race, although at present their ideas of morality are rather in a confused state." He added that "the lazy Mexicans . . . lying in the sun with their naked children, give anything but a brisk or business-like air to the place [the lower border]."[180] The Abbé Domenech himself, perhaps out of a European bias for farmers, remarked that "rancheros are just as indolent as their countrymen of the town."[181] The so-called indolence of the Mexican was one stereotype that became deeply engrained in the minds of Anglo observers, but there were others. A. B. Clarke, a traveler on his way to the gold mines of California, made landfall at the small island of Brazos Santiago, a former military depot during the war with Mexico. It was there where he "first saw specimens of the Mexican, or 'blanket race.' I noticed some small company sitting on the ground playing at monte, and other favorite games of chance, and passing the 'pesos' freely."[182] C. C. Cox, a prominent Nueces Valley rancher, reminisced that "as a rule [Mexicans] are generous [and] faithful to their obligations—industrious as industry goes in this Southern clime—grateful always for favors, & appreciative of confidence in their integrity and naturally gifted in the school of politness [*sic*]. In my investigations I cannot claim to have discovered any new or commendable traits in the Mexican character, but must agree with the established opinion, and pronounce ignorance, indolence and cowardice to be the predominant characteristics of these people."[183] John McAllen, who had sought and lost the office of county judge in Hidalgo County in 1884, brought a legal proceeding against the victor, Thaddeus M. Rhodes, to enjoin him from taking office (both were married to Hispanic women and had long lived among the settlers). In his pleadings to the state appellate court, McAllen asserted that "the commissioners court was composed of ignorant and unscrupulous [Mexican] men, only one of whom could read, write, or speak the English language."[184] His language was more blatant than most Anglo politicians of that era, but it reflected a common belief that *mejicanos* were unworthy citizens because they were ignorant, untrustworthy, and illiterate. Such stereotypes easily played into the hands of some of the new settlers. It is not, then, altogether surprising that at times relations between the two groups soured and violent attacks on each other occurred with dire consequences, as attested by such well-known events as the Cart War and the Salt War.

Some Anglo settlers believed that their archenemy was a Mexican thief. This easily fostered the *bandido* stereotype that has persisted to this day. A prominent Brownsville citizen, G. D. Kingsbury, who was postmaster in that town after the Civil War, voiced contempt toward Mexican settlers. Writing his sister prior to the sectional conflict (in 1858), he declared that "the population of [Cameron] county is about 7,000 no less than 6,000 of which is Mexican of which 5,000 may be recorded as theives [*sic*]."[185] Mrs. Chapman came much closer to the truth when she argued that some Mexicans committed petty thefts out of desperation.[186] Court records support her contention.[187]

TEARS IN THE FABRIC OF TEJANO SOCIETY

The fabric of Tejano society in south Texas was by no means perfect. Quarrels, disputes, lawsuits involving property rights, and the usual transgressions of the small criminal element in the populace were commonplace in a society whose members eagerly sought to defend their position. Initially, however, the region suffered little in the way of serious or rampant crime, except for Brownsville, where gold-rush travelers on their way to California camped, attracting a motley crowd of newcomers and Mexicans to the town, making the new town ripe for misfortune. While historians and other social scientists, basing their work on the memoirs of settlers and frontier commissions sent to the border, depict the society in south Texas as crime-ridden, lawless, and inept in the administration of justice, this was not a universal nor omnipresent condition. It is important to recognize the inadequacy of this thesis, for, in fact, crime and punishment exhibited considerable variation during the first half-century of U.S. rule in the Southwest. At times, little crime occurred, while at other times a sort of "crime wave" affected the populace. Those convicted found themselves in jail or eventually in the state prison at Huntsville. In general, however, the bulk of the population in the region was law abiding and peaceful.

Some years were officially reported as very quiet ones. In 1850 the census enumerator tallied no paupers and two crimes each by natives and foreign-born residents in the entire Lower Valley, excluding Nueces County. Also, two natives and nine foreign-born were reported to be in prison. And in the summer of 1860, when the census was taken, Cameron and Hidalgo counties reported no paupers and no one in jail, while Brownsville counted only two persons in jail, both foreign born.[188] Statistics of criminal courts confirm the low occurrence of crime. In the 1850s only seven cases were tried in the Webb County district court at Laredo. These included aggravated assault charges in two cases, and one case each of burglary, larceny, malfeasance in office, cattle stealing, and selling liquor without a license.[189]

Much of the same kind of lawless behavior present in Webb County was typical of the region. For example, while some of the crimes alleged to have been committed by settlers in Hidalgo County included murder and attempted murder, most of them involved assaults and thefts. Cases that actually came to trial involved the theft of one or two head of livestock. Occasionally, sundry crimes such as adultery, taking cattle out of the county without inspection, selling a hide without inspection, killing unbranded and unmarked stock, and selling liquor without a license resulted in indictments.[190] These totals possibly underreport the extent of the crimes committed, but there is no way of knowing to what degree. It is true that there was a high rate of dismissals of court cases and that law officers were not very successful in finding those who had been indicted. Consequently, those indicted often never appeared before a court of law to determine their fate. And even the few who were prisoners sometimes escaped from lawmen. In 1861 Sheriff Sixto Domínguez of Hidalgo County submitted a small claim for safekeeping prisoners, a standard practice in those days when the sheriff housed, fed, and guarded prisoners, but the court disallowed the claim because his "prisoners got away."[191]

Anglos blamed Tejanos for this seeming inefficiency in the administration of justice. Yet this condition resulted largely from factors beyond the control of local officials, whether Mexican or Anglo. Among the more important factors were the rapid changes in county administrations, the migratory composition of its settlers, the rural nature of the region, its large area, and its proximity to safe haven in Mexico. Anglos also asserted that the low number of cases tried was due to the *mejicanos'* lack of knowledge of the English language and because a jury could not be seated when the defendant was a familiar citizen. The first argument is questionable because, in fact, courts usually employed interpreters. The latter is valid in that the settlers tended to know each other, or to be related in many cases, but it should be noted that the more notorious criminal cases were often tried in an adjoining county, on a change of venue. Still, dismissal of court cases was common, and clerks cited a variety of reasons for this action.[192] Ironically, in the last quarter of the nineteenth century, crimes against Mexicans and infringement of their fundamental constitutional protections were serious problems that local Anglo officials ignored, unless pressed by the U.S. government as a result of Mexican diplomatic initiatives.[193] Further study would clarify the nature of crime, its prosecution, and punishment in south Texas.

Civil cases concerned minor matters, but occasionally important disputes over valuable property and other kinds of claims arose. Sometimes lawsuits involved Tejanos and Anglos. In the early 1890s, Thaddeus M. Rhodes and Don Florencio Sáenz, two of the most respected stockmen and Hidalgo County officials as well as neighbors, faced each other in a district court in Brownsville, in a bitter dispute concerning some lands in the Llano Grande grant.[194] At other times disputes involved Tejanos and other *mejicanos.* Mercurio Martínez mentions a 1912 lawsuit in Zapata County, in which a local court denied adverse possession rights to *mejicano* settlers who he claims were given permission to clear land for fields by the Uribes, prominent landholders.[195]

Occasionally, gangs of outlaws who were usually called bandits or desperadoes, as well as notorious individuals who operated on their own, struck fear in the settlers. In 1875, the district court in Edinburg took note of the "great risk of [a prisoner's] escape or rescue by organized banditti now infesting the country between the Río Grande and the Nueces rivers."[196] Consider the case of one Pancho Garza, who in 1899 "was riddled with buckshot" in the town of Hidalgo by deputy sheriffs Valente Rodríguez and Albert Tagle. Allegedly a notorious horse thief, Garza had earlier attacked the Reynosa police and wounded two men. He was lured to the *jacal* of his mistress, where Garza and the two deputies exchanged gunfire. A local newspaper reported the results cautiously, saying that "it is believed that he is either dead in the brush or badly wounded." Yet the newspaper headlines read "Pancho Garza Killed."[197]

Those engaged in large-scale rustling and other serious crimes were usually never caught by anyone, not even the Texas Rangers, although those who were actually captured were often killed "while fleeing." If, however, the bandit problem had been as severe as claimed by stockraisers and their apologists, why then did herds increase so rapidly (as reported in assessment rolls) at the same time that ranchers were trailing massive numbers of livestock to distant markets? Once again, the literature is so biased that the history of the so-called destruction of the herds in the 1870s is a serious misrepresentation. This does not mean that stock was not stolen, for it was, but these activities were not as well organized and continuous as some writers have asserted. I do not mean to contradict, however, the thesis that there were times, such as during Reconstruction, when in fact rampant lawlessness took over and no legitimate officials on either side of the border could contain the perpetrators of such disorders. Yet it is inaccurate to view all or much of the post-1848 period as a time of uncontrollable crime.

Some writers have made much of Indians and Mexican raiders. My criticism of this older historiography is not meant to detract from the fact that settlers—both Hispanic and Anglo—were suddenly subjected to attacks by Indian and Mexican raiders in which lives were lost, children and women taken captive, and property looted or destroyed. However, it is my assertion that the new settlers, especially Anglos and Europeans, emphasized the danger of living on the frontier to such an extent that much of it may have been self-serving, and consequently their reports of Indian raids and Mexican banditry or fears of invasion by Mexicans must be used with caution. One striking irony of the persistence in labeling *mejicanos* as bandits is general omission of the fact that, following the Texas Revolt, young Anglo men called cowboys stole gentle and wild herds belonging to the old *rancheros* and Anglos settlers not only in east Texas, but also in the western area of the state, the mostly Hispanic area around San Antonio and the Trans-Nueces.[198] A classic example of Anglo paranoia about Mexican invasion and insurrection is the so-called Río Grande City riots of September 23–24, 1886. Local Anglos reported to the secretary of war that the situation involved "hourly" fighting and a threatened uprising of fifteen thousand to twenty thousand Mexicans, who evidently would cross the river to perpetrate a rampage of murder against the few Anglo men, women, and children who lived in the Lower Valley. According to their reports, the "uprising" or "riots," alleged to involve "hourly fighting," began as a result of an incident involving U.S. customs inspector Victor Sebreé. Actually, Sebreé had engaged in a gunfight with two *mejicanos*, including Catarino Garza, a newspaper editor and leader of the Mexicans. Anglos who corresponded with the secretaries of war and the treasury asserted that Garza was a dangerous instigator who advocated the belief that the Trans-Nueces lands belonged to the

Mexicans and that the Anglos were interlopers. Upon investigation, Lt. Col. D. R. Clendenin, military officer at Fort Ringgold, Texas, reported that no such mob or riots existed, but he acknowledged that "politics has a great deal to do in the matter, and that it is not 'a war of races' as is claimed by some Americans. Some of the best and most prominent Mexicans are on the side of law and order." In spite of this assessment, the Anglos had stirred things up enough that a military force of four hundred troops was placed on alert, and it was used to monitor elections in Starr County in November 1888.[199] As this Río Grande City incident demonstrates, some elements of the new settlers went to grave extremes to foster a belief that they were nearly always beleaguered by Indians or Mexicans. The problem with this kind of general alarm was that those who were asked to assist the citizens in putting down disorders rarely ever scrutinized the latter's claims.

In fact, early careful observers noted the nature of frontier disturbances and the inability of the inhabitants to defend themselves and to maintain order. As early as 1850, Lieutenant Vielé described Río Grande City as "a great filibustering rendezvous."[200] Following his inspection of U.S. posts in Texas, Colonel J. K. F. Mansfield (1856) concluded:

> It is across this river [the Río Grande] at various points that Smuggling is carried on, and bandits of both Indians and Mexicans commit *at times* [my emphasis] depredations. . . . But little or no dependence can be placed on this population [of Mexican stockraisers and American traders] as a community to preserve order and enforce the laws.[201]

Other observers also noted this breach of the norm, explaining that since contraband in goods enriched local merchants no one dared to oppose it. The chaos of the civil wars in both the United States and Mexico at midcentury facilitated smuggling operations, some of which involved respected business and political men of all nationalities.[202]

A second kind of distortion that permeated Anglo thinking concerned the almost constant indictment of "bad" Indians and Mexicans. Some *mejicanos* in the lower border country occasionally gave tacit support to such generalization. However, a perusal of citizen petitions to the state and national government as well as testimony submitted to U.S. frontier commissions sent to investigate "border problems" reveal a pattern of statements charging Indians and Mexicans with various offenses in very general terms. It is nearly impossible in most cases to determine how many raiders were involved, who they were, where they went, and exactly what they took.[203] There were so many such instances of general confusion and alarm among the settlers that even contemporaries admitted not knowing who was actually committing the crime. An early Corpus Christi resident, Englishman Thomas John Noakes, noted in his diary, in 1861:

> The country is greatly excited at present, occasioned by the murderous depredations of what are reported to be Indians, the country, according to reports being full of them and several persons being killed. Mr. Bryden [an area resident] has had one shepherd killed and everything at his ranch thrown into the greatest confusion. His Mexicans will not leave the house and his flocks of sheep are all mixed up. The accounts are so conflicting, however, and the rumors so little to be depended on that I really doubt whether these murders were committed by Mexicans or Indians. One thing is certain, there are very many people of bad sort, mean enough to do this.[204]

Naturally, Tejanos were not solely responsible for crime, for Anglos and European newcomers too committed offenses. Take, for instance, conditions during the early years of the founding of Brownsville, where observers reported considerable lawlessness, involving Anglo newcomers and travelers to the California gold fields. The Abbé Domenench condemned Americans for their involvement in lawless activities, calling them "the very scum of society." He also asserted that the local sheriff in Cameron County treated the *mejicanos* badly and that no land grant was safe because "impartiality [was] not considered by Texas judges a duty." The clergyman attributed the greater part of the murders to Texas Rangers, and he condemned the rampant lawlessness as well as the application of "lynch law" to those suspected of committing crimes.[205] Lieutenant Viele was paraphrased in *De Bow's Journal* in 1850 as saying that "besides the regular [Anglo] Texans [there] are a class of vagrant Americans who give a bad name to Texas."[206]

Actually, at times both Anglos and Mexicans committed wanton murders that led to mob rule. In 1850, "lynch law" made its appearance in Cameron County, although reports also indicate that two Mexicans and one Anglo were formally tried before the district court in Brownsville prior to their hanging in early January 1851. It is not clear how long mob rule or vigilantism prevailed in the area because newspapers in New Orleans, in May 1852, citing a Brownsville newspaper as its source, indicated that one American and nine Mexicans were executed "without the sanction of any law, save that of a hastily assembled and incensed multitude."[207]

There were, of course, other less drastic ways of dealing with alleged criminals. The county commissioners' minutes of April 29, 1854, simply recited that one Elisha Throughman, the constable of Precinct 2 in Hidalgo County, "was driven out of the county for horse stealing."[208]

CONCLUSION

Most Tejanos in south Texas functioned well in a changing society. Adaptation to Anglo influences occurred, but there was no large-scale assimilation. Adversity and transformation in the social and political order had essentially conditioned the citizens since the Spanish era to accept change. Thus, after 1848 the settlers continued to devise their own strategies to deal with the social and economic changes around them. Adaptation was essential for the survival of the Tejano's group identity. As such, they exhibited a resiliency that helped them to adjust to a volatile world that was becoming increasingly linked to larger, social, political, and market forces, one in which some succeeded and others failed. As individuals and as a group, Tejanos were largely a free, self-directed, dynamic people who did not suffer universal oppression at the hands of new settlers from the United States and Europe. The Anglo perception that Mexicans lived in "pastoral simplicity and contentment," in "unique contrast to the opposite character of their American neighbors," was at best only partly accurate.[209] Race and class distinctions certainly affected the everyday rhythm of life among Tejanos. They were not all alike, although in the minds of many "outsiders" this view persisted. Yet regardless of social or class distinctions, a common ethnic and cultural identity united the settlers into a Tejano community. Life was not static but ever-changing, especially for landholders, although those who did not own property experienced a similar history. True, the family remained at the center of society. At times, however, disputes weakened its sanctity, although among landholders the importance of landownership strengthened collective bonds. Culturally, *lo mejicano* persisted in an array of social activities, and immigration from Mexico reinforced many of its elements. Still, as Tejanos became more acquainted with American traditions and institutions, some of them gradually adopted new customs, attitudes, values, and expectations. They learned to negotiate their presence and participation in an evolving society sanctioned by Anglo customs, legal traditions, and social institutions, but one that had a strong Spanish and *mejicano* foundation. In short, after 1848 Tejanos experienced flux and transition in the first half-century of American rule, for they continued to live in familiar ways while adapting to the changes brought about by annexation and Anglo and European settlement. At the same time, some newcomers from the United States and Europe also assimilated Hispanic social values, not to mention the all-important economic activities.

South Texas was a Tejano homeland, a place where Tejanos constituted the major component of the population and where being first-in-place on the basis of settlement gave them advantages over newcomers. What this meant was that Anglos could never dissolve the cultural loyalty of Tejanos to their Spanish and *mejicano* heritage. This was one aspect of Tejano life that differed from the experiences of other groups, such as the *californios* and the Mexican settlers of Arizona, both of whom were quickly overrun by Anglo newcomers. Whereas Hispanic New Mexico consisted mostly of villages, the Tejano experience was based largely on *ranchos*, towns, and cities, instead of villages.

Tejanos who interacted with Anglos, especially large landholders and other economic elites, underwent a process of acculturation, but full assimilation rarely occurred. Nonetheless, interethnic cooperation was essential for bringing about a level of social and political stability necessary for economic progress in the region. Yet violence and interethnic conflict periodically shattered peace and tranquillity in the lower border country. For the most part, however, it was not a lawless society, despite the persistent depiction of society in south Texas as one in which rampant banditry and ignorant Mexicans, manipulated by political bosses, held sway. Despite the general acceptance of Tejanos in most places during most of the time, poor and dark-skinned *mejicanos* succumbed to Anglo cultural and ethnic intolerance and prejudice. Tejano–Anglo accommodation slowly gave way in the final years of the nineteenth century to discrimination and even separation in a few districts of the region. By 1900 social and class divisions between the Tejano and U.S.- and European-born settlers were much more rigid than at any time in the previous century, an omen that did not bode well for the future of ethnic relations.

Several important dynamics were part and parcel of the adaptation of Tejanos to incorporation into the life and culture of the United States after annexation. One key factor was the continuity of *lo mejicano.* The persistence and strength of Mexican culture in south Texas was due to the large Tejano population and a general acceptance of *lo mejicano* by most newcomers. Still, the arrival of new settlers from south of the border not only augmented the Tejano population, it also contributed to a more complex social milieu. Socially, this post-1848 wave of immigration from Mexico reinforced Hispanic culture, giving Tejano society a new vibrancy. Some newcomers from the United States and Europe were Hispanicized to a degree, absorbing social and cultural elements of the old *mejicano* settlers, such as the leisurely style of life, use of the Spanish language, intermarriage and adoption practices, and acceptance of social rituals including *compadrazgo*, or co-parenthood. Moreover, a significant number of *rancheros* engaged in friendly and fair business and political contacts with Anglos. However, as newcomers ascended politically and economically and as Tejanos lost status in the last twenty or so years of the nineteenth century, some changes in Tejano–Anglo relations occurred. For instance, few Anglos chose Hispanic women as marriage partners; the latter no longer provided a way to enhance the newcomers' or their children's opportunities for material advancement, as local Tejano women had done during the earlier period of American incorporation. As a consequence, the reality of Tejano–Anglo cooperation in the economic and political order for the sake of regional development became primordial, replacing the earlier style of interethnic relations, whose foundation was primarily socioeconomic.

The second key element of Tejano adaptation to an ever-changing society in south Texas dealt with their adjustment to new habits, attitudes, and goals introduced by the coming of Anglos to the region. At best, adapting to Anglo ways in the social, economic, and political arenas was an ongoing process in which individuals chose the extent to which they were willing to acculturate. Still, several factors unique to the region limited the opportunities for assimilation. Of these, the most important were the early arrival and ubiquitous presence and permanency of Tejanos in the region. Nearly everywhere sizable Tejano communities could be found or, at the very least, a small enclave of Mexican workers, such as a small *ranchería* or town *barrio.* Also, after the initial contact between *mejicanos* and newcomers in the early and mid-nineteenth century, little assimilation occurred through intermarriage with Anglos and Europeans.

De Léon and others argue that some Tejano communities underwent a process of acculturation, which they term *biculturation.* This social history of Tejanos shows that most kept their cultural traditions and that only a few who lived in proximity to Anglos, or who had longlasting or meaningful social and economic ties to them, embraced habits, attitudes, values, and aspirations of the United States. The better-off Tejano *rancheros* and their cohorts in business and professional life attained some semblance of adaptation to the American way of living, especially in the educational and political arena. Protestantism made few converts, while the Catholic church struggled to enhance its loyalty among Tejanos by offering familiar and new services to them. In short, some assimilation took place in the ever-changing society, but not very much. At the start of the twentieth century, south Texas remained a predominately Tejano region.

CHAPTER FIVE

LOSING GROUND

Anglo Challenges to Mexican Landholders and Land Grant Adjudication in South Texas, 1846–1900

It is impossible to fully understand the anxiety that weighed heavily on Mexican landholders whose lands and other material possessions remained on the north side of the Río Grande during the war with Mexico and the immediate postwar years. Still, it was certain that this difficult period would bring about Mexican–Anglo confrontation because the newly annexed lands offered few immediate rewards other than the possibility of utilizing the fertile grasslands, the navigable Río Grande and its port, and the possibility of appropriating the abundant herds of domestic and wild livestock. Understandably, Mexicans did not want to give up their property easily. This situation caused competition, controversy, and conflict between Mexicans, who sought to maintain ownership of their lands and livestock, and the newcomers from the United States and Europe. At the end of the war, the older Mexican landholders on the north bank of the Río Grande often found themselves uncertain as to their rights to the lands, despite what Mexicans believed to be specific guarantees to their property and civil rights under Articles 8 and 9 of the Treaty of Guadalupe Hidalgo. The treaty itself provided no standard for validation of land grants. Consequently, land-grant adjudication proceeded in a piecemeal fashion, with the federal government determining the procedures for the validation process in the new American Southwest, except that under a special case by virtue of its prior claim to the Trans-Nueces, the state of Texas controlled the process in the newly annexed lands.[1] Not surprisingly, some Anglos used new laws and the courts to their advantage to gain land, and occasionally resorted to devious means to subvert the Mexicans' position as dominant landholders.

This chapter addresses several facets of the history of land-grant issues in south Texas, including early attacks on the rights of Mexican landholders, the short-lived Anglo drive to establish a territorial government for the region and its effects on landholding, and the processes involved in land-grant adjudication. It is my purpose here to clarify the historiography on Tejano land tenure because the Tejano interpretation of land-grant adjudication differs from the Anglo view of this issue. Above all, it is important to assess what significance land-grant adjudication held for both *mejicano* claimants and Anglo and European competitors. Still, it is true that the costs of adjudication served as a barrier to regaining their property, perhaps one that *mejicano* landholders had not foreseen under their interpretation of the treaty rights. Moreover, as this chapter and the following case study of landholding in Hidalgo County shows, Tejano land loss was a complicated and gradual process, one that resulted in varying rates of displacement from the *ranchos* and a more complex land-tenure system in the region.

EARLY AMERICAN CHALLENGES TO TEJANO LANDHOLDERS IN THE LOWER VALLEY

The war with Mexico brought not only soldiers to the Lower Valley, but also a host of Anglo Americans who began almost immediately to challenge the Mexicans for control of the land. Among these new residents were ex-soldiers, adventurers, and others from the United States and Europe who stayed in the Lower Valley, augmenting the local population of *mejicano* settlers and the older Anglo and European merchants and artisans. While merchants and artisans were content merely to restart the Mexican trade and reopen their shops, many of the newcomers from the United States and Europe had loftier economic and political ambitions, resorting to conflict to gain an upper hand among the newly annexed inhabitants. Some of them were interested in what they could take from the Mexicans, particularly the fertile delta lands and rich pastures where large numbers of livestock grazed. They often manifested a greediness and anti-Mexican bias that stirred up trouble and widened the chasm between the Mexicans, on the one hand, and the Anglos and Europeans, on the other.[2]

The prevalence of uncertainty created confusion, as can be seen in the first contacts between Mexicans and Anglos in Laredo. Although the *mejicano* citizens of Laredo had experienced relatively less aggression than other communities in northeast Mexico during the war, Mexicans were still apprehensive about Anglo rule. They had initially accepted Anglo Texan occupation of their territory and the creation of Nueces County in November 1846. In adjusting to U.S. sovereignty, they had also participated in the election of city officers in the summer of 1847. Yet they remained distrustful and suspicious of the American newcomers. On October 2, 1847, Laredoans petitioned the Texas legislature for assurances that their property rights would be protected. Prior to the ratification of the Treaty of Guadalupe Hidalgo (May 1848), city officials also forwarded petitions to both the American and Mexican authorities, asking that Laredo remain a part of the Mexican republic. Their appeal consisted of several arguments: that under the Texans there had been a lack of dependable protection against the Indians, a violation of property rights, and unacceptable American ways of dealing with wild livestock. However, once Mexico ratified the treaty, Laredo became a part of Texas and of the United States. By then Anglo Texan volunteers had been mustered out of service, and as the town returned to civilian rule, with the Mexicans in control, fears about American domination were allayed.[3]

Prior to the adjudication of land grants under the laws of Texas, Anglo-American officials in the Lower Valley were among the first to question the validity of continued Mexican ownership of land grants on the north side of the Río Grande. Judge Rice Garland, a former jurist and congressman from Louisiana who sold lands and bought land certificates in Matamoros, advertised in Brownsville's *American Flag* on June 2, 1847, that "Mexican law and authority are forever at an end" in the Nueces territory and that "by the laws of Texas no alien can hold real estate within its limits." In the same ad, he declared in Spanish that all original owners of land must have their lands surveyed and possess deeds. He warned Mexican owners that "preparations are being made to locate other claims on the land covered by such titles."[4] As later events showed, Mexicans were not about to give up their land claims so easily, although in some instances they were forced to take steps to protect their property rights.

The movement of Mexican squatters to the lands north of the river in the Brownsville area, which began in 1847, jeopardized the title of some Mexican landowners. A *ranchero*, Rafael García Cavazos, who claimed a share of the Espíritu Santo grant, was greatly distressed when squatters located *labor* rights on his land. The latter asserted their rights to the land on the basis of awards made by the city government of Matamoros. García Cavazos contended, however, that the *labor* grants were invalid because the local government had never paid landholders for the expropriation of the lands in 1826. In an advertisement in the *American Flag*, he warned the squatters to leave and promised to resort to the law to protect his rights.[5]

At the same time that he was attempting to ward off squatters, the *ranchero* faced a much more powerful challenge from merchant Charles Stillman, whose plans were to found a new townsite, near Fort Brown, on the lands encompassed within the *labores*. Despite the fact that the local federal court had voided those titles, Stillman continued to buy up squatters' titles. During the legal struggle that ensued between García Cavazos and Stillman, from 1848 to 1850, the judge ruled in favor of the *ranchero.* When Stillman threatened to appeal, García Cavazos opted to sell to Stillman's lawyers, Elisha Basse and R. H. Hord, because further court costs would have been prohibitive. In return for the land, the seller took a note for thirty-three thousand dollars. After extensive litigation among various parties involving these original settlers and buyers, the García Cavazos descendants were eventually paid for the land.[6] This case typified the kind of legal conflicts over land waged by newcomers who desperately wanted to gain control of valuable real estate. An unexpected consequence of the García Cavazos–Stillman dispute was Juan N. Cortina's 1859 revolt against what he called Anglo usurpers.[7]

There were several other well-known legal battles between Mexican landholders and Anglo newcomers. One of these cases disputed ownership of La Sal del Rey, a salt lake in the San Salvador del Tule grant. Competing claims for this valuable salt deposit set the stage for this suit. An adventurer, J. N. Reynolds, claimed the tract on which the lake was located, on the basis of land scrip that he held under the Republic of Texas. H. M. Lewis, another claimant, held a certificate of the same government issued earlier to another party. Reynolds purchased Lewis's interest and took possession of the salt lake. José Salvador Cárdenas, who had acquired the land grant by purchase from the family of the original grantee, sued both Reynolds and Lewis in the U.S. district court, but to no avail. In some cases, sales of land made during the Mexican-American War appear ostensibly legitimate, but, as labor economist Paul S. Taylor argues, such sales were often made under duress because Anglo newcomers challenged the Mexicans to stay in the Trans-Nueces at the same time that General Zachary Taylor was preparing a large invasion force. Early transactions between Mexican sellers and Anglo buyers sometimes went awry as a legal subterfuge turned out to be an actual deed. Such was the case concerning Blas María de la Garza Falcón's Chilipitín grant in Nueces County. His heirs were forced twice to defend their claim in the courts, because an Anglo claimant asserted ownership rights to the land on the basis of a mortgage rather than a deed.[8] These lawsuits were a prelude to a long history of legal battles over land that would divide family, friends, and foes alike.

ADJUDICATION OF LAND GRANTS IN SOUTH TEXAS

Realizing that settling the issue of validity of land titles in the Trans-Nueces was a pressing problem, the state of Texas took control of the adjudication process shortly after the signing of the Treaty of Guadalupe Hidalgo. Those in the middle of this issue included *rancheros*, who were concerned about their property rights, and Anglo and European newcomers, who had acquired *derechos*, or undivided interests in the land, during the Mexican-American War. The latter were mostly merchants who had sought out grantees or heirs as well as previous purchasers of the grants and for a few dollars had bought from them the undivided rights, or *derechos*. Except for an isolated case or two—like the merchant John Young, who claimed three Reynosa *porciones*—new settlers did not usually purchase an entire grant. It was too risky to do so in view of the unsettled conditions and the lack of effective legal jurisdiction by the authorities of the United States or, for that matter, Texas. Nonetheless, they evidently anticipated that the lands along the Río Grande frontier would be more valuable once the war was over. In fact, during the conflict some merchants located stores and warehouses on the north bank of the river. Others desired the new lands, for purposes of speculation. Their interest in acquiring land was probably influenced by the fact that in contrast to California and New Mexico, Spanish and Mexican officials hardly ever granted land to Anglos and Europeans in the province of Nuevo Santander and in Tamaulipas, although the colonization law of Tamaulipas allowed for foreigners to acquire land grants settled under *empresario* contracts.[9] Newcomers, in particular, must have sensed that there was no free land for them to take, in view of the long history of *ranchero* occupation of the Lower Valley. Thus, those claiming vested interests and those interested in the acquisition of land grants insisted that public policy would be best served if the state took rapid steps to validate the land grants.

The uncertainty of rights to Spanish and Mexican land titles in the newly annexed Trans-Nueces became manifest at the start of American control of the region. For instance, despite the return to civilian rule in Laredo, Mexicans in Webb County remained uneasy about their rights to the land. In late 1848, they sought to have their titles recorded in the county, only to have Hamilton P. Bee, the county clerk, refuse to do so. Bee defended his action on the grounds that he was unsure if Texas law required titles to be recorded in the state's General Land Office in Austin or if they needed only to be registered prior to having them recorded by the county clerk. The clerk advised the Mexicans to send their titles to the Land Office, but many objected to sending these documents across territory controlled by the Indians. Prior to Bee's inquiry, George W. Smyth, commissioner of the Land Office, had refused to record and register any document that purported to be a land title issued by Spain or Mexico. Unsure of what to do, he had asked the Texas attorney general for his legal opinion. Smyth believed that the state constitution and laws contemplated that the Land Office should be the repository of land titles, but he did not think that every unauthenticated document to come along should be accepted. The attorney general agreed with Smyth that nothing in the laws of the state explained how documents were to be authenticated for recording and registration. He urged legislative action in this area. This situation, as well as pressure from individuals who sought to locate land certificates issued to them by the Republic and State of Texas in the Trans-Nueces area, led Smyth to inform the governor that if the legislature did not act, he would be compelled to issue patents to those desiring them in the region.[10]

Governor Peter H. Bell responded energetically. In a message to the Texas legislature on December 26, 1849, he noted the urgency of "settling upon a secure and permanent basis the land titles of the country," and recommended that the legislature establish a board of commissioners to investigate titles. In the debate that followed, it became apparent that some people did not like the idea of a special commission and particularly objected to Governor Bell's recommendation to limit investigation of claims to those where evidence of title was already in Texas. This would effectively bar the claims of those who lacked original records but whose titles were longstanding. Another concern was a belief that Article 8 of the Texas Constitution—which allowed for the confiscation of land if a person had left or had refused to participate in the Texas independence movement, or had aided the Mexicans—would be used against them. The intent of this article was to punish Texans of Mexican descent who had sided with Santa Anna or who had remained neutral. However, an amendment requiring an affidavit that a claimant or person under whom they claimed title had not borne arms or aided the enemy during the Texas Revolt was voted down in the House of Representatives by a vote of 23 to 19. The bill's opponents argued that it was unfair to demand the allegiance of Mexicans to whom no protection had been offered during the course of the fighting.[11]

THE TERRITORIAL MOVEMENT IN THE LOWER VALLEY, 1850

Prior to the conclusion of these proceedings in Austin, a movement had emerged in the Lower Valley to create a Río Grande territory separate from Texas. Meeting in Brownsville on February 2, 1850, the leading separatists or territorialists included merchants, lawyers, politicians, adventurers, and, at least initially, Mexican *rancheros*, although the role played by the latter is unclear. Perhaps they, too, were perplexed by the motives of distant Texan officials, toward whom they had always been suspicious and hostile since the Texas Revolt of 1835. The key participants and driving force behind the movement included Colonel Stephen Powers, a lawyer and local political chief who founded the Democratic party in south Texas; the lawyers Basse and Hord; major merchants like Sam A. Belden and Charles Stillman; and Joseph R. Palmer, editor of Brownsville's *American Flag*, and an ardent supporter of filibustering and Manifest Destiny. Richard King and Mifflin Kenedy, prominent steamboat operators and soon-to-be powerful landowners, also supported the idea of organizing the Río Grande territory. These men asserted that the state of Texas never had jurisdiction over the region and warned that it might annul land titles in the "Nueces Strip" or impose on residents there "expensive and ruinous lawsuits" to defend their property. They proposed that Congress be petitioned to allow the creation of a territorial government that would quickly and fairly adjudicate land titles so that land with a clear title might then be purchased for less money than it would cost to obtain it under a certificate from the state. The meeting concluded with a call for a convention to form a provisional government until the U.S. Congress could be petitioned.[12]

Despite two petitions to the U.S. Congress, the Brownsville separatists failed to secure what they wanted. The first petition evidently received wide support from Mexicans. Nearly all of the names affixed to it were of Spanish origin except for three, including that of the local sheriff, J. G. Browne. It is not clear what the Mexicans were offered or promised for joining in the petition, but apparently they too wanted to protect their property under the new regime. Texas's U.S. senator Thomas J. Rusk dismissed the petition as the work of men "engaged in directing their action to their own purposes," but he did not disclose their objectives. The second petition consisted of a similar appeal to the Congress. It had seventy-four signatures, mostly from men who had lived but three or four years on the border, although the list includes King, Kenedy, Power, Basse, and Hord. Very few Mexicans participated in this petition. We can only surmise that they were not asked to sign.[13]

The separatists' actions precipitated a countermovement. Its leaders included elected officials who expressed confidence in the state of Texas and who denied the separatists' charges that Texas had neglected and acted in bad faith with regard to the interests of the Lower Valley. Its key leader was Judge Israel B. Bigelow, the chief officer of Cameron County. Evidently, some Mexican landholders, such as the important Ballí family supported this group, although their motives or objectives are unknown. Two Ballí family members were officeholders, and they served as bondsmen for key leaders like Judge Bigelow. Meeting on February 5, 1850, they adopted resolutions that recognized Texas's sovereignty over the territory between the Nueces and Río Grande, and denied that they had ever submitted to the jurisdiction of Texas previous to the annexation of the Trans-Nueces. The assembly also urged that one or more tribunals be established by the state to investigate "legal and just titles to land situated between the Nueces river and the Río Grande," and applauded the governor for proposing, in a message to the Texas legislature on December 26, 1849, the creation of a commission to investigate titles to land in the region.[14]

Fortunately for Bigelow and his supporters, on February 8, 1850, just three days after their meeting in Brownsville, the state legislature passed an act providing for the appointment of a special commission to investigate claims of all Spanish and Mexican grants west of the Nueces River. On February 22, 1850, Governor Peter H. Bell, in a letter to the people of the new counties in south Texas, stated that the commissioners would investigate and recommend for confirmation to the state legislature claims that originated in equity and fairness. He also assured the people that the work of the commission would promote the prosperity of the area.[15]

Before the work of the commission got underway, the separatist movement was entirely bankrupt. Senator Rusk told the Senate, on March 11, 1850, that the Mexicans had been duped by individuals who only recently had come to the area and had exploited the prejudices of "Mexicans who were originally and always adverse to Texas." Obviously, the senator was cognizant of the lingering legacy of conflict between Mexicans and Anglo Texans, a conflict that had intensified bad feelings between the two groups ever since the Texas Revolt of 1835 and the war with Mexico. Texans generally condemned the separatists for engaging in dirty politics and for currying the support of Northerners, whose motives Texans detested. Evidently, some of the separatists had given only lukewarm support to the movement. For example, Jack R. Everett, a lawyer at Roma, admitted his error and disclaimed any further ties with the movement.[16] Despite these developments, the work of the commission was hampered in some localities by the suspicions aroused by the separatists.[17] It is likely that such suspicions complicated the investigation and adjustment of claims that followed.

THE BOURLAND-MILLER COMMISSION, 1850–1851

Under the act of February 8, 1850, two commissioners and an attorney were appointed to "take cognizance of all claims . . . [which] originated in good faith . . . , " and the procedures for investigating claims were spelled out. William H. Bourland and James B. Miller, experienced public officials in Texas, were named commissioners, and Robert Jones Rivers, a well-known lawyer and judge, served as the board's attorney. Under the law, the claimants to Spanish and Mexican land grants were required to submit a full and written description of the land claimed, along with all of the evidence of title and rights on which the claim was based. They also had to provide an affidavit that documents submitted were not forged or antedated. Witnesses could be summoned to testify before the commission. Once this phase of the investigation was complete, the commissioners were to report where the titles were perfect. In case of an imperfect claim, the commission could recommend confirmation if it concluded that all requirements for perfecting the title would have been met had there not been a change in national sovereignty. The board was required to prepare an abstract on each claim, together with a recommendation on whether it should be confirmed or rejected. The abstract and supporting evidence would be submitted to the governor, who, in turn, would give the documents to the legislature for final action.[18]

After several delays, the three members of the commission opened for business at Laredo on July 15, 1850. Laredoans, suspicious of the commissioners, did not want to present any claims. Upon being assured by County Clerk Bee of the board's honest intentions, however, *rancheros* submitted fifteen claims from Webb County. Sensing the urgency of showing good faith to the Mexican people of Laredo, Bourland felt it wise to present the claims for immediate confirmation, although the board had a year to report. Bourland returned to Austin and submitted the list to Governor Bell on August 24, 1850. On September 4, 1850, the state legislature confirmed the *rancheros*' fifteen claims. In the meantime, Miller and Rivers had proceeded to Río Grande City.[19]

At Río Grande City, Miller and Rivers received an inhospitable welcome from the Mexican residents, who refused to submit a single claim. In frustration, Rivers resigned from the commission and Miller vowed that he would not return to Río Grande City. He moved on to Brownsville, where a letter from Bourland found him, requesting him to return to Río Grande City. As a result of this unfavorable stay, no claims were presented at Río Grande City.

From Austin Bourland proceeded to Brownsville, where Miller was taking testimony. From there, Bourland wrote to the governor that because of the demise of the separatists' movement they were being treated with respect, and he was confident no trouble would arise. When the board finished its work in Brownsville, Miller decided to return to Austin by sea, on the steamer *Anson*, making the voyage from Port Isabel to Galveston before going overland to Austin. Two days out, the *Anson* sank fifteen miles from Matagorda. Miller lost his trunk, the original titles, and about eight hundred dollars in fees from the claimants. Because of this loss, he urged the governor to amend the law to make the commissioners' decision final. Miller's suggestion was not accepted and, as a result, the commission had to redo all of its work in procuring duplicates and other evidence.[20]

Following an adjournment of several months in the spring of 1851, Bourland went on his own to Eagle Pass, Laredo and Río Grande City. He then traveled to Corpus Christi, where he held his last session in the summer of 1851.[21]

LEGISLATIVE CONFIRMATION OF LAND GRANTS IN SOUTH TEXAS, 1852

In accordance with the law, the governor on November 20, 1851, sent his report on the work of the commission to the legislature, where a select committee examined the testimony. On February 10, 1852, the legislature, closely following the commissioners' recommendations, confirmed 194 claims in the names of the original Spanish and Mexican grantees, including those transferred to heirs and legal assignees or purchasers. Very few claims were confirmed for Anglo or European claimants, such as the merchant John Young of Brownsville. The claims confirmed included those to 31 tracts in Webb County, 134 in Starr County, 56 in Cameron County, 21 in Nueces County, and 2 in Kinney County.[22]

The validation of land grants apparently satisfied not only *rancheros*, but anyone claiming an interest in or desiring to acquire land. As Montejano asserts, confirmation of title ostensibly incorporated the landed elites into the new political fabric of the region, so that at least the old conflicts between Mexicans and Anglo Texans were temporarily set aside.[23] Perhaps more important in the long run to Tejano landholders, the way was now opened for renewed land transactions as well as for lawsuits among parties claiming title to the same lands.

Several of the claims that the commissioners refused to recommend were nonetheless confirmed by the state legislature in 1852. These included the claims to Llano Grande (1790) and Las Mesteñas (1794), both large land grants located in Hidalgo County. It is interesting to speculate why the legislature overrode the commission. Perhaps the fact that the two grants were well settled and that they belonged to the influential Hinojosa and Ballí families may have persuaded the legislature to confirm them. Besides, the confirmation of these two grants facilitated acquisitions by other interested parties and served to ease suspicions on the part of the old settlers and those wanting to purchase the land from them.

LEGISLATIVE AND JUDICIAL ADJUDICATION OF LAND GRANTS IN SOUTH TEXAS AFTER 1852

The important work of the commission and subsequent confirmation by the state, however, did not entirely bring an end to the issue of settling Spanish and

Mexican land grants, mainly because seventy grants were not adjudicated either in 1851 or in 1852. In addition, the commission rejected a small number of claims. Thus, after completion of the commission's work, further adjudications by the courts and the state legislature were necessary to deal with these claims.[24]

In regard to rejected and unadjudicated claims, Texas responded in two ways: (1) allowing claimants the right to sue in the district courts for validation and confirmation, and (2) making individual legislative confirmations. Of these two methods, the former approach was by far the most commonly used. Special state laws enacted in 1860, 1870, and 1901 provided the procedures under which claims could be presented. Under the first act, suit had to be brought in the state district court in which the grant was located. The second and third acts permitted the bringing of suit in the district court of Travis County (Austin).[25]

Sixty-eight land grants ended up in the courts under the three acts. Of these, fifty-three were approved by the courts without having to resort to any other adjudication procedure. Except for seven grants, which were adjudicated under the 1901 act, all of these claims were presented under the 1860 and 1870 acts. Thus, the claimants acted relatively quickly. Only two grants were rejected by the courts.[26]

Among the more important claims denied by the Bourland Commission, but later approved by the district courts, was that to San Salvador del Tule (1797), one of the largest land grants in south Texas. This claim had a history similar to those usually rejected by the commissioners on the grounds that the land grant had originally being occupied by the grantees and other purchasers who made improvements on the land, vacated it temporarily, and subsequently reoccupied it.[27] After annexation, Mexican *ranchero* landholders in the San Salvador del Tule grant raised considerable livestock on the grant's abundant prairies. When this claim was first presented to the Bourland Commission in 1852, it had been rejected on the basis of abandonment of the grant in 1811, due to Indian attacks. Yet James B. Miller, in a dissenting opinion to the governor, recommended confirmation. Miller asserted that the grantees and descendants soon returned to the grant, the cattle had greatly increased, and "the amount of land now in cultivation, owning to the long continuity of settlement, and the great number of occupants is very considerable." He urged that the grant be recognized since rejection would work a great hardship on the settlers. He said that he did not favor depriving them "of their long cherished homes or [*sic*] to anull their titles, which, for three quarters of a century have been respected and considered valid."[28] In 1904, the district court in Austin ruled in favor of the claimants, forty-seven landowners, most of whom were well-known Tejano *rancheros*.[29]

Gil Zárate y Bayarena's claim, La Blanca (1835), consisting of five leagues of land in north central Hidalgo County, was also denied by the Bourland Commission. The commission refused to recommend the claim to the legislature on the grounds that the claimant had initiated a settlement, but had abandoned it after making only a few improvements.[30] Under the 1901 act, the state of Texas instituted suit against those holding land under this grant. James B. Wells defended the suit, resulting in a judgment in which the district court of Travis County confirmed the grant to six leading Anglo ranchers.[31] It is unclear how these ranchers acquired the land. It is possible that realizing the claim had been rejected earlier by the Bourland Commission, they bought undivided interests from the original claimants and/or squatted on the land as they moved their herds from place to place. Documents in the papers of lawyers for Richard King and Mifflin Kenedy indicate that, in fact, these ranchers actively acquired undivided interests in land grants that had not been adjudicated, and often for relatively small amounts of money that were less than most regular sales of land within the same grant.

The courts also confirmed another seven grants that had been recommended initially by the commissioners, but not confirmed by the state legislature in 1851 and 1852.[32] Due to the loss of the original records of the Bourland Commission, the loss of the legislative committee report that examined the commissioners' recommendations, and a lack of social or legal histories of these grants, it is not possible at this time to assess why confirmation did not take place in 1851 and 1852.[33] A possible hypothesis is that the original Mexican claimants vacated the grants and Anglo newcomers squatted on the land and/or acquired *derechos.*

Interestingly, six land grants had to be adjudicated and validated by both a court and the legislature of the state. In the Lower Valley, the Ballí claim to Padre Island suffered this fate.[34] It is not clear why this sort of double confirmation took place in these cases. Perhaps the claimants did not hold the grant as original grantees, but rather as purchasers of undivided interests or as holders under the legal doctrine of adverse possession. Consequently, their rights were not as secure. Further study would be necessary to determine the status of their holdings and the reasons for the lengthy and duplicate confirmation process.

Texas courts originally rejected only two claims. One of these, the claim for the *ejidos,* or commons, of Reynosa in Hidalgo County, rejected outright by the Bourland Commission in 1851, was eventually overturned after considerable litigation. Initially, two separate courts agreed with the commissioners' judgment that the *ejido* lands reverted to the Mexican government when the old town of Reynosa was broken up, and that Mexico claimed the land in October of 1836, when Mexicans bought it. But as a result of winning its independence in March 1836, Texas claimed the land so that (the logic goes) the Mexicans had no right to it. Obviously, this case was a travesty of justice because Texas never had effective control over the Trans-Nueces prior to 1848. Following legislative confirmation under the 1901 act, the state sued the Tejano claimants to recover the two leagues, but lost in the appeals court and state supreme court.[35] A claim for a *porción* in the jurisdiction of Revilla (Guerrero), downriver from Laredo, became only the second claim to be rejected by the courts. The reason for this decision is unknown.[36]

Long after the completion of the work of the Bourland Commission and subsequent validation and confirmation by the state legislature and the courts, fifteen land grants, all of them *porciones*, were adjudicated and confirmed by special legislation. Eleven of these confirmations involved Laredo *porciones*, all of which were approved by the state legislature on March 31, 1921. Only one of these grants had been originally recommended by the commissioners in 1851. Because of the limited information in the General Land Office files and in the House of Representatives *Journal*, where the bill (H.R. 496) originated, it is not clear why these *porciones* had not been adjudicated earlier. However, the notes on *porciones* 34 and 57, two of the eleven *porciones*, state that these grants had been vacated, probably due to Indian attacks, which were common in Laredo in the late colonial era. This led to the commissioners' decision not to recommend validation.[37] It is likely that the other grants had a similar history and determination. Then, why were they finally confirmed in 1921? It would appear that equity dictated this result, in view of the fact that people continued to hold onto the land well into the twentieth century.

After 1921, four other *porciones* received legislative adjudication and confirmation. *Porciones* 39 and 40 in the jurisdiction of Guerrero (formerly Revilla) had evidently never been adjudicated, despite the fact, the Bourland Commission wrote, that they were "older and subsisting grants" than those of 1767. They were finally confirmed by the legislature on March 25, 1927. The third *porción*, also in Guerrero, had been recommended in 1855, but evidently the legislature took no action. As a result, it too was validated and confirmed at a late date—March 11, 1930. The last *porción* to be validated and confirmed by the legislature was *Porción* 69 in the jurisdiction of Mier, which received confirmation on June 16, 1965.[38] Again, it is likely that as the lands in these grants were held by either descendants or others in good faith, equity demanded their approval.

Despite the availability of the Bourland Commission, the state courts, and the legislature, twenty-four land grants in south Texas, such as Juan Garza Díaz's grant, Vargas, and Joseph Antonio Cantú's *Porción* 55 in Hidalgo County, were never adjudicated.[39] Although the reasons are unknown, a few theories can be advanced. It is possible that the holders of the grants temporarily vacated the land, and therefore they missed the commissioners. It is also possible that the expense of hiring a lawyer to seek confirmation through either the courts or the legislature was too prohibitive. Some claimants might not have wanted to pursue adjudication, believing or knowing that the grant was subject to challenge. What is important to note, however, is that in these cases people continued to hold land and to make transactions that they recorded in the county where the land was located. So while the state of Texas has no knowledge of the land because no record of title and patent exists in the General Land Office, the lands are of record in the county to this very day.[40]

CONCLUSION

Early Mexican–Anglo contacts in the Lower Río Grande Valley of Texas produced conflict over land claims, even before the all-important matter of land-grant adjudication had taken place under the direction of the state government. As illustrated herein, some of these conflicts involved Anglo newcomers who opposed continuation of Tejano landownership on the basis of the inherent right of United States dominion as a result of the war with Mexico. Others took advantage of the threat of war to acquire land at very cheap prices. Still, there were others who, through purchase and the use of the courts, sought to obtain lands already claimed by Tejanos, such as the Cavazos García lands in the Espíritu Santo grant and the Chilipitín grant. Mexicans did what they could to prevent losses by resorting to the courts, but the courts were new and based on Anglo law. While not always winning these battles in the courts, Tejanos clearly were intent on holding their ground. They could not be accused of being passive, as Anglo newcomers challenged them to rich pasturelands and *porciones* that had sustained their way of life for several generations.

Regardless of how newcomers acquired land or *derechos* to land grants, formal validation of land titles was a pressing issue, and one that the state of Texas addressed almost concurrently with rise of a territorial movement in the Lower Valley. Contrary to popular history, the adjudicatory process concerning land grants in the Trans-Nueces was generally quick and it favored Mexican land tenure. In the vast majority of the Spanish and Mexican land grants located in south Texas, the state acted swiftly to validate land-grant claims presented to the commissioners in 1851 and 1852. Later, the state courts adjudicated claims at three different times in the period from 1860 to 1901. Thus, by 1852 the legislature confirmed 209 claims, with only a handful of outright rejections. The state courts validated an additional sixty-seven claims. The courts rejected only two claims. In addition, in the 1920s the legislature confirmed fifteen additional claims, mostly of Laredo *porciones.* As noted above, special circumstances prevailed in that area, resulting in this late adjudication. Equity, however, favored Tejano landholders for the most part. In the end, only twenty-four land grants were never adjudicated, and for sundry reasons. In sum, Mexican landholders, for the most part, successfully pressed their claims to the nearly 350 land grants located in the region. This shows that, by and large, Tejano landholders decided to cast their luck in Texas and not return to Mexico. This insured the persistence of a Tejano social and economic legacy that remains alive to this day in south Texas.

Obviously, Tejanos could not protect their claims without resorting to American lawyers and other friends who understood the new legal system. Some proved to be loyal friends whose fees were well earned, while others preyed on them. Well-known men, such as Stephen Powers and Edward Dougherty, evidently profited from the validation proceedings by receiving land as a fee for representing claimants before the commissioners.[41] In short, except for individual cases in which newcomers acquired certain interests in land grants and Anglo lawyers profited from defending land-grant claimants before the Bourland Commission and the courts, the bulk of the Tejano landholders maintained control of the land in the initial period of incorporation. The lack of free land, a condition that resulted from extensive Spanish and Mexican settlement, meant that new settlers would have to acquire land from Tejanos for whom landownership was essential to a ranching economy—an economy that gained importance as time went on and helped to nurture the Tejano identity.

CHAPTER SIX

A CASE STUDY OF TEJANO LAND TENURE IN HIDALGO COUNTY, TEXAS, 1848–1900

As noted above, land-grant adjudication by the state of Texas resulted in the confirmation of the vast majority of *mejicano* claims to Spanish and Mexican land grants. Once this had occurred, newcomers from the United States, Mexico, and Europe pressed their efforts to gain land from the original grantees and their descendants because prior to confirmation it had been too risky to purchase rights to land grants that were, in essence, in a state of limbo. The displacement of Mexican *ranchero* landholders was a complicated process because it involved social, economic, and even political forces. Yet substantial Tejano landholdings in much of the Lower Valley persisted for a considerable time after the Mexican–American War. One way of understanding the changes in land tenure is to examine, quantitatively and qualitatively, the dynamics involved in a particular place and over a significant period of time. With this in mind, I offer the following case study of Hidalgo County to demonstrate how landholding changed during the first half-century of American rule, a process of change in land tenure that was more complex than commonly realized. This chapter then describes and analyzes landholding patterns among Mexicans, Anglos, Europeans, persons of mixed Hispanic-Anglo and European ancestry, and Blacks. For our purpose here, I am more concerned with understanding how Hispanics became minority landholders in their native land and the pace of their displacement. Subsequent chapters offer a complete discussion of the overall effects of the growth of the commercial ranching economy and of other developments on Tejano landholders.

COMPARATIVE LANDHOLDING IN HIDALGO COUNTY, 1852–1870

During most of the period from 1852 to 1870, Mexicans made up the largest group of landowners in Hidalgo County, and their rate of landholding exceeded the combined landholding of Anglos, Europeans, and other ethnic and racial groups. As noted in Table 6.1, nearly 80 percent of all landholders were of Mexican descent during this time. Their number increased from 41 in 1852 to 116 in 1865. Yet by 1870 only 79 Mexican landholders appear on the tax roll, which appears to be missing a few pages (although the statistical summary at the end of the tax document is evidently complete). The reason for this decline is not clear, although a considerable number of the smallest landowners were no longer holding land. Their displacement reflected the effects of consolidation among larger landholders as the pace of commercial ranching quickened.

The number of non-Mexican owners grew from thirteen in 1852 to twenty in 1870, and the amount of land claimed by these settlers varied considerably during this period. Table 6.2 shows that Anglo and European newcomers claimed 16.5 percent of the land in 1852, a mere four years after the end of the Mexican-American War, although they constituted less than 5 percent of the population in the county.[1] By the mid-1860s Anglos and Europeans owned approximately half of the land in the county. It is likely that the unsettled conditions during the Civil War years fostered this anomaly in landholding that favored new settlers quickly acquiring land. As the data for the postwar years show, this was a temporary setback for *mejicano* landholders. The Anglo share of the land in the county declined from 26.8 percent in 1865 to a more moderate 14.6 percent in 1870. At the same time, the share owned by Europeans also decreased, but not as sharply. What all of this means is that the few Anglo and European newcomers, who arrived early, made determined efforts to acquire land quickly, but they could not entirely dispossess the Mexicans, the more numerous and older settlers.

A number of factors facilitated Anglo and European acquisition of land in south Texas in the 1850s and 1860s. Merchants and steamboat operators, like Charles Stillman, Richard King, Mifflin Kenedy, José San Román, and others operating out of Brownsville, made handsome profits during these years, which they invested in lands. Also, Anglos had actively worked to create the new county governments and they controlled key political offices. These circumstances made it relatively easy for them to take advantage of the largely Spanish-speaking Tejanos. Without native Spanish-speaking lawyers and judges, Mexicans resorted to hiring Anglo lawyers, whose fees sometimes were paid in land but oftentimes in money obtained from the sale of livestock and other "prod-

Table 6.1 Landholders in Hidalgo County, by Ethnicity, 1852–1900

	Mexican		Others		Total Owners
	No.	%	*No.*	%	*No.*
1852	39	75	13	25	52
1855	41	82	9[a]	18	50
1865	115	84	22	16	137
1870	79	79.8	20	20.2	99
1875	137	88.4	18	11.6	155
1880	193	87.7	30	12.3	220
1885	254	86.7	39	13.3	293
1890	364	86.3	58	15.7	422
1895	260	83.3	62	16.7	312
1900	363	83.3	73	16.7	436

Source: Hidalgo County, *Tax Rolls*, 1852, 1855, 1865, 1870, 1875, 1880, 1885, 1890, 1895, 1900.

[a] Excludes 2 landowners whose ethnicity could not be determined due to the illegible writing in the manuscript of the tax rolls.

Table 6.2 Percentage of Land Held in Hidalgo County, by Ethnicity of Landholders, 1852–1900

Year	Mexican	Anglo	European	Black	Blend
1852	83.5	6.1	10.4	—	—
1865	48.7	26.8	24.5	.5	—
1870	62.2	14.6	22.6	[a]	[a]
1875	72.2	15.9	12.3	[a]	[a]
1880	73.7	20.5	4.5	1.3	[a]
1885	40.0	38.0	19.7	1.4	[a]
1890	38.5	38.2	22.2	[a]	[a]
1895	33.6	50.0	16.0	—	—
1900	29.0	57.5	7.4	—	6.1

Source: Hidalgo County, *Tax Rolls*, 1852, 1865, 1870, 1875, 1880, 1885, 1890, 1895, 1900. There is a gap in the records from 1860 to 1864, probably due to the Civil War, so the 1865 data might not be as precise as it should be.

[a] Less than 1 percent.

ucts of the country." Likewise, the turmoil of the Civil War offered opportunities for both Anglo and European newcomers, who gambled on acquiring land from Tejanos.[2]

In the mid-1850s, Black landholders appeared in the county, although they never became numerous and eventually most intermingled with Tejano settlers. The origin of this group was the settlement of a handful of mostly Southern whites who had Black or mulatto wives. This community began in 1855, when John F. Webber, a native of Vermont who had lived near Austin with his Black wife and children, purchased two leagues of land in the Agostadero del Gato, a five-league grant located in southeastern Hidalgo County along the Río Grande. Other newcomers who found themselves in the same situation as Webber joined his settlement, which appropriately became known as Webber's Rancho. These settlers farmed some of the land and called themselves farmers, but they generally herded small numbers of livestock. The racially mixed community's share of the land was less than 1 percent of the county's total acreage.[3]

Between 1852 and 1870, all four major ethnic and racial groups of landholders gravitated toward owning large tracts of land (four thousand acres or more) instead of small parcels. This was particularly true of Anglos and Europeans, but to a large extent true of Mexicans as well. As noted in Table 6.3, a majority of the Anglos and Europeans owned more than four thousand acres of land.

The Mexican pattern of landholding changed gradually during this nearly twenty-year period (1852–1870). At first Mexicans held the land in common, so that in the years prior to 1865 one individual, usually the family patriarch, claimed the entire tract, either a *porción* or a larger land grant. Common landholding meant that the descendants of the original land grantee or a subsequent buyer continued in possession of the land without any formal partition. (These grants were not community grants as in California and New Mexico, where groups of Hispanic settlers or Indians received a grant.) A typical example of continuity in common landholding can be found in testimony, given to the Bourland Commission in 1851, that *Porción* 51 (1767) in present-day Hidalgo County was a grant to the grandfather of the applicant, Juan N. Bocanegra, and that the grant was occupied and cultivated by the applicant and other heirs.[4]

Other cases support the assertion that land was held in common without any partition. In 1852 Rafael Flores García was listed as the sole taxpayer on two tracts, *Porción* 41 having 4,870 acres and Los Guajes, a Spanish grant, 11,070 acres—probably because he was the patriarch, as evidenced by his appearance before the Bourland Commission in 1851 as the applicant for those tracts. In 1865, ten individuals with the surname Flores claimed land in equal shares in

Los Guajes, indicating that the grant had been divided among relatives. Since there is no evidence of a partition suit, the division was probably informal.[5]

There were several reasons for the persistence of common landholding in south Texas. In the Spanish and Mexican period, formal partitions were rare and generally few sales were made to outside persons. Moreover, sales that were made during this time were typically of *derechos*, or undivided interests to the whole tract. Some persons did not bother with legal transactions, which would have had to be conducted in the *villas* of the Río Grande. In fact, attorneys were not always available in the frontier towns to draw up the proper documents. For example, José Francisco Guerra Chapa of Reynosa, who appeared before the Bourland Commission in 1851 to present his claims, died in September of 1853, leaving a wife and three children as heirs as well as several grandchildren who were the heirs of one of his daughters who had died previously. His heirs asserted that he had made an oral will prior to his death, specifying how his lands were to be distributed among the heirs. On July 9, 1857, the heirs filed an agreement in Spanish ratifying Guerra Chapa's oral will at the courthouse of Hidalgo County. The agreement covered eight Reynosa *porciones*, none of which were grants to Guerra Chapa. Evidently, he had acquired these lands by purchase over a considerable period of time. The one grant made to Guerra Chapa, Loma Blanca, was not even included in the agreement, but it was later adjudicated in the district court of Starr County and confirmed to his heirs.[6] In this case, all of the heirs collectively owned a large number of tracts. However, partition suits of lands became more common as the number of owners grew and the commercial ranching economy placed more pressure on landholders to sell their *derechos*.

The tradition of common landholding accounts for very few *mejicanos* owning or claiming acreages of less than two thousand acres. For example, as noted in Table 6.3, in 1852 only seven out of forty-one Mexican landholders (17 percent) owned less than two thousand acres. In time, however, Mexican landholders followed a practice of breaking down the larger units of land, either through inheritance or sales of land.

However, as noted in Table 6.3, by 1865 the pattern of widespread large common landholdings had changed, as 74 out of 116 (73.8 percent) of the Mexican landholders were assessed on less than two thousand acres of land, leaving only 42 out of 116 (26.2 percent) still claiming two thousand or more acres. The latter class of landholders represented *ranchero* elites of the county. For the most part, their ownership of the land would persist for at least one or two more generations. In 1870, forty-two out of seventy-nine (slightly more than 50 percent) of the Mexican landholders owned less than two thousand acres.

Non-Mexican landholders preferred to acquire entire tracts, usually a league

Table 6.3 Landholders in Hidalgo County, by Size of Holdings and Ethnicity, 1852–1870[a]

	Class							
Mexicans	1	2	3	4	5	6	7	8
1852	—	4	2	1	5	4	6	19
1855	—	3	2	1	7	1	7	20
1865	30	13	18	13	8	5	17	12
1870	6	8	16	12	7	7	11	12
	Class							
Others	1	2	3	4	5	6	7	8
1852	—	—	—	—	1	—	2	10
1855	—	—	1	—	—	—	—	8
1865	—	1	1	1	1	—	3	15
1870	—	2	1	1	3	—	2	11

Source: Hidalgo County, *Tax Rolls*, 1852, 1855, 1865, 1870.

[a] Class 1 equals 50–199 acres, Class 2 equals 200–499, Class 3 equals 500–999, Class 4 equals 1,000 to 1,999, Class 5 equals 2,000–2,999, Class 6 equals 3,000–3,999, Class 7 equals 4,000–5,999, and Class 8 equals more than 6,000.

of land (4,428 acres) or a *porción*. In 1870, only four out of the twenty non-Hispanic landholders claimed less than 2,000 acres of land. Also, the number of heirs who inherited and therefore had to divide the land might not have been as many for Anglos and Europeans as for Mexicans, because the Mexicans had been on the land longer and they had extended families as opposed to immigrants who arrived single.

Despite the gradual development of a small class of Hispanic and non-Hispanic landholders owning tens of thousands of acres and ranching on a large scale, the acquisition of the intermediate and large Spanish grants (over two leagues of land) generally did not take place at this time. However, in the case of John Young, John McAllen and his wife, Salome Ballí McAllen (whose first marriage was to Young and lasted until his death), there was a systematic attempt to acquire the Santa Anita, one of the largest Spanish grants located in the county. Young had previously initiated the process by acquiring *derechos* to this grant from the Domínguez family members, who were heirs to the grant. His first acquisition took place in late 1849, when he obtained from Doña Guadalupe Domínguez a one-half league interest that she had inherited from her father, Estanislado Domínguez. Ten years later, Young acquired Sixto Domínguez's undivided one-fourth interest in the grant after a series of transactions involving lawyers at Brownsville who had been parties to the separatist or territorial movement in 1850. Between 1858 and 1861 Young and his wife, Salomé Ballí Young, acquired undivided rights from four other Domínguez heirs. After Young's death, John McAllen and Salomé Ballí McAllen continued to add to their holdings, buying up the balance of the Santa Anita. According to a local historian, Florence Johnson Scott, Salomé Ballí McAllen wanted the land because it had originally been granted to one of her relatives. By 1880 the McAllens had acquired a large chunk of the Santa Anita—about 65,420 acres of the total grant of 93,000.[7]

The boom in stockraising that took place in the 1870s and early 1880s did not immediately alter the stable pattern of landholding among the five population groups who claimed land in Hidalgo County, although there were perceptible changes. As noted in Tables 6.1 and 6.2, Mexicans remained the most numerous landowners as well as the dominant landowners in terms of acreage owned. Mexicans claimed 72.2 percent of the land in 1875 and 73.7 percent of the land in 1880. The share held by Anglos rose from 15.9 percent in 1875 to 20.5 percent in 1880. They increased their share largely at the expense of Europeans, whose share dropped from 12.3 percent in 1875 to only 4.5 percent in 1880.

The fluctuation in European land tenure in the last quarter of the nineteenth century reflected several factors. First, European immigration to Hidalgo County was practically insignificant. Very few settled in the county, and those who did tended to be merchants, professionals, or artisans. It is true that a merchant or two eventually acquired land. For example, Manuel Samano, a Spanish merchant in the town of Hidalgo, claimed two tracts totaling 1,700 acres in the 1890s and engaged in stockraising on a small scale.[8] Second, some Europeans, like their Anglo counterparts, held on to the land for a brief time and then sold it. For example, Leonardo Manso, a Spaniard, was one of the first non-Mexicans to claim land in Hidalgo County at the time of its organization in 1852, a five-league tract in the Llano Grande grant, where he engaged in stockraising. By 1875 his acreage had declined to one league, and five years later he owned only one-half of that amount. John B. Bourbois, a Belgian immigrant, claimed a *porción* from 1860 to 1880 and half of an adjoining *porción* in the latter year, both in the southwestern part of county. Although the combined tracts totaled 7,875 acres, the value of his livestock was only three hundred dollars in 1880. Before 1880 he had not been assessed on any livestock. A farmer and artisan, Bourbois evidently did not ranch on his land, although he may have leased it to others. By 1885 Bourbois had disposed of his landholdings.[9] Third, European landholders who stayed in the county married Mexican women, so in the next generation the land was owned by their children of

Table 6.4 Landholders in Hidalgo County, by Size of Holdings and Ethnicity, 1875–1885[a]

	Class							
Mexicans	1	2	3	4	5	6	7	8
1875	15	25	22	28	8	5	16	18
1880	26	35	31	33	16	3	25	24
1885	54	52	39	43	22	5	21	18
	Class							
Others	1	2	3	4	5	6	7	8
1875	—	—	3	1	5	2	2	5
1880	—	1	3	—	7	1	5	13
1885	2	3	4	1	9	5	10	5

Source: Hidalgo County, *Tax Rolls*, 1875, 1880, 1885.

[a] Class 1 equals 50–199 acres, Class 2 equals 200–499, Class 3 equals 500–999, Class 4 equals 1,000–1,999, Class 5 equals 2,000–2,999, Class 6 equals 3,000–3,999, Class 7 equals 4,000–5,999, and Class 8 equals more than 6,000.

mixed ancestry, or "blends." The best example of this is the case of Salomé Ballí and her two children. Upon the death of her first husband, her son, John B. Young, inherited one-half undivided interest in his father's estate. During her second marriage to John McAllen, she bore a second son, James B. McAllen. Her first son and John McAllen conducted the ranching operations as a partnership until 1896, but a partition of the property was not effected until 1907. By 1900 James B. McAllen also owned land, which he had inherited from his mother, who died in 1897.[10] In this manner a small number of children of Mexican-Anglo or Mexican-European descent acquired land.

In the case of Blacks, after the early acquisitions of land in the mid-1850s there tended to be no other purchases. As a result, the initial large tracts became divided and subdivided among descendants, most of whom married among themselves or with Mexican women, and some sales were made to newcomers who joined the mixed community.[11]

The 1870s saw a continuing growth in the number of landholders among all groups, particularly among Mexicans and Anglos; a further erosion of large landholdings (more than two thousand acres) among Mexicans; and a persistence in large landholdings among Anglos and Europeans. As noted in Table 6.1, Mexican landholders increased from 79 in 1870 to 137 in 1875 and to 193 in 1880. Considering that the Mexicans' share of landownership remained fairly constant during the decade, it is clear that large landholdings were being broken down through sale or inheritance. As noted in Table 6.4, the result is that whereas before 1865 about 50 percent of Mexican landholders claimed two thousand or more acres, by 1880 only 20 percent claimed that amount. More and more, Mexicans purchased or received through inheritance relatively small tracts of land (under two thousand acres).

FACTORS CONTRIBUTING TO THE GROWTH IN THE NUMBER OF TEJANO LANDOWNERS, 1875–1900

Two reasons explain the rapid growth in the number of Mexican landowners. First, the stockraising boom encouraged some individuals to buy land. It appears that a number of new *rancheros*—some of whom were also grocers or merchants—did well enough to purchase land instead of leasing it in order to continue their ranching operations. One or two cases illustrate this point. By 1870 Julio Guzmán grazed cattle and horses along the Río Grande in the vicinity of the Santa Ana grant. In 1880, this *ranchero*'s personal wealth totaled 1,416 dollars, most of it in livestock since he owned no land. In 1885, he claimed 10,860 acres of land in the same locale. The value of Guzmán's personal and real property amounted to 8,395 dollars, of which 60 percent represented the value of his land and the balance the value of his livestock. According to the tax assessor's report of 1896, Guzmán had only inherited 111 acres in two parcels, out of six parcels of land totaling 6,244 acres. Although his acreage and the value of his livestock declined after 1885, he still owned 3,173 acres in 1900.[12] A self-made *ranchero*, Guzmán evidently invested his profits in the purchase of land during the good years of the expanding commercial ranching economy.

Another new *ranchero* who achieved considerable prominence in Hidalgo County was Macedonio Vela. Vela had immigrated from neighboring Reynosa, Mexico, in 1857, during the wars of the Reforma. An industrious man, he worked as ranch foreman at a site called El Tule, evidently near the old river settlement of Peñitas. He then started ranching near the McAllens' Santa Anita ranch, in the center of the county at a place called Buena Vista. In 1865, Vela reported the value of his livestock as 2,300 dollars. Five years later he still owned no land, but his livestock had increased in value to 4,995 dollars. About this time he purchased his first league of land for 1,000 dollars from John and Salomé Ballí McAllen, and he steadily increased his stockraising activities. His *rancho*, known as Laguna Seca, grew into a community of ranchers, *vaqueros*, and laborers, with a store, school, and post office. According to family tradition, Vela mounted a cattle drive to Dodge City, Kansas, in about 1878, although San Antonio was the preferred marketplace for Vela and his brothers, who also founded large and prosperous ranches in the county during the same time. In the meantime, he proceeded to acquire additional land. Between 1880 and 1885 his landholdings rose from 6,642 acres to 31,456 acres. By 1896 Vela had purchased six tracts of land, totaling 52,000 acres, on which he raised large herds of cattle, horses, and mules. Vela raised the latter from forty different herds of mares, shipping donkeys to Cuba from the ports of Corpus Christi and Galveston.[13] These examples show that Mexican immigrants and landless Tejanos aspired to and developed their own *ranchos*. This was particularly true during the period of recovery and boom in the ranching economy that lasted from about 1852 to the 1880s.

A second reason why the number of Mexican landowners multiplied is that as older *rancheros* died their wives and children partitioned the land among themselves, usually informally, or after ranching in partnership for a period of time, they opted to sell. For example, in 1895 Macaria Pérez and her four children received varying amounts of land following the death of Juan Sabas Pérez, a Camargo *ranchero* who owned about 3,500 acres in three separate tracts in northern Hidalgo County. Pérez, who had obtained his land by purchase, had been moderately successful in ranching in the county for over thirty years.[14]

Land sales facilitated the growth in the number of stockraisers and landholders. As noted above, upstart *rancheros* benefited tremendously because land was readily available for acquisition at very cheap prices, even during the height of the ranching boom. Typically, sales occurred in cases involving widows who did not live on the land, or persons who were unable to manage their estates due to disabilities of one kind or another, such as lunacy, or because they were minors; and when no will was left under which to distribute the real estate. For example, when the widow Maxima Longoria de Ochoa, who was childless, was declared a lunatic in early 1885, her guardians disposed of her real and personal property to pay for the expenses of caring for her. On November 8, 1887, the well-known rancher Ramón Vela purchased a tract from her estate for 150 pesos in Mexican silver coin.[15]

New *rancheros* arose as they inherited land from one or both of their parents. For instance, María del Refugio Cavazos Gutiérrez inherited a large acreage from the estate of José Narciso Cavazos in the San Salvador del Tule grant. For many years Refugio and his co-heirs held the tract, about 53,136 acres, in common and engaged in stockraising. By 1896, however, three heirs held the land individually and in about equal acreages.[16]

Large land units still held in common were sometimes put up for sale, especially by the descendants of land grantees who were not raising livestock or otherwise using the land. The buyers were sometimes men entering the ranching business for the first time, while others had been involved for a long time. For example, the heirs of José Francisco Guerra Chapa, the grantee of Loma Blanca (1831) in the northwest corner of Hidalgo County, began to dispose of their undivided rights in 1873 by making sales of large parcels of land to groups of Mexican buyers. The heirs, who lived at Matamoros, evidently had no personal use for the land, although the confirmation of title in 1872 by the district court of Starr County recognized that they had been using the land and paying taxes on it for the last forty years.[17] When one of the Cavazos Gutiérrez heirs died in the late 1880s, the four children inherited an estate consisting "of about 10,000 acres undivided interest in San Salvador del Tule." However, their father, who was the guardian, claimed that "he [did] not [have] actual possession of more than 2,000 acres minus Moises [Cárdenas's] share who [was] no longer a minor." Twice he petitioned the court to sell the land "because they derive no income from said lands," and he needed money to support, care, and educate his children. On May 10, 1900, he informed the court that he had sold 7,488 acres to Mrs. Henrietta M. King.[18]

LANDHOLDING IN HIDALGO COUNTY, 1880–1900

After 1880, land tenure among the five cultural groups in Hidalgo County experienced considerable change, resulting in a significant deterioration in Mexican landholding and a corresponding expansion in Anglo landholding. Table 6.2 shows that by 1885 Mexicans no longer owned a majority of the land in the county. By that year their share of total acreage had dropped to 40 percent and it steadily decreased to 29 percent in 1900. The principal beneficiaries of the decline in Mexican landholding were Anglos, whose rate of landholding increased from 20.5 percent in 1880 to 38 percent in 1885, to 57.5 percent in 1900.

CAUSES OF THE DECLINE IN LANDHOLDING AMONG MEXICANS, 1880–1900

What explains the decline of the Mexicans and the rise of Anglos as the dominant landholding group? A variety of economic and social factors played a major role in the loss of Tejano-owned land. As discussed below, prosperous times enticed Anglos and a few Europeans to engage in ranching activities in the region. Thus, men like D. R. Fant, William Sprague, and Edward C. Lasater, who made their appearance in the region in the late 1880s and 1890s,

Table 6.5 Landholders in Hidalgo County, by Size of Holdings and Ethnicity, 1890–1900[a]

	Class							
Mexicans	1	2	3	4	5	6	7	8
1890	106	87	63	49	14	10	15	20
1895	79	54	41	30	15	10	14	17
1900	177	59	46	32	14	9	11	15
	Class							
Others	1	2	3	4	5	6	7	8
1890	5	4	4	1	9	1	9	25
1895	7	10	5	6	7	2	4	21
1900	6	11	4	6	6	4	10	26

Source: Hidalgo County, *Tax Rolls*, 1890, 1895, 1900.

[a] Class 1 equals 50–199 acres, Class 2 equals 200–499, Class 3 equals 500–999, Class 4 equals 1,000–1,999, Class 5 equals 2,000–2,999, Class 6 equals 3,000–3,999, Class 7 equals 4,000–5,999, and Class 8 equals more than 6,000.

acquired by lease and purchase massive tracts of grasslands, particularly the Spanish and Mexican land grants of intermediate size. The land purchases of Fant offer a good illustration of this process. By 1885 Fant claimed two tracts, one containing 37,464 acres and the other 9,344 acres in the northern sector of Hidalgo County. In the next five years, he acquired all or part of nine other tracts, totaling nearly 90,000 acres of land.[19] Gradually, there was a rise in the number of Anglos who claimed land in Hidalgo County: fourteen in 1875, thirty-seven in 1890, and fifty-three in 1900. Twenty-five percent of the Anglos did not reside in the county, but most were Texans, like Lasater and Fant, who engaged in stockraising elsewhere in the state.[20]

As discussed in chapter 8, below, the deterioration in stock prices and wool that began in the early 1880s, and the environmental calamities that affected the region in the late 1880s and 1890s, combined to break Mexican *rancheros*, particularly small producers and those who had borrowed extensively. These circumstances facilitated land loss among undercapitalized *mejicanos* who did not have the luxury of waiting until stock prices rebounded in the late 1890s.

A further consideration is that a growing number of Mexican landowners in Hidalgo County continued to acquire land either by inheritance or through purchase. While not always buying from Mexican landowners, it may have been easier to buy from them because older *rancheros* were hard pressed due to

Table 6.6 Manner in which Land Was Acquired in Hidalgo County, by Ethnicity and Residency, 1896[a]

Ethnicity and Residency Status	Inheritance	Purchase	Both	Other
Mexican Resident	105	90	9	4
Anglo Resident[b]	5	11	—	2
Mexican Nonresident	16	13	3	—
Anglo Nonresident[b]	3	6	1	—

Source: Hidalgo County, *Tax Rolls*, 1896.
[a] Excludes a small number of persons who did not render an assessment to the tax office.
[b] Includes other non-Mexican landholders. Most, however, were Anglo.

the bad market conditions. Also, the more powerful Anglo ranchers who had liquid reserves or who could tap lenders were not willing to give up at this time, making it harder to buy or lease land from them.

Land sales, however, definitely accelerated. Table 6.6 points out, for example, that in 1896, the only year in which the county tax assessor recorded the manner by which a person acquired possession of land, fully 50 percent of the resident Tejano landowners had obtained land through inheritance. About 48 percent had received land by deed, which indicates that the transaction was probably by purchase. In a small number of cases, 9 out of 199 individuals, Mexicans obtained land under both kinds of transactions. Among Mexican landholders who did not reside in the county, 16 out of 32 (50 percent) also acquired land through inheritance. While some Anglos also inherited land, they were twice as likely to hold land under a deed of purchase than through inheritance.[21]

Thus, the alienation of Mexican-owned land was an ongoing process. In the 1870s and 1880s, it accelerated in response to favorable market conditions in ranching, population growth, partition suits, and traditional inheritance practices. The deterioration in the prices of cattle and wool, which began in 1883, and a prolonged economic recession that followed in the early 1890s combined to produce further sales of land as well as tax and mortgage foreclosures. Individuals—Tejano and non-Tejano—with access to capital usually acquired the foreclosed land. Toward the end of the nineteenth century, the King ranch's access to creditors allowed it to obtain foreclosed properties, enlarging their already vast holdings. Also, Anglo ranchers sometimes lent money to Tejanos and, when the latter could not make their payments, the lenders foreclosed on them.[22] The result was a long, gradual process in which Mexicans lost their land.

To make matters worse, the percentage of Mexicans holding large acreages declined considerably after 1875, while the overall number of Mexicans holding land increased. As noted in Table 6.1, Mexican landholders claiming large land tracts of four thousand acres or more declined from 30 percent in 1875 to 14 percent in 1890, to 11.2 percent in 1900. At the same time, the number of Mexican landholders rose from 79 in 1870 to 137 in 1875, to 193 in 1880, to 254 in 1885, and to 364 in 1890. A temporary decline to 260 Mexican landholders occurred in 1895—evidently a correction in the rapid erosion of Mexican land tenure as some landholders, especially Anglos, consolidated their properties at the expense of small *rancheros.* In 1900 the number of Mexican landholders rebounded to its prior peak, reaching 363. The significance of this rapid growth in Mexican landholders—slightly more than a 500 percent increase between 1870 and 1890—is that Mexicans acquired smaller tracts of land at a time when ranching necessitated larger and larger units of land to be successful. As noted in Table 6.2, in 1875 only 25.8 percent of the total number of Mexican landholders claimed small tracts of between 50 and 499 acres. By 1900, as Tables 6.1 and 6.5 show, 54.1 percent of the total number of Mexican landholders held similar units of land. In absolute numbers this means that whereas only forty Mexican landholders claimed between 50 and 499 acres in 1875, the figure had soared to 236 owners in 1900, nearly six times the 1875 number.

While Mexican landholding was increasingly concentrated in small acreages, the evidence indicates that the Anglos continued to hold large tracts. In 1875, thirteen out of fourteen Anglo landholders held two thousand or more acres of land. In 1890, thirty out of thirty-seven claimed the same amount of land. Ten years later (1900), thirty-six out of fifty-three Anglos were assessed on two thousand or more acres. (At the same time, only ten out of fifty-three Anglos owned between 50 and 499 acres.) Clearly, Anglos tended to acquire large parcels of land. As a result, they were in a better position to reenter commercial ranching once it became profitable again at the turn of the century, or to sell their landholdings once the price of land increased.

A critical question, then, is why the number of Mexican landholders increased so dramatically after 1875. The best explanation is a steady rise in the Mexican population, which produced pressures to sell land to new buyers as well as to grant land to descendants. As noted earlier, an egalitarian tradition persisted stubbornly among Mexicans of dividing land equally among heirs. Thus, as each new generation inherited land the unit of land held by the parents was reduced by as many children as they had raised. A perusal of the abstract of title to the Loma Blanca grant shows that the descendants of José Francisco Guerra Chapa took undivided equal rights to the land in 1872. A study of the sales made by his heirs, beginning in 1873, discloses a similar pattern of the new buyers' children inheriting undivided interests that, no matter how small, were in turn sold to other buyers.[23]

Partition suits quickly increased the number of Mexican landholders. Common holdings were not a very practical way of landholding, because with the passage of time the number grew of those individuals who were entitled to undivided interests in the whole land grant. This was especially true in cases in which buyers were not related to the land-grant owners and their descendants and in cases in which purchasers were expanding their landholdings and wished to have their lands surveyed prior to making costly improvements. A partition suit in which the court designated specific shares for individual claimants represented the most common solution to the growing problems presented by common landholdings. A perusal of courthouse records and files of leading Lower Valley lawyers involved in the "land business" discloses a growing number of partitions of land grants in the 1880s and continuing into the early twentieth century.[24]

Partition suits and subsequent sales of lands (both divided and undivided rights) augmented the number of landholders, many of whom ended up owning small tracts. Tax records and wills indicate that in the late nineteenth century this was a fairly common occurrence among Tejano *rancheros*, most of whom owned two, three, or more of these tiny parcels of pasturelands. In time, these very small holdings were also sold. For example, Gregorio Chapa Zamora, a country merchant and small-scale rancher in southwestern Hidalgo County, owned at the time of his death in 1895 three small tracts of land in *Porción* 73, another tract of 124 acres in *porciones* 74 and 75, another 89 acres in *Porción* 74, rights in the *ejidos* of Reynosa and rights to the Lampazitos ranch of "quantity unknown" because they were undivided, and 221 acres in *Porción* 76. The administrator, in his report of the sale of these lands, noted that they "were not a desirable investment" because they were "unimproved, unenclosed, and fit only for grazing," and that they were "undivided and being and forming part of four different large grants (*porciones*)."[25]

CHANGES IN LANDHOLDING AMONG NON-MEXICAN LANDHOLDERS, 1875–1900

The last quarter of the nineteenth century also saw changes in the pattern of land tenure among Europeans, Blacks, and "blends." As noted in Table 6.2, the landholdings of Europeans fluctuated most between 1875 and 1885, probably due to the effect of the boom in stockraising, as both Anglos and Mexicans purchased land to raise stock. However, their position stabilized after 1885. In 1890, Europeans held 22.2 percent of the land in Hidalgo County. Thereafter their holdings declined, so that by 1900 it they held only 7.4 percent of the total. Much of this drop was due to the inheritance of their holdings by Mexican spouses or children. Table 6.2 also shows that Black landownership increased slightly in the early 1880s, but began to decline in 1890. By then the individual tracts owned by Blacks were relatively small in acreage, with few persons owning more than two thousand acres.

As this study of land tenure in Hidalgo County shows, two crucial dynamics were at work in producing changes in landholding traditions even before the ink was dry on the Treaty of Guadalupe Hidalgo. One aspect of the process involved the erosion of the amount of Mexican landownership. The second entailed increasingly greater control of the land by newcomers from Mexico, that is, Mexicans who were likely born in Mexico based on census and other records, as well as new settlers from Europe and the United States.

Essentially, the transfer of land from Mexican landholders occurred in three ways: (1) legitimate inheritance and/or sales of land under varying market conditions; (2) a variety of legal procedures other than private sales between parties, such as foreclosures and sheriff's sales; and (3) extralegal means. The latter process naturally produced the most resentment among the former Mexican landowners, but it is very difficult to document except, in most cases, by oral histories that are not too reliable. The more scrupulous buyers of real estate—both Mexican and non-Mexican—shied away from deception and other legal ruses, paying whatever price the market commanded. *Mejicanos* had a long history of buying and selling land to each other. Men like Julio Guzmán and Florencio Sáenz acquired land in southeastern Hidalgo County largely as a result of their considerable stockraising experience. In fact, Sáenz purchased five separate parcels in the Llano Grande grant, four of them from James B. Wells. These tracts totaled about 15,000 acres. His fifth tract consisted of 653 acres that he bought from Leonardo Manso.[26] Later on, in the 1880s, moderately successful ranchers like Jesús María Vela and Basilio Pérez, who refused to give up ranching even as prices for livestock tumbled, purchased sections of land from railroads along the northwestern boundary of the county. Shortly before 1900, Basilio Pérez displaced a number of small *rancheros* from Loma Blanca, acquiring by purchase nine tracts totalling 4,547 acres, which he then sold in 1897, in one transaction, to Mrs. King for $5,683.75.[27] In some cases—a few, to be sure—Mexicans who were merchants on either side of the Río Grande purchased land from other Mexicans.

While Anglos and Europeans often acquired considerable acreage by purchase, they were not reluctant to use the legal system to control land formerly owned or still claimed by *mejicanos.* Anglo ranchers like King and Kenedy directed their Brownsville lawyers to purchase as many *derechos* as they could find. These lawyers hired agents to locate people who had undivided interests in land grants. The pressure that lawyers and land buyers could apply was probably intense. For instance, James G. Kenedy, son of Mifflin Kenedy, wrote James B. Wells, exhorting him to greater efforts in obtaining a *derecho* that seemed to be slipping away. He urged Wells not to "lose sight of our interests in Mestinas [*sic*][grant], I understand [that] Mrs. Lira has brought suit to recover. Use every means in your power to defeat Mrs. Lira."[28] Without an in-depth study, it is difficult to assess the work of lawyers who defended Mexican land grantees while at the same time representing or assisting Anglo and European purchasers. However, there is evidence that lawyers took advantage of the confusion inherent in the incorporation of lands previously granted to Spanish and Mexican settlers in a new order dominated by Anglo newcomers.[29] Typically, however, Anglos, Europeans, and some *mejicanos* acquired property at sheriffs' sales, when *ranchero* landholders became delinquent in their tax payments. In Hidalgo County, as early as 1854 the commissioners' court discussed the possibility that "some of the lands would have to be sold for taxes due."[30] The early records of the court lack sufficient precision to determine how soon the county exercised its right to sell at auction properties that were delinquent. However, in the 1870s, Sheriff Alexander Leo regularly sold delinquent Tejano properties. Many of the purchasers were county officials, some of whom were Anglo. The sums paid were usually very small and represented the exact amount of taxes due and court costs. For instance, in 1877 Thadeus M. Rhodes, a perennial officeholder (county commissioner and judge), acquired, in a tax sale, a deed to 3,087 acres of land belonging to Doña Josefa Cavazos for the sum of $16.50.[31] This manner of acquiring land was legal, but it worked against Tejanos who were unable to find monies to pay their taxes or to redeem their properties after they were sold by the sheriff.

The more successful merchants usually enjoyed an advantage in having a surplus of capital to invest in land acquisitions. As noted previously, Brownsville merchants were especially active in controlling large tracts of land. Some were purely bent on speculation, while a few actually utilized their land for stockraising or engaged in commercial farming along the delta of the Río Grande.

During the height of the cattle boom, Anglo ranchers from other sections of the state expanded their operations into south Texas. A small number of them, in fact, controlled so much land in the northern half of the county that by the 1890s they had displaced a considerable number of Mexican ranchers not only off the land but also out of stockraising. There is very little evidence that these landless Mexicans leased land from the new Anglo owners. For example, in

1900 Mrs. Henrietta M. King leased two hundred acres for a period of two years to a *ranchero* who earlier had sold her the same tract. This was the only lease that she made on the Loma Blanca grant, although by this time Mrs. King had acquired half of the five-*sitio* grant.[32]

Gross thievery of Tejano-owned land is difficult to prove, but some individuals—usually Anglos—did obtain land from Mexicans through fraud, intimidation, and other illegal means.[33] According to *mejicano* oral tradition, aggressive ranchers, both Mexican and non-Mexican, sometimes acquired land by extending their fences beyond their lands and into someone else's property.[34] Except for cases in which police or court records or other evidence is available, the illegal fencing of land can only be documented through oral history.

Despite all of the changes in landownership, continuity in *mejicano* landownership remained strong. Much of it was due to the good fortune of some *rancheros* that Anglos did not desire certain lands or that the *rancheros* were economically strong enough to resist the inroads of newcomers.[35] In other cases—where large land grants had not been broken down by sale or partition, or where the heirs were few instead of numerous—*mejicanos* persisted in holding onto the land past 1900. For example, Amado Cavazos of La Noria Cardeneña and Refugio Cavazos Gutiérrez of San Manuel, descendants of native-born Tejanos, continued to ranch through the good and bad times, but they too suffered from the aggressive grabs of their more powerful neighbors, such as Mrs. King. Consequently, they adapted their system of landholding. By the 1890s, according to Ramón V. Vela, a descendant of Macedonio Vela, old *rancheros* in the central and northwestern part of the county, such as Jorge J. Cavazos, Arcadio Guerra, Macedonio Vela, and Juan de la Viña Sr., had sharecroppers—many of them former cowboys—growing corn and cotton on their land. Some of the large *ranchos* contained fifteen or more families who worked the land on shares.[36] When stock prices rebounded in the second half of the 1890s, the remaining Tejano ranchers enjoyed a measure of prosperity, for it was difficult for "king cotton" to thrive in the semiarid plains of south Texas.

CONCLUSION

The decline of Tejano landholding in Hidalgo County during the years from 1852 to 1900 was a gradual process that involved multifaceted and sometimes interrelated causes. Among the most important were competition for grasslands, traditional inheritance practices of *mejicanos*, and other social, economic, and political factors. In the early years of American rule, skilled "land lawyers" assisted Brownsville merchants and other capitalists in acquiring large tracts, especially in Cameron, Nueces, and Hidalgo counties. At times they merely speculated, selling to other Anglos as well as to Mexican buyers. Other newcomers followed the lead of Richard King and Mifflin Kenedy, amassing ranching domains and eventually passing on their legacy to Anglo Texans. To be sure, however, Anglo ranchers were few in number because they seldom migrated to the area and they tended to have few children, in contrast to the Mexican *rancheros* who often had large families and other collateral heirs.

By the 1880s most *ranchero* elites, except for a few families like the Velas of Laguna Seca, saw their landholdings dwindle through friendly family partitions and sales. Contrary to popular belief, Mexican landholders were actively involved in selling land to each other and to upstart *rancheros* who had livestock but no land. As the *rancheros*' livestock increased, it was more logical for them to purchase *agostaderos*, or pasturelands, as a measure of security. The cases of Macedonio Vela and Julio Guzmán, among many others, represented this classic rise of new *ranchero* landholders. The good ranching years from about 1870 to 1883 further promoted land sales, while the bad years spanning the mid-1880s and early 1890s accelerated land loss, as Mexican *rancheros* scrambled to pay off debts and taxes by selling some of their holdings, or unable to pay, lost their holdings to foreclosures by lenders and tax sales by the county.

Moreover, as old *rancheros* died, it became more difficult to keep their landholdings intact. In cases where a surviving spouse remained, the ranch holdings continued as one unit, although sometimes a widow would sell her share and that inherited by her children. This was especially true of childless widows, or widows with minors who, unable to manage and administer a ranch, moved back to the old towns of the Lower Valley. Many a guardian also sold the land belonging to his wards—usually his children, grandchildren, or other relatives—to pay taxes and debts of the estate and to pay for the care and education of the children under his or her guardianship. However, because so much land became available for sale during the depressed years of the late nineteenth century, estate administrators and executors as well as guardians wisely preferred to sell livestock rather than land in the hope that prices for pastureland would eventually improve. This occurred in most cases in which the estate was modest in value, say several thousand dollars, and other resources were available to keep the remaining descendants solvent. If an estate had little value, land was readily sold to pay off debts of the estate and/or for the support of minor children and widows.

In cases where a widow and her children continued to operate a ranch, as in the case of Juan Sabas Pérez, subsequent probate proceedings or a partition suit led, in due time, to a ranch of several thousand or several hundred acres becoming a multiplicity of small landholdings. Tracts consisting of small acreages were not conducive to commercial ranching activities. These were eventually sold for a few dollars.

By 1885 Mexicans in Hidalgo County had definitely become "strangers in their native land." At this point, they controlled slightly under 50 percent of the land. Social and economic dynamics had produced considerable land loss at the same time that the number of landholders had increased dramatically. Tejano *rancheros* desperately needed capital to survive the depressed conditions of the 1890s. To stem their complete collapse, they continued to borrow from each other and from border merchants with whom they had dealt before. But the hard times in commerce and ranching dried out the traditional sources of liquid funds. Moreover, few Tejanos could convince San Antonio-based brokers to lend them money because of the risky condition in the marketplace and the fact that many landholders still held land in common. Anglo ranchers faced similar hard economic circumstances, but they could withstand the depression by continuing to borrow until the market improved because most of them were large-scale producers with a history of access to brokers. Others survived by selling some of their land and herds to pay off pressing notes.

The position of Mexican landholders in Hidalgo County rapidly evaporated after the mid-1880s. Prosperous new Anglo ranchers, like Edward Lasater and William P. Sprague, took up the rich prairie lands in the northern part of the county. Smaller but enterprising *rancheros* also grazed herds there, buying vacant lands from railroad companies, public lands from the state of Texas, and surplus lands from ranchers who needed to dispose of some of their properties. By 1890, however, Mexican *rancheros*—descendants of grantees and immigrant owners—held slightly under 40 percent of the land in Hidalgo County.

The 1890s witnessed a further drop in Mexican landholding, as the deepening depression in stock and wool prices forced stockraisers to reduce their herds and more and more Mexican landholders retreated to small farms and *ranchos*. Years of drought also wreaked havoc with stockraisers. After ten more years of losing ground, Tejano landholding dropped to 29 percent of the land in the county in 1900. The future looked bleak, for without prosperous times the Mexicans could not continue as *rancheros*, much less displace the few but more powerful Anglo ranchers who had become dominant in the Tejanos' native land. In sum, land loss among Mexicans in Hidalgo County (as well as throughout the region) was a gradual, complicated, and a relatively late process.

This case study of land tenure in one key county in south Texas challenges the traditional historical interpretation of Tejano land tenure. Whereas historians such as Acuña and others see Tejano land loss as a rapid blow and one that was directed by powerful and shrewd merchants and Anglo usurpers, the evidence shows that, in fact, a multiplicity of factors account for the displacement of Tejanos and that the process was gradual and incomplete, even after fifty years of Anglo competition for the grasslands of south Texas.[37] The vast majority of both Anglo and Mexican newcomers acquired lands from Tejanos by purchase, although some obtained land by intermarriage and other legal ways, such as sheriff sales and foreclosures. Other than Tejano oral histories, it is difficult to uncover illegal acquisition of Tejano-owned land by Anglos for several reasons. A major problem for researchers is the lack of written documentation and/or accessibility to private collections controlled by descendants or agents of powerful Anglo landholders. In addition, some of the records—public and private—are evidently missing.

Historians and other social scientists have largely neglected the effects of social causes, relying, as Montejano does, on changes in the market economy to explain Tejano displacement from the land. Anglo and *mejicano* immigrants certainly placed pressure on landholders to sell, which was especially true during the heyday of the stockraising boom; but bad times also resulted in land loss. Market forces alone, however, did not destroy the favorable position of Tejano stockraisers. Social factors, such as the persistence of egalitarian landholding traditions among Tejanos and the growth of the population, accounted for much of the subdivision of the original land grants. Partible inheritance was a practice that evolved from centuries-old Spanish law. Still, all of these factors—social, economic, and political—eventually worked against most Tejano and *mejicano rancheros.* As a group, they were never fully displaced from their native land. It is this continuity that has helped to make south Texas a unique region of the state, in contrast to the rapid loss of land and status that Tejano landholders experienced in San Antonio, Goliad, and Nacogdoches. The evidence for Hidalgo County challenges McWilliams's thesis that Mexicans continued in control of their land and destiny in south Texas past the start of the twentieth century.

This study of Hidalgo County also shows that, while Tejano land loss was a gradual process, it occurred at a faster pace beginning in the 1880s. Tejanos had become minority landholders in Hidalgo County between 1880 and 1885, and evidently even earlier in other districts such as Nueces County. This finding allows us to date more precisely the time period in which Tejanos were no longer the dominant landholders, in contrast to the earlier scholarship of McWilliams, Montejano, and Weber, which addressed this point in very general terms. The crucible of the Mexican American experience occurred during the 1880s and 1890s, when much of the Tejano-owned lands were lost. This change in ownership of the land set the stage for their subordination as second-class citizens at the start of the new century.

CHAPTER SEVEN

RECOVERY AND EXPANSION OF TEJANO RANCHING IN SOUTH TEXAS, 1848–1885

The Good Years

Even before the war with Mexico, United States economic penetration had been felt in some areas of northern Mexico, including coastal California, northern New Mexico, and the Lower Río Grande Valley of Tamaulipas. The presence of a small but influential group of Anglo-American and European merchants and artisans at Matamoros since 1820 was a portent of future events in the economic history of the area. With the end of the war, a new era began for the Mexican populace who had settled north of the Río Grande.[1] The United States or American side of the Río Grande grew gradually, taking on its own peculiar development. The new settlements quickly became intertwined with the old river *villas*, and they continued to be influenced by events that took place on the border and in Mexico. However, as time went on, economic changes pulled the region more and more into the market economy of the United States. After annexation, the resurgence of the mercantile trade based on the Río Grande and the accelerated commercialization of ranching, and to a lesser degree farming, in the post–Civil War period ushered in profound economic changes that reshaped society in south Texas.[2] Commercial ranching, in particular, became the dominant economic activity of the bulk of the population. Much of the history of stockraising in south Texas in the second half of the nineteenth century is a story of Tejano ranchers and their adaptation to a changing economy and society in which competition for resources between Tejanos and Anglos intensified.

This chapter, then, addresses two key phases of Tejano ranching in the post-1848 period: (1) the initial recovery of stockraising in the period 1848–1865;

and (2) the boom in livestock and wool production in the period 1866–1885. My objective here is to delineate the key elements of Tejano ranching in south Texas during a dynamic period of expansion. To understand the important role that Tejanos played in the ranching economy, I discuss here the early trade in livestock, the return of the *rancheros* to their lands, the system of registration of marks and brands, the temporary disruption of the recovery during the period from 1859 to 1865, the advantages that facilitated the expansion of commercial ranching, the variation in ranching activities across the region, and the market effects on livestock and wool production and marketing strategies of Tejano *rancheros* in the post–Civil War years. I have also included a detailed case study of ranching in Hidalgo County during this period (1852–1885) and identified a number of successful Tejano *rancheros* who operated in south Texas.

THE EARLY LIVESTOCK TRADE OF THE REGION, 1848–1850S

Following the turmoil of the Mexican-American War, an initial period of recovery in commercial ranching set in, only to be halted with the outbreak of the Civil War. Two interrelated factors promoted this phase of stockraising: (1) an increase in local sales and exports of livestock and livestock by-products, especially hides, tallow, and wool; and (2) the return of Mexican *rancheros* to the north side of the Río Grande to reclaim their lands and reorganize their ranching enterprises. The California gold rush of 1849 brought travelers passing through on their way overland to the Pacific Coast. To outfit their traveling parties, company leaders bought goods from local traders and livestock from *rancheros.*[3] By the early 1850s a number of tallow factories were also in operation along the coast. For example, John Peter Schatzell and H. S. Kinney owned one at the Rincón del Oso, near Corpus Christi, valued at eight thousand dollars in 1854.[4]

Commerce at the Río Grande grew rapidly with annexation. The customs collector at Brazos de Santiago reported that the value of imports from Mexico during the fiscal year ending June 30, 1858, included nearly 430,000 dollars in livestock, hides, and wool. For the eleven months ending May 31, 1859, the same imported products saw a rise in value to 490,000 dollars.[5]

Not all agricultural products, however, were exported through Brazos Santiago. The German merchant John Zirvas Leyendecker, who located in Laredo in the mid-1850s, purchased corn, beans, and flour as well as thousands of pounds of hides. He sold some of these products to merchants in San Antonio, but most of the hides were marketed in New Orleans through the port of Corpus Christi, which was closer to Laredo than Brazos Santiago.[6]

With increased settlement by both Anglos and Mexicans in the region, the sale of herds intensified. Some sales occurred upon the demise of the settlers. Probate records of this early period indicate that this was quite a common occurrence throughout the region.[7] Also, a handful of the early newcomers to the region who were interested in starting a ranching business began to buy significant numbers of stock from local *rancheros.* Richard King and his partner, Gideon K. Lewis, started to build up the Rancho Santa Gertrudis in this fashion beginning in 1854. The ranch's first account book itemized five separate livestock purchases from Manuel Ramírez of La Bóveda, amounting to 799 dollars. In addition, other *rancheros* sold stock to that ranch, including Mariano Munguía of Hidalgo County, whose sales totaled 683 dollars. The account book also lists a sale of two hundred cows for 1,200 dollars from Lewis to Rancho Santa Gertrudis. Lewis, an ex-Texas Ranger and part-owner of a storehouse and wharf at Corpus Christi with John Willete, traveled the countryside scouting good bargains.[8] He had evidently purchased these cows from other *rancheros,* but their names are unknown. Rancho Santa Gertrudis also relied on commission buyers, such as Louis Mallet and E. D. Smith, who purchased stock from local *rancheros.*[9]

In the early 1850s, as the process of readjustment to U.S. sovereignty continued, Mexican *rancheros* began to return to their lands with their livestock north of the Río Grande. John L. Haynes, a member of the state legislature who represented the Lower Valley, estimated that by the early 1850s the Trans-Nueces counties had at least 10,000 horses, 100,000 horned cattle, and 200,000 sheep and goats. These numbers were much larger than those reported by the census of 1850, which had been taken in the summer of 1849, partly because Indian raids had forced *rancheros* to take their herds into Mexico temporarily. While the exact character of the commercial transactions involving livestock are not clear, significant sales of livestock took place at this time. For Haynes reported that in a twelve-month period prior to his writing (October 1859) stock buyers from Missouri, Illinois, Kentucky, and Tennessee bought from local as well as Mexican ranchers 30,000 horses and 300,000 sheep, which he valued at 1,050,000 dollars.[10]

VARIATION IN THE RECOVERY OF STOCKRAISING IN THE TRANS-NUECES, 1848–1860S

Dependent on a number of factors, the recovery of stockraising varied from one county to another in the region. For example, already by 1860 Cameron County's total value of livestock stood at 815,725 dollars, whereas in neighboring Hidalgo County—a less settled and developed zone—it totaled only 109,765 dollars. North of these two counties, Nueces County stockmen reported that the value of their livestock was 612,394 dollars.[11] Thus, stockraising had become well established along the eastern half of the coastal plains. West of Cameron and Nueces counties—a drier, less settled district—livestock production had also gained momentum as *rancheros* returned to their lands. For example, in 1860 Starr County *rancheros* were assessed for taxes on 2,347 horses, 15,729 cattle, and 65,155 sheep, with a total value of 213,895 dollars.[12] Unfortunately, the agricultural censuses for other western counties in south Texas are incomplete, but it is likely that livestock production there followed the Starr County pattern because of similar terrain and climate.

REGISTRATION OF STOCK MARKS AND BRANDS DURING THE RECOVERY AND EARLY BOOM YEARS OF THE RANCHING ECONOMY, 1848–1870

A strong indication of the ongoing recovery in ranching activities is also reflected in the swift increase in the number of livestock marks and brands registered in the new county courthouses in south Texas. Cameron County lists 254 brands for the years 1852–1861, with hundreds more added after the start of the Civil War.[13] Starr County records indicate that from 1848 to 1849—less than two years after the creation of the county—109 brands were registered. From 1850 to 1860, an additional 299 brands were recorded at Río Grande City. During the entire period from 1848 to 1860, most owners of marks and brands in Starr County were Tejanos or Mexican immigrants—373 out of 408—but, as in Cameron County, a small minority of the early stockmen and cattle and/or wool buyers were Anglos or Europeans.[14]

A similar proliferation in the registration of stock marks and brands can be found in Webb and Nueces counties. From 1848 to 1860 the Webb County clerk filed and recorded a total of 109 marks and brands. Of these, 91 belonged to Mexican males, 7 to Mexican females, and 11 to Anglos. The latter presented their marks and brands mostly for the years 1853–58. As in other parts of the Trans-Nueces, Tejanos were the first to engage in stockraising in the Laredo district. Their predominance in ownership of marks and brands continued into the following decade (the 1860s) and indicates the extent to which Tejanos dominated livestock production during the recovery and early years of the boom in the ranching economy. During the period from 1861 to 1870, the Webb County records indicate that Mexican males claimed 291 marks and brands, Mexican women—including four married to Anglos—claimed 33, and Anglos another 34.[15]

TEJANO USES OF MARKS AND BRANDS IN THE RANCHING ECONOMY

The registration of marks and brands accelerated after 1848 because of the expansion of the livestock industry in south Texas. Long regulated by Spanish and Anglo legislation, the registration of marks and brands served to ensure the property rights of stockmen and dealers in stock, for such instruments represented a marketable property interest that could be sold, traded, inherited, and even discontinued. Marking and branding livestock was also intended to prevent the loss of animals to a thief and assisted legitimate owners in protecting their rights to animals claimed by someone else. While every humble *ranchero* owned at least one *fierro,* or branding iron, to brand his stock, riding horse or milk cow, important Tejano stockmen usually registered several brands. Tejanos and Mexicans whose herds were established in Texas often registered their marks and brands more than once, or they registered several different ones. They also filed registrations for their children and others who could not come to the county seat from their *ranchos.* Husbands and wives often recorded their separate marks and brands. *Rancheros* also registered brands in several counties, especially if they conducted ranching in adjoining counties, or if they moved their stock from place to place, as happened during times of drought. Take the case of José María García Villarreal, who resided in San Antonio. In September 1874, he declared to the clerk of Hidalgo County that his stock grazed on the Lucero and Buena Vista *ranchos* in the northern part of the county. According to the clerk's notes, the *ranchero*'s brand "has been in use by him since the 15th of February 1858, and . . . he has used and still owns the brand of his deceased father[,] Nicolás García Longoria," that brand having been recorded on January 25, 1853, and another brand recorded on October 6, 1868. García Villarreal then added that both of these brands were "now discontinued by him and the one in the margin is to be used by him exclusively for the future." On the same day, Toribio García, a resident of Camargo and evidently a kinsman of José María, with stock at the same places, recorded his brand and ear mark, which he said were "first recorded in Book A [*Record of Marks and Brands*], page 99, August 18, 1858, in Starr County."[16] There are other examples of multiple registrations of marks and brands from other counties. In 1859, Marcelo Pérez y García of Cameron County recorded four separate brands, one for Rancho San

Antonio, one for Cinco Señores, one for La Noria or El Rosario, and another for stock that was sold.[17]

Sometimes *rancheros* sold, canceled, replaced, or gave away their marks and brands. Francisco Fuentes Farías of Cameron County, who had first registered his mark and brand on January 13, 1858, sold them to Richard King on November 19, 1879.[18] Juan Telles of Webb County recorded a new brand on August 4, 1869, because he had sold his original brand to Pablo Telles, his son.[19] Similarly, an Anglo rancher, Thomas J. Lee, sold his brand to Jesúsa Rodríguez of Webb County in 1871.[20] In many cases, contracts between ranchers involved the sale not only of the livestock, but also the mark and brand. On March 26, 1874, Agapito Longoria sold Richard King all of his horned cattle as well as his brand and earmark for 500 dollars. Five years later, Don José Longoria of Rancho El Sáuz, Cameron County, sold King 269 horses for $1,277.75, and for 25 pesos the "*derecho y acción a mi fierro*," that is, his right and title to his brand.[21] In the spring of 1875, Eligia Martínez of Peñitas, Hidalgo County, replaced a mark and brand that she had previously used with another *fierro*, and Agustín García of the same county registered an ear mark and brand that he had previously recorded.[22]

Tejano (and Anglo) ranchers also registered the marks and brands of their minor children, kinsmen, and children for whom they usually served as legal guardians. On January 12, 1859, Severo de la Garza presented to the Cameron County clerk the marks and brands of his four female children for recording.[23] Similarly, in Webb County Lazaro de la Garza filed for registration five different marks for his three sons and two daughters in 1867. In the same year, J. K. Anderson, the guardian of J. M. Vela, a minor, recorded the latter's mark and brand at Laredo. Three years later, E. F. Hall, Webb County's district clerk, filed the marks and brands of his wife, Nieves Salinas, and that of the couple's "infant child," Carolina Hall.[24] In May 1874, the guardian of Andrea and Rómula Garza of Peñitas, Hidalgo County, recorded their brand; they were the minor children of a deceased *ranchero*, Luis Garza, who had left a small estate consisting of land and livestock.[25]

Brands were also recorded because they were used solely for specific commercial purposes. Some *fierros* were designated as specific brands, such as those belonging to partnerships or companies, for stock which was sold to others, and for marking and branding the increase of a herd. One important specific use was that of the "road brand." By law, anyone who drove cattle to market beyond the boundaries of Texas was required to place "a large and plain road brand composed of any device" on the left side of the back behind the shoulder. Every person using a road brand was also required to place it on record, along with other brands, in the county from which the animals in question would be trailed and before such removal from the county occurred.[26] The so-called road brands grew in popularity as commercial ranching became more viable after the Civil War.

EARLY TEJANO BUSINESS ARRANGEMENTS IN STOCKRAISING, 1848–1870

Throughout the region Tejanos and newcomers who were engaged in raising stock as well as buying and selling livestock and wool created a variety of business arrangements. While most Tejanos participated in the ranching economy as sole owners of their herds and sundry enterprises, by 1852, if not earlier, partnerships and companies were already in existence. Cameron County counted at least four Tejano partnerships prior to 1870: Anastacio Bernal and Antonio Sandoval in 1852; Manuel Treviño and Santos Coy in 1867; and Alvino Salinas and Refugio Ramírez in 1868. In the same year Alvino Salinas also formed another partnership with a brother.[27] In Starr County the first to file a company brand was Rafael López, in 1866.[28] In Hidalgo County three Tejano *rancheros* organized Cárdenas & Co. and made Rancho La Noria Cardeneña their headquarters, with the company recording its brand on January 30, 1867. Three days later, Rosalío López and Faustino Rodríguez registered their company brand in the same county.[29]

In Webb County, three Tejano and one Tejano—Anglo partnerships are of record prior to 1870, with the earliest formed in 1848 by Cristóbal Benavides and Antonio Vela. At the start of the new year in 1867, two *rancheros,* one Sánchez and one Salinas became partners. In 1868 Atanacio Viduarri, a well-known and successful stockraiser in the century-old José Vásquez Borrego grant, and J. B. Bell registered a partnership brand. In 1869 Agustín Ayala and Juan Benavides also filed a company brand at Laredo.[30]

As noted above, some of the partnerships and companies were composed of Tejanos and newcomers. For example, in Starr County Samuel J. Stewart of Río Grande City and one Garza filed a partnership brand in 1860.[31] Without further study it is difficult to say whether these partnership and company businesses were short-lived or lasted many years. Still, it shows the degree to which Tejanos adjusted to the changing dynamics of commercial stockraising. In fact, these arrangements were even more numerous after 1870, as ranching activities accelerated across the Lower Valley.

Tejano women were also directly involved in the ranching economy after annexation of the Lower Valley. It is difficult to say how many were widows who were continuing ranching operations after the deaths of their husbands—

though in some cases the order of surnames in tax records indicated that status—and how many were simply married or single women who "owned their own separate mark and brand" through inheritance or purchase. In any case, they too were involved in the business of ranching, depending on either adult male children or on hired workers for assistance. Overall, what is important to note is that a variety of livestock business arrangements worked out during the first decades persisted for many years, and among Tejano men and women the preference was for sole ownership of their stockraising operations.

THE PREDOMINANCE OF TEJANO STOCKRAISERS IN SOUTH TEXAS, 1848–1870

In this early phase of commercial ranching, small and medium-size stockraising enterprises were much more numerous than the activities of the so-called cattle kings, and such ranchers were more likely to be Tejanos rather than Anglos, Europeans, Blacks, or "blends," that is, persons of mixed heritage.[32] In his economic history of the Lower Valley, Leroy Graf asserted that up to the Civil War only three Anglo ranchers resided within one hundred miles of the Río Grande.[33] Actually, there were a handful more and perhaps a score or two in the Corpus Christi area, 150 miles north of Brownsville. Thomas North, who spent five years in Texas in the mid-1860s, noted that southwest Texas was filled with a "lively and active race of stock-raisers." Lieutenant William Chatfield, who spent several years at Fort Brown in the early 1890s, observed that for Mexicans stockraising seemed almost an "inherited instinct" because of their long tradition of ranching.[34] Both the tax rolls and federal censuses for south Texas counties reveal the presence of many Mexican stockraisers. These ranchers were either Texas born or born in Mexico, but they were identified by their surnames.[35] For example, in 1860 Cameron County had 354 Tejanos who claimed livestock, compared to only 32 who were either Anglo or European. Of the latter, most were primarily merchants, storekeepers, or officials, though a handful owned "*ranchos.*" In the same year, neighboring Hidalgo County counted 190 stock owners, of whom 178 were Mexican and only 12 Anglo or European. Even in Nueces County, where Anglos had gained control of large tracts of land, fully 33 percent of the 174 landholders who claimed livestock in 1860 were Tejanos.[36]

In Starr, Zapata, and Webb counties, nearly all of the stockraisers were Mexican. It was indeed rare to find more than a score of non-Mexican stockmen and/or buyers in that large district, and these were usually merchants who imitated the activities of Mexican *rancheros.* In Starr County, for instance, the enumerator of the agricultural census in 1859 listed 133 owners of stock, of whom 121 were Mexican and 12 were Anglo or European.[37] Regardless of whether Mexican stockmen devoted their energies to raising sheep, cattle, or horses, a variable that depended on conditions at any given time, the fact remains that *rancheros* were a major force in the development of stockraising in the region.

After annexation of the Trans-Nueces region, the first successful stockraisers were Mexicans, primarily the descendants of original land grantees or men with experience and capital sufficient to purchase land from the grantees or from their descendants. As such, they followed the tradition of their forefathers, who had pioneered stockraising in northern New Spain in the seventeenth century. This can be illustrated by identifying early stockraisers. Consider, for instance, the case of Hidalgo County. Members of the Ballí, Hinojosa, Cano, Leal, and Domínguez families were leading ranchers in the southeastern quadrant of the county in the 1850s and 1860s. In southern Hidalgo County, along the Río Grande, Prudencio Cantú was an old stockraiser. In the southwestern zone of the county, many old *rancheros* could be found, including members of the Ochoa, Munguía, Villarreal, Flores, and Salinas families. In the central part of the county, the massive San Salvador del Tule grant was the headquarters for many ranchers, most of whom were related by blood or marriage. When that grant passed from the Ballí to the Cárdenas families, as a result of a judicial sale in 1829 to satisfy an estate indebtedness, a number of ranches were founded, with the headquarters receiving the name of La Noria Cardeneña. The Cárdenas, Cavazos, and Chapa families made this district one of the most successful ranching areas in the county. North and northwest of this district, Mexicans also were involved in ranching in the mid-nineteenth century on land grants that dated to the late Spanish period and the early Mexican period. Mexicans held on to their land grants and continued to engage in stockraising until Anglo ranchers came into the northern sector of the county, as they expanded and consolidated their ranching operations in the late nineteenth century.[38]

To a large extent, similar dynamics in land tenure operated throughout the core areas of the Lower Valley, where the Tejanos held on to much of the land. A few examples show the early entry and persistence of these *rancheros.* With the purchase of the El Grullo grant in 1853 and the La Boveda grant in 1856, Manuel Ramírez Elizondo of Matamoros initiated a large-scale ranching enterprise involving cattle and horses. In early 1869, Ramírez filed an inventory of his property in which he claimed two thousand horses and mules, four thousand cattle, eighteen hundred sheep, and one hundred head of jacks and jennies.[39] In spite of the fact that his mother had her own *rancho*—and from her he eventually inherited three leagues of land in the Espíritu Santo grant—

Sabas Cavazos, who resided in Brownsville, went on his own as did many of his fellow *rancheros.* In 1858, Cavazos purchased El Pasadizo, a Mexican grant containing three leagues of land and located in Nueces County, from the grantee's heirs. Before his death, in 1879, he had acquired several other parcels of land in Cameron County, and he also owned other unlisted properties in Mexico. He raised large numbers of horses, cattle, and sheep.[40]

Zapata County, a semi-dry plains district devoted to mixed ranching, usually had a handful of very successful *rancheros* whose herds expanded with the growth in demand for wool and livestock. Among them were Blas María Gutiérrez, Cosmé Martínez, Pedro Flores, and Hipólito García. Of these, García became the largest producer of livestock and grew quite wealthy. His story is typical of this group of *ganaderos,* or stockmen, whose success occurred during the years of recovery and expansion. Acquiring land during the Mexican era, García started slowly, as reflected in the first county tax data for Zapata County (1858), in which he claimed 130 cattle and 112 horses. Two years later he reported owning 225 cattle, valued at 1,350 dollars, and 200 horses, valued at 2,000 dollars, as well as 1,800 dollars in land. In spite of the commotion of the Civil War years, García remained fully committed to stockraising, buying up additional lands. By 1867 he controlled 35,531 acres of land, and his cattle and horse herds totaled nearly 2,000 head. He continued to enlarge his landholdings and herds until near the end of his life, when he conveyed much of his property to his wife. One measure of his success can be seen in the fact that by the late 1880s he had 50,000 dollars on hand, miscellaneous property worth 20,000 dollars, 200 horses, and 6,000 cattle, and the total value of his property for tax purposes was 144,188 dollars.[41]

José María Valadez is also representative of the class of new *rancheros* who started early and whose descendants continued in the ranching business after the death of the patriarch. Valadez was born on his family's ranch near Camargo, in the early nineteenth century. He married in 1841, constructed a *jacalón,* or large adobe home, and started farming on the *vegas* of the Río Grande at Rancho de Valadeces, Tamaulipas. He then moved to Matamoros, where he went into business with a *lancha,* or launch, a small rowboat that he used to take people to the U.S. side of the border. He then returned to San Pedro de Roma, Tamaulipas, and began a carting business by acquiring several *carretas,* or large wooden carts. His *carretas* were involved in transporting cotton from Texas, from as far as Arlington during some of the Civil War years. About this time, Valadez and several of his relatives were impressed into transporting weapons for the Mexicans fighting the French, and they were not released from this duty until July 1865. Valadez, who had traveled with his carts to Corpus Christi and other points in Texas, was impressed with the abundant pasturelands in Nueces County, and he purchased property east of Palito Blanco, where he founded Rancho La Laguna de las Calaveras and started raising stock in 1864. He acquired sheep under a lease agreement with Don Gregorio Villarreal of La Grulla, Texas, and was soon raising large numbers of sheep and some horses and cattle. As his ranching operations grew, Valadez decided to acquire more land, purchasing a large tract from the heirs of Vital Hinojosa, a land grantee whose grant was located in Duval County. This second ranch was christened Rancho La Bandera. Valadez died in Camargo in 1880, but his nine children continued to live and raise livestock on those two *ranchos*.[42]

Such evidence of the dominant presence of Tejano stockraisers in south Texas in the 1850s contradicts Terry Jordan, who has asserted that by the middle of the nineteenth century Tejano *rancheros* had "very nearly disappeared." Probably Jordan's failure to look at county tax and probate records prevented him from correctly assessing the presence of Tejano ranchers. In addition, the census data that Jordan did examine is not complete, and as the census enumerator noted in the summer of 1849, the Mexicans had removed their herds to the south side of the river to prevent further losses to raiding Indians.[43]

DISPLACEMENT OF STOCKRAISERS IN THE RECOVERY PERIOD

During this period of recovery, some areas began to witness the first major displacement of small and moderate livestock producers, as the consolidation of ranching began to emerge with the beginning of the cattle drives north after the Civil War. That is, as the demand for livestock accelerated, producers responded by raising larger herds. This, in turn, resulted in increased competition among ranchers for the better lands. As the commercialization of ranching gained momentum, producers with less economic clout were displaced. For example, the data for Cameron County reveal nearly a 50 percent drop in the number of resident Tejano stockraisers from 1859, when 244 were counted, to 133 in 1870.[44] The precise dynamics of this displacement are unknown, but it is likely that some *rancheros* sold their herds to others, and those who may have been squatters, using the open range, opted to leave ranching as legitimate landholders demanded their lands solely for their own use. Also, widows of *rancheros* sometimes did not continue stockraising activities for a number of reasons, but especially when they had no male children or when the children were too small to help out. They usually sold out to relatives or others.

CONTRARY WINDS: "CORTINA'S WARS," THE CIVIL WAR, AND LAWLESSNESS IN SOUTH TEXAS, 1848–1870S

Two events hampered the full recovery of the region's stockraising economy, namely, Juan N. Cortina's raids in the Lower Valley and the effects of the U.S. Civil War. Generalized banditry was part and parcel of the activities associated with these two events. In the summer of 1859, Cortina, a respected *ranchero*, witnessed the pistol-whipping of a Mexican laborer by an Anglo city marshal in Brownsville. Cortina, who knew the victim, intervened and shot and injured the lawman. Branded an outlaw, Cortina then took refuge at his mother's ranch. This incident soon triggered instability and conflict along the Lower Valley.

Angered by the discrimination against Tejano landholders and Mexicans in general, Cortina and a band of followers attacked Brownsville in September 1859, killing three Anglos. In several public proclamations, Cortina alleged that his actions were in response to the inequitable and high-handed manner in which certain Anglo politicians and lawyers injured the rights of Mexican landholders north of the Río Grande. For a period of five months, Cortina waged a rebellion in order "to defend ourselves," he said, "and to mak[e] use of the sacred right of self-preservation . . . because the supremacy of the law has failed to accomplish its object," namely, justice. Those who had perished in the fighting, Cortina claimed, "form, with a multiple of lawyers, a secret conclave for the sole purpose of despoiling the Mexicans of their lands and usurp[ing] them afterwards." Vowing to continue his resistance, Cortina acknowledged the precarious condition of Mexican landholders as "strangers in their own country." As he gained followers, Cortina's conviction of his right to take up arms emboldened him to proclaim that "as to land, Nature will always grant us sufficient to support our frames and we accept the consequences that may arise. [But] our personal enemies shall not possess our lands until they have fattened with their own gore."[45]

Driven across the Río Grande and into Mexico by United States troops, Cortina continued to wage intermittent attacks along the border. According to Anglo Texans, Cortina was the leader of roving bandits who committed atrocities and stole cattle in south Texas. Because of the extreme biases in contemporary reports from both sides of the Río Grande, it is not entirely clear how much blame for the cattle thefts must be attributed to Cortina. Still, there is no doubt that Cortina's activities bred more lawlessness, as conflict between Anglos and Mexicans intensified in the 1860s and early 1870s. Moreover, the Civil War in the United States, which was concurrent with French intervention in

Mexico, only served to heighten anxiety and fear along the international border at the Río Grande.

South Texas was a distant and insignificant theater of the Civil War, except for the use of neighboring Mexico as a funnel for the cotton trade of the South. It is estimated that three thousand *carros*, or vehicles, were employed in transporting Southern cotton to Mexican border towns, as far upriver as Eagle Pass and Del Rio, Texas, prior to being sold at Bagdad and Matamoros. This economic activity brought in 3 million pesos in trade to Nuevo León alone and greatly enriched Confederate cotton agents and the merchant class with whom they worked, both in south Texas and in northern Mexico.[46] Consequently, Confederate and Union forces in south Texas waged a sporadic conflict, in which they sought to destroy any property of value to the other, particularly cotton and livestock. Tejano soldiers in the Union army recalled after the war, when some were charged with cattle rustling, that during the war they had been encouraged to steal cattle from the Confederates.[47] In 1863, when the Confederates began to feel desperate, they too directed army patrols to drive all stock, especially beef cattle and horses suitable for cavalry service, north of the Nueces River.

The availability of immense herds of livestock also led the state legislature to suspend the operation of stray laws, authorizing anyone to appropriate unfenced or unbranded cattle for his own use. Such chaotic conditions further encouraged rustling. Along the Río Grande, the Confederate Thirty-second Texas Cavalry fed itself almost entirely on beef cattle, seldom giving impressment vouchers to the owners of the stock. The loss of thousands of cattle due to the Texas drought of 1864 forced the Texas legislature, in November 1864, to pass a resolution calling upon the Confederate authorities to prohibit the exportation of cattle to Mexico and to limit the impressment of beef cattle. Texas ranchers also sought means of resisting impressment, but the military officials reacted by resorting to large-scale rustling, ignoring both the spirit and the letter of the impressment laws as they drove herds off to the slaughterhouses without issuing vouchers to or paying the rightful owners of the stock. Despite the owners' protests, only the end of the war brought impressment to a halt.[48]

After the Civil War, border disturbances continued to plague south Texas, and each national government blamed the other for the problems on the frontier. In 1872, two United States commissions and one from Texas sent to the border squarely put the blame on Mexico for its failure to control the border, singling out Mexican officials who condoned Cortina's activities. In 1873, a Mexican frontier commission sent to investigate border conditions blamed the difficulties on revolutionary bands of "undisciplined and immoral" men who, they claimed, joined General Cortina and other commanders. These men, the commissioners argued, deserted their forces and crossed the border to commit robberies and other crimes. In addition, the Mexican commissioners argued that much of the banditry involved local bands and officials from the Texas side. Because of limited and often conflicting evidence on Cortina, it is impossible to determine his precise role in the raiding. Still, Cortina was a complex frontier figure who strongly influenced conditions along the border from 1859 to the early 1870s. These conditions made it possible for opportunistic raiders from both Texas and Mexico to continue intermittent criminal activities. However, in the mid-1870s, Mexico clamped down on disorders along the Río Grande, as Don Porfirio Díaz solidified his power in an attempt to obtain American recognition and investment. At the same time, Anglo Texans finally gave up on the idea of fomenting another war of aggression for the purpose of acquiring more territory from Mexico. For the more chauvinistic Texans now reasoned that a peaceful and secure border would allow them to obtain economic benefits without the trouble of having to invade Mexico and govern its *mestizo* people.[49]

GENERAL TRENDS IN THE DEVELOPMENT OF STOCKRAISING IN SOUTH TEXAS, 1865–1885

After the Civil War, a resurgence in commercial ranching in south Texas produced a new wave of prosperity. With the termination of the war, soldiers returned home eager to rebuild their lives and to restore a shattered economy. In spite of the adverse effects of the conflict on the ranching industry, not to mention such other factors as drought and rampant lawlessness, cattle were abundant. It is estimated that at the end of the Civil War there were five million cattle in Texas, most of them in the territory south of San Antonio.[50] Cattle drives to midwestern and western markets, meant to satisfy the demand for beef cattle and to stock new ranches, provided the initial impetus for the expansion of ranching in south Texas. Its ranchers soon found a new source of wealth in the sale in distant national markets, not only of large numbers of cattle, but also horses, mules, and sheep, as well as thousands of pounds of wool. For a period of about twenty years, the livestock industry enjoyed a renewed and unprecedented prosperity that transformed the region socially and economically.[51]

The growth in the pastoral economy during the period 1860–1900 was characterized by a rapid rise in livestock production in the core counties of south Texas. Cameron County led in cattle and horse production, although some of its ranchers occasionally raised moderate numbers of sheep. As late as 1890, livestock in Cameron County included 18,338 horses, 93,727 cattle, 155 jacks, 26,129 sheep, and 3,016 goats, all valued at 828,432 dollars. Nueces and Hidalgo followed the trend of Cameron County with large cattle and horse herds. Sheepraising represented a more moderate economic activity in these counties.

By far the most consistent large-scale sheepraising took place in Starr, Zapata, Webb, Encinal, and Duval counties. Located on the western half of the Río Grande plains, these counties were mainly devoted to sheepraising, although cattle and especially horses were raised in large numbers. Their role in the sheep industry contributed toward making the Río Grande Plains region the center of the greatest concentration of sheep in Texas during the great boom of sheep ranching, lasting from about 1860 to 1890. In 1880, the Río Grande plains contained 1,644,266 sheep—45 percent of all sheep in Texas. with about 600,000 sheep in Zapata, Webb, and Duval counties.[53]

In addition, considerable Tejano ranching took place in the rest of the Trans-Nueces. In the 1870s and 1880s, the San Diego area of Nueces County was a major sheep ranching district, although some Tejanos engaged in mixed ranching, raising horses and cattle as well as sheep and goats. Tejano *rancheros* also persisted into the 1880s in the Petronila, Los Olmos, and Casa Blanca areas of Nueces County.

FACTORS FAVORING THE DEVELOPMENT OF STOCKRAISING IN SOUTH TEXAS

In addition to a strong market demand, other cultural, economic, and natural factors promoted commercial stockraising of cattle and horses. The more important advantages favoring stockraising included a long tradition of ranching among the Mexican settlers; the availability of cheap pastureland, most of which remained unfenced until the 1880s; a mild, semitropical climate that encouraged a rapid growth of native grasses; and the presence of immense herds of livestock in the outlying districts of northern Mexico, where stock could be obtained cheaply.[54] Aided by these conditions, ranching spread through the countryside, bringing south Texas increasingly into the ambit of the expanding market economy of the United States.

Much has been written about the origin of the American cowboy, especially about his debt to the Mexican *vaquero*. J. Frank Dobie and many other writers, including ranchers and trail drovers, agree that the *vaquero* was unsurpassed as a horseman and as a skilled worker was essential to the livestock industry.

Dobie corrected much of the earlier, more biased descriptions of *vaqueros* by Anglos. He did, however, consider the vaquero to possess a mixture of qualities; he found him to be "superstitious, a bit cruel to animals, close to nature, faithful, and hospitable."[55] Américo Paredes likewise asserted that a *vaquero*'s skills were so treasured that in the folklore of south Texas he was esteemed and held in high regard and never considered to be a common worker or peon.[56] In fact, the tradition of the *vaquero* was frequently passed from one generation to another.[57] In time a *vaquero*'s skills were passed on to Anglo cowboys, who came to equal his talents for herding and horsemanship.[58]

The persistent literary preoccupation with the cowboy as a romantic hero as well as Hollywood's portrayal of western settlers, especially ranchers, as macho men has eclipsed recognition of the reality that ranchers everywhere depended on a variety of skilled and unskilled workers other than cowboys in order to make stockraising a successful operation.[59]

There is some evidence that suggests both a degree of paternalism and of mutual respect in the relationships between ranch owners and employees. Consider, for instance, the memories of Roberto Vela, a descendant of Don Macedonio Vela. Roberto Vela fondly reminisced about some of the workers at Rancho Laguna Seca. Cowboys, he said,

> were of all races and they were experts at camplife. . . . The cooks were . . . El Indio Serapio, El Pelón Senobio, Santiago Munguía and several others. . . . Other servants, employees and persons of many talents were Samuel Bentacourt and Octavio Alemán. . . . The servant of the main house was a gentleman by the name of Pacífico Ochoa, who married Anastacia Díaz. Anastacia Díaz was my *pilmama* or as is known in English my nanny. It hurt me deeply when she left me to marry him. Don Pacífico worked at the Hacienda [Rancho Laguna Seca] all of his life, and died there close to the age of 70. In other words, he lived at Laguna Seca Ranch from childhood until his death.[60]

Emilia Schunior Ramírez likewise noted that in ranch communities where one or several large landholders and a community of workers resided numerous opportunities presented themselves for communal activities, such as special days for baking bread, quilting parties, and the slaughtering of livestock as well as the customary religious and secular holidays.[61] It should be noted that in the memory of the second and third generation Tejanos, class distinctions are evident but the manner of address and relationships among owners and employees indicates that the social system of the *ranchero* elites was not so rigidly structured that it prevented the existence of a mutual sense of respect and appreciation. Yet unskilled common workers, sometimes called peons, developed close bonds with their employers. *Vaqueros*, however, did not see themselves as peons because of the special skill required to do their various tasks.[62] Also, villagers who lived in the communities along the Río Grande tended to be small landholders, artisans, or landless workers. In general, these settlers enjoyed a greater degree of independence of pursuit than those whose lives were spent working on large *ranchos*.[63]

While some workers at Laguna Seca and elsewhere became lifelong dependents of one rancher, the evidence suggests that for many, if not most, their work history included employment with various ranchers. This, of course, tended to lessen the degree of paternalism that some authors attribute to the rancher-*vaquero* relationship.[64]

As invaluable as cowboys were to ranchers, their wages and working conditions changed little during the half-century after 1848. Cowboy wages in south Texas doubled from the middle of the nineteenth century to the last quarter of the century. Edward Dougherty informed the U.S. commissioner of patents in 1852 that one *vaquero* was required to care for two to three hundred cattle and that he received six dollars per month and one dollar of corn as a ration.[65] In the late 1860s most cowboys at the King ranch earned ten dollars per month, and if they were working in a camp or outfit, they were provided with food and a cook.[66] By the last quarter of the century, cowboys earned from eight to twelve dollars a month plus board.[67] Actually, wages paid to Tejano *vaqueros* varied on account of the specialized work they were required to do, but fell within the general range. These tasks were divided into herding, caring for, gathering, and branding horses and cattle as well as "breaking and gentling" horse stock. Driving stock to market was also considered a separate activity.[68] In the 1870s, Don Francisco Curiel, *caporal* of the horse stock of Rancho de la Rosita near Corpus Christi, earned twelve dollars per month and a ration of two *almudes* of corn every eight days. Don Juan Curiel, a servant of the ranch, earned ten dollars per month and the same ration of corn as workers at Rancho Laguna Seca.[69] The added risks of such a long drive, the constant care of the herd (including night duty), and the fact that the men were away from their families for extended periods necessitated the payment of higher wages to cowboys who trailed cattle north.[70]

Away from the core counties, such as Dimmit County, a dual wage system prevailed. According to the Texas commissioner of agriculture, in the early 1880s the "wages of pastores and vaqueros [there] averaged $12.00 per month for Mexicans and $15.00 for Americans."[71] Without further study of ranch records, it is not clear whether a system of dual wages based solely on ethnic or racial classification was pervasive or an atypical fact. Historian Richard Slatta also notes the existence of dual wages in Texas, but he does not cite the location.[72] At the same time, there is some data that suggests that even in counties that were away from the heartland of the Tejano population a relaxed social setting could be found. For example, at San Roque in Dimmit County, in 1880, two *vaqueros* lived as boarders in the homes of Anglo cattlemen.[73]

Land was also essential for ranching, particularly large-scale ranching. Throughout much of the Southwest, including Texas, public land was readily available and easy to get.[74] In south Texas, however, the long history of Spanish and Mexican land tenure meant that except for the upper reaches of the Nueces River, where hardly any grants had been made, the land was privately owned, but it could still be obtained through fair or devious means. When legitimate leases or purchases were made from private persons and from the state, land for grazing was still cheap.[75] Also, Tejanos for generations had bought and leased land from each other. The public records document hundreds of land sales but few leases, perhaps because the latter were based on oral contracts among kinsmen and others whom they knew and trusted. Before the proliferation of hundreds of *ranchos* in the 1870s and 1880s, the units of land sold to Tejanos and newcomers were generally large. A *sitio* or a fraction of one was the typical standard. For example, Sanforth Kidder, an American residing in Matamoros, filed a Mexican deed dated in Nueces County in 1847, in which he bought two *sitios* of pastureland from Juan José Treviño, the grantee of Los Torritos, a Tamaulipan grant located downriver from Reynosa. According to the deed, Kidder paid four hundred pesos for the land—two hundred pesos per *sitio.* Francis J. Parker, one of the earliest Anglo stockmen and a partner with William Hale at Santa Rosa, claimed that frontier raids in the 1870s had affected the price of land so that "Mexican owners are offering five leagues of land as good as ours with perfect title in our immediate neighborhood for six hundred dollars . . . "[76] In the mid-1890s, when wool and livestock prices were depressed, Edward C. Lasater, a major stockraiser in the northern part of Hidalgo and Starr counties, boasted that he paid one-half what Mexican ranchers had paid among themselves when they sold land to each other one generation earlier. Lasater claimed that he paid fifty cents an acre on most properties that he purchased at this time.[77] As late as 1900, grazing lands in both Cameron and Hidalgo counties was usually valued at one dollar an acre for tax purposes. In fact, men like Richard King often acquired thousands of acres of land at less than one dollar an acre. D. R. Fant, an experienced and leading stockman, testified in a suit between a bank and several stockraisers that in the 1890s the "reasonable rental value" of pastureland in south Texas was seventeen and one-half cents per acre per year.[78]

Ranchers also needed substantial sums of capital to buy the land to grow with the cattle business, especially as ranching became more and more a commercial enterprise. Fortunately, in the last quarter of the nineteenth century stockmen who wanted to buy land or build up their herds had access to lenders, such as local merchants and bankers or brokers who represented foreign investors. At least one major lending firm, Francis M. Smith and Company of San Antonio, which later became known as H. P. Drought & Co., believed so strongly in the potential of south Texas grasslands that they invested considerable sums in ranching. According to Smith, investments in ranching rather than farming were preferred because the latter was too risky because of the fluctuation in labor and the vagaries of the weather. Smith, who had learned his business as a lender to Midwest farmers, also thought that Texas bankers were more willing to lend to ranchers than to farmers. When pressed by investors, he presented a host of arguments in favor of lending in Texas, dwelling on such matters as the fertility of Texas land, the climate, the immense railroad mileage, and the potential for immigrant settlement.[79]

Favorable tax policies and other kinds of favoritism were a boon to large stockraisers. County governments, the most important taxing bodies in the region, annually set assessment rates for both livestock and land. Political bosses along the border who courted powerful landowners as one of their chief constituencies served them in a number of causes. Above all, politicians favored limited urban development, thereby forestalling an increase in land values. Making use of their political muscle, ranchers also had their property undervalued so they would pay less taxes than those who lacked friends in the county tax offices. Thus, when Cameron County placed an $8.00 value on cattle belonging to the King ranch, the manager, Robert J. Kleberg, wrote to its lawyer, James B. Wells, asking for his help in reducing the assessment to $7.50 per head because, he argued, such was their value in Nueces County and the cattle in Cameron were farther from market. Politicians not only made sure that tax rates on land were kept as low as possible, they also classified the lands in the county in such a fashion as to benefit large landowners. For example, in Hidalgo County, the commissioners wrangled over tax rates for land each year. Large tracts of Anglo-owned pasturelands located north of the *porciones*, which were mostly Tejano owned, were usually assessed at one-half the rate of the river grants. According to historian Evan Anders's classic history of boss politics in south Texas, in the worst cases certain persons did not pay taxes, although receipts were provided to them.[80]

Other than these tax advantages and opportunities to acquire land cheaply, ranchers needed an adequate amount of rainfall and good weather for their herds to multiply. Because of its location, south Texas generally enjoyed excellent weather conditions for breeding livestock. According to Joseph Nimmo,

Jr., perhaps the leading United States expert on the western range, cows in Texas calved successfully at a rate of 90 percent versus 50 to 70 percent in northern ranges. This made the state a major supplier of young stock exported to establish new ranches in the West and Northwest. Freezes rarely occurred, and as long as the customary amount of rainfall continued, the land produced luxuriant grasses particularly suited for raising stock. In fact, most of the soils in south Texas were rich in nutrients to sustain the varieties of both short and tall grasses that were grazed by thousands of stock. According to V. W. Lehmann, a King ranch biologist, under normal rainfall conditions tall sage grasses, known as bluestem, grew in the rich, well-drained alluvial soils of the Río Grande delta. North from there and past the brush country were the inland sands where the so-called climax grasses, a type of tall grass, also thrived. Tall grasses could be found from the San Fernando Creek, which crosses the King ranch, northward to present-day Nueces and San Patricio counties. Along the coastal sands and inland on the plains of the Nueces (and the San Antonio River), tall grasses thrived on sandy and black waxy clay soils.[81] Nearly every astute observer of the grasslands of south Texas found them to be premier grazing lands. Major W. H. Emory reported in 1853 that "all the region between that river [Nueces] and the Río Bravo is . . . a fine grazing country." However, others who traversed the desolate western side of the Río Grande Plains region during times of prolonged dryness or in the short winter months found it barren, with the terrain consisting of "rather . . . infertile prairies and . . . completely deprived of forests."[82] Thus, while the eastern half of the Río Grande plains produced tall grasses that were excellent for raising cattle and horses, the western half, which received less rainfall, became the sheepman's domain because of the prevalence of short grasses.[83]

Water was also crucial for both man and beast, but not much was available in south Texas. Indeed, there were very few permanent streams, of which the most important were the Río Grande and the Nueces River, although *arroyos* or creeks, which were often dry, were numerous.[84] Adequate rainfall was critical for the grasslands in south Texas to produce enough grass to sustain large numbers of livestock. The rainy season was from late summer to early fall, though some rain fell during the spring. Records indicate that 26.29 inches of rain fell in the Laureles and Santa Gertrudis divisions of the King ranch over a nine-year average covering the first decade of the twentieth century. In Brownsville, 27.07 inches of rainfall was the average for a thirty-seven-year period from the 1880s to about 1910. These averages made the coastal districts the best-watered lands in the region.[85] Depressions in the land, known as *lagunas*, served to collect rainwater. Wells were also dug, and later, toward the 1880s and 1890s, modern well-drilling equipment was used to bore artesian wells. Where they were able to do so, *rancheros* built *presas*, or dams, along creeks, utilizing limestone and caliche deposits from which *sillares* were quarried and used in construction for damming or lining creeks and other waterways. Some of these *tanques*, or tanks, are still in use today. One of the earliest man-made lakes or reservoirs was the one built by Don Hipólito García of Randado.[86] Still, the greatest danger to stockmen was a persistent drought, which occasionally did wreak havoc upon the ranchers.[87] Despite these natural limitations, many Mexican *rancheros*, and later a good number of Anglos, committed themselves to large-scale ranching in south Texas.

One additional advantage to ranchers in south Texas was the proximity to the northern Mexican states of Tamaulipas, Nuevo León, and Coahuila, where stock could be purchased. American consular reports indicate that Tamaulipas and Nuevo León exported cattle to Texas at the height of the industry's expansion. Stephen H. Smith, consul at Nuevo Laredo, claimed that Tamaulipan cattle were mostly "beeves exported [by] small owners near the point of export [with] all most [*sic*] all exports to points in Texas for fattening." The consul at Monterrey, Robert C. Campbell, reported that one-third of Nuevo León's cattle was "exported to Texas and other states [New Mexico and Arizona] in the last two years [of 1881 and 1882] . . . " He also noted that many horses, especially mares—perhaps 25 percent of Nuevo León's total—were shipped to the United States. He added that good-sized mules averaging fourteen and fifteen hands were "bought by Americans and shipped to Texas this year [1883]." Consul General Stephen H. Sutton of Matamoros made similar observations concerning Mexican cattle exports to Texas. He gave the value of live animals exported to the United States as 314,272 dollars in 1881 and 455,917 dollars in 1882.[88] Mexican exports of livestock continued to grow despite a 20 percent duty on beef cattle. Matías Romero reported that cattle exported to the United States from Mexico totaled about 400,000 in 1896 and 1897, and they averaged about fifteen dollars in Mexican silver per head.[89] He lamented the small size of the Mexican cattle and urged Mexicans to introduce shorthorns and to utilize feeding corn, along with the traditional cotton-seed meal, for proper fattening and marbling of the meat.

Factors Favoring Sheep Ranching in South Texas

Whereas *rancheros* had a long history of raising sheep and goats in Nuevo León and Coahuila, and later in Nuevo Santander, the Anglo and European newcomers to Texas learned to appreciate this branch of the pastoral economy with the shift in the world market demanding more wool. Thus, when the price of wool accelerated in the late 1860s due to tariff protection, Tejano and Anglo and European stockmen quickly opted to engage in large-scale sheepraising on the plains of Texas. Texas wool, the first to reach the market in the spring, generally meant that it commanded a good price. In 1890, Texas wool was the highest priced in the West and was still in demand on the market.[90]

But good prices alone did not make for successful sheep ranching. Contemporary experts claimed that with a relatively small amount of capital, one could start a sheepraising enterprise since grasslands were cheap; the wages of *pastores*, or shepherds, were low; and foundation herds could be obtained easily and inexpensively from *rancheros*. The new sheepraisers believed that these conditions meant that large profit returns could be made within a short period of time. These same observers noted optimistically that future prospects seemed even brighter in 1890, as the population was on the upswing, transportation facilities were improving, and the demand for domestic wool was rapidly increasing.

The most obvious natural qualities in Texas beneficial to sheep ranching were its climate and its immense plains. Texas's dry, mild climate, consisting of a short or virtually nonexistent winter (with the absence of snow or blizzards), proved to be favorable for sheep year-round. As early as 1848, a Mr. Gilbert of the *Matagorda Tribune*, writing in *DeBow's Journal*, noted that according to the practical experience of ranchers, sheep were found to "improve in vigor and wool in the lower latitudes." He claimed that experiments had shown that for unknown causes sheep did poorly along the western side of Matagorda Bay in southeastern Texas, but he concluded glowingly that "the prairies of Western Texas present the best facilities for sheep raising of any part of the world."[91] Plentiful water and adequate natural shelter for the protection of the sheep during winter were also factors that made sheep husbandry in Texas attractive.

Initially, ranchers expressed some concern about various diseases that could have been harmful to sheep. However, since sheep ate range grasses closely, eradicating waste grasses, those diseases that had originally threatened flocks became an insignificant variable.[92] *Rancheros* also liked sheep and goats because they were good scrubbers, eating the foliage of the brush plants and trees, or *chaparro*.[93]

Like *vaquero* wages, a shepherd's wage varied in the second half of the nineteenth century. In 1850, a shepherd in the Lower Valley cared for two thousand sheep in return for $5.00 per month and $1.00 of rations.[94] In 1878, F. W. Shaeffer, a highly respected sheepraiser in Duval County, estimated the wages of shepherds at $11.00 per month and rations.[95] The cost for shearing in 1878 was, according to Shaeffer, $3.50 per hundred. In 1890, according to reports submitted by stockmen to the federal government, wages paid to shepherds continued to vary in south Texas. This is how they described conditions:

"Mexican herder is not a high-priced worker. Some of them work by the month for $7 in Mexican money, 2 bushels of corn, 4 pounds of coffee, 4 pounds of sugar, and a goat [for meat] occasionally. The average wages range from $10 to $20 per month, and on the Mexican border still lower. In the larger holdings a superintendent has charge of the various flocks and herders, and he frequently receives $1,000 per year." Shearers called *tasinques* received from three to six cents per animal in south Texas.[96]

The availability of Mexican sheep in Texas and Mexico was also a key factor in the development of the sheepraising industry in the state, although it is obvious that new breeds were quickly introduced to upgrade the Mexican stock. Gilbert, for example, reported that ranchers had successfully crossed the Merino and South Down with the *churro*, or Mexican sheep. He estimated the value of the crosses at $2.50. He also claimed that in the San Antonio area "Mexican sheep can be purchased at $1 [to] $1.25 per head, perhaps less just now, as we understand that large droves have recently passed over the Rio Grande into Texas."[97] Edward Dougherty, in his report to the commissioner of patents (1852), likewise noted the presence of significant sheep herds in the Lower Valley and the initial attempts to breed new crosses. The half-breeds resulted from the use of Merino, Bakewell, and Saxon rams. He gave the following prices: native sheep, fifty cents per head; fat sheep, $1.00–$1.50; half-breeds, $1.50; lambs, twenty-five cents; and wool twelve and one-half cents per pound.[98]

With the passing of time, the base Mexican sheep were gradually upgraded by stockraisers.[99] Already by 1878, nine-tenths of the flocks in Texas, the third largest sheep-producing state, were mostly Merino, although the *churro* was evidently still dominant in south Texas.[100] The improved stock produced a better quality wool and a higher average per pound yield.[101] The price of wool naturally rose and fell because of numerous factors. For Texas growers, wool averaged twenty-one cents per pound in 1878. In 1890, medium fine and light fine wool earned from thirteen to twenty cents per pound.[102]

As a business venture, sheep ranching in Texas involved some risks. A number of problems were evident to sheepraisers, but the most severe obstacles to guaranteed prosperity were: (1) the vulnerability of the territory to Mexican and Indian depredations; (2) losses to destructive wild animals, mainly coyotes, bobcats, mountain lions, and wolves; and (3) inadequate tariff protection for American-produced wool. As frontier settlers, most stockmen viewed hostile raids as an impediment to successful ranching. Consequently, they favored tough measures to deal with raiders. While protection laws existed in hopes of eradicating these wild animals, fifty cents per bounty was not much of an incentive. As a result, wild animals were responsible for more than 500,000 dollars in sheep and goat losses during 1891. Ranchers throughout the wool districts of the American South were aware that their industry could succeed only if the U.S. Congress enacted tariff legislation with a watchful eye on competitors. This concern was political in nature, and it was a gamble that sheepraisers would eventually lose.[103]

LIVESTOCK AND WOOL PRODUCTION IN SOUTH TEXAS, 1860–1900

In the second half of the nineteenth century, Mexican stockraisers in south Texas tended to favor raising large livestock over sheep and goats, although a number of them were engaged in mixed ranching, herding both kinds of livestock on their lands. And as noted below, sheepraising was important for about a thirty-year period, from the 1860s to about 1890,[104] but horses, mules, and cattle were more valuable than sheep and goats.

Some controversy surrounds the origin of Texas cattle. Terry Jordan and other writers have recently asserted that the origin of the cattle industry in Texas is of South Carolinian background. Yet they note that migrating Anglo herdsmen experienced many occasions when their cattle intermingled with Spanish or Mexican cattle.[105] John E. Rouse, in *The Criollo: Spanish Cattle in the Americas*, shows convincingly that, in fact, the so-called Spanish and Mexican cattle were the basic stock of what northern cattlemen called "Texas" cattle or "longhorns." According to Rouse, the impact of southern herders' Native American cattle on Spanish cattle was very minor when the Anglos reached Spanish Texas in the 1820s.[106] Longhorns became the leading type of cattle herded until new breeds were gradually introduced by cattleraisers to upgrade their longhorn herds in the last third of the nineteenth century.[107]

As a result of varying market and weather conditions, the figures on livestock and wool production varied from year to year across the south Texas range. Table 7.1 gives an idea of the variability in the number of cattle grazed in the Lower Valley over a thirty-year span for which the data are accurate.

As noted in Table 7.1, in 1900 there were nearly two and one-half times as many cattle in south Texas as in 1880. High prices provided an incentive to ranchers in the region to market as many head of beef cattle as possible in the period from the close of the Civil War to the early 1880s. These prices prevailed due to increasing consumer demand for beef in the North, at a time when cattle were in short supply and stockraising had not fully developed in the West. The large numbers left on the range in 1890 and 1900 largely reflected a depressed market from 1892 to 1896 and the return of sheepraisers to cattle raising following the debacle in the price of wool, especially in the large sheep-

Table 7.1 Number of Cattle in South Texas in Selected Years, 1870–1900[a]

Year	Number
1870	277,846
1880	144,092
1890	242,882
1900	440,503

Source: *U.S. Census of Agriculture*, 1860, 1880, 1890, 1900; *U.S. Census of Population*, 1870.
[a] Excludes milk cows.

raising district of Starr, Zapata, Webb and Duval counties.[108] As noted in Table 7.2, the value of livestock in 1900 reached an unprecedented level of nearly 9 million dollars as large numbers of cattle and horses were being produced, but the market remained sluggish. But before that decline in the market came about, the livestock business was the most important economic activity in south Texas.

The volume of livestock, wool, hides, and other agricultural produce reached record amounts during the boom years, and these products continued to be marketed after the halcyon years of the ranching economy. By 1876, for example, the annual export of cattle and wool in the Brownsville district totaled 3,870,000 dollars, a sum that included imported Mexican cattle and wool shipped through that port.[109] At San Diego, sheep ranchers normally marketed 400,000 pounds of wool annually, but in 1873 the amount of wool brought there for export soared to 2 million pounds. In the upper part of the Río Grande Plains region, San Antonio (whose produce was exported through Galveston, including 600,000 pounds of wool in 1876 and 2,000,000 pounds in 1877) and Corpus Christi served as the principal marketing centers for livestock and livestock products from Nueces and neighboring counties. The exports of wool through Corpus Christi were 600,000 pounds in 1866 and an expected shipment of 6,500,000 pounds in 1878.[110] As late as 1890 Corpus Christi was still exporting considerable livestock and other agricultural produce, including 500 carloads of cattle, 1,500,000 pounds of wool, 250,000 pounds of hides, and 2,000 bales of cotton.[111] About this time, other marketing centers in the region reported a sharp increase in wool and livestock production.[112]

The best prices for cattle came in the 1860s and 1870s, during the heyday of the cattle drives, and in general lasted until 1885. In 1867, a three-year-old steer worth less than ten dollars in Texas sold for thirty-eight to forty dollars in Kansas and Illinois.[113] In 1870–71 an older steer—one five-year-old—sold for ten dollars in Texas and twenty dollars in Kansas. Of course, market prices

Table 7.2 Values of Livestock, Farm Products, and Farm Implements in South Texas, 1870–1900

	Value of Livestock	Value of Farm Products	Value of Farm Implements
1870			
Nueces	$1,063,658	$ 224,539	$ 7,905
Duval	$ 75,735	$ 26,522	$ 300
Encinal	$ 16,305	$ 19,030	$ 160
Webb	$ 131,599	$ 163,178	$ 2,258
Cameron	$ 444,900	$ 157,770	$ 12,355
Hidalgo	$ 139,188	$ 50,460	$ 3,950
Starr[a]	$ 18,320	$ 1,450	$ 75
Zapata	$ 108,733	$ 10,268	$ 437
1880			
Nueces	$ 446,099	$ 74,908	$ 3,640
Duval	$ 554,451	$ 51,144	$ 9,227
Encinal	$ 355,301	$ 208,054	$ 200
Webb	$ 303,031	$ 128,492	$ 925
Cameron	$ 367,658	$ 20,300	$ 19,175
Hidalgo[a]	$ 78,677	$ 41,095	$ 2,330
Starr	$ 257,613	$ 21,490	$ 1,513
Zapata	$ 150,353	$ 51,365	$ 2,173
1890			
Nueces	$ 324,250	$ 102,530	$ 7,520
Duval	$ 293,640	$ 31,760	$ 4,490
Encinal	$ 582,100	$ 77,420	$ 790
Webb	$ 684,600	$ 232,060	$ 18,200
Cameron	$ 279,632	$ 121,070	$ 16,757
Hidalgo	$ 715,220	$ 156,330	$ 14,620
Starr	$ 141,330	$ 53,170	$ 14,440
Zapata[a]	$ 20,869	$ 9,130	$ 1,865
1900			
Nueces	$2,360,490	$ 433,838	$ 52,310
Duval	$ 583,314	$ 234,319	$ 22,340
Encinal[b]	—	—	—
Webb	$1,002,290	$ 320,371	$ 34,370
Cameron	$2,972,023	$ 517,337	$ 40,270
Hidalgo	$ 824,794	$ 155,332	$ 30,340
Starr	$ 682,749	$ 218,368	$ 14,860
Zapata	$ 274,326	$ 26,603	$ 7,160

Source: *Ninth, Tenth, Eleventh, and Twelfth Census of the United States*, 1870, 1880, 1890, 1900.

[a] Incomplete.

[b] Not organized.

varied somewhat. One immigrant merchant who was also involved in stock-raising, Joseph H. Vale, reported that beeves were selling at twelve dollars in the Corpus Christi area in 1870.[114] A Texan who drove eleven hundred cattle to California in the spring of 1870 and later sold the herd in Reno, Nevada, recalled that "we paid $10.00 for grown steers in Texas, [and] got $30.00 after driving them 2,000 miles."[115] Prices did not stay this high once the drives north accelerated and the western range was stocked with Texas cattle. Except for temporarily depressed years when the market was saturated, prices for cattle during the period from about the mid-1860s to the mid-1880s generally ranged from twenty to thirty dollars, and occasionally up to thirty-five dollars, producing a bonanza in cattle ranching from south Texas to Montana.

During the boom years of the livestock industry, *rancheros* usually sold their cattle, horses, and mules in San Antonio, Corpus Christi, Rockport, and Brownsville, or to buyers from the East or from Texas who traveled the ranch country. The more successful Mexican *rancheros* drove cattle to the Indian Territory and other distant places. Sheep were raised primarily for their wool, and large shipments of wool were exported annually from south Texas ports, such as Brownsville and Corpus Christi, to the Atlantic. Some wool was also sold to Mexican buyers who, in turn, produced woolen goods. Stockmen also purchased sheep as breeding stock.[116]

Size of Tejano Ranchos

How successful were *rancheros* in south Texas? Moderately successful Tejanos claimed livestock worth a few thousand dollars, say one to five thousand dollars, but every county had a few stockmen ranching on a larger scale, owning stock worth five thousand dollars or more. Among the latter, some raised as many as several thousand head of cattle or horses and ten thousand head of sheep or more, and their pasturelands covered thousands of acres. Based on a quantitative study of Hidalgo County's tax rolls from 1852 to 1900, at best only about 15 percent of the stockraisers reached these moderate and large-scale levels of production. On the basis of U.S. agricultural census data and county tax records, I believe that this pattern was typical for the entire region. Table 7.4 shows that in 1860 only 12 out of 633 Tejano ranchers owned herds valued at five thousand dollars or more. The number rose to 35 out of 417 in 1870 and to 52 out of 830 in 1880. While the data are not totally complete, because the reports were not returned or remain incomplete for some of the counties, it is evident that Tejano ranching involved mostly small-scale, family-owned enterprises. As noted above, some Tejanos formed partnerships or companies, but these persons were usually larger stockraisers who had access to capital. Thus, I disagree with Montejano, who based his history of south Texas on the "large self-sufficient ranches," asserting that such *ranchos* were typical and determined the pattern of class relations for the entire region. Since 85 percent or so of the Tejanos were small *rancheros*, the nature of their society was markedly different than that represented by Montejano's analysis. More on this point will be discussed below.

SUCCESSFUL TEJANO *RANCHEROS* IN 1870: A BRIEF LISTING

Examples of leading *rancheros* in 1870 can be found in all of the region's counties. In Cameron County the most productive *rancho* belonged to Pedro Longoria, who owned 12,015 acres. His activities were exclusively devoted to ranching, as he raised barely 300 bushels of corn. His stock consisted of 700 horses, 50 mules, 10 milk cows, 14 oxen, 60 sheep, 40 swine, and 4,400 cattle. The total value of his livestock was reported as fifty-four thousand dollars, but it should be recalled that these dollar values were based not on market value, but on local assessment rates that were usually kept very low.[117] Among all Tejanos in south Texas, Longoria owned the largest single herd of cattle at this time. In neighboring Hidalgo County only four Tejanos had livestock over 5,000 dollars in value: Simón Garza, 9,200 dollars; Macedonio Vela, 6,450 dollars; Salvador Guerra, 7,450 dollars; and Sabas Pérez, 12,720 dollars. All of them herded cattle and horses, with only Guerra reporting fifteen hundred head of sheep in addition to large livestock.[118] Albino Canales, in Duval County, reported that he owned fifteen hundred horses, eighty milk cows, and fifteen hundred sheep, all with a value of 17,120 dollars.[119]

A number of successful *rancheros* can also be found in Nueces County. The most outstanding Tejano there was Alejos Pérez, who claimed ownership of 1,000 horses, 50 mules, 45 milk cows, 165 cattle, and 3,000 sheep, worth 14,945 dollars. He paid 500 dollars in wages and his wool clip amounted to 6,000 pounds. Since he reported owning only 320 acres of improved land, it is very likely that he was ranching on a relative's land, or that he leased land from other Tejanos. As previously noted, because of the abundance of land, grazing land was rented at very cheap rates throughout most of the second half of the nineteenth century. Pablo Pérez, who owned 11,220 acres, a bit more than two and one-half leagues of land, rounded his herd to 500 horses and 500 cattle. At this time the county assessed cattle at 4 dollars and horses at 9 dollars, so that his entire stock was valued at a modest 6,500 dollars. Santos Moreno still owned 9,152 acres, upon which he grazed 275 horses, 1,540 head of cattle, and 2,000 sheep, with the stock having a value of 9,650 dollars. José María Valadez,

Table 7.3 Value of Livestock Owned by Mexicans and Others in South Texas, 1860, 1870, 1880 (in Dollars)

	Cameron		Hidalgo		Starr	
	Mexicans	*Others*	*Mexicans*	*Others*	*Mexicans*	*Others*
1860						
$1–999	226	9	163	11	100	6
$1,000–1,999	61	7	13	—	9	2
$2,000–4,999	45	5	2	1	2	3
$5,000 or more	11	11	1	—	—	1
1870						
$1–999	48	11	25	6	ND[a]	ND
$1,000–1,999	24	5	29	2	ND	ND
$2,000–4,999	37	2	7	—	ND	ND
$5,000 or more	22	2	4	1	ND	ND
1880						
$1–999	40	2	74	12	133	1
$1,000–1,999	30	7	11	—	28	—
$2,000–4,999	27	4	6	1	27	—
$5,000 or more	9	7	1	1	11	—

	Zapata		Webb		Duval	
	Mexicans	*Others*	*Mexicans*	*Others*	*Mexicans*	*Others*
1860						
$1–999	I[b]	I	I	I	ND	ND
$1,000–1,999	I	I	I	I	ND	ND
$2,000–4,999	I	I	I	I	ND	ND
$5,000 or more	I	I	I	I	ND	ND
1870						
$1–999	103	3	10	—	36	3
$1,000–1,999	19	—	8	2	11	—
$2,000–4,999	4	—	12	—	9	3
$5,000 or more	1	—	7	1	1	2
1880						
$1–999	130	2	46	—	71	2
$1,000–1,999	24	—	3	—	50	3
$2,000–4,999	11	—	8	1	55	6
$5,000 or more	5	—	11	4	15	7

Source: *U.S. Census of Non-Population, 1860, 1870, 1880*, ms.

[a] No data.

[b] Incomplete data.

a *ranchero* relatively new to the region, claimed 20 horses, 100 cattle, and 4,000 sheep that produced 8,000 pounds of wool. His stock was reported to be worth 4,500 dollars.[120]

The largest stockraiser in Webb County at this time was Nicolás Sánchez, whose stock included 100 horses, 4 mules, 200 milk cows, 24 oxen, 776 cattle (note that the total cattle stock is a neatly rounded 1,000 head), and 7,500 sheep, with the value of livestock being 13,065 dollars. The county's largest sheep rancher, however, was Ramos [Ramón?] Martínez, whose 10,400 sheep produced 20,000 pounds of wool. His expenses for wages totaled 1,750 dollars. Another important sheepraiser was Cayetano de la Garza, who owned 9,300 sheep as well as 60 horses, 2 mules, and 560 cattle; he reported paying 1,500 dollars in wages. Santos Benavides, the ex-Confederate soldier-leader, reported owning 100 horses and 1,500 cattle, all valued at 6,760 dollars.[121] There were, of course, many small-scale *rancheros* whose herds had a value of a few hundred dollars and considerable numbers whose livestock was valued in the middle range from one thousand to five thousand dollars.

A variety of marketing dynamics involving large numbers of Tejano producers as well as Tejano and Anglo buyers characterized the pastoral economy. By resorting to the records of bills of sale of livestock in Hidalgo and Webb counties, I believe that several Tejano marketing patterns are evident for the last three decades of the nineteenth century, the time period for which this kind of documentation is available.[122] First, the data for Hidalgo County in Appendix 3 indicates that sales and drives to various marketplaces, mostly in Texas, were seasonal. Also, Tejano producers sold to both Tejanos and Anglos. These persons were sometimes other ranchers, but not always; some were commission men representing livestock buyers in distant markets. In Hidalgo County, buyers also tended to purchase small herds from several Tejano *rancheros* in a given district or ranching community. Apparently, larger stockmen like Macedonio Vela, Simón Garza, and others drove their own herds, eliminating middlemen and earning a better return on their sales. These activities were not reported in the Hidalgo County bills of sale because the fact that the owners drove their own stock to market precluded their inspection by the county's hide and animal inspector. Unfortunately, the bills of sale rarely gave precise prices for stock sold. However, local sales were usually made at lower prices than those for which *rancheros* herded stock northward. This factor accounts for the greater economic success among the larger stockmen, for whom long drives were practical. Few transactions involving sheep and goats are of record in Hidalgo County, but, as noted above, it did not generally produce large numbers of small livestock.

The data for Webb County, a very large land district devoted to mixed

Table 7.4 Leading Tejano Sheep Ranchers, Webb County, 1880 (by Family)

	Acreage	*Total Value of Land*	*Wages*	*Value of Farm Production*	*Sh/g*	*Wool/lbs*	*Cattle*	*Horses/Mules*
Benavides								
Santos	5,314	$ 20,400	$ 2,833	$ 4,831	14,700	18,000	631[a]	91
Eulalio	5,640	$ 8,000	$ 800	$ 6,000	7,000	21,000	0	15
Cristóbal	—	$ 14,300	$ 4,000	$ 8,000	14,000	21,000	0	31
Refugio	—	$ 11,240	—	$ 3,750	10,000	15,000	180	35
Porfirio	9,524	$ 12,851	$ 2,500	$ 4,440	12,600	16,000	263	0
Benavides Totals:	20,478	$ 66,791	$10,133	$27,021	69,800	91,000	1,074	172
de la Garza								
Cayetano	6,700	$ 12,540	$ 1,712	$ 5,990	15,300	22,500	0	0
Lázaro	1,411	$ 3,000	$ 2,000	$ 2,540	1,000	0	0	47
de la Garza Totals:	8,111	$ 15,540	$ 3,712	$ 8,430	16,300	22,500	0	47
Sánchez								
Nicolás	—	$ 32,000	$ 6,000	$12,500	32,000	50,000	100	150
Santiago	—	$ 6,500	$ 1,456	$ 4,061	6,000	12,000	100	75
Roberto	6,000	$ 5,678	$ 600	$ 2,500	5,150	10,000	60	30
Margarito	6,100	$ 920	$ 500	$ 600	0	0	105	12
Sánchez Totals:	12,100	$ 45,098	$ 8,556	$19,661	43,150	72,000	365	267
3 Family Total:	40,689	$127,429	$22,401	$55,112	129,250	185,500	1,439	486

[a] Santos Benavides claimed he had lost 200 cattle.

ranching, shows a strong contrast with the patterns of Hidalgo County. Appendix 4 reveals an early predominance in cattle ranching, involving the sale of both locally raised stock as well as imported cattle from nearby Mexican *ranchos* and *haciendas*. Whereas Hidalgo County producers sold small numbers, Webb County *rancheros* marketed large herds, some over one thousand head per individual transaction. What does this mean? The bills of sale point to the presence of the same buyers and sellers in Webb County. The Tejano stockraisers in Webb County were not as numerous as those in Hidalgo County. However, the fact that they were generally very large landholders, in turn, made it possible for them to produce and market large herds. As in Cameron County, such powerful ranchers monopolized the pastoral economy. The small-scale *ranchero*, while not completely gone from the scene, played a minor role in Webb County. Again, price data on the individual sales is incomplete, but the larger producers of cattle in Webb County do not appear to have received high prices because they were usually selling to other Texas ranchers or middlemen, and they evidently did not drive their own herds north to eliminate buyers.

Also, it is apparent that sheep ranching on a large scale was an important pastoral enterprise in Webb County. In fact, a number of transactions are of record in the bills of sale. There were some Anglo producers, particularly in sheepraising, as they too sought to enter the industry during the booming years. But again, Tejano producers played a pivotal role in sheepraising. As noted in Table 7.4, in 1880 the Benavides, de la Garza, and Sánchez families, controlled a sizable share of wool production in the county because of their large sheep herds. Collectively, these three families owned about 129,000 sheep, out of 181,616 sheep in the county, or nearly 73 percent of the total, and their production of wool totaled 185,500 pounds. The Benavides family claimed 20,000 acres, on which they herded 69,000 head of sheep (and goats), which produced 91,000 pounds of wool during the spring clip. They reported that their farm production was worth a bit over 27,000 dollars. The Sánchez family was second in the value of farm production, with nearly 20,000 dollars, and the de la Garza brothers were in third place with a value of 8,430 dollars. It is likely that these figures do not represent sales of horses, mules, and cattle.

COMPARATIVE LIVESTOCK PRODUCTION AMONG MEXICANS AND OTHERS IN HIDALGO COUNTY, 1850–1885

The entire pattern of recovery that occurred shortly after annexation and the subsequent boom in the ranching economy can be viewed in a case study of Hidalgo County, where the initial pace of recovery was definitely slower than in Cameron, Starr, and Nueces counties. According to the tax data for Hidalgo County, few ranchers owned more than fifty cattle in the period from 1852 to 1865: eight in 1852, six in 1855, and forty-two in 1865. During this period all of the ranchmen were Mexican, except for two Anglos and two Europeans.[123] Tejanos raised 74 percent of the cattle in the county in 1865, but the largest cattle ranch belonged to Salomé Ballí McAllen and John McAllen, a native of Scotland who had come to the Lower Valley in the 1840s. In 1865 Rancho Santa Anita had eighteen hundred cattle.[124]

Similarly, horse and sheep ranching were relatively small operations during this initial period of economic reconstruction. Few stockmen in Hidalgo County owned more than fifty horses: one Mexican rancher in 1852, none in 1855, and fourteen Mexicans and one European in 1865. In the latter year, five *rancheros* herded between 100 and 150 horses. In 1852 Petra Hinojosa, a widow, owned the largest herd, with 2,000 sheep. Three years later, John Young, an English merchant in the Lower Valley, grazed 5,000 sheep, probably along the Río Grande, where he was quickly accumulating land. Only eight other small herds were assessed by the tax assessor.[125] Of a total of 11,095 sheep and goats in 1865, only nine ranchers, all of them Mexican, owned more than 500 sheep and goats.

Rancheros in Hidalgo County dominated cattle ranching from 1865 to 1885. Mexicans made up the largest number of ranchers in the county, increasing from 67 in 1870 to 115 in 1880. In addition to Mexican *rancheros*, there were a few Anglo, European, and Black stockmen. The expansion of the ranching economy in the county during the post–Civil War period is reflected in the proliferation in stock marks and brands recorded in the county courthouse at Edinburg. In the years from 1866 to 1873, a total of 423 marks and brands were filed. Of these, 371 belonged to Mexicans, 38 to Anglos and Europeans, 12 to Blacks, 1 to a Mexican-Anglo stockman, and another to the Oblate missionary priests who had a *rancho* at La Lomita, upriver from Edinburg.[126]

The next five years saw a similar pattern of Tejanos dominating the registration of marks and records. From 1873 to 1877, Mexicans recorded 409 marks and brands, of which 85 belonged to women, and an additional brand was registered by a Mexican-Anglo rancher. Anglos filed 28 marks and brands, and Blacks 2.[127]

The role of Mexican *rancheros* figured importantly during this period of rapid livestock expansion. As noted in Table 7.5, Mexicans produced the majority of the cattle raised in Hidalgo County during this period: 73 percent in 1870, 81 percent in 1875, and 91 percent in 1880. Up to 1880, Anglo stockmen raised less than 6 percent of the cattle. The presence of John McAllen in the ranching business meant that Europeans produced more cattle than Anglos. However,

Table 7.5 Cattle Production in Hidalgo County, by Ethnicity of Owners, 1865–1885

Year	Total No. of Cattle	Mexican	Anglo	European	Black	Blend
1865	7,881	73	1	25	0	0
1870	14,444	74	3	22	[a]	[a]
1875	11,022	81	4	14	1	[a]
1880	14,438	91	5	[a]	2	[a]
1885	38,467	68	18	12	1	[a]

Source: Hidalgo County, *Tax Rolls*, 1865, 1870, 1875, 1880, and 1885.
[a] Less than 1 percent.

the prosperous early 1880s stimulated Anglo expansion into Hidalgo County. As a result, in 1885 Mexican stockraisers produced only 68 percent of the cattle. At the same time, Europeans lost about 10 percent of their share in cattle production. The decline in Mexican and European production was made up by the entry of Anglo ranchers, who increased their share to nearly 18 percent.

The expansion in ranching in the Lower Valley is also reflected in the increase in the number of ranchers and the greater diversification of ranching, as some ranchers became increasingly oriented to commercial stockraising instead of raising livestock for local markets only. Tables 7.6 and 7.7 show the distribution of ranchers by ethnicity and size of cattle herds in Hidalgo County for the period 1870–1885. In order to analyze the development of commercial ranching in Hidalgo County, the ranchers are classified according to classes. A small herd is defined as either class 1 or class 2. While farmers or ranchers owning between 1 and 24 head of cattle (class 1) may not have been commercially oriented, those herding between 25 and 99 head of cattle (class 2) were probably involved in marketing livestock to either stock buyers or other ranchers. Ranchers in class 3 (100–199 head of stock) were medium-size breeders. The larger ranchers are defined as those whose herd numbered more than 200 head of cattle (class 4).

As noted in Table 7.7, in the post–Civil War years Mexicans in Hidalgo County raised mostly small herds. From 1870 to 1885 almost 80 percent of all cattle herds owned by Mexicans were either in the class 1 or class 2 category. About one-third of the small herds consisted of 25 to 99 head. The biggest absolute gain in small herds took place between 1880 and 1885. Small herds jumped from 189 in 1880 to 506 in 1885. The fact that small herds were so common indicates that it was easier to enter herding on a small scale.

Table 7.6 Ethnicity of Owners of Cattle Herds in Hidalgo County, 1870–1885

	Mexicans		Others		Total
	No.	*%*	*No.*	*%*	*No. Owners*
1870	151	92.1	13	7.0	164
1875	225	94.0	15	6.0	240
1880	217	93.9	14	6.1	231
1885	576	93.7	39	6.3	615

Source: Hidalgo County, *Tax Rolls*, 1870–1885.

Table 7.7 Size of Cattle Herds in Hidalgo County, by Ethnicity of Owners, 1870–1885

	Mexican							
	1870		1875		1880		1885	
Class[a]	*No.*	*%*	*No.*	*%*	*No.*	*%*	*No.*	*%*
1	65	39.2	113	47.1	101	43.7	339	55.1
2	55	33.1	86	35.8	88	38.1	167	27.2
3	16	9.6	20	8.3	19	8.2	43	7.0
4	15	9.0	6	2.5	9	3.9	27	4.4
Total	151	91.0	225	93.7	217	93.9	576	93.7
	Other							
Class	*No.*	*%*	*No.*	*%*	*No.*	*%*	*No.*	*%*
1	5	3.0	5	2.1	4	1.7	14	2.3
2	6	3.6	8	3.3	6	2.6	12	2.0
3	2	1.2	1	.4	3	1.3	6	1.0
4	2	1.2	1	.4	1	.4	7	1.1
Total	15	9.0	15	6.2	14	6.0	39	6.4
Grand Total	166		240		231		615	

Source: Hidalgo County, *Tax Rolls*, 1870–1885.

[a] Class 1 equals 1 to 24 head. Class 2 equals 25 to 99 head. Class 3 equals 100 to 199 head. Class 4 equals more than 200 head.

Table 7.8 Horse Production in Hidalgo County, by Ethnicity of Owners, 1865–1885[a]

Year	Total No. of Horses	Mexican	Anglo	European	Black	Blend
1865	2,166	95	1	4	0	0
1870	5,547	90	2	7	1	[b]
1875	10,057	88	5	5	2	[b]
1880	13,380	99	2	[b]	[b]	[b]
1885	24,517	86	5	[b]	[b]	[b]

Sources: Hidalgo County, *Tax Rolls*, 1865–1885.

[a] Excludes jacks (donkeys), most of which were owned by Mexicans. This stock was used for breeding mules.

[b] Less than 1 percent.

Table 7.7 also shows that the number of Mexican *rancheros* grazing medium and large herds remained fairly constant throughout the 1870s. The number grew in the early 1880s, however, when about 20 percent of the Mexican cattle herds were either medium or large. Medium herds ranged from 16 in 1870 to 19 in 1880, but by 1885 56 herds qualified as class 3 herds (100 to 199). Large herds fluctuated from 15 in 1870 to 6 in 1875, rising to 9 in 1880. By 1885 the number of large herds owned by Mexicans had increased to 27 in number. The decline of medium-size herds in the 1870–1875 period reflects the impact of the 1873 panic, which evidently led some ranchers to cut back or sell their herds. However, this situation was corrected by 1885, when both medium and large-size herds increased in number. The more successful Mexicans owned these herds and prospered from the better times. Also, by this time eleven Anglos—most of whom did not reside in Hidalgo County—now herded medium- and large-size cattle herds, whereas before 1880 only one Anglo owned a medium-size herd.

As noted in Table 7.8, Mexican ranchers dominated horse and mule production in Hidalgo County for nearly a quarter-century after the Civil War. Even as the numbers of these kinds of livestock increased, Mexicans continued to breed a disproportionate share of them. During the entire twenty-year period Mexicans accounted for an average of 90 percent of all horses and mules raised. While some ranchers raised only horses and mules, it appears that most also herded cattle alongside the horse stock. Steady prices for horses and mules made this branch of the livestock industry popular with *rancheros*.

During the ranching bonanza of the 1870s and early 1880s, the sheer number of Mexicans involved in breeding horses and mules also increased dramatically.

Table 7.9 Ethnicity of Owners of Horse Herds in Hidalgo County, 1870–1885

	Mexicans		Others		Total
	No.	%	*No.*	%	*No.*
1870	160	92.0	14	8.0	174
1875	218	92.0	19	8.0	237
1880	280	94.2	17	5.8	297
1885	576	92.6	46	7.4	622

Source: Hidalgo County, *Tax Rolls*, 1870–1885.

As noted in Table 7.9, the number of Mexicans who raised horses rose from 160 in 1870 to 280 in 1880 and 576 in 1885. Moreover, an average of 92 percent of all owners of horse herds in Hidalgo County were Mexican.

Nearly 85 percent of the Tejanos herded small herds and the rest of the *rancheros* owned medium or large herds of horse stock. As noted in Table 7.10, the number of Mexicans who claimed more than 25 horses and/or mules soared from 54 in 1870 to 244 in 1885. In the 1870s, however, most Mexican stockmen raised small herds in the range of 25 to 99 head. For example, in 1875 only 10 out of 54 Mexicans herded medium- or large-size herds of horses and mules. Five years later only 18 out of 114 Mexicans reported owning medium or large herds of horses and mules. While the number of Mexicans who were assessed on medium and large herds of horses and mules increased to 32 in 1880 and 51 in 1885, the number of Mexicans who owned small herds rose moderately to 118 in 1880 and then soared to 193 in 1885. Obviously, the ranching boom led to an expansion in the size of some ranchers' herds, but during the same period many more *rancheros* entered ranching, rapidly augmenting the numbers of small-scale producers.

The *rancheros* most successful in breeding horse stock were Macedonio Vela and his brothers, Rafael and Salvador, Amado and Refugio Gutiérrez Cavazos, Vicente Cárdenas, Antonio Cano, Esteban Garza, Lino Hinojosa, Lucas Cantú, Rafael Flores Salinas, Pedro Villarreal, Martín Hinojosa del Toro, and a few others. Esteban, Sebastián, and Gregorio Dávila, who apparently were nephews of Antonio Cantú Sánchez, received an inheritance from the latter in 1875, and they became prominent cattle and horse breeders. Cantú Sánchez's *rancho*, La Piedra, consisted of land in Hidalgo County that bordered on the Río Grande and extended north five or six leagues; this land is in the San Salvador del Tule grant. He had also purchased, from the heirs of Yreneo

Table 7.10 Size of Horse Herds in Hidalgo County, by Ethnicity of Owners, 1870–1885

	Mexican							
	1870		1875		1880		1885	
Class[a]	*No.*	*%*	*No.*	*%*	*No.*	*%*	*No.*	*%*
1	106	60.9	106	44.7	130	43.8	332	53.4
2	44	25.3	96	40.5	118	39.7	193	31.0
3	8	4.6	15	6.3	25	8.4	37	5.9
4	2	1.1	3	1.3	7	2.4	14	2.3
Total	160	91.9	218	92.8	280	94.3	576	92.6
	Other							
Class	*No.*	*%*	*No.*	*%*	*No.*	*%*	*No.*	*%*
1	11	6.3	10	4.2	9	3	34	5.5
2	2	1.1	5	2.1	7	2.4	7	1.1
3	—	—	2	.8	—	—	2	.3
4	1	1.5	2	.8	1	.3	3	.5
Total	14	8.9	19	7.9	17	5.8	46	7.6
Total	174		237		297		622	

Source: Hidalgo County, *Tax Rolls*, 1870–1885.

[a] Class 1 equals 1 to 24 head. Class 2 equals 25 to 99 head. Class 3 equals 100 to 199 head. Class 4 equals more than 200 head.

Zamora, one-half of a *porción.* Cantú had loaned his nephew, Don Sebastián Dávila, 175 pesos for the purchase of the other half of the Zamora *porción*, where he evidently had his *rancho.* Esteban and Gregorio apparently operated their ranches in the lands of La Piedra. These *rancheros* customarily raised from one hundred to five hundred horses, excepting Macedonio Vela, who eventually raised up to one thousand horses. As with successful cattle raisers, the good fortune of these men and their wives rested not only on large landholdings, but also was the result of disciplined work and an early entry into the ranching economy. There is no clear evidence that they borrowed large sums of money, but apparently they returned much of their profits from sales back into ranching.[128]

During this time, only a handful of Anglos and Europeans raised horses and mules. Except for John McAllen, all of these stockraisers herded small or medium-size herds. Thus, up to 1885 horse and mule production was basically a Tejano economic activity.

There was very little change in the number of sheep and goats from 1865 to 1870, when the total reported in the tax rolls was 11,646. Again, only twenty-eight ranchers were assessed on sheep and goats, nine of whom owned 500 or more head of sheep and goats. Only five ranchers, all of them Mexican, were assessed on more than 1,000 sheep and goats. The stable sheep and goat population reflected the fact that the demand for sheep and goats was not strong enough to entice ranchers to raise them in larger numbers.

In response to better prices for wool and breeding sheep in the 1870s, ranchers in Hidalgo County began to increase their sheep and goat herds, so that by 1880 their numbers were nearly triple the total for 1870. Sheep and goats increased to 14,198 in 1875, and doubled to 28,279 in 1880. Of the two, sheep were more numerous, accounting for 87 percent of the total. Mexican stockmen usually raised both sheep and goats, instead of one or the other. The main reason was that both kinds of livestock were cared for in the same manner, and goat kid was a favorite meat among the Mexican populace, especially among shepherds who lived in the pastures tending the sheep.[129]

Nearly all of the larger sheep and goat raisers were Mexican. In 1875, of six ranchers who herded more than 500 sheep all were Mexican except for Edward C. Dougherty, who had a herd of 1,200 sheep.[130] The largest herds belonged to Teodoro Guerra, who grazed 3,000 sheep, and Esteban Garza Garza, whose sheep herd numbered 3,500. In 1880 fourteen ranchers reported owning herds over 500. Of these, all were Mexican, except for two owned by Anglos. The three largest sheep herds were owned by Esteban Garza Garza, 2,000 head; and Gabino López and Jesús Rodríguez, both grazing 4,000 sheep. Five other Mexican ranchers raised more than 1,000 sheep.

Goats were raised in increasing numbers in the 1870s and 1880s, but not in as large a number as sheep. Except for an occasional Anglo merchant, such as Brownsville's H. M. Fields, who grazed 600 goats in 1880, nearly all goat raisers were Mexican ranchers.[131] Few raised more than 500 goats, but one did in 1880 and four in 1885.

Sheep and goat ranching peaked in 1885, when there were 52,314 sheep and goats in Hidalgo County, nearly double the 1880 total; and 82 percent of this stock were sheep. Mexican ranchers owned 72 percent of the sheep and 92 percent of the goats. Only fourteen of the Mexican stockmen raised between 500 and 1,000 sheep. Ten of the eleven herds with more than 1,000 sheep and goats were owned by Mexicans. However, the largest herd belonged to John McAllen, who grazed 4,000 sheep at Rancho Santa Anita. Among the more enterprising Mexican ranchers, Esteban Garza Garza continued to engage in commercial sheep ranching, herding 3,000 sheep. Another Mexican, Eduardo Villarreal, a well-known cattle rancher, reported owning 3,584 head of sheep in 1885.

The success of Mexican sheep ranchers paralleled the rapid rise of sheepherding that coincided with high prices for wool and sheep. Post–Civil War prices for south Texas wool were generally high, reaching thirty cents or more per pound. In 1878 the price dipped to twenty-five cents, and in 1880 to twenty cents per pound, which was still quite profitable. Sheep advanced in value from two dollars per head in 1858 to three dollars in 1878. However, by 1882 sheep could be purchased for one dollar to two dollars each because of their overabundance.[132] And as world wool production rose after 1885, prices tumbled and stockmen in the United States felt the pinch. Even for Lower Valley ranchers who seemed to be oblivious to world economic trends, the changing market economies brought havoc to their way of life.

Few non-Mexicans played a major role in the ranching economy of Hidalgo County before 1885. Two of the earliest arrivals were John Young and John McAllen. Young, a Scottish merchant at Brownsville and upriver at Edinburg, married Salomé Ballí, great-granddaughter of Doña Gregoria Hinojosa de Ballí. Young succeeded in merchandising, and he began to acquire *derechos* to land as well as buying land at sheriff sales prior to the work of the Bourland-Miller Commission. In 1852 he claimed ownership of about 35,000 acres. Young died in 1859, leaving a large estate to his wife and son, including about 100,000 acres. McAllen, who was Young's clerk, continued to manage Young's store at Brownsville and the trading post at Edinburg.[133]

In 1861, McAllen married Salome Ballí de Young and, together, they continued to operate the various businesses. Depending on his father-in-law and other Ballí relatives and on an Anglo foreman, Charles C. Thompson, McAllen became a rancher. After his foreman and father-in-law died in 1868 and 1869, respectively, McAllen began to spend considerable time at his ranch, Santa Anita, most of which he had acquired by 1879. For many years McAllen and his stepson, John Ballí Young, operated their ranch as a partnership, running several thousand head of livestock.[134] In 1880 Rancho Santa Anita was a prosperous settlement of ninety-three persons, with nearly all of the adults working as *vaqueros* or laborers.[135]

Before 1885 only a handful of Anglos lived near the river, most of whom farmed bottomlands and raised small numbers of livestock in contrast to their Mexican neighbors.[136] One exception was Thaddeus M. Rhodes, a North Carolinian who had served in the American army during the war with Mexico and stayed in the Lower Valley at the end of the conflict. He conducted farming and ranching activities at Rancho Relámpago, in the southeastern corner of the old Llano Grande grant.[137] Rhodes started on a small scale and gradually increased his herds, and in this respect he was typical of the many Mexican *rancheros* whose prosperity paralleled the booming ranching economy. In 1870 Rhodes owned 50 cattle and 3 horses. His cattle herd increased to 125 head in 1875, and in 1890 reached a peak of 1,000. Following the drought of the early 1890s, Rhodes was assessed on only 300 cattle in 1895. In 1900 he owned only 250 cattle. A similar pattern of production is evident in his horse stock, which increased from 20 in 1875 to 80 in 1880, reaching a peak of 150 horses in 1885 and 1890, and declining to 40 horses in 1895. Like most moderately successful ranchers, Rhodes raised sheep alongside his herds of horses and cattle.[138] He also tried his hand at corn and cotton farming on the river's bottomlands.[139]

CONCLUSION

The significant participation of Tejanos in the ranching economy of south Texas during the years 1848–1885 reflected the continuing importance of land to these settlers and their determination to earn a decent living from their own endeavors. Possessing a long history of stockraising that dated to the Spanish period, they continued to utilize much of their expertise as well as adapt to new challenges that arose with the change in sovereignty in 1848 and the growing commercialization of stockraising. They were able to adjust to chaotic political conditions affecting them, responding as best they could until the more normal times returned after the Civil War era and the end of intermittent banditry. The initial period of recovery of stockraising in the region began concurrently with land-grant adjudication of Tejano claims to Spanish and Mexican land grants in the 1850s. That this was the case is understandable because landholders did not feel secure in returning to their lands until the issue of validation of title had been resolved. Also, Indian depredations initially hampered the movement of herds from the south side of the Río Grande into the region. However, the growth in the number of livestock and the successful sale of stock accelerated the resurgence of ranching enterprises. During the first ten years or so of this development (1848–60), Tejano ranchers were clearly dominant throughout the region, except for the rise of an incipient Anglo ranching enclave in the Corpus Christi area, where Stillman, Kenedy, and King founded their ranches. This peripheral entry of Anglos saw no real expansion until the 1870s and 1880s, when other newcomers from the United States and Europe entered ranching. The large number of brand and ear mark registrations, the proliferation of new *ranchos*, and even Tejano—Anglo partnerships reflected the noticeable expansion in the ranching economy. By 1860 this growth was most apparent in Cameron, Nueces, and Starr counties, but these activities were also occurring in the rest of the region, as reflected in the large numbers of livestock assessed for tax purposes by the various counties. Suddenly, problems loomed, and stockraising nearly came to a halt.

Cortina's raid of 1859 and subsequent interborder conflict between Mexicans and Anglos resulted in chaos, hampering the success of normal ranching operations. The Civil War years (1861–65) and turmoil in Mexico, for all practical purposes, stalled the recovery, although Tejano stockmen and women did not disappear from the land. In fact, nearly all official reports indicate that both Tejano and non-Tejano owned herds increased rapidly during this time, as well as during the years of Reconstruction, contrary to the argument of powerful ranchers such as King and Kenedy and others who claimed that their herds were devastated by bandits from Mexico.

The full acceleration of the ranching economy, with its growing commercial character, occurred in the post–Civil War years. By the 1870s ranching in much of Texas, including the southern part of the state, was a major business. What I mean by this is that stockraising was an economic activity that demanded considerable expertise and resources in order to be successful in an ever-changing marketplace. Good management, luck, ambition, and the acquisition of valuable grasslands and a cooperative nature were essential for the success of small and large enterprises. The traditional markets in nearby Mexico and key markets in Texas and Louisiana continued to receive Tejano-owned or Tejano-produced livestock and wool. With the demand for beef cattle and other livestock and wool after the Civil War, Tejanos entered new, distant markets, selling stock in the Indian Territory, Missouri, Kansas, and even Cuba. The evidence shows that about 15 percent of Tejano ranchers engaged in large-scale livestock production. These stockmen grazed herds that numbered hundreds and thousands of head of cattle, horses, and sheep. The wealthier *ranchero* class had a permanent workforce that included servants, general laborers, artisans, *caporales*, *vaqueros*, and shepherds, but they did not generally have a peon class because they were not farmers as such. *Vaqueros*, in particular, as throughout Latin America, saw themselves as tough and independent men whose skill ensured them a measure of respect and independence. Most *rancheros*, however, were small-scale and moderate producers whose livestock were valued at under five thousand dollars. It is for this reason that few Tejanos fit Montejano's description of a *hacendado* or large-scale *ranchero*. Thus, the vast majority of *rancheros* in south Texas were indeed self-employed proprietors who, during peak seasons, hired free workers as cowboys and shepherds. The tiny villages that grew around a large *rancho*, like Randado or Laguna Seca, and the social and economic activities that took place there never really resembled the classic *hacienda* of Latin American *latifundios.* The region was mainly an enclave of small ranchers, rather than *hacendados.* In many ways, this was a logical development in view of the persistence of partible inheritance and the Spanish–Mexican pattern of land tenure in which *porciones* and land grants of less than four or five leagues were dominant. The fact that independent *rancheros* were numerous has helped to perpetuate the Tejano memory of the *ranchero* tradition.

Many factors contributed to a *ranchero*'s success. As in the colonial and Mexican period, adequate land and other natural resources were vital. While the eastern section of the region enjoyed tall grasses conducive to the raising of large animals, the western section consisted of short grasses and a more difficult topography because of low hills, rocky soils, and deeper *arroyos.* The rainfall of a normal season was adequate, but ranchers devised other ways to cope with the potential of drought. Access to capital was important to *rancheros* whose initiative and ambition drove them to acquire more grazing lands and herds. Unfortunately, few Tejanos in the Lower Valley qualified for loans from the more important brokers, such as H. P. Drought and Co. of San Antonio. Thus, local merchants, bankers, and friendly relatives served as lenders. In any case, the histories of individual *rancheros* presented here are indicative of those who already owned land or arrived early in the region and who worked hard to establish large, prosperous *ranchos.* In the Webb County area, a relatively small class of Tejanos, descendants of the colonial families introduced by Escandón, monopolized landholding and virtually excluded the entry of small *rancheros.* There, *rancheros* remained dominant throughout the good years and the bad times that were to come later in the nineteenth century. In the rest of the region, the number of *rancheros* grew rapidly, although consolidation of landholding, which was directly affected by the commercialization of stockraising, saw the displacement of smaller producers.

In short, the ranching business was lively and far reaching in its social and economic impact upon Tejanos and others. A variety of commercial transactions involving the buying and selling of stock and wool and the financing of ranching operations characterized the pastoral economy. Stockraising itself was conducted by both small and large *rancheros.* South Texas was not and never had been the home of Chevalier's classic "powerful men of the north," nor for that matter did a Sánchez Navarro estate develop in the region. Yet it had evolved into much more than merely herding, as in the days of Abraham. The dominant type was the *ranchero,* usually a self-made man who entered ranching in the initial period of recovery and remained in the business thirty, forty years, or more. The bulk of their number were small-scale producers, but every district had a few men whose herds were extensive. Tejanos in south Texas, more than in other regions of the state, had played a crucial role in the recovery and expansion of stockraising in the period from 1848 to 1885, thereby contributing to the growth of the national economy. The last fifteen years or so of the nineteenth century would rapidly transform the ranching economy.

CHAPTER EIGHT

THE DECLINE OF TEJANO RANCHING

Its Social and Economic Bases, 1885–1900

Whereas the 1870s and early 1880s were good years for Mexican as well as Anglo ranchers throughout south Texas, by the mid-1880s declining prices in the marketplace and other problems began to adversely affect Tejano *rancheros.* As the new century approached, the ranching economy remained largely stagnant, and new changes were in the offing as the movement to convert the rangeland to farmland gained momentum. Eventually, all of these changes affected Tejano *rancheros* and those who depended on them for their livelihood. Gradually, the region's economy converted to a dual farming and ranching society, but that story is one that belongs more to the twentieth century, when intensive, large-scale irrigation projects resulted in intensive farming along the delta lands of Río Grande.

This chapter focuses on the factors that produced a rapid loss of the Tejano dominance in the ranching economy of the region. I have again utilized the tax data on livestock in Hidalgo County to document these brief fifteen years of the shrinking ranching economy, especially the Tejano sector. Particular emphasis is placed on Anglo competition, the decline in stock and wool prices, the effect of bad weather, lending practices, and the negative economic impact of partible inheritance on Tejano *rancheros* and the response of Tejanos to the decline in stockraising. Historians have often noted the overall effect of the changes in the marketplace and the weather on the livestock industry, but few have examined how these factors affected Tejano stockraisers. Moreover, historians have rarely examined how inheritance and intermarriage affected Tejano landholding.

TEJANO STOCKRAISING IN HIDALGO COUNTY, 1890–1900

Ironically, one aspect of stockraising that reached its apex as the good fortune of Tejano stockmen was about to change was the proliferation of Mexican-owned cattle herds. Table 8.1 shows that in Hidalgo County, in 1890, Mexicans claimed 532 cattle herds. Within five years, the downturn in stockraising eliminated many producers—more than half—as Mexicans owned only 213 herds of cattle. The number of Mexican-owned cattle herds changed slightly in the next five years, rising to 229. Obviously, few new or old cattlemen entered stockraising because of the poor market prospects.

Another aspect of Tejano cattle ranching in the 1890s that reached the highest level was the growth of small cattle herds. As noted in Table 8.2, in 1890 *rancheros* owned 459 small herds. Two interrelated factors account for the rising number of small cattleraisers: the profitable 1870s and 1880s enticed many settlers to raise cattle, while the decline in the acreage owned by Mexicans—many owning tracts of only a few hundred acres—made large-scale stockraising impossible. During the rest of the 1890s, Mexicans still owned an average of 80 percent of the small herds, but the number of stockraisers declined considerably, to about two hundred cattleraisers. This decline reflected the worsening conditions that affected ranchers as prices tumbled and the drought brought havoc to the grasslands of south Texas.

During the same period, the total number of medium and large-size Mexican operators dropped drastically from seventy-three in 1890 (or 13 percent of all cattleraisers) to seven in 1895 and twenty-one in 1900. In the latter year, only 8 percent of all cattle herds in the medium and large classes were owned by Mexicans. Thus, by 1895 Mexicans had suffered a serious decline in cattle ranching.

Tejanos who raised *caballadas*, or horse herds, during the last decade of the nineteenth century succumbed to the same fate as the *mejicano* cattleraisers: after 1890, fewer and fewer *rancheros* were involved in breeding horses, in comparison to the booming years of the 1870s and 1880s, and their herds were generally smaller. As noted in Table 8.3, throughout the 1890s Mexicans raised an average of about 88 percent of all horse herds in Hidalgo County. Of a total of 509 horse herds in 1890, 469 (or 92 percent) were owned by *rancheros*. The number of Mexican-owned herds dropped sharply to 207 in 1895, rising slightly to 233 in 1900. Of the Mexican-owned herds, about 82 percent were in the small class category throughout the decade. As noted in Table 8.4, the decline in horse raising was evident as the number of Mexican-owned medium and large-size herds dropped from 32 in 1890 to only 9 in 1900. Not surpris-

Table 8.1 Ethnicity of Owners of Cattle Herds in Hidalgo County, 1890–1900

	Mexican		Other		Total Owners
	No.	*%*	*No.*	*%*	*No.*
1890	532	92.8	41	7.2	573
1895	213	88.4	28	11.6	241
1900	229	85.1	40	14.9	269

Source: Hidalgo County, *Tax Rolls*, 1890, 1895, 1900.

Table 8.2 Size of Cattle Herds in Hidalgo County, by Ethnicity of Owners, 1890–1900

	Mexican					
	1890		1895		1900	
Class[a]	*No.*	*%*	*No.*	*%*	*No.*	*%*
1	273	47.7	172	71.4	156	58.0
2	186	32.5	34	14.1	52	19.3
3	37	6.5	4	1.7	10	3.7
4	36	6.3	3	1.2	11	4.1
Total	532	93.0	213	88.4	229	85.1
	Other					
	1890		1895		1900	
Class	*No.*	*%*	*No.*	*%*	*No.*	*%*
1	14	2.4	18	7.5	19	7.1
2	10	1.7	1	.4	7	2.6
3	8	1.4	—	—	—	—
4	9	1.6	9	3.7	14	5.2
Total	41	7.1	28	11.6	40	14.9
Total	573		241		269	

Source: Hidalgo County, *Tax Rolls*, 1890, 1895, 1900.

[a] Class 1 equals 1 to 24 head. Class 2 equals 25 to 99 head. Class 3 equals 100 to 199 head. Class 4 equals more than 200 head.

Table 8.3 Ethnicity of Owners of Horse Herds in Hidalgo County, 1890–1900

	Mexican		Other		Total Owners
	No.	*%*	*No.*	*%*	*No.*
1890	469	92.1	40	7.9	509
1895	207	88.0	26	12.0	233
1900	233	84.4	43	15.6	276

Source: Hidalgo County, *Tax Rolls*, 1890, 1895, 1900.

Table 8.4 Size of Horse Herds in Hidalgo County, by Ethnicity of Owners, 1890–1900

	Mexican					
	1890		1895		1900	
Class[a]	*No.*	*%*	*No.*	*%*	*No.*	*%*
1	275	54.0	155	66.0	187	67.8
2	162	31.8	42	17.9	37	13.4
3	22	4.3	6	2.5	6	2.2
4	10	2.0	4	1.7	3	1.1
Total	469	92.1	207	88.1	233	84.5
	Other					
	1890		1895		1900	
Class	*No.*	*%*	*No.*	*%*	*No.*	*%*
1	26	5.1	19	8.1	30	10.9
2	8	1.6	3	1.3	7	2.5
3	1	.2	3	1.3	2	.7
4	5	1.0	3	1.3	4	1.4
Total	40	7.9	28	12.0	43	15.5
Total	509		235		276	

Source: Hidalgo County, *Tax Rolls*, 1890, 1895, 1900.

[a] Class 1 equals 1 to 24 head. Class 2 equals 25 to 99 head. Class 3 equals 100 to 199 head. Class 4 equals more than 200 head.

ingly, small herds also fell from 437 in 1890 to 197 in 1895, before rising slightly to 224 in 1900.

The number of sheep and goats grazed in Hidalgo County in the 1890s not only fluctuated widely, but also declined from the previous highs of the mid-1880s. Overall, the number of sheep and goats dropped to 35,208 in 1890 and to 22,202 in 1895. By 1900 a slight improvement in the total number of sheep and goats occurred as the industry made a brief comeback. Sheep and goats numbered 32,680, a 40 percent increase in five years, but still less than the total for 1890. As a percentage of the total, sheep steadily declined from 80 percent in 1890 to 58 percent in 1900, reflecting the prevailing downward trend in sheep-raising as prices for wool fell and the industry moved out of the south Texas plains and into the rugged Edwards Plateau.

Still, in the closing years of the nineteenth century, Tejanos continued to dominate sheep and goat raising, but 80 percent of the herds numbered fewer than five hundred head. After 1895, *rancheros* in Hidalgo County pursued a familiar strategy of cutting back sharply on sheep and goat production. In 1900 only 101 farmers and ranchers raised sheep, a decline of 20 percent in ten years. Even with a brief rebound in production, few ranchers grazed large herds. Only nine ranchers herded 500 or more sheep. Goat production followed the pattern of sheepraising, with small numbers of farmers and ranchers engaged in goat-raising on a relatively smaller scale than before.

THE GROWTH OF ANGLO COMPETITORS IN RANCHING IN HIDALGO COUNTY, 1880S–1900

Toward the end of the ranching boom in the late 1880s and during the continuing consolidation of ranching in the 1890s, Anglos began to graze large herds of cattle in big sections of the various south Texas counties. Consider, for example, the case of Hidalgo County, where grazing herds were owned by, among others, William P. Sprague of Hidalgo County; Mary C. Russell, Nueces County; Cornelius Stillman and A. J. Bloomberg, both of Cameron County; D. R. Fant, Bexar County; J. M. Chitham and A. Parr, a partnership of Bexar and Duval counties, respectively; Jot Gunter and Thomas Jones, a partnership of Bexar County; E. C. Lasater, Starr County; and King and Kenedy. Like their more prosperous Tejano counterparts, nearly all of these large-scale Anglo ranchers had been in ranching for a considerable time.

The best known, besides King and Kenedy, were probably Dillard R. Fant and Edward C. Lasater. Fant, who was raised in Goliad County, Texas, started out as a teamster after the end of the Civil War, moved on to become a cattleraiser in Goliad County, and then combined a successful career as a rancher, a livestock contractor, and a trail driver. One of the largest landowners in Hidalgo County in the late 1880s and 1890s, with nearly a quarter-million acres, Fant grazed thousands of head of cattle in the county, fattening them before shipping them to northern markets.[1]

Lasater was born in 1860 in Goliad County, Texas, home to a number of leading cattle drivers during the heyday of the cattle drives. His father, Albert H. Lasater, was born in Arkansas and moved to Texas in 1857. He engaged in horse and mule raising until the Civil War. In 1865, he set up a mercantile business in Goliad. When the elder Lasater's health declined, his son took over the sheepraising business. Following his father's death in 1882, Lasater settled his father's debts and liquidated his sheep herds.[2]

After he settled the estate debts, Lasater became a horse and cattle trader, selling horses as far east as New York and Connecticut. Then, in 1890 and 1891, he was involved with a livestock commission business, shipping cattle from south Texas to the New Orleans market. In 1893, Lasater contracted twenty-five thousand cattle for delivery. He picked a bad year, with the prices plummeting during the depression. Cattle that had sold for twenty-five dollars per head in 1884 dropped to six dollars per head in 1893. After selling the cattle, he incurred 130,000 dollars in debts. Lasater felt that he could still make a fortune, and in late 1894 he contracted to deliver thirty thousand head of cattle in the spring of 1895. Placing his faith in the recovery of the livestock industry, Lasater also began to obtain credit to buy land and stock.[3]

When the livestock business rebounded in 1895, Lasater continued his large-scale ranching operations. In 1895, Francis Smith and Co. financed Lasater and his father-in-law's purchase of the Matías García tract of 25,709 acres. Riding the good times, Lasater continued to expand his ranching and land-buying operations. In 1901, when he sought a 130,000-dollar loan from H. P. Drought & Co. (the successor to Francis Smith and Co.), he owned 220,000 acres in south Texas, most of it in Hidalgo and Starr counties, and he had 66,000 acres under leases. After selling 330,000 dollars worth of cattle, most of it in Kansas, Lasater's ranches were still stocked with 12,000 cattle, 500 horses, 60 mules, and 450 sheep.[4]

Like Lasater, William P. Sprague entered the ranching business late in the nineteenth century. Born in Rhode Island, Sprague apparently settled in Texas sometime after 1880 and started in the mercantile business. By the 1880s he was living in Hidalgo County, where he was involved in ranching and politics, serving as county commissioner for many years. Sprague started ranching on a small scale. In 1885, he was assessed on 100 cattle and 250 horses. He rapidly built his stock and in 1890 he had 800 cattle and 500 horses. Five years later,

Sprague's holdings had dropped: his horse herd totaled 404 and he reported having 520 cattle. By 1900 Sprague was again investing in stockraising, grazing 3,000 head of cattle at Rancho La Coma, in central Hidalgo County, in response to the favorable price of beef at the time.[5]

Like other Anglo ranchers in south Texas, Sprague had a penchant for acquiring large tracts of land. By 1885 he had gained control of 15,500 acres and his wife, Harriet B. Sprague, claimed ownership of 9,965 acres of land, all in the San Salvador del Tule grant. By 1900, Sprague's landholdings amounted to 100,738 acres. Since he did not graze extremely large numbers of livestock, like Lasater or Kenedy, Sprague was largely a land speculator looking to the future, when land prices would rise. As this did not occur immediately, Sprague remained tied to county politics and continued as hinterland rancher and merchant.[6]

In the 1880s and 1890s, a small number of other Anglo and European stockraisers and merchants were attracted to stockraising in south Texas. While these new stockmen did not rival King, Kenedy, or Lasater, the lure of cheap pastureland and inexpensive stock, coupled with profitable stock prices, encouraged new ventures. For example, Cornelius Stillman, a Brownsville merchant and brother of Charles Stillman, ran large numbers of cattle in Hidalgo County, while at the same time he owned large tracts of land in Cameron County.[7]

Other Brownsville merchants who invested in ranching in Hidalgo County included, A. J. Bloomberg (who resided in New York) and his local partner, G. M. Raphael; the Spanish merchants Manuel Fernández and Manuel Barreda; and J. S. and M. H. Cross. The enterprising attitude of these men can be seen in the case of Barreda, a dry-goods merchant who had started out as a store clerk in Brownsville. He rented a ranch in Cameron County, which he stocked with two thousand head of cattle and horses. According to Lieutenant Chatfield, Barreda was optimistic that he could compete for eastern buyers. About this time, he also grazed another herd in Hidalgo County. The Crosses were a father and son who owned two stores, a bakery, and three ranches totaling nine thousand acres, on which they grazed three thousand head of livestock in 1890. Except for some of the merchants or their descendants, such as Fernández, who continued to ranch into the twentieth century, most merchants tended to stay in the stockraising business as long as the good times made it profitable.[8]

As more and more Anglos ventured into the northern half of Hidalgo County, they began to account for a greater percentage of the livestock. As noted in Table 8.5, by 1890 Anglo cattlemen and women produced 33 percent of the cattle, with Mexicans owning 57 percent of the cattle. In 1895, Anglo ranchers claimed 46 percent of the cattle, compared to 36 percent for *rancheros*. This was the first time that Anglo stockmen owned more cattle than Tejanos. The seriousness of the decline among Mexican stockraisers was even more

Table 8.5 Percentage of Cattle Production, by Ethnicity of Owners, Hidalgo County, 1890–1900

Year	Total No. of Cattle	Mexican	Anglo	European	Black	Blend
1890	53,803	57	33	8	[a]	[a]
1895	22,694	35	46	18	[a]	[a]
1900	45,065	18	73	4	[a]	6

Source: Hidalgo County, *Tax Rolls*, 1890, 1895, 1900.
[a] Less than 1 percent.

apparent in 1900, when they accounted for only 18 percent of the cattle, compared to 73 percent for Anglo ranchers. In absolute numbers, Mexican stockmen claimed only 8,100 cattle in 1900, compared to 30,600 in 1890. Only in the production of horses, mules, goats, and sheep did Mexican *rancheros* maintain a high level of production, raising between 50 percent and 80 percent of these kinds of livestock during the post-1885 period.[9] However, as noted in Table 8.6, the decline in the absolute number of horses and mules clearly shows the worsening condition of Tejano stockmen. Tejanos barely raised 4,500 horses and mules in 1900, compared to 16,000 in 1890.

The same decline is evident in neighboring Cameron County. Tejanos and other Spanish-surnamed persons, mostly Spanish-Mexican individuals, reported that in 1890 they owned 22,493 cattle, or 23 percent of the total cattle herd, which numbered 98,000. In 1900, their share of cattle dropped to 9,842, or 20 percent of the total production of 50,200 cattle, which had plummeted due to the droughts of the 1890s. Tejanos herding cattle dropped from 400 in 1890 to 117 in 1900. Obviously, few Tejano ranchers were able to maintain the previous levels of high production and many small producers were quickly pushed out of ranching.

Horse and sheep production showed a similar displacement of Tejano producers in Cameron County. Whereas Tejanos and other Spanish-surnamed stockmen raised 7,966 horses and mules in 1890—62 percent of the total production—in 1900 they reported owning only 2,680, or 43 percent of the total number assessed for taxation. Tejanos still raised sheep, but in small numbers, and total production declined about 50 percent from 1890 to 1900. In 1890, they reported owning 10,893 sheep. Ten years later, the number of Tejano-owned sheep stood at 5,030, an insignificant number for the production of marketable wool.[10]

Throughout the region, Tejano persistence in horse, mule, and sheep production was probably due to two factors. First, mules were more and more in

Table 8.6 Percentage of Horse Production, by Ethnicity of Owners, Hidalgo County, 1890–1900

Year	Total No. of Horses	Mexican	Anglo	European	Black	Blend
1890	19,778	81	12	7	a	a
1895	7,211	68	19	13	a	a
1900	7,230	63	20	9	a	9

Source: Hidalgo County, *Tax Rolls*, 1890, 1895, 1900.
[a] Less than 1 percent.

demand as some ranchers began to raise corn and cotton to offset the losses in the sale of livestock, enticing former cowboys to become sharecroppers. Second, small livestock were more adaptable to living off the scanty grasses, and they did better during the drought of the early 1890s because they consumed smaller amounts of water compared to cattle.[11]

THE DECLINE OF TEJANO RANCHERS: BAD WEATHER, FALLING PRICES, AND LACK OF CREDIT, 1880S–1900

A variety of sources noted the worsening environmental and marketing conditions, in which ranchers and merchants—who gave credit to stockmen and bought agricultural produce from them—found themselves. The most important merchants were still based at Brownsville, men such as Bloomberg and Raphael, the Fernández, the Celayas and H. M. Field, whose brother was Marshall Field, the famous Chicago merchandise entrepreneur.[12] *Rancheros* often wrote to merchants, such as Field, to ask for credit or to seek help in selling or acquiring livestock or farm produce. Field also received numerous inquiries from stockraisers about stock prices, and the latter usually described prices and the condition of the grasslands in their vicinities.[13]

The first adverse weather to affect south Texas was the humid, cold winter of 1880–81. A sleet storm that blanketed the region in November 1880 killed lambs, which were highly susceptible to cold, wet temperatures. Then, in January 1881, a blizzard killed adult sheep, which already had been weakened by the previous freezing weather. This storm also caused some loss of cattle, although longhorns were sturdy and adaptable to such rapid climatic change as occurs in Texas winters. An extremely cold winter occurred in 1886–87 and it was followed by a drought. Such abnormal weather also caused a rapid deterioration of pastures, which resulted in the production of poor-quality livestock.[14]

Eventually, the inclement weather and disease took a toll on sheep herds. The U.S. Census of Agriculture reported that in 1890 Hidalgo County sustained a loss of 7,498 sheep, leaving 20,906 on its farms and ranches. Starr County still had 50,966 sheep, but its losses amounted to 9,033 sheep. There were barely 3,000 sheep—this figure is probably an incomplete total—in Cameron County and only 10,000 in Zapata County, a perennial leader in wool production during the heydays of the boom in wool prices.[15]

A long and devastating drought that began in 1891 afflicted south Texas nearly the entire decade. Drought, of course, had been a rancher's curse in the plains all too often. Jorge Alaniz, a rancher in the San Diego area, gave away eight hundred head of cattle because he was unable to feed them during the drought of 1893.[16] In 1895, Commissioner Mills blamed the drought for the people's suffering, remarking that "the extreme drought of the past seven years has probably rendered them [Mexicans in the Lower Valley] more poverty-stricken than they have been for generations . . . "[17]

Stockraisers were again affected by the 1898–1899 drought. N. L Wood wrote from D. R. Fant's Santa Rosa ranch on November 8, 1898: "[Cattle] are cheap around Alice [a major shipping point on the railroad from Corpus Christi to Laredo]. I have bought a good many up here since I left Brownsville. There is no grass in that country [between Brownsville and here]. Dick King has all of his cattle here in the Santa Rosa pasture and Bob Driscoll is pasturing 3,000 near here. We have plenty of grass but it is [damn?] dry here. We are watering everything out of wells and it sure helps things to get them watered."[18] Conditions worsened as the drought continued into 1899. Fant simply informed Field in March 29, 1899: "No water, no grass."[19] Because of the prolonged drought, livestock production declined, although larger producers persisted in stockraising at a lower volume.[20]

Both Anglo and Mexican *rancheros* were hampered not only by bad weather and disease, but also by falling prices. Stock prices were indeed depressed. According to Lieutenant Chatfield, in 1891–92, stock to start a cattle ranch could be bought in the Lower Valley for four dollars per head.[21] H. M. Field's letterbooks also recorded a number of livestock sales, indicating low prices. On December 11, 1893, he sold some of his livestock, forty-eight animals at $8.00 each.[22] A bit over a year later, he listed a sale of 248 cattle for $1,423.50, slightly less than $6.00 per animal, the going price John McAllen had reported in the depression of 1870.[23] Thus, between late 1893 and early 1895, the already depressed prices tumbled about 25 percent more. Similarly, poor market conditions affected sheep, whose value declined from $3.00 in 1878 to $2.00 in 1882. During the 1893 depression, ranchers in the region reported that the most they could get for sheep was $1.00–$1.25 per head and sometimes less than $1.00.

Goats sold for $1.00. Wool prices plummeted, more abundant than ever as new producers such as Argentina and Australia reached world markets. The once profitable twenty cents per pound for wool in 1880 decreased to fourteen cents in 1887, seven cents in 1893, and three to four cents in 1897.[24] Unable to earn a profit as cattleraisers or sheepraisers, some ranchers quit or allowed their herds to multiply, despite the limited opportunities for a better market during the 1890s. These prices could hardly keep a *ranchero* in business, especially when one recalls that in the boom days beef cattle were easily worth anywhere from ten to thirty-five dollars or more and goats and sheep as much as two to three dollars each.

As marketing livestock became more difficult, a feeling of despair overcame both Anglo and Tejano ranchers. The old settler Thaddeus M. Rhodes, writing from Rancho La Jara on December 1, 1898, was desperate. "I have a little grass in my pasture but no water in water holes. Should there be a buyer [of stock] please inform him that I have from 80–100 head [of livestock]—1, 2, 3, and 4 year old[s] and some cows. I wish to dispose of and will deliver when wanted. I want the money by the 15th of January as my note and taxes will be due."[25] Fant himself wrote Field from Rancho Santa Rosa on March 29, 1899: "What is cattle worth down there? They are damn cheap here. If you have any buyers down there, send them up here."[26] Exactly two months later, Don Florencio Sáenz, who also owned a general merchandise store at Rancho La Toluca in Hidalgo County, echoed the ranchers' plight. Writing to Field, he asked, "Do you know of anyone who might want to buy one- or two-year old steers in good condition?" And he added, "I can sell 150 to 200 [steers]. I will sell the increase of my herd, if there are no buyers for the steers. I will also sell fairly good cows for slaughtering."[27]

An important factor in the decline of ranching among the Mexican *rancheros* was their inability to obtain substantial sums of capital to weather the bad times. In the colonial period, *rancheros* had traditionally resorted to lease arrangements involving livestock, as well as borrowing monies from merchants and elite landholders and/or political leaders. With annexation, new sources of capital appeared in the form of local merchants and bankers who opened businesses in south Texas. Still, others borrowed money in San Antonio, where the major lenders were located. Generally, as long as prices held steady, local sources could be counted upon to lend money to *rancheros*, offering chattel mortgages on their real and personal property. Smaller numbers of *rancheros* succeeded in borrowing from the better-established brokers and bankers because these lenders were highly selective in their lending policies. For instance, the records of H. P. Drought & Co. of San Antonio disclose that during the period from about 1885 to 1908, out of hundreds of loans only thirty-nine loans were made to *rancheros* south of the Nueces River. Most of the loans were modest, with few over ten thousand dollars. It is clear, however, that those *rancheros* who did take out loans were usually among the more successful elite. Chattel-mortgage records for Encinal and Starr counties show that a significant majority of the loans obtained by Tejanos were for less than one thousand dollars. Between 1888 and 1899, less than one-third of the loans obtained by inhabitants of Encinal County were for one thousand dollars or more. The figures were even more dismal for those who resided in Starr County. Out of several hundred loans secured by Starr County residents between 1880 and 1900, only sixty were for more than one thousand dollars. Demonstrating the dominance of large-scale *rancheros* during this period, it is interesting that out of sixty loans for one thousand dollars or more, Manuel Guerra, a Starr County *ranchero* was the recipient of twenty-three loans. Guerra's large landholdings and herds, as well as his good business contacts in banking and livestock marketing centers, made it possible for him to obtain loans not only in the Lower Valley and San Antonio, but also in Kansas City and Chicago. His case, however, was atypical, for most *rancheros* borrowed only in Texas.[28]

Why did Mexicans receive so few loans? The overriding factor in making loans, for example at Drought & Co., was the preference for properties that had a perfect title. Lenders also preferred to lend to large landowners with perfect titles, stipulating long payment periods in the mortgage. Except in cases where only a few persons owned a grant or large shares of one or more grants, *rancheros* who still retained ownership of their land were at a definite disadvantage with regard to these requirements. First, some grants had been or were still in litigation either for confirmation by the state or for partition among heirs. Second, toward the end of the nineteenth century many grants had already been divided informally among the heirs or partially broken up by sale. This was especially detrimental to the owners of *porciones* and the intermediate-size land grants. The passage of time led to many persons—usually relatives—holding undivided shares in these lands. This situation could easily, and often did, complicate the matter of clear title. Lenders shied away from taking risks with those parties. Third, ranchers generally had a strong bias against borrowing because lenders insisted on long-term payments to maximize their interest at the expense of the borrowers. Aware of volatile market prices, ranchers preferred not to gamble on long-term borrowing arrangements for fear of losing their land, which served as security for their loans.[29] Consequently, *rancheros* were clearly at a disadvantage in borrowing money vis-à-vis the larger and newer Anglo ranchers, such as Fant and Lasater, who borrowed extensively.

As the end of the nineteenth century approached, Tejanos resorted to familiar strategies for marketing their livestock. Some, like Mauricio González of the

Palito Blanco area, near Alice, shipped and drove cattle to the Indian Territory.[30] Since the 1880s Alice had become the principal railhead for sending livestock and wool to market from south Texas. J. Nimmo, Jr., reported that by the mid 1880s "stockmen [were] more willing to pay freight charges than drive" their stock to market. This was evidently true even of Tejano *rancheros* who sent stock from Alice to the Indian Territory and Missouri by rail.[31] However, some ranchers, like A. Peña of San Diego and Ramón Vela of Laguna Seca, followed time-honored traditions, driving cattle and horses to nearby markets in Corpus Christi and San Antonio.[32] As late as 1899, some Tejano ranchers from the Benavides area drove horse stock to east Texas, where they were unable to sell due to the economic hardships there.[33] Some Tejanos continued to sell to livestock contractors, including local Tejanos like Luis Ramírez of Cameron County, who advertised in Spanish on his letterhead that he "buys stock at the best prices."[34] Both Fant and Lasater were major stock buyers in the 1890s, and Tejanos supplied them with large numbers of livestock.

Again, it is obvious that a drop in the price paid for beef cattle, sheep, goats, and wool, the impact of abrupt climate changes, and a lack of credit affected most Tejano ranchers. It could be argued that *rancheros* could wait out the poor market conditions and build up their herds. However, in the case of Hidalgo County the evidence shows that they did not do this because their lands had been reduced and credit was not readily available to them.

INHERITANCE PATTERNS AMONG *RANCHEROS* AND THEIR DETRIMENTAL EFFECT ON THE RANCHING ECONOMY: THE SOCIAL FACTOR

Adherence to Spanish tradition and law regarding property rights strongly affected the ranching economy by fostering constant divisions of Tejano *ranchero* property. One aspect of this continuing legacy involved husbands who openly acknowledged and respected the property rights of their wives and children. In 1876, Antonio Cano, a successful *ranchero* who resided at Rancho de Guadalupe in Hidalgo County—his herds were worth about sixteen thousand dollars and he owned 8,095 acres—declared that his wife "brought to the marriage twenty two-year old fillies valued at thirty pesos and one three-year old cow valued at five pesos for which purpose it is my wish that the sum of their values be paid out of my property[.] [S]aid sum which will be taken out being thirty-five pesos and the sum shall be returned to her one year after my death."[35] The acknowledgment of a wife's separate property was in some cases more general in character. Cipriano Hinojosa, a well-known and respected *ranchero*, declared in

1878 that "I am the owner of my own brand and my wife of her [brand,] my wife not having any right to intervene in my property she being the owner of her brand and interests which exists in her property [*sic*]."[36] The few Anglo newcomers who had married Mexican women also affirmed the right of their wives to their separate property. On a business trip to central Texas in 1879, John O. Thompson gave to his wife, Felicitas Longoria de Thompson, "all live animals of every kind and description bearing her brand . . . and which is of record in the County Clerk's Office of Hidalgo County hereby declaring such property as her own separate property."[37] One Norberto Días [*sic*], in his inventory and appraisement of his wife's estate, reported two lists, one the "Separate Property of Guadalupe Rivas de Días" and the other the "Community Property of Guadalupe Rivas de Días and Norberto Días."[38]

Imbued with a strong sense of egalitarianism, *rancheros* usually left their estates to their wives and children. In the case of surviving wives, the estates sometimes were theirs only for the duration of their lives, that is, a life estate. Although Antonio Cano provided for his children's inheritance in his livestock and lands, he excepted his homestead at "Rancho de Guadalupe with its appurtenances of houses, lots, corrals and fields which I give to my wife for her life estate." In addition, he declared "that the cash money [that I have] I grant to my wife for her own use and without any devolution whatsoever to my children."[39] In 1880, Félix Cano, a son of Antonio Cano and also a resident of Rancho Guadalupe, distributed his property in a more general way, declaring that his wife, María Higinia Cantú, "by all rights . . . should have one-half of all my capital" and that "the other half shall be and I leave to my children or heirs . . . "[40] Four years later, Felipe Villanueva Garza of Rancho Tampacuas declared that it was his wish "that one-half of all my capital or property shall be exclusively of my wife, and that the other half of said capital shall be divided in equal parts among my seven children, whom I declare my legitimate heirs."[41]

While some *rancheros,* such as Félix Cano and Ceferina Fernández's husband, distributed property more generally to their wives and children, others were more specific in declaring how they wished their property distributed. The old *ranchero* Antonio Ballí Cavazos agreed, in 1887, to "grant and donate to my children . . . my property which consists of land which I have inherited, and of the property which I have bought, half belongs to my wife, Doña Manuela Rubalcava de Ballí. The horse and cattle stock that have my brand and mark . . . shall also be divided among my above named sons and daughters."[42]

If they did not have children, husbands and wives tended to leave their estates to each other or to other relatives. That this custom was long a precedent in the Río Grande Valley frontier can be seen in a number of wills. Writing in 1838, Don Leandro de la Garza, a Reynosa *vecino,* explained that "on account of not having any surviving children . . . we make ourselves mutual heirs of each other of all that exists so that at the death of the first one the surviving spouse have and use generally everything . . . " When he died in about 1853, Don Leandro left an estate appraised at 1,913 dollars, consisting of two tracts of land totaling three-quarters of a league in Hidalgo County, 3,000 sheep and goats, and 120 cattle. His wife, Doña Josefa de Hinojosa, continued the *rancho* until she died in 1855.[43] Shortly before he died, the *ranchero* Antonio Guerra of Rancho de La Habana made an oral will (in 1875) in the presence of four witnesses, including an Anglo, saying that "of all that is mine I acknowledge but one heir, my wife, Doña Chepita Garza y Guerra." He declared that his wife was entitled to all that "we have done together and all that pertains to me through my [inheritance from my] father and mother." He claimed land in four different locations.[44]

Rancheros without children usually left their property to their wives and/or other relatives. For example, the estate of Don Ignacio de Ochoa consisted in part of 336 head of horse and cattle stock. According to the 1885 report of the partition judges, after reserving 45 head of stock to cover the expenses of administration, his wife received one-half of the stock as her share and the other half went in equal shares to ten heirs "who make up the family of Don Tomás de Ochoa, brother of Don Ignacio de Ochoa."[45]

Rancheros typically left equal shares of their property to all of their heirs, regardless of sex or age. Before he died, Marcos Guzmán dictated a will in Spanish at Rancho de Toluca on May 11, 1899. He acknowledged that his wife was already deceased and that they had had thirteen children, eight of whom were dead, six having died as children. He named his surviving children as heirs, and he declared that all of the property that was left "[was] to be divided in equal parts among all of the heirs."[46]

Even in cases in which some of children had preceded their parents in death, parents followed the tradition of granting the share in the inheritance belonging to the deceased son or daughter to their respective heirs. For example, Mauricia F. de Cano of Rancho Toluca, wife of the old patriarch Antonio Cano, shortly at the turn of the century acknowledged that they had had five children of which one son and two daughters had preceded her in death, each of them leaving children as heirs. Claiming that she had property worth four thousand dollars, mostly in claims due her, she wished her estate to be divided "in five equal parts between my two surviving sons and the children of my three deceased ones . . . "[47]

This practice of treating all children equally was also true in cases in which Tejano parents had already distributed certain property to some of their children in anticipation of receiving a share in the inheritance. In 1876, Antonio

Cano declared "that two of my sons, Guillermo and Félix and my daughter Susana have received in anticipation of their share of the inheritance the following: ten two-year old heifers, fourteen two-year old fillies, one stallion, one selected tame horse, one selected three-year old colt, and one yoke of bulls for oxen; it is my desire that each one of my other daughters be given equal shares and that what is necessary be taken out of my property." Barely six months after their Cano's death, his children and Luis Solis, father and guardian of the children of Susana Cano, who had also died, "confessed to having received from Don Martín Hinojosa [del] Toro [the administrator], the full share that belongs to us and devised to us by our father according to his will to our entire satisfaction."[48]

Some *rancheros* wisely distributed their estate or part of the estate to their children during their lifetimes. According to Jesús María Vela, temporary administrator of the estate of Macedonio Vela, the old *ranchero* had "during his lifetime" distributed all stock "to his children to each of them to their entire satisfaction." Known as *inter vivos* gifts, these forms of distribution were probably common in view of the fact that such gifts averted family disputes after the death of the grantor, as well as eliminating costly court proceedings. Such gifts may have been even more popular among *rancheros* owning small estates, since few of them are recorded in the probate files of the courthouses.[49]

In cases where some children had already received their share of the inheritance prior to the father or mother's death, treating the remaining children equally with regard to inheritance was common. Cipriano Hinojosa noted in 1878 that two sons and one daughter of his first marriage had each received ten cows, with their calves, as their inheritance, and the other three children, two daughters and one son, were to be given the same so that they would all share equally. Hinojosa, a respected *ranchero,* also made a special provision to take care of his youngest child, Dorotea, a daughter by his second marriage. He declared that the balance of his stock in the community property was to be given to her, and he also appointed his son, Manuel, as guardian of her and another minor sister, Rafaelita; *rancheros* were especially careful in safeguarding the property of their minor children. One year after Cipriano Hinojosa's death, his children filed an affidavit with the probate court stating that they were in agreement with the partition of the property effected by the executor of the estate, Thaddeus M. Rhodes.[50]

In addition to leaving their property to their loved ones, some *rancheros* also demonstrated their concern for their families and relatives in other ways. Husbands sought appointment as administrators of their wives' estates obviously on the belief that they could better manage the mundane affairs related to lands and stockraising. When, for example, the *ranchero* Marcos de Ochoa of Ojo de Agua died in 1884, Higinio Longoria, the husband of the deceased man's only daughter, petitioned and qualified as administrator of the estate of Marcos de Ochoa.[51]

Rancheros also showed devotion and care for their ailing wives. In 1882, J. N. Cantú made an application to the probate court to administer the community property belonging to him and his deceased wife, Manuela Guzmán de Cantú. He informed the judge that he had married his wife at Rancho Nuevo, Cameron County, in 1868. They resided there until 1873, when they moved to Rancho Sardinas in Hidalgo County, remaining there until 1878. He then explained "that on April 30, 1878, Manuela became ill, confined to her bed, [and] because of her illness [he] took her to Reynosa to obtain medical care." She never recovered and died shortly afterward. He had three small children who resided with him at El Capote ranch, near Edinburg.[52]

PROTECTION OF *RANCHEROS'* PROPERTY BY RELATIVES

There are also many cases in which widows protected their own interests in the community property, and especially the property inherited by their children. Usually, this involved receiving monies for their care, maintainance, and education. Sometimes, it also involved selling some of the property in order to pay the costs of the children's upbringing.[53] In some cases, wives served as administratrices, as in the case of Mary C. Leo because her husband, A. J. Leo, died without a will. At other times, wives proceeded as executrixes in cases in which their husbands left wills and testaments.[54]

As old *rancheros* died, their sons or other relatives disposed of their property according to their wills, or if they left no will according to the laws of the state. With the organization of the new county governments, Mexican settlers petitioned the probate court for appointments as administrators or executors of a deceased *ranchero*'s estate. Some administrations involved very small estates, such as the first few noted in the probate records of Hidalgo County in which the cases were actually filed in Cameron County in 1850. But some estates were much more valuable and involved well-known families. Such estates were often quite complex, although few complete documents survive. Take, for example, the case of Juan José Hinojosa, a chief justice of Reynosa, who died in about 1810. In 1850, his grandson, Yndalecio Domínguez, qualified as administrator of the estate. The appraisers valued the estate, which consisted of eleven parcels of land and one claim on an account of about 5,000 dollars, at 7,900 dollars. In some cases, administrating a father's estate involved considerable time and talent. For instance, upon the death in 1884 of José María Mora, a *ranchero* and storekeeper at Rancho Relámpago, his son, Melchor Mora, served as administrator of an estate that was subject to a few large debts owed to wholesale merchants located in Brownsville. Melchor not only had to care for the assets of the store, but also manage the real property and livestock belonging to the estate. Moreover, his father had left several minor children and a wife who was ill, and as administrator, Melchor Mora had to safeguard as much of the assets and the homestead from execution because of several lawsuits against the estate. Fortunately, the state homestead law provided modest protection, and he was able to protect enough assets, worth 1,357 dollars, to keep the family from becoming impoverished—a fact of life not always possible when the estates were relatively small and the debts high.[55]

There are many other such cases in which a relative administered the estate of minor children. When the *ranchero* Juan Cantú of Rancho Rosario, in Hidalgo County, died in 1869, Don Cipriano Hinojosa served as the administrator of Cantú's estate as well as guardian of his small son, Gregorio Cantú. The deceased man had left an estate worth about one thousand dollars, which consisted of household furniture, livestock, corn, and other produce. As grandfather of the child, Don Cipriano qualified as guardian, and according to him, the child resided with his grandmother at his *rancho.* Based on his reports to the court, Don Cipriano faithfully discharged his duties, selling off all of Juan Cantú's estate and placing the money on loans to other *rancheros,* so that by April 1872 the rates on monies that he had loaned had risen to "12% and [were] secured by mortgages on real estate."[56] In 1888, J. N. Domínguez sought the appointment of a guardian on behalf of the three minor children of Archibald A. Johnston and Manuela Domínguez de Johnston, stating that he was their grandfather and that "he tried to collect rents from parties living in the houses [which belonged to the minors and were located in Laredo] and they refused to pay them without his being appointed guardian."[57]

Some appointments of guardians involved very small estates, but in any case, relatives usually sought them or were appointed by the probate court to administer such estates. For example, in 1889, Ramón and José Tijerina, two young brothers who were orphans, asked the court to name their uncle, Tomás Bustamante de Tijerina, as guardian of a small estate left by their father Hilario Tijerina and consisting of cash and cattle worth about 150 dollars.[58]

Needless to say, a surviving parent often served as guardian of their children, a duty that involved a number of time-consuming tasks.[59] In 1900, Vicente Cárdenas, who had already served ten years as guardian of his minor children, petitioned the court for an order allowing him to sell their undivided interest, consisting of about ten thousand acres, because "he ha[d] no funds to maintain or educate them or to pay debts . . . " Usually, as in this case, the court allowed the petitioner to sell the property at a private sale in order for the seller to secure a good price.[60] In many cases, *rancheros* left personal estates consisting of livestock, which were subsequently sold by guardians of minor children. When Gregorio Quiroga died in about 1892, an inventory of his estate disclosed that he had 196 head of livestock, valued at twelve hundred dollars. He left three children and a wife, who subsequently married James L. Dougherty, a well-known county official. In 1903, the court discharged Dougherty and his wife as guardians because the three children had "reached the age of majority, [and] the guardians . . . have long since delivered to them their property of their father."[61] When her husband, L. H. Box, died in 1881, Louisa Box became first executrix of the estate, serving as such until 1893, and then as guardian of her children. During an eighteen-year period, she paid off the estate debts, sold some of the land, and used the remaining balance for the education and maintainance of the children. In 1903, she reported to the court that her children, who were now of legal age, still owned in common with her two tracts of land totalling nearly fifty-five hundred acres.[62]

Older brothers were also selected by minor siblings to be their guardians. Under the laws of the state, children over fourteen years could choose their own guardians. Crisanta Garza, for example, petitioned the probate court in 1882 to obtain the appointment of her brother, Juan Garza, as her guardian.[63]

In the 1870s and 1880s, *ranchero* Gregorio Dávila served as guardian for the children of his brother-in-law, Manuel Fuentes. As guardian, he disposed of two tracts of land in Victoria County, Texas, lands that the children had inherited through their maternal grandfather.[64] In 1882, Doña Higinia C. de Cano, the wife of Don Félix Cano of Rancho Guadalupe, named Martín Hinojosa del Toro as executor and Don Florencio Sáenz of the same *rancho*, her *concuño*, or brother-in-law, as guardian of her seven children, without the requirement of a bond. Shortly after her death in September 1883, Don Florencio received from Don Martín 1,932 dollars for the benefit of the children.[65]

DISPUTES OVER INHERITANCE AMONG TEJANOS AND BETWEEN TEJANOS AND NEWCOMERS

Despite the overall code of fairness that permeated Tejano distribution of inheritance, serious disputes arose among family members and nonrelatives. There is some evidence that inheritance issues had long existed among the old residents of the *villas* of the Río Grande. For example, Victoria Ballí, the widow of Don Benigno Leal, noted in her will of 1887: "although I and my late husband by written agreement each of us willed our estate unto the survivor of each other, the immediate relatives of my husband initiated a claim against the inheritance, annulling the agreement. By an accord celebrated in a transaction with the representative of my deceased husband's brothers, five hundred dollars were paid [to settle their claim]."[66]

At times, however, conflicts resulting from various claims of family and friends escalated into court proceedings, an indication that the normal channels of resolving time-honored contests over property were no longer operative. Disputes did occur between family and non-family members over the administration of an estate or over the guardianship of an adult or minor children and their property, but on the basis of a careful examination of nearly one hundred files in Hidalgo County and other probate records of south Texas counties these instances were not preponderant.

However, one case in which the administration of an estate was challenged involved Virginia Longoria, the widow of Leonardo Longoria, and his brother, José Longoria. José Longoria declared to the county court that he was a merchant at San Román in 1883 and sole owner of "all goods, houses and land." Accoring to José Longoria, his brother was a destitute whom he employed as a clerk in the business and remained so until May 1888, when José made him an equal partner "giving him one-half of the goods, subject to debts and one-half of the storehouse, not including the land." The estate was appraised at $2,142.72. According to José, his brother had one young daughter by a previous marriage, and she lived in Duval County, Texas, with her mother. Virginia Longoria had married his brother on about August 22, 1888, and José asserted that she "had no property and brought none into the marriage." This argument served as his basis for refusing to yield possession of the store to her. Although the widow hired counsel to defend her interests, she lost the case after "much litigation and expense." The administrator, José Longoria, in fact, charged the estate two hundred dollars for attending court and defending the interests of the estate. He attended court for forty-two days during the period from February 4, 1889, to May 5, 1890, riding on horseback from San Román in the backcountry to Hidalgo, a one-way distance of seventy-five miles.[67]

The case of Ignacio de Ochoa is illustrative of the divisions among family members over the management and disposition of property rights. When Ignacio de Ochoa died on April 19, 1884, the *ranchero* from Rancho Ojo de Agua left a small estate consisting of about 336 head of cattle and horses, a few farm implements, and three tracts of land. Upon the petition of two of the dead man's nephews, the court appointed them joint temporary administrators. During this time, a commission of three partition judges named by the county judge gave one-half of the estate to his elderly wife, Doña Máxima Longoria de Ochoa, who was eighty or eighty-five years of age, and one-half to ten Ochoa heirs, "who consist of the family of Don Tomás de Ochoa, brother of Don Ignacio de Ochoa, deceased." Shortly afterward, the widow was declared a lunatic by the county court, setting the stage for a feud over the guardianship of Doña Máxima.

The appointment of her brother, Ysidro Longoria, was challenged by Nasaria Longoria de Villarreal and her husband, Gregorio Villarreal. A sister of Doña Máxima, Nasaria argued that she could best render attention and care to her sister because she was of the same sex and asserted that her sister would live "most unhappily and unpleasantly" if she were not under her control. She also claimed that one of Ysidro's sons, Diego Longoria, was already controlling and managing the widow's property. In fact, Diego was one of two previously court-appointed temporary administrators, the other being Cornelio de Ochoa, a nephew of Ignacio de Ochoa.

Ysidro Longoria asserted that his sister had resided with him since the death of her husband and that "he [had] always given his undivided attention to his sister['s] . . . Person and Property [*sic*] . . . " In an amended plea to the court, he also alleged that part of his sister's property consisted of livestock that needed immediate attention.

After a hearing in which each side was represented by an attorney, the court appointed Longoria guardian of the person and estate of Doña Máxima on February 6, 1885. Two months later, Longoria resigned for "personal reasons," and the court appointed Cornelio de Ochoa as temporary guardian of Doña Máxima. Then, on November 13, 1885, the court appointed the Villarreales permanent guardians of the estate and person of the widow. While the Ochoas had supported Ysidro Longoria and had served as his sureties on his bond, the Villarreales' bonds were endorsed by two Anglo newcomers, Dr. A. M. Headley and J. M. Franz.

By June 1890 the estate of Doña Máxima, under the Villarreales' management of the guardianship, had dwindled to one tract of land and a small number of livestock. In fact, the guardians claimed that the estate was indebted to them in the amount of 730 dollars. Probably because of this sorry state of affairs, the Longorias attempted one more time to gain control of her estate. On July 8, 1890, in their application to the court they charged that Gregorio Villarreal had "squandered and converted to his own use a large quantity of the property of the Estate." The court evidently agreed with the Longorias, for it again appointed Ysidro Longoria as guardian. By this time, however, it was too late for them to correct any wrongdoing. Longoria reported to the court that Villarreal had control of her remaining property and that the latter refused to make a final report.[68]

When friends were designated as heirs and/or executors of estates, problems over heirship sometimes arose, but few such cases are of record, perhaps because *rancheros* usually had extensive family or collateral descendants. A case in point concerns the estate of Bárbara López de Solis. A widow without children, she had purchased some land and acquired some as the survivor in the community of her deceased husband, Domingo Solis. The land was located in north-central Hidalgo County. On January 22, 1890, at Rancho de San Francisco in the jurisdiction of Camargo, she wrote a will in Spanish witnessed by a number of persons, including J. R. Monroe, an Anglo lawyer from Río Grande City, Texas. In the will, she left one-half of her property to a friend, Antonia Villarreal de Díaz, wife of one Casiano Díaz. The other half she bequeathed to the children of Fernando López, who was deceased. She also named as executor one Rufino Domínguez. All of these named parties resided at Camargo, but this, of course, did not prevent their involvement in the probate of the will. Although Rufino Domínguez hired counsel—James B. Wells and J. R. Monroe—he did not prevail in his application to be designated executor in early 1891. The court, instead, named Agustín Salinas as temporary administrator. The county judge sided with Salinas because his wife, Camila López de Salinas, and Felipe López de Garza were evidently next of kin of the deceased, and he had obtained a power of attorney from them to make the application to the court.

The estate, which had been inventoried and appraised by Domínguez at about five thousand dollars, was evidently in the hands of Salinas until early 1903, when he died. At that time, an Anglo lawyer in the county named James H. Edwards applied to the court to serve as administrator. On November 10, 1904, Edwards submitted to the court a final report in which he stated that "Salinas had sold off and disposed of all livestock to parties unknown and without authority" because he had never obtained an order from the court to do so. All that remained of the estate was a tract of land containing 738 acres, for which he sought a court order to sell in order to pay taxes, attorney fees, and court costs. One can only speculate that Salinas's actions may have benefited those parties Bárbara López de Solis had designated as heirs, although an injustice was done to the executor whom she had selected for her own reasons.[69]

Another example of conflict between relatives and nonrelatives involved the estate of Felicitas Solis Zamora, who died, at the age of twenty-three or twenty-four, on April 12, 1897. At the time of her death, she had been living with the family of the former county judge, Thaddeus M. Rhodes. According to court testimony, Rhodes claimed that she had been raised by his family since she was two or three years of age. Upon her death, Rhodes dispatched a servant and *vaquero* of the young woman to the county court, directing a letter dated April 22, 1897, to the county judge, J. M. de la Viña. Rhodes informed Judge de la Viña that "this estate [of Felicitas Solis Zamora] require[s] immediate attention on account of disorders in the ranch where her . . . personal property is [located]." He also urged the appointment of a temporary administrator "because the Estate is subject to loss and also for the purpose of paying of nurses['] charges and funeral expenses." He ended the letter by telling the judge that "my daughter [María] Rafaela Rhodes was appointed Executrix and sole heir to the Estate."

On April 24, 1897, Melchor Mora, who, like Rhodes, resided at Rancho Relámpago, was appointed temporary administrator. Mora estimated the value of the estate to be $1,500.00, but his inventory reduced its value to $761.56. Although the estate was relatively small in comparison to other *rancheros*, it became the center of controversy between Rhodes and one Rufino Zamora, evidently a relative of the deceased woman.

Zamora was drawn into the legal fight over the will following the application of María Rafaela Rhodes to the court in September 11, 1897, in which she sought to probate the will. In early November of 1897, Zamora contested the will by contending that Felicitas Solis Zamora had been of unsound mind when she wrote the will on her deathbed in the Rhodes home. Judge de la Viña heard the testimony of various neighbors and other persons who had known Felicitas, including Manuel Alemán, who, at the request of Mr. Rhodes, had signed the will as a witness, but said that he "was not present at the writing of the will." He was contradicted by José Sáenz, who said he was present at the signing of the will and testified that Felicitas had been of sound mind. Mr. Alemán's wife, a niece of Mrs. Rhodes, testified that the will was "not signed by Miss Solis, and [that she] did not designate anyone to do it being more dead than alive . . . " This evidence was supported by Genoveva Sosa, the nurse who had cared for Felicitas. Sosa testified that she was present in the room when a will was brought in and that it "was not approved or disapproved" by Felicitas because "she was more dead than alive." Though the testimony was inconsistent, Judge de la Viña denied the application of María R. Rhodes on the basis that Felicitas, "at the time of making [her will] she was incapable of making a valid bequest."[70]

Quarrels over estates sometimes pitted children against parents. Illustrative of this situation is the case history of the fight over the management of the estate of Plácida Cantú de Johnston. Plácida, who was married to George W. Johnston, a well-known resident and former official of Hidalgo County, died on March 4, 1882. The family lived in the town of Hidalgo and owned horse and cattle stock valued by the appraisers of the estate at $2,115.94, excluding "a small amount, number unknown, [of] wild *caballada* stock," some of which were unbranded, "scattered and may never be caught or herded." Shortly after her mother's death, Josefa Johnston de Odell and her husband, William Odell, petitioned the court for appointment of a receiver to safeguard and look after the assets of the estate of Plácida Cantú de Johnston. One of two married daughters, Josefa alleged that her father was unfit to be the guardian of her minor siblings because he had taken up with a "woman of low character and reputation for wife, she being a married woman." In addition, she charged that Johnston was depriving the children of their share of the property of the estate, teaching the minor children bad morals by his conduct, and disposing of stock by selling it. In July 1882, a fellow townsman, Manuel de Alcalá, who operated the ferry at Hidalgo, was appointed receiver of the estate. He was immediately challenged in court by Johnston, who claimed that de Alcalá had damaged the estate by "penning the cattle for days together and keeping them without food or water and running them in hot weather . . . " In spite of this plea, the probate court judge ruled against him, finding the charges to be correct. Judge Rhodes then proceeded to place the estate in receivership. It remained in the hands of the receiver until December 2, 1882, when the parties arranged an amicable settlement. Under the agreement, Johnston was named administrator and he was ordered by the court to pay off the community debts, which were small, and then to "pay over one-half the surplus" to Plácida Cantú de Johnston's heirs.[71]

CLAIMS OF CREDITORS AGAINST TEJANO ESTATES

In some cases, individuals due monies or having claims of one sort or other petitioned the court to serve as administrators of the estates of deceased *rancheros* or their heirs. Economic self-interest was a strong motive behind the manner in which administration proceedings regarding the estate were conducted. The death of Jacinto Olivares in Camargo, in September 1878, prompted Hidalgo County merchant F. O. Rench to ask the court that he be appointed administrator of Olivares's estate, estimated to be worth two thousand dollars. Judge Rhodes agreed with the petition and set a bond of four thousand dollars on Rench. The sheriff, A. J. Leo, and an immigrant farmer, John B. Bourbois, a justice of the peace, served as Rench's sureties on the bond, which was approved on March 18, 1879. On June 17, 1879, John McAllen and Angel de la Vega, the two appraisers, filed an inventory and appraisement of the estate with the court. According to them, Olivares's estate consisted of sixty horse stock valued at $174.00, with the appraisers placing very low values on the livestock. They valued mules at $6.00 each, mares at $3.00, and stallions at $6.00. Two years previous to this case, Rhodes, as the executor of the estate of Cipriano Hinojosa, had placed a value of $4.50 on mares and $10.00 on stallions. Mules at that time were valued at $15.00 to $20.00 each. The appraisers also listed 553 acres in Gil Zárate's grant as belonging to Olivares, which they valued at ten cents per acre. As it turned out, McAllen, who had been one of the appraisers, had a claim of $50.00 against the estate for pasturing Olivares's horse stock. To pay off claims against the estate, Rench quickly petitioned the court to sell the livestock belonging to Olivares. John B. Young, McAllen's stepson, bid the identical sum that the appraisers had placed on the livestock. Then, on September 30, 1879, McAllen purchased the 553 acres for $22.12 in cash, not even half of the already low value the appraisers had decided upon. According to Rench's final accounting of his administration, dated March 26, 1880, the sales of Olivares's property totaled $196.12, a much lower sum than the estimated value Rench had earlier placed in his petition to the court. What is particularly interesting about this case is that administrators and executors usually gave reliable estimates of the worth of the property of an estate, and usually property of the estate was sold for a greater value than the original estimate as well as the estimate that appraisers set in their inventories. Rench's final accounting showed that he had paid the following estate debts: $50.00 to McAllen for pasturing horse stock, $29.91 in court costs, $50.00 in legal advice to A. J. Leo, $27.41 in additional court costs, and $35.29 on his 10 percent commission for receiving the property and paying off claims against the estate. At this point, the estate had a balance of $5.00, which was insufficient to pay Rench's bill of $20.00 for the care and management of the estate. In view of the insolvency of the estate, on May 17, 1880, Rhodes accepted the final settlement offered by Rench. Thus, in this case, McAllen, as creditor, and his stepson took advantage of a deceased *ranchero* for whom no one appeared to defend the interest of the estate.[72]

Very small estates belonging to *rancheros* were not immune to disposition by creditors. Juan Camacho died in 1888 and left real property valued at about one hundred dollars. Charles Schunior, his creditor, applied to the court, alleging Camacho's indebtedness to him and claiming that the deceased man's property was "going to waste." He received permission from the court to sell the land in question—seven and one-half *varas* fronting on the Río Grande—which he did, for forty dollars in Mexican coin.[73] Despite all of these cases involving controversy or quarrels over management and distribution of property and cases involving greed—a minority of the reported cases—the probate records are filled with cases in which sound management and fairness predominated.

THE RESPONSE TO THE DECLINE OF RANCHING: CROP EXPERIMENTATION AND TENANT FARMING, 1880–1900

The decline of ranching in south Texas during the 1880s was partly offset by a renewed interest in subtropical farming in the Lower Valley delta counties that led to the development of sharecropping and the beginning of experimental commercial farming.[74] These changes were reflected in a sharp rise in the number of farms and ranches, an increase in tenant farmers and sharecroppers, a rise in the value of farm products, and an increase in the value of farm implements in the last third of the twentieth century.

The number of farms and ranches in the Lower Valley delta counties of Cameron, Hidalgo, Starr, and Zapata expanded from 667 in 1860 to 1576 in 1900.[75] Because the data are incomplete, it is not possible to assess precisely this growth in farming and ranching enterprises. As noted previously, however, stockraising accelerated in the mid-1860s and continued growing through the 1880s until market and environmental problems set in. Even during this period, old ranches were subdivided and new ones founded. As a result, the number of landowners multiplied rapidly, which explains, of course, the initial rise in the number of farms and ranches in the Lower Valley delta counties. The second factor that led to an increase in the number of farms and ranches is ironically a consequence of the decline of ranching. In response to that decline, by 1890 a greater number of persons began to take up sharecropping and irrigated farming along the delta of the Río Grande. In fact, very few tenant farmers lived in the Lower Valley delta district prior to 1880, but their numbers increased rapidly after 1890. As noted in Table 8.7, only 65 out of 362 farms were rented for a fixed value or farmed on shares in 1880. The main reason for the low figure was that during the height of the ranching economy most persons owned or leased land. Those who leased land apparently used it to graze herds for brief periods, and subsequently either purchased land or dropped out of ranching. Consequently, the rate of tenancy—18 percent in 1880—was relatively low. As ranching declined, however, more persons entered into tenancy arrangements. These persons evidently used the land for farming since the acreage leased for a fixed money value or rented for a share of the products seldom exceeded fifty acres. For instance, in 1890 only 8 out of 136 farms (5.9 percent) rented for a fixed sum comprised more than one hundred acres. Except for 1 out of 114 sharecroppers, all of them leased farms of fifty acres or less.[76] As Table 8.7 shows, in 1890 three times as many tenant farmers resided in Cameron County as in Hidalgo County. This disparity reflected the fact that in Cameron County fifty-six Anglo and European landowners owned tracts of one thousand acres or more. Their combined acreage totaled about 90 percent of the land area in the county, which meant that very little land was available for farming.[77] Since these large landholders monopolized landholding, Tejanos resorted to leasing land.

The hard times in stockraising and the impact of declining commerce with Mexico accelerated the sharp rise in tenancy, even in parts of the Lower Valley

Table 8.7 Classification of Farms in Four Lower Valley Counties, by Type of Ownership, 1880–1900

	No. of Farms	Owner	Tenants	Managers
1880				
Cameron	113	93	20	—
Hidalgo	117	87	30	—
Starr	132	115	17	—
Zapata[a]	—	—	—	—
1890				
Cameron	271	82	169	—
Hidalgo	237	186	51	—
Starr	157	157	0	—
Zapata	133	123	10	—
1900				
Cameron	500	161	310	29
Hidalgo	490	221	248	21
Starr	382	302	66	14
Zapata	204	195	3	6

Source: *Tenth, Eleven, and Twelfth Census of the United States, 1880, 1890, 1900.*
[a] No Data.

where tenancy had not previously existed. The lack of jobs in ranching, the growing concentration of landownership in the hands of a few ranchers and merchant-speculators, and the poverty of Mexican immigrants all combined to offer scant possibilities for farm ownership. For those who disliked tenant farming, the only other option was migration north. Apparently many people chose that option, since geographic mobility was a strong feature of the regional population. By 1900 tenants operated three-fifths of all farms in Cameron County and about 54 percent of the farms in Hidalgo County. Starr County reported 66 tenant farmers out of 382 (17.3 percent) in 1900, whereas previously the county had not reported even 1 case of tenant farming. Zapata County had 3 tenants out of a total of 204 farms and ranches. Obviously, the western part of the Lower Valley delta had not been affected by the rise in farm tenancy as much as the eastern part. This was largely due to the fact that Mexican landowners were still the majority landowners in Starr and Zapata counties, with a ranching economy predominant there, in contrast to the minority landholding status of Mexicans in Cameron and Hidalgo counties and the diversifying farming economy in that part of the Lower Valley.[78]

The farming economy of the Lower Valley made fairly impressive gains in the last third of the nineteenth century. To be sure, farmers faced technological, financial, and transportation barriers that hindered the growth of large-scale commercial farming. The lack of railroads with which to tap distant markets represented a serious obstacle to agriculture's rapid expansion. *Rancheros* also lacked the capital needed to build expensive irrigation systems, as Lieutenant Chatfield had urged in the early 1890s.[79] Most Lower Valley delta farmers lived near the Río Grande to take advantage of the water, using a Nile-like system of irrigation in which low-lying areas called *ancones* were seeded annually. The perennial deposit of silt enriched the soil so that if enough moisture was captured crops would easily grow. Thus, for instance, in 1880 in Hidalgo County 22 out of 43 of the principal *ranchos* were devoted to farming, and all were located in the southern part of the county along the river or a few miles to the north. A few of these *ranchos* were actually small villages of 200 to 300 persons. A total of 172 farmers and 467 laborers resided in these farming communities. Only 6 stockraisers and 14 herdsmen lived in this farming zone.[80]

Observers often commented on how the area's mild weather made possible the growing of two crops per year. Lieutenant Chatfield wrote that for a farmer in the delta of the valley "there is always something he can do every day from January to December, and most of the time can be spent in the fields." Even in the ranching sections, stockraisers and laborers raised garden and field crops, using wells to irrigate land as well as to provide drink for humans and livestock.[81]

Despite the region's long growing season, crop production varied considerably. In some years the rainfall was inadequate or did not come in time to produce a substantial yield. The severe drought of 1891–92, for example, impoverished many small *rancheros* in south Texas. Newspapers reported that *rancheros* suffered so greatly that communities outside the region provided emergency relief to them in the form of provisions and corn.[82]

In spite of these problems, farmers raised crops for themselves and for local markets. For instance, the city market in Brownsville offered consumers all year round a variety of local produce, including bananas and citrus fruits. Some farmers tried to grow grapes and tobacco commercially, but the main products continued to be corn, sugarcane, and cotton.[83] Corn was the most important crop in the Lower Valley delta. Two harvests per year yielded an average of 115 bushels per acre—somewhat more than in other farm areas of the state. Normal corn harvest averaged about one-third of a million bushels per year.[84] It was consumed locally, as was sugarcane in the form of brown sugar or *piloncillo*. The yield per acre of sugarcane was reported to be four thousand pounds, comparable to Louisiana production. As late as 1890, however, the settlers in the Lower Valley imported a considerable amount of foodstuffs, as farming remained largely dependent on nature for its success. Not until 1905—when the first major land companies were formed with midwestern capital—were irrigation systems constructed on a scale large enough to make commercial agriculture truly practical. The small cotton crop and somewhat larger wool crop of the late nineteenth century were exported to eastern markets and to northern Mexico, especially Monterrey and Saltillo, where mills produced various kinds of apparel.[85]

As noted in Table 7.3, in the years from 1870 to 1900 farmers in the four Lower Valley delta counties reported a steady rise in the value of their farm products and in the value of their farm implements, except for the anomalous year of 1880. The largest growth in farm production took place in the 1890s, with the value of farm products rising nearly threefold from 339,700 dollars in 1890 to 917,640 dollars in 1900. This growing farm economy, however, did not totally compensate for what the ranching economy had lost, since stockraising had been a profitable venture over most of the countryside, while farming pretty well had to be confined to the narrow band of delta lands. According to the U.S. Census of Agriculture in 1899, the recorded sales of livestock and the value of slaughtered stock on farms in the Lower Valley totaled about $800,000.[86] Thus, while the value of farm products exceeded the value of livestock transactions, that statistic is misleading as to the ranching industry's actual dominant role. For the census data also reveals that the value of livestock on farms and ranches had risen dramatically from 1,157,051 dollars in 1890 to 4,753,892 dollars in 1899.[87] That is, the hard times in marketing livestock had led to a swift increase in the number of livestock. Obviously, this situation financially harmed not only ranchers, but also those supported by the money that circulated as a result of livestock sales. No wonder ranchers began to turn to farming as a way to reduce their dependency on stockraising.

Investments in farm tools and equipment in Cameron, Hidalgo, Starr, and Zapata counties also soared in value from about 17,000 dollars in 1870 to 92,630 dollars in 1900. The increase in tillable acreage as well as in the use of farming equipment and irrigation works accelerated the rise of commercial farming, which would eventually convert much of the rangeland into farmland.

In the last decades of the 1800s, the introduction of irrigation machinery and experimental farming gradually changed the character of agriculture in the Lower Valley. The efforts of a score of men provided the initial stimulus for commercial farming that adapted Mexican practices and relied on traditional crops such as cotton and sugarcane. In 1876, George Brulay became the first person to use a small pump to irrigate sugarcane, bananas, and other crops near Brownsville. Another early commercial farmer was a French immigrant, Celestin Jagou, who marketed citrus and other fruits from his irrigated farm six miles downriver from Brownsville.[88]

By the early 1890s a few men had built irrigation canals and erected pumps along the river. For example, during the drought years of 1889 to 1895, John Closner built canal laterals and set up a twenty-five-horsepower centrifugal pump and portable steam engine to irrigate two hundred acres at his San Juan Plantation, which was located east of the town of Hidalgo on the Río Grande. At about the same time, Emilio C. Forto, a Spanish-born politician in Cameron County, and the Longoria brothers of Brownsville built a seven-mile canal to irrigate three thousand acres in the Santa María area. These improvements, in turn, stimulated more crop experimentation and resulted in the cultivation of diverse commercial crops. Planters in Santa María, near the Cameron–Hidalgo county line, grew tobacco and sea-island cotton, sugarcane, grains, and vegetables. Soon several thousand acres of cotton were grown. The cane was milled at the Río Grande plantation belonging to Brulay.[89] Because of the high interest in cotton, farmers occasionally found it difficult to obtain seed. Thaddeus M. Rhodes, for instance, purchased five hundred pounds of seed in Matamoros because H. M. Field delayed in filling his order.[90] Some farmers planted sugarcane, which grew remarkably well in the rich soils of the delta. Soon a number of farms and plantations became showcases, and their proprietors' success brought attention to the potential of large-scale commercial farming.[91]

While Corpus Christi and San Diego attained greater success in cotton production and truck farming in the last decades of the nineteenth century, optimism for large-scale irrigated farming in the Lower Valley delta district was high. Ranchers and promoters, in particular, dreamed and talked about building railroads and irrigation systems to revitalize the economy.[92] But persisting problems like a lack of markets and capital for internal development projects would have to be resolved before the ranchers and land developers could realize their fortunes.

CONCLUSION

The last fifteen years of the nineteenth century represented almost a complete reversal in the fortunes of Tejanos, as a combination of social, economic, and environmental factors eroded their dominant position as livestock producers and majority landholders in nearly all districts of the Lower Valley. At the same time, the overall malaise that affected stockraising set in motion a transition to commercial irrigated farming in the delta counties of the region, a new development that came into full fruition in the early twentieth century.

The continuing commercialization of ranching, which was dependent on large sums of capital, was detrimental to most Tejano *rancheros*. By the mid-1880s ranching assumed an entirely new dimension characterized by corporate management instead of a simple family enterprise. As J. Nimmo, Jr., noted in 1885, Texas cattle ranching was "largely a ranch business" that was "carried on within enclosures belonging to cattlemen," as distinguished from ranchers who utilized the open range of the public domain.[93] Clearly, Anglo ranchers like King and Kenedy took advantage of their contacts with bankers and other lenders in Brownsville, Corpus Christi, and San Antonio. They tended to maintain their ranches intact during the good and bad years. Loans secured in the latter years essentially bought them time in which they hoped to see the market improve. Tejanos had traditionally borrowed from local merchants and bankers as well as other *rancheros*. Few, however, had recourse to major lenders in San Antonio mainly because the criteria for lending did not favor small landholders or those whose title to land was held by numerous owners.

While the detrimental effects of severe weather and the vagaries of the market economy in the 1880s and 1890s affected all ranching enterprises, small *rancheros* were the first to be displaced. These men and women drifted into the towns of the region or found employment with the more successful ranchers. However, the erosion of the land base of the *ranchero* class, particularly elites, represented the most crucial factor in the ultimate decline of the Tejanos. Because large tracts of land were essential to engage in commercial stockraising during this period, Tejano *rancheros* found themselves at a serious disadvantage at a critical time.

My study of the individual *ranchero* histories shows that with each new generation of *ranchero* descendants, the tendency was to break down the larger *ranchos*. On the one hand, this continuous subdivision of landholdings served social utilitarian purposes for a society that depended on the land for much of its social and economic life. On the other hand, it had an adverse effect on Tejanos because commercial ranching demanded access to large acreages and ultimately to capital during periods of rapid expansion, to join in the growth, as well as during tight economic periods in order to survive the distress. Moreover, *ranchero* estates were also subject to claims by creditors and others. Estate administration, even when carried out faithfully, resulted in the sale of herds and small tracts of land. By 1900 only a few Tejano landholders could in fact compete for loans or wait out the depressed economy until stock prices improved to reenter ranching on a moderate scale.

The transition to commercial farming involving corn, cotton, sugarcane, and other crops, which began on an experimental basis in the 1880s and 1890s, had several effects on Tejanos. Some landholders converted rangeland to farmland even in districts such as central Hidalgo County, districts away from the delta lands. A few introduced irrigation technology, but most did not, probably because they lacked capital. Consequently, much of the farming remained *de temporal* or seasonal. Large *rancheros* also adapted to the decline in ranching by adopting a system of tenancy that allowed Tejanos formerly engaged in the ranching economy to become tenant or sharecropper farmers. This was evident even in districts such as Starr County, where nearly everyone involved in agriculture, previous to the bust in stockraising, was a landholder.

Eventually, the overall decline of Tejano landholding that took place in the last quarter of the nineteenth century made it impossible for them to engage in large-scale stockraising. There were, of course, exceptions so that, in fact, some *rancheros* held their own, awaiting improvements in the marketplace. What all these changes in Tejano stockraising meant was that the social and economic fabric of Tejano society at the start of the twentieth century looked very different from the mid-nineteenth century, when nearly all stockmen and landholders were Tejano; in fact, they had lost much ground as the ranching economy had become capital-intensive and subject to worldwide factors beyond their control.

CHAPTER NINE

TEJANO RANCHEROS AND HISPANIC LANDHOLDING IN THE SOUTHWEST, 1848–1900

Most historians, such as David F. Weber and Rodolfo Acuña, agree that the crucible of Mexican American history is the period from 1848 to 1900, when the old settlers, the Mexicans, and the new arrivals from Europe and the United States forged significant relationships that shaped the society and economy of the region. With land as the basis of wealth for most of the settlers, competition between the two groups intensified, and as Mexican Americans lost control of these lands, they lost wealth and status in society. One of the central questions guiding this study of Tejanos in the Lower Valley is their displacement from the land. Specifically, I have examined the issues of the timing and manner in which land loss occurred in south Texas. This final chapter presents a brief comparative study of *mejicano* or Hispanic land tenure in the Southwest in the second half of the nineteenth century. What follows then is a short description and analysis of Hispanic land-grant history and adjudication and land loss in New Mexico, Arizona, California, and Texas. Lastly, I address the question whether, comparatively speaking, the experience of the Lower Valley regarding land tenure was as harsh as asserted by historians and other social scientists.

THE NEW MEXICAN EXPERIENCE

As the oldest and one of the most isolated former Spanish–Mexican settlements in the far northern frontier, New Mexico's land-tenure system evolved with unique peculiarities. Three or four developments stand out. First, due to the length of occupation, about one thousand land grants were made in New Mexico during the entire span of Spanish–Mexican rule. Second, the majority of the land grants were made in the names of a group of settlers instead of individuals. These grants were basically community grants intended for the benefit of all *vecinos* who were party to the grant of land. Third, settlers in New Mexico's frontiers retreated back and forth to their lands as a result of Indian attacks, which resulted in the same land being granted over and over to settlers. Fourth, the property rights of the preexisting Pueblo communities were respected.

The Hispanic land-grant dynamics can be viewed in the history of the Cañones region of north central New Mexico, where the first lands were granted in the 1730s. The first grant there was awarded to a Spanish soldier, and the second to three Montoya brothers from the town of Abiquiu. The Montoya family acquired the rights from the soldier, but in 1745 Ute Indians attacked and forced the settlers to leave the frontier. The original Montoya grant, Piedra Lumbre, was reoccupied in 1760 by a relative of the Montoyas named Pedro Martín Serrano. Martín Serrano then requested and obtained from the governor a grant de novo to the land. A cousin of Martín Serrano also asked for and received a grant south of Piedra Lumbre. This grant was smaller in area, but on the lands of a previous grant, the Polvadera, which the Montoyas had acquired earlier, in 1740. In the early nineteenth century, a third grant was made in the area, and it too experienced a similar history. This grant, the Cañones or Pederales, was a grant to Juan Bautista Valdéz, his family, seven companions, and presumably, their families. In 1818, Navajos drove the settlers away, and the lands were later reoccupied. On April 1, 1824, the new settlers, now led by the eldest son of Juan Bautista Valdéz, took formal possession of the land from the *alcalde*.[1]

Partly as a result of the complex history of New Mexican land tenure prior to the war with Mexico, land-grant adjudication consumed more time in New Mexico than anywhere else in the American Southwest after 1848, and the methods and rules adopted were not only burdensome but ultimately unfair. In New Mexico, land claims were subjected first to a legislative process in Washington, D.C., and then to a judicial system in which the standards for judging claims were rigorous. By imposing such a process and placing the burden on the claimants, the chances of obtaining confirmation were slim and those for defeating claims were high. Consider the evidence. Of the 1,000 or so land grants in New Mexico, claimants asserted their rights to only 212 grants. Prior to 1891, the U.S. Congress confirmed 48 claims out of the 212 presented to the surveyor general for determination. The federal government then patented 22 out of the 48 claims, totaling about 2 million acres, leaving 35 million acres of land in an unsettled status.[2]

'As a consequence of the gross disparity in confirmation of Hispanic claims under the surveyors general, many claimants eventually pressed their rights before a second adjudicatory body, the Court of Private Land Claims located in Santa Fe. This special court was created in 1891 because of the slowness with which the United States Congress reviewed and validated land-grant claims: 116 land grants awaited congressional action in 1889, and no grants had been confirmed by Congress since 1879. The Court of Private Claims adopted strict legal rules and requirements for confirmation. As a result, the claims were carefully scrutinized and a majority were defeated because the court rejected several presumptions in favor of a claim—presumptions that the surveyors general had followed previously in their work. The court did not complete its work until 1904.[3]

Community grants in New Mexico complicated matters because the Court of Public Land Claims repeatedly refused to recognize the entire acreage of a community grant, treating common lands as public-domain land subject to the right of the government to dispose of as it desired. Consequently, New Mexicans who were successful in proving their claim often received title to individual tracts—usually cultivated strips in narrow river valleys—that were relatively small in acreage. Moreover, community grants were especially preyed upon because the documents often named only the key settler on the title papers, rather than all of the grantees and those incorporated into the community, or *plaza.*

The slowness of the adjudicatory agencies in examining Hispanic claims in New Mexico allowed both Anglos and Mexicans to speculate in land, particularly prime tracts or those that could easily be acquired by manipulating the imprecise title to a grant. In the latter case, speculators purchased the undivided interests of landholders, particularly those in community grants, and then proceeded to force a judicial partition, which usually resulted in the sale of the entire grant to one or more speculators for a fraction of its real value.[5]

In New Mexico, technical details related to a land-grant title also undermined the validity of a claim. The most common such details were the inexactness of the grant, overlapping grants, lack of archival evidence warranting the granting of land, lack of a proper conveyance or title, and lack of a proper authority to grant title. Not surprisingly, many claims in New Mexico were never presented to the surveyor general or to the court.[6]

Victor Westphall's comprehensive study of land grants in New Mexico asserts that the court heard claims for 231 grants, totaling 34,653,340 acres, of which 82 claims comprising 1,934,986 acres were confirmed. Westphall concluded that 10,741,243 acres of land were ultimately granted by the Congress and the Court of Private Claims, while the court rejected 22,718,354 acres of land. Of this amount, he estimates that 70 percent of the rejections, or nearly 16,000,000 acres of land, were unfair.[7] As the final avenue for land-grant claimants, resorting to the Court of Private Claims again proved costly, burdensome, and inequitable as many claims were defeated.

Ultimately, a combination of social, legal, political, and cultural factors greatly diminished the landholdings of New Mexico's *hispanos.* According to historian Roxanne Dunbar Ortiz, settlers in northern New Mexico had lost 80 percent of the land by 1900—somewhat more than Tejanos, who lost about 60 to 70 percent of their landholdings in south Texas. The role of the courts in effecting a sharp decline among Hispanics in New Mexico is strongly documented by studies of individual grants. The incompatibility of the Spanish and Mexican laws and customs and Anglo-American common law regarding land acquisition and use presented enormous difficulties. This was in sharp contrast to Texas, where the state had adopted, in fact and in law, the land system that Spain and Mexico had imposed in order to make its vast plains productive. As elsewhere in the Southwest, lawyers also played a key role in bringing about land loss in New Mexico. They usually asked for one-third of the grant when they represented land-grant claimants. Unfortunately, lawyers and most of the surveyors general of New Mexico also speculated in land grants—they were not totally disinterested in the presentation of Hispanic claims. Gradual economic penetration by the railroads and by lumber and cattle companies dealt a severe blow to some landowners. The notorious Santa Fe Ring consisted of well-to-do and politically powerful Anglo newcomers and some Mexican *ricos* who dispossessed landholders.

Ortiz also argues for the persistence of a different cultural tradition of land tenure among the New Mexicans. Whereas *hispanos* valued the land for its intrinsic value in producing what it could yield for their survival, Anglos appreciated the land for its speculative value. Thus, she argues, the latter were more interested in market value rather than in use value, and because of these different orientations toward land use the two systems of land tenure clashed violently. Ortiz's arguments, however, are not supported by the historical experience of New Mexico's *pobladores.* The latest case studies of individual land grants indicate that, in fact, New Mexicans themselves sold land to each other and that they engaged in economic activities oriented to profit making, despite the fact that the bulk of land in New Mexico was not oriented to large-scale commercial agricultural economy. As a consequence, the majority of the New Mexican landholders farmed and grazed stock at a subsistence level. Eventually, they too would feel the pressures of Anglo economic expansion and the encroachment of the U.S. government. Many *hispanos* ended up as owners of small plots in river valleys.[8]

THE ARIZONA EXPERIENCE

The smallest number of land grants made by Spain and Mexico in the Southwest were in Arizona, but the history of land-grant adjudication there was similar to New Mexico. These grants were found south of Gila and along the Santa Cruz Valley, and to the east in the San Pedro Valley. They were first occupied in the 1820s and 1830s, evacuated in the 1840s and 1850s due to Apache raids, only to be subsequently reoccupied by Mexican and Anglo cattlemen. Mexican land tenure was therefore of short duration, and the Mexicans quickly sold their interests to newcomers. Like the case of New Mexico, the surveyor general of Arizona worked slowly, beginning his investigation of the claims in 1871. By 1888 he had reported on all but a half-dozen claims. He recommended to the U.S. Congress thirteen claims and disapproved two claims, but Congress did not act on his reports. Consequently, the Arizona claims likewise ended in the Court of Private Claims in Tucson. When the court finished its work in 1904, it confirmed eight land grants and rejected ten. The confirmed grants awarded title to only 116,540 acres out of the 837,680 acres claimed. Much of the disallowed land was known as "overplus" land, which was not part of the formal grant but had been used over the decades for stockraising.[9]

THE CALIFORNIAN EXPERIENCE

While only thirty-four grants for *ranchos* were awarded to individuals during the entire Spanish period in California, the Mexican era saw a proliferation of several hundred land grants. Officials in California awarded a small number of land grants in community to Indians so that the bulk of the grants went to individual *californios*.[10] In fact, as in south Texas, a few *californios* received multiple grants that resulted in impressive landholdings, with some *rancheros* owning up to 300,000 acres.[11] In addition, the more greedy *californios* and Anglos took advantage of the secularization of the missions in the 1830s to acquire highly valuable and developed lands, causing the disintegration of the natives' communities.[12]

The U.S. Congress appointed a surveyor general for California in March 1853, but the agency that actually determined the validity of a claim was called the Board of Land Commissioners, which had been created under the Land Act of 1851. The land commission eventually received 813 claims. The California claims comprised 588 grants, totaling over 12 million acres—probably the most productive lands in the state. Because of the long interval between the creation of the commission and the end of war with Mexico, some *californio rancheros* suffered hardships. Paul W. Gates asserts that in 1851 between a quarter and a third of the land grants had already changed hands. It is likely that the pressures to alienate their property rights reflected the *californios*' fears that their lands would not be protected by their conquerors. Under the Land Act of 1851, claims denied by the land commission could be appealed to the state district court and then to the United States Supreme Court. In spite of the swift turn of events in California with the discovery of gold and rapid immigration, the land commission confirmed grants totaling about 8,850,000 acres.[13]

A host of factors facilitated the decline of *californio* landholding during and after adjudication. As in New Mexico, technicalities served as serious impediments to the validation of some California claims. Most of these involved fraudulent titles or rights that were not fully vested in accordance with Spanish and Mexican colonization laws, and claims for grants for which there was no satisfactory documentary evidence of a title. In California, however, considerations of equity saved many claims.[14] While legal fees were not exorbitant, many *rancheros* paid with land, with lawyers customarily getting one-quarter of the claim. Economic factors proved to be more critical in northern California because of the rapid settlement that took place there after the discovery of gold. *Californios* in the southern part of the state suffered from erratic markets and environmental setbacks. High taxes and high interest rates on loans were also factors. The extravagant spending of some *rancheros* also may have been a cause for their decline.[15]

THE TEJANO EXPERIENCE IN THE LOWER VALLEY

As previously noted, prior to 1848 Spain and Mexico awarded over 350 land grants in the Lower Valley of Texas over the span of a century. These grants were all given to individuals, with some persons receiving multiple grants. The *porciones* were allotted along the Río Grande for town settlers. The larger grants or *mercedes* were intended for *agostaderos* or stockraising, and by the third generation the *pobladores* had occupied much of the region to the Nueces River. The few mission properties in the Lower Valley were secularized in the 1790s. As a consequence of these patterns of landholding, the lands in the region were individual properties of the descendants of Escandón's colony and new arrivals from nearby districts in northern New Spain and later Mexico.

After 1848, land-grant adjudication of lands in south Texas opened a new chapter in the lives of the *mejicano* settlers, most of whom desired to continue in possession of their lands and other properties. In contrast to the other jurisdictions in the Southwest, the state of Texas, by virtue of its previous claim to the territory extending from the Río Grande to the Nueces River, created the machinery for adjudicating the validity of claims to the lands in the so-called disputed territory. The Bourland Commission, the state district courts, and the state legislature all served as adjudicatory agencies. The first large number of land-grant confirmations by the state legislature in 1851 and 1852 was the work of this commission. The state district courts then followed up its work, and in a small number of sundry cases, the legislature itself served both as an adjudicatory tribunal and the authority that granted confirmation of title. Overall, very few claims were denied confirmation, and in the end only twenty-four grants in the region were never adjudicated, and for unknown reasons.

TEJANO LAND LOSS IN THE LOWER VALLEY

Tejano land loss in south Texas began very slowly in the 1840s and continued at a gradual pace until the depression in livestock and wool and in commerce began in the late 1880s, continuing into the first half of the 1890s. The trying years became a wedge used by wealthier Anglo and European ranchers and merchant-speculators to take up more land from hard-pressed *rancheros*. As a result, land loss accelerated. While some *rancheros* persisted in owning large tracts of land past 1900, considerable displacement took place throughout the region. Some districts, especially along the coastal counties of Cameron and Nueces, saw a sharp decline in Tejano landownership, whereas the displacement of *rancheros* proceeded much more slowly in Starr, Zapata, Webb, and Duval counties.

Social, economic, and political factors undermined the initial high levels of Tejano landownership in south Texas following the initial confirmation of their land grants. The rise in population put pressure on Tejano families that still owned land to grant it to their descendants as inheritance or to sell to new settlers. The population in the Lower Valley jumped from nearly ten thousand persons in 1850 to ninety thousand in 1900. The growth in friendly and unfriendly partition suits, which began in earnest in the 1870s and continued at an accelerated pace into the early years of the twentieth century, also resulted in a larger number of landholders. A few examples will suffice to illustrate the effects of partition suits. As a result of a suit brought by Richard King against the heirs of María Josefa Cavazos, the Espíritu Santo was partitioned in 1889 into thirty-two shares. And in 1900 the district court of Starr County partitioned two land grants, totaling 112,483 acres, into eighty separate shares. A small number of shares were awarded to two lawyers, probably as compensation for their work. The San Antonio broker, Francis Smith, an intervenor in that partition suit, received thirteen separate shares, most under one thousand acres, but a few large shares—land that the firm had previously obtained from Tejanos under foreclosure proceedings.[16] Consequently, the number of Tejano farmers and ranchers in 1900 was greater than ever before, but the majority now owned tracts of land that were less conducive to successful commercial ranching. As time passed, only efficient ranchers who practiced scientific management of their lands and herds could compete on relatively small acreages. Few Tejanos appear to have made this transition by 1900. As a result of this sharp decline in landholding, many *rancheros* became landless and powerless. The future did not look promising since the next boom would rest on the value of irrigable land, land adjacent to or near the river where much of it had already been lost to new settlers from the United States and Europe.

As new settlers entered the Lower Valley during the ranching boom, economic competition for the land accelerated. This competition sometimes involved friendly sales, such as Tejanos selling land to new immigrants from Mexico. As the case of Don Florencio Sáenz indicates, Anglos also sold land to Mexicans. Macedonio Vela's first purchase of land was from John McAllen and Salomé Ballí McAllen. These transactions occurred mostly during the good years of the cattle economy, from the mid-1860s to the early 1880s. During the difficult years in the post-1885 period, Mexicans were so hard pressed to pay off debts that large-scale Anglo ranchers, such as D. R. Fant, Henrietta B. King, and Edward C. Lasater and land speculators such as the merchants A. J. Bloomberg and G. M. Raphael, Jeremiah Galvan, Francisco Yturria, Henry M. Field, and others, acquired large tracts of land from Tejanos.

As noted above, conflict over land between Tejanos and Anglos involved a variety of forms, such as lawsuits, fraud, intimidation, and violence. Regrettably, much of the evidence documenting the worst tactics used to drive Tejanos from their lands is difficult to obtain and evaluate, mainly because many of the source materials are presently unavailable or inaccessible for research. Also, some documents are missing from both public and private sources. For example, there is a gap in the commissioners' court records of Hidalgo County for the Civil War years.

At times, Anglos used laws, the courts, and other officers to their advantage to expel Tejanos from their lands, sometimes illegally. For example, Tejanos, who lacked familiarity with the American legal system and with the English language, resorted to Anglo lawyers at different times in the adjudicatory process as well as after confirmation of their claims. Thus, *rancheros* retained lawyers to represent them before the Bourland Commission as well as in other legal matters, often paying with land. The first large transfers of Mexican landholdings to Anglo newcomers were the result of such arrangements. Lawyers continued the practice of taking land as a fee in later lawsuits under the special legislative acts. Lawyers also took land as a fee in defending Tejanos charged with crimes. Probate judges and sheriffs also helped Anglos acquire valuable lands and herds from Tejanos, in ways that often took advantage of the latter. Consider, for example, the case of the estate of Manuel Ramírez Elizondo. After this *ranchero* died sometime in 1874, one John McClane of Nueces County went to the probate court presided over by the county judge. He petitioned the court to be appointed administrator of the *ranchero*'s estate. The judge agreed and Richard King and Reuben Holbein, King's agent and secretary, served as sureties for McClane, who received the desired appointment. The surety was set at 130,000 dollars, which indicated that the *ranchero*'s property was quite valuable. On December 29, 1874, the three-member board of appraisers filed their inventory and appraisal. They included one Tejano *ranchero* and two Anglos, G. W. Pettigrew and Reuben Holbein. They valued the estate at 56,000 dollars. Cattle were valued at $3.50 per head, horses at $10.00, and donkeys at $3.00. Except for the horses, these values were set low, but the administrator claimed that there was no market for the beef cattle. Barely two months later, on March 1, 1875, McClane reported that he had sold the cattle to King at the appraised value.[17] No mention was made of the other stock.

Newcomers sometimes enriched themselves with thousands of acres of land by virtue of their positions in government. A case in point is John Closner, who arrived penniless on the border in 1884, after building railroads in Porfirian Mexico. Selected by James B. Wells of Brownsville, a King attorney and the reigning Democratic political boss of south Texas, to mediate the disputes between two warring factions in Hidalgo County, Closner first served as deputy sheriff and later became sheriff and tax collector.[18] The tax rolls show that he owned no land in 1890, but he began to acquire small parcels of acreage in 1893. By 1900 he claimed sixty thousand acres of land, of which he farmed two hundred.[19] At the turn of the century, Closner became a land speculator and investor in farmland development, until he embezzled large sums of money from the county and left office.[20]

The use of barbed-wire fencing and laws related to fencing land were detrimental to Tejano *rancheros.* For example, in Hidalgo County voters cast ballots to adopt ordinances requiring the fencing of sheep and goats in the 1890s. While Anglo ranchers who migrated in south Texas benefited from such laws, some *rancheros* who had formerly utilized the open range were displaced. Both Tejano and Anglo ranchers in that county were often required by the county commissioners' court to open roads that they had closed by fencing and to built gates to facilitate the movement of herds from one place to another. However, it should be noted that there is very limited evidence that "fencing wars" between ranchers and other landowners occurred in the region, although such conflict was common in central Texas during the last quarter of the nineteenth century. Still, attempts to enter a landholder's range was usually met with a vigorous protest, physical threats, violence, and costly lawsuits.[21]

GENERALIZATIONS ABOUT HISPANIC LANDHOLDERS IN THE SOUTHWEST

While circumstances varied from jurisdiction to jurisdiction, several generalizations can be advanced about the process of land-grant adjudication in the Southwest. Texas and California profited from the relatively more prompt and liberal adjudication of land grants than did Arizona and especially New Mexico. The fact that both Texas and California were states rather than territories—and were under intense pressure by settlers who wanted land, especially in northern California—speeded up the process of validation. Moreover, both Texas and California benefited from the more common practice of individual private grants instead of community grants, a practice that was more common in New Mexico. Also, Tejanos, to a greater extent, benefited from the relative degree of liberality of the adjudicatory agencies in Texas than did *californios* and *hispanos* in New Mexico, who faced the same burden of having to prove their claims.[22]

The worse aspect of land-grant adjudication involved the rejection of a claim or a sharp reduction of acreage in a validated land grant. More than in south Texas and California, Mexicans in New Mexico and Arizona sustained considerable land loss in the adjudicatory process. In California the land commission often faced problems in determining the size of a grant and even its location. Problems arose partly because the Spanish and Mexican land systems were not as precise as Anglo-American law. Claims not only suffered from indefinite and overlapping boundaries, but also from incomplete confirmation of a grant by the proper authorities. While all of these difficulties created costly delays in the examination of a claim, the outright rejection of a claim led to more expensive appeals in the courts. It is clear that New Mexican claims were defeated on the basis of very similar problems. Why were land grants in south Texas spared these challenges? Even though similar land laws operated in all of these jurisdictions, it seems to me that Anglo familiarity with Hispanic land-grant practices in Texas dating to Austin's colony in the 1820s, as well as the fact that the population pressures from outsiders in the Lower Valley were not as intense as in California, figured importantly in a more equitable and prompt adjudication of Tejano claims.

The length of time that a grant had been held was also a crucial factor in determining whether the claim was valid. For example, historians have noted that some California grants were in the possession of the *californios* for a short time, usually less than ten years and in some cases only one or two years. In New Mexico, Governor Manuel Armijo granted over half of the 31 million acres granted under Spain and Mexico in a brief period from 1837 to 1846.[23] These facts make the California and New Mexico claims different from the south Texas claims, which had been in the possession of their owners for at least twenty or thirty years at the time of validation and in many cases for nearly one hundred years—settlers on the river *porciones* having received title in 1767. As the Bourland Commission noted in 1851, with regard to the claim of the descendants of José Miguel Ramírez for an eight-league tract called Agua Nueva de Arriba (1831) in present-day Jim Hogg County, "the original grantee and his family have held peaceable possession of the land for sixty or seventy years." That this knowledge of Tejano landholding was kept for generations in the oral tradition is illustrated by the histories recorded in the twentieth century by Mercurio Martínez. He recalled his family's land-tenure history of the Dolores lands, saying that in 1859 his grandfather had bought the Dolores subdivision of the Vásquez Borrego Grant from Antonia Viduarri, the widow of Hipólito Peña, a Borrego descendant.[24] A long history of land tenure definitely facilitated validation and confirmation of land grants in the Lower Valley.

While the adjudication process presented troublesome problems in the Southwest as a whole, competition for the land—once titles were confirmed (or for that matter denied or not adjudicated)—produced the deepest conflict and the erosion of the Mexicans' landholdings.[25] The most acceptable and subtle means for displacing Mexican *rancheros* involved "purchases" of undivided interests in a grant.[26] Anglo ranchers employed the best lawyers, who, in turn, relied on shrewd land agents to protect their economic interests, especially in obtaining titles or *derechos* to land. How some of these agents worked can be gleaned from a brief letter from E. B. Raymond, a land agent and ranch foreman for the King ranch, to James B. Wells, the ranch's attorney in 1898. "Old Tom Trevenio [*sic*] has been Bellyacheing [*sic*] for a long time about that 250 acres of land and every time he hears of your being in Brownsville he wants to leave his work here and go to see you. . . . I am about geting [*sic*] tired of his damn foolishness and expect will yet have to fire him out of here. Please decide the matter with him one way or the other and start him out of Town. As he has a camp outfit and ought to be with it attending to his work. If you make him a Deed to any Land at all it should be given him off in some corner where he can be fenced and nail to the Cross for good."[27]

Hispanics throughout the U.S. Southwest struggled to maintain control of their landholdings at the end of the war with Mexico. While the factors that reduced landownership varied from place to place, a common experience pitted the original *pobladores* and their descendants against the new arrivals from the United States and Europe. Change in land tenure was a key element that shaped the history of each jurisdiction in which Hispanics held land. Based on my study of land-grant adjudication of Tejano claims in south Texas and this brief comparative analysis of other jurisdictions in the Southwest, I believe that *rancheros* did not suffer as harsh a treatment as is commonly depicted in the popular literature, historical memory, and scholarly literature. Still, for Tejanos the most critical time period that produced drastic changes in land tenure was the post-adjudication years, when the process of land loss unfolded. The general view has been that Texas was a particularly harsh place for *mejicanos.* The fact that land grants in the Lower Valley have been studied superficially has helped in perpetuating a distorted history of Tejano land tenure and in relating this history to other Hispanics in the Southwest.

One of the central questions in the history of the Tejanos is their displacement from the land following the events of the Texas Revolt of 1835 and the Mexican-American War. As discussed earlier here, the causes of land loss in the Lower Valley were complex, and it is clear that rapid displacement in much of the region occurred after 1880. Recently, new research, especially that of Carolina Castillo Crimm on Victoria, investigated the history of Tejano land tenure. However, little is still known about important districts such as Nacogdoches, the San Antonio-Goliad complex, Refugio-San Patricio, and even the El Paso Valley. Research concerning those districts should be undertaken in order to ascertain how Tejanos fared under their new rulers.

EPILOGUE

Over a period of 150 years (from the 1730s to 1900), the settlers in the Lower Valley proved to be hardy, resilient, and adaptable to changing circumstances, qualities that helped most of them adjust to a variety of changes. A difficult climate, nomadic Indians, shifts in the marketplace, changes in sovereignty, and conflict with Anglos did not dent the spirit of a people who for generations had lived on the frontier. Originally, the settlers saw themselves as Spanish and *mestizo* because their colonial experience in New Spain involved the conquest of the nomadic Indians. After the war with Mexico, these settlers called themselves *mejicano*, but gradually identified with their evolving historical identity and ethnicity as a Tejano people. The Tejanos shaped a distinct society, culture, and economy in south Texas.

Good fortune and initiative brought success to some settlers, while others experienced limited opportunities to improve their lives during the course of the century and a half of Hispanic settlement. Those who utilized the most important resources of the land—its people and its vast grasslands—benefited materially. A small class of merchants and officials gained wealth from their activities. *Rancheros* who owned or acquired significant landholdings and herds did well in the pastoral economy, which was always susceptible to ups and downs. Naturally, good years brought prosperity and expansion, while bad years brought economic contraction and even displacement from the land. Some other settlers lived a harsh reality, in which advantages were few and fleeting, but they too survived the good and bad times. For all of them, however, their lives were enriched by the rhythm of everyday activities and important events that transcended their personal lives. Their historical experience grew out of a long tradition of adaptation to frontier life that, in time, resulted in a rootedness in the land, a sense of place that was dear to them and their descendants.

THE COLONIAL LEGACY IN THE LOWER VALLEY

The colonial period saw the implantation of the basic structure of Hispanic society and economy in Nuevo Santander, which has had lasting implications for the Lower Valley to the present day. Nuevo Santander represents the foundation for the Spanish–*mejicano* origins of the Lower Valley. Escandón's enterprise (1747–1767) was remarkable because it achieved its objective of the imperial consolidation of an unsettled territory through conquest and colonization. The Spanish–Coahuiltecan Indian encounter yielded tragic consequences for the Indians in two important ways: (1) the number of Indians in missions declined rapidly, and (2) only a few Indians were eventually absorbed into the already heterogeneous colonial population, furthering *mestizaje* among the settlers. In effect, the Indian cultural element was largely erased, compared to other provinces of New Spain where their communities remained intact. As a result, *lo español* was given greater worth and importance, while *lo indio* was deprecated. As other historians have shown, this colonial framework polarizing two distinct human cultures played itself out similarly across the northern frontier, as the non-Spanish negotiated their way in a society dominated by the so-called *gente de razón.*[1]

Outside of beleaguered Laredo and the perennial trouble spots in the Tamaulipan sierra regions, the settlers were mostly successful in defending their frontier from Indian warriors. With a long history of fighting Indians in this distant frontier, the settlers were hardened frontiersmen and women. Nonetheless, the costs in loss of property and human lives were often high. This military-militia tradition of the settlers left a legacy that is often apparent in the bravery of Tejano and other *norteño* soldiers who have fought in America's wars in this century as well as those who participated in Mexico's revolutions.

While semimilitary in origin, the civilian settlers provided the impetus for the colony's growth. In the Lower Valley, it is important to recognize the *villas del norte,* founded in the eighteenth century, as the key source of the Tejano population for the region. In addition, by 1848 hundreds of Spanish and Mexican land grants had been made in the region between the Río Grande and the Nueces River. These land grantees or subsequent buyers were nearly all citizens from the *villas del norte.* For these reasons, the history of Tejanos in the

Lower Valley began with Escandón's colony, although some livestock operations began as early as the 1730s. The endurance of a Hispanic population in the Lower Valley of Texas after 1848 owes much to this early history of settlement and land tenure.

Oakah L. Jones, Jr., and other historians have depicted Nuevo Santander as a frontier society with few distinctions. However, new research, such as that of historian Lisbeth Hass on southern California, shows that Spanish–Mexican frontier societies were more complex and dynamic than commonly believed.[2] Similarly, the evidence for Nuevo Santander suggests that the society was fluid in nature, but differences in sex, wealth, and to some extent, race made for variation in the status of the citizens. Evidently, some rivalry existed among settlers initially, as was the case in Laredo, but intermarriage and the need for unity in the face of Indian attacks dissolved those conflicts. De la Teja documents a very similar situation in San Antonio, except that there the rivalry existed between Canary Islanders and the so-called *agregados*, or soldier-families, who came from Nuevo León and Coahuila.[3] *Mestizaje* reduced racism, but it was not totally absent. Initially, all settlers, including married women and widows, who desired to become town dwellers received land grants as an inducement to occupy this *frontera*. Some men enjoyed the fruits of first-class citizenship. They owned land, voted in local elections, and provided leadership in town government as well as in their community or *rancho*. These men became the principal patriarchs in a hierarchical society sanctioned by both the Catholic church and the state for the purpose of maintaining social and political stability.[4] Since the colonial period, women had also exercised leadership roles in their families and communities, especially landholding women; however, more study is needed to clarify their private and public roles.

Continuity of a civic tradition of responsibility among key landholders, merchants, and political elites was an important feature of Hispanic society. Laredo, for example, witnessed a rotation of officeholding among Hispanic patriarchs and their descendants from its founding until very late in the nineteenth century, when Raymond Martin rearranged the political order by instituting a system of one-man bossism in place of the traditional Hispanic oligarchy. The fact that Matamoros was a port since the 1820s meant that newcomers also entered the town's leadership; some of the men were non-Hispanic.

During the Spanish and Mexican periods, the settlers in the Lower Valley region engaged in trade, commerce, and ranching. Most of the settlers, however, survived off the land as small farmers, as hunters, and especially as ranchers. Each facet of economic life involved a variety of practices. Spanish policy restricted trade to internal markets, but there were gaps in enforcement. The rise of a more complex market economy that began in the era of Bourbon reforms and continued with the expansion of international trade in the early nineteenth century, coinciding with the growth of internal markets as the population increased, meant that *rancheros* and merchants had to be attuned to changes in the marketplace. The larger and more ambitious *rancheros* and merchants benefited from these opportunities, but ancillary workers also gained from the improved opportunities resulting from fewer trade restrictions and wider demands for the "products of the country." There is evidence of this development in Saltillo and other places in the northeastern provinces of New Spain, including Nuevo Santander; however, more study of this process and its effects on the settlers is needed.[5] In any case, landholders and merchants were practical in their activities, holding on to their goods, lands, and herds even in unfavorable conditions such as wars, raids, and droughts. Weber, in his study of Mexico's far northern frontier during the period from 1821 to 1846, characterizes its settlers as a pragmatic people who, despite isolation from the core and Indian raids, developed socially and economically in ways that represented fundamental change compared to the center of Mexico.[6] It seems to me, however, that in the Lower Valley and other places in northeastern Mexico, this development occurred prior to the early Mexican–Anglo contacts of the 1820s.

During the Mexican war of independence, unofficial ports in the Gulf of Mexico, such as Tampico and Matamoros, brought new activities that ushered in international commerce. In the Lower Valley, Matamoros grew quickly to become the entrepôt of the Río Grande trade that expanded into northern Mexico. In general, a measure of prosperity occurred, benefiting those involved in the "Mexican trade."

It was the land, however, that occupied the attention of most of the settlers. The availability of large tracts of virgin pasturelands facilitated the growth of stockraising during the years spanning Spanish and Mexican rule. Ranching practices reached far into the colonial and Iberian past. Survival in the pasturelands north of the Río Grande delta required adaptive environmental and economic strategies. Some practices had long been customary among *rancheros*, but others evolved, partly as new technologies became available in the last quarter of the nineteenth century. As in Mexican California, a few stockmen did acquire multiple land grants, but no significant *hacendado* class arose in Nuevo Santander. Very few individuals had the resources to undertake the founding of *haciendas*, as did José Vásquez Borrego of Coahuila. Occasionally, an enterprising merchant and/or rancher acquired *derechos* to a number of grants, but eventually such landholdings were broken up by inheritance and sales. Even though some grants exceeded the standard five leagues required for establishing a *hacienda*, settlers developed a tradition of individually owned *ranchos* that were worked by the *ranchero*, by his sons, and occasionally by hired workers. Consequently, most stockraising operations were on the level of a *rancho*, and Tejano *rancheros* did not live in a quasi-feudal Mexican hacienda society, as Montejano asserts.[7] The importance of this development is that it opened opportunities for sons and daughters to continue their father's ranching operations or to found their own independent enterprises. Also, landholdings were continuously subdivided among the heirs, precluding the growth of a small class of powerful landed elites, as occurred in Coahuila and San Luis Potosí.[8]

Two distinctive elements in the colonial history of the Lower Valley distinguish it from New Mexico and California. First, the settlers in the Lower Valley came from common *norteño* roots, mostly in neighboring Nuevo León and Coahuila. This gave the settler population a predominant Spanish culture and ethos that was distinct from the core culture of Mexico. From the beginning, there was a partial incorporation of the local nomadic Indian population, a fact more common to New Mexico and southern California, where large numbers of sedentary Indians had lived for hundreds of years. The continuing survival of Indian identity in those places meant that tension persisted longer, adding to the complexity of the society.[9] This *norteño* origin has had lasting consequences for the formation of a Tejano identity, which arose in the last decades of second half of the nineteenth century as conflict between Tejanos and Anglos intensified. Second, a large number of *pobladores* received land grants for stockraising in the Lower Valley, which made for a more egalitarian social and economic society than southern New Mexico, where a few settlers received very large land grants. Moreover, New Mexicans were not major livestock producers; they were mostly self-sufficient agrarians, especially in the northern part, where the bulk of the grants were community grants. *Californios*, who received very few land grants in the Spanish period, were awarded several hundred in the Mexican period, facilitating the ascendancy of a *ranchero* class in the 1820s and 1830s. The *californios*' land-grant history is more akin to that of the settlers of the Lower Valley, but there is one important difference. At the time of annexation, they were mostly first-generation landholders, as compared to a large number of third generation-Tejano landholders, who were such by virtue of the 1767 land grants as well as a few awarded before that time. However, this long history of Tejano landholding fostered a deep economic and psychohistorical attachment to the land, still cherished today and similar to the *nuevo mejicano* and *californio* tradition of land tenure. There are, of course, other similarities among all four Hispanic groups (including Arizonans) in the Southwest, but these are sociocultural and not economic.

TEJANO ADAPTATION TO A CHANGING WORLD

The Tejano experience in the Lower Valley was one of substantial adaptation to changing circumstances in politics, education, culture, and the economy. Tejanos, in particular, played a dynamic role in the society and economy of south Texas for much of the nineteenth century. Tejano—Anglo accommodation in social and economic life was widespread, despite the existence and persistence of competition for the natural resources of the region. Gradually, conflict set in as Tejanos lost control of their destinies with the erosion of their landholdings. As a result, their historical identity as Tejanos emerged late in the nineteenth century, as Anglos gained control of the region's resources and conflict between the two groups intensified. In short, during the first fifty years of U.S. rule, Tejanos maintained an appreciation for the past while embracing the inevitable march to a more highly competitive, urban, and modern society.

The Tejano social fabric was characterized by strong nuclear and patriarchal families. The population was both native-born as well as foreign-born, but there was little distinction because the social and cultural milieu of the Mexican immigrants was similar to that of the Tejanos. Intermarriages between Anglo males and local Hispanic women was often positive. Adoptions were common, and the presence of family networks suggests that competition for resources existed. At times, divisions arose, especially with regard to the inheritance of land, herds, and money. Crime was not absent, but it was neither chronic nor rampant, except in the imagination of some contemporary observers who stood to gain by stereotyping the Tejano as a *bandido*, similar to the situation facing the *mejicano* in California, where the archetype criminal was the ubiquitous Joaquín. In fact, those who committed crimes, including the notorious cattle thieves, were both Hispanic and Anglo.

Culturally, *lo mejicano* persisted in religious and secular customs and traditions, reminding the settlers of their past and giving them a sense of group identity. The river did not so much separate as unite socially and economically the settlers of the old *villas* and the new towns. In a special sense, proximity to the old homeland facilitated the transmission of ongoing Mexican cultural forms, so the Lower Valley conveniently served as a sort of *cuna* or cradle for much of what became part of the Greater Mexico culture that Américo Paredes has written about. This process occurred early in the Lower Valley, as compared to southern California and other places in the Southwest, primarily because Texas, especially the southern part of the state, had received such large numbers of immigrants from Mexico in the second half of the nineteenth century. Yet it is true that a few Tejanos with strong social or economic ties to Anglos were acculturated to Anglo customs, habits, and attitudes, but most were not. The growth of public and private education, politics, and joint Tejano–Anglo business activities promoted acculturation in American life. More than anything, limited opportunities for intermarriage between the two groups prevented the kind of assimilation that other groups experienced in the United States.

The fact that Tejano landholders were numerous and that *mejicanos* made up a very large percentage of the population ensured a participatory role for Tejano leaders in politics. Even then, however, factions among Tejanos were prevalent, aiding political bosses throughout the region. Thus, I disagree that the bulk of the Tejano voters were "corralled" by Anglo politicians, the assertion that Evan Anders makes in his valuable study of boss politics in south Texas. In any case, the Tejano *ranchero* and business class continued to play a key role, but with varying degrees of success, in town and county governments throughout the region after 1848. It is possible that this early tradition of local participation, while broken up by the arrival of Anglo citizens in the era of town and farm development, served as a memory that a later Mexican-American generation could emulate in its quest for full citizenship in the twentieth century.

Tejano *rancheros* played a leading role in the growth of stockraising in the Lower Valley during the period from 1848 to 1900. They returned to their lands and engaged in commercial ranching in various ways. Initially, in the period from 1848 to 1865, they encouraged the recovery of ranching by reintroducing herds into the Lower Valley and quickly expanding production. This phase was also marked by initial sales that completely reoriented the region's trade, with its markets in Mexico redirected to the north. The boom in wool and stockraising that began in the post–Civil War era lasted to the middle of the 1880s. During this time, Tejanos diversified their production and entered new and distant markets. They practiced mixed ranching, a tradition that went back to sixteenth-century colonial origins in stockraising districts northeast of Mexico.[10] The last phase of the ranching economy (from the middle of the 1880s to 1900) saw a considerable contraction of Tejano ranching, which paralleled their loss of land. This event, however, was a very late development, particularly when compared with what happened to *californios*, who were, with the Tejanos, the most important *rancheros*. The most serious disadvantage to Tejano ranchers was the lack of capital at a time when prices for wool and livestock tumbled and drought affected the region. Yet it is evident that stockraising was a capitalist activity that experienced ups and downs, as it had historically in northern New Spain. What this history of Tejano *rancheros* suggests, then, is that they were adaptable producers, not dependent on one kind of livestock, which hurt some *rancheros*, such as the *californios*, after annexation.[11] Also, Tejanos were by and large small and moderate producers, men and women who owned their own land and worked it themselves. This is very similar to the tradition that existed in northern Mexico during the Porfiriato but whose roots also date to the late colonial period, when settlers were given land to prevent incursions from raiding Indians and later to halt U.S. expansion.

The ranching economy of south Texas employed hundreds of workers, especially cowboys and shepherds. As Frederick Katz points out, these workers, most of whom came to Texas when work was not available in northern Mexico, were basically the most free; their skills and the proximity to work in the United States set them apart from the rest of the workers in Mexico.[12] That the Lower Valley had no substantial use of peon labor is a direct result of this long historical development of stockraising.

After the war with Mexico, the profitable Mexican trade expanded and offered employment opportunities on both sides of the Río Grande. It remained in place until the 1880s, in spite of various difficulties. High tariffs in Mexico traditionally encouraged smuggling, although American merchants and officials seemed to have accepted this reality. Still, by the 1850s regional trade markets with northern Mexico had grown in importance, as key commercial cities, such as Monterrey and Saltillo, increased in population and became primary markets for European and then increasingly American goods. As a new outlet to world markets, principally in the United States, the port of Matamoros had begun to reorient trade north instead of the traditional orientation to the south. The Civil War in the United States also disrupted the established manner of conducting commerce and trade, as Confederates used Mexico's bordertowns, including Monterrey and Saltillo, as bases for selling cotton and buying greatly needed supplies for the South. Still more upsetting to Lower Valley merchants on the American side of border was the continuation of a free-trade zone in Tamaulipas, which had been established in the late 1850s. From Mexico's perspective, this initiative shored up business and kept the population on its side of the border, but Americans, especially Lower Valley merchants, objected on the grounds that free trade bypassed them, harming them economically. Eventually, this arrangement proved too difficult for Mexico's national government, which was under attack by merchants in its interior cities as well as by the U.S. government. Forced to act, Mexico terminated the free-trade zone, relegating its border merchants to their own devices to survive the new conditions.[13]

A general economic decline in the 1890s, reflecting worldwide problems, affected merchants and stockraisers in the Lower Valley. Their situation deteriorated, and soon nearly the entire region fell into a worsening recession and depression from which merchants and stockraisers could not shake themselves. In short, Tejanos did not experience widespread economic or political losses until the 1880s and 1890s.

TEJANO LAND-TENURE HISTORY

One of the central problems in understanding Tejano history is the persistence in the literature of the myth of a "no-man's-land" and the Tejano rejection of that interpretation. It is important to observe that although historians and other writers have often labeled the movement of *rancheros* from their land grants back to the Lower Valley towns as "abandonment," their landholdings and herds were only temporarily left behind. Throughout the nineteenth century, Tejanos usually returned to their lands once the immediate danger had subsided. Regrettably, this aspect of the region's history has shaped much of the historiography of Texas; historians as well as settlers new to the region continue to assert that south Texas was a "no-man's-land." Such assertions have served as a convenient rationale for dismissing Tejano efforts and claiming Anglo superiority on the basis of the 1848 conquest. What I assert and demonstrate is that *rancheros* who were caught up in periodic movements back and forth to the *villas del norte* did not give up their claims, for their lands and herds were the main sources of their wealth. Moreover, after 1848 they remained permanently on their land grants. The fact that nearly all of the land grants in the Lower Valley adjudicated by the Texas legislature and courts were confirmed for Tejano claimants underscores my argument that they did not abandon their lands. Furthermore, as long as stockraising remained profitable, Tejano landholders were numerous in the Lower Valley. It is this long history of land tenure in the grasslands of the region that gives Tejanos a strong sense of place, one that even today is easily observed among much of the population.

Contrary to previous assertions that Tejanos were an oppressed people subordinated to Anglo domination very early after 1848, the decline of most Tejano landholders was a very late development, and one involving a greater complexity than previously acknowledged. In fact, the displacement of Tejano landholders in the Lower Valley region varied from place to place. In the 1850s and 1860s, some Tejanos in the coastal area between Brownsville and Corpus Christi saw their lands taken up by a handful of new Anglo ranchers. Later, in the 1870s, a few Anglos and Europeans acquired lands around San Diego, and they also occupied the desolate upper Nueces River Valley. Central and northern Hidalgo County and parts of Webb County saw the arrival of large Anglo ranchers in the last twenty years of the nineteenth century. What this means is that Tejanos lost land to Anglos and Europeans mostly in fringe areas of the region where the *mejicanos* were few in number or where large tracts of adjacent public land remained available for purchase. And in some districts, Tejanos were never totally displaced from the land.

Land loss was a complicated process that involved social, economic, and political dynamics. The most important factors contributing to Tejano land loss included: initial confusion over the status of land grants, competition over the best lands, extensive litigation of land grants after the initial adjudication of 1851–52, sheriffs' sales, fraud and other illegal seizures of land (and herds), frequent division of Tejano landholdings either by purchase or through inheritance, limited accessibility to capital and credit, and the deterioration of the ranching economy after 1885. Crucial social factors not previously addressed by historians, such as the growth in the landholding population, the persistence of partible inheritance, and intermarriage, significantly altered Tejano landholding patterns. By 1900 the number of Hispanic landholders who owned or claimed large acreages (over two thousand acres) had been drastically reduced. Many others had been totally displaced from the land, while a few others remained isolated in small *ranchos*.

Tejano landholding persisted despite adversity late into the nineteenth century, but not at the initial high levels experienced in the first quarter after annexation. Still, a Tejano sense of place endured in many locales, and while many individual *rancheros* lost their lands, their participation in the ranching economy has long remained a source of pride for their descendants. In a very important way, then, Tejanos may lament the loss of their lands, but not in the manner that John R. Chávez describes in his thesis of the lost-land image held by Chicanos in the Southwest. Chávez's argument fits in well with an ideological interpretation of the Chicano struggle for civil rights, but it does not explain the rich and varied Tejano experience of landholding and participation in the commercial ranching economy of the Lower Valley.[14]

The general explanations previously offered to explain Tejano land tenure are too simplistic, and the assertion that the Tejano experience in the Lower Valley was particularly harsh requires qualification. McWilliams's "persistence" thesis is simply too generous to the Tejanos of south Texas, for, in fact, too many *rancheros* lost their land at various times in the second half of the nineteenth century, especially toward the end of the century. As a result, some of them moved to the towns and cities of the region in search of steady urban employment. Those who persisted as landholders have continued to modernize their agricultural economy, as has the whole region. My findings parallel Pitt's "decline" thesis for the *californios*, but it should be clear that land loss among Tejanos was a much more gradual and slower process, similar to the New Mexican experience, as reported by Westphall and Ortiz. Acuña, Weber, and Montejano also address the land-loss controversy, but in a general way. For this reason, it is important to undertake more careful documentary and quantitative studies of land tenure in order to see what factors proved to be critical in producing land loss. The same, however, can be said of the studies on New

Mexican and particularly Californian Hispanic land tenure because one is often left with the impression that only large landholders operated in those regions of the Southwest. Jordan is incorrect in subscribing to the "no-man's-land" thesis because, in fact, most of the land in the region south of the Nueces River was still claimed and used by Tejano *rancheros* during the period from 1810 to 1870. Finally, Weber, De León, and Montejano are too harsh in the analysis of the Tejano experience. The diversity of the settlers' social-cultural and economic activities and their success in those endeavors shows these factors shaped much of their lives, notwithstanding oppression, discrimination, and ethnic conflict.

While the notion that conflict between the Tejanos and Anglos was omnipresent should be tempered by the evidence of widespread positive interaction between both peoples, Anglo antagonism toward *mejicanos* did exist. Social conflict over land and political power was common. For the most part, Tejano landholders were considered equal or first-class citizens. The difficulty arose when many *rancheros* lost their land. This situation was perfect for the growth of social conflict. The growth of the new science of racial thinking and the ideology of Manifest Destiny in the middle of the nineteenth century did much to sustain the negative attitudes and actions toward *mejicanos* throughout the Southwest. Historian Hass has recently documented how this unfolded in southern California,[15] and there is evidence that this occurred in the Lower Valley. For instance, there is a persistent Anglo belief that Tejanos were ill-prepared to serve as officeholders and on juries because they there were ignorant and untrustworthy. The result of such thinking is, of course, stereotyping. Conflict was sometimes sporadic and specific in nature, while at other times general and seemingly directed toward individuals rather than toward the entire Tejano community. It was often more the result of the actions of a few misdirected, prejudiced, and selfish persons than the result of the actions of all Anglos or Europeans or Tejanos. Texas Ranger abuses should be singled out as a distinct form of overt violence and discrimination against the Tejano because the Rangers and their apologists assert that their actions were moral and civilizing. The evidence of Anglo racial bias is scanty: the segregation of schoolchildren in Corpus Christi and the restriction in the sale of lots in that same town during the 1890s. Thus, interethnic relations consisted of intricate interactions between the two groups.

There is limited evidence of how Anglos treated workers, but it appears that their treatment was not especially harsh. Neither the Tejanos nor the Anglos resorted to the use of peons to a significant degree. Cowboys and skilled rural workers never considered themselves to be peons. Moreover, even in the case of hacienda-type ranch operations like King's and Kenedy's, there was a high turnover in the labor force; peonage would not have tolerated such a condition. For these reasons, De León's argument for the oppression of Tejanos should be moderated, and Montejano's claim that the social and economic order was conditioned by *patrón*–peon relationships is at best applicable to very few actual ranching enterprises among both Tejano and Anglo ranchers. The strong role of the Tejanos as ranchers, farmers, *vaqueros*, merchants, storekeepers, and artisans, and their participation in other economic activities and as officeholders speaks not only to their resiliency, adaptability, and continuity, but also to the fact that they were a people largely free of open oppression. What is significant in the Tejano historical experience is that most of them were self-directed human beings. Naturally, they also had shortcomings, as disclosed by the existence of a small Tejano criminal element and the occurrence of family disputes over property. All in all, however, Tejanos functioned well in a society that was adapting to a changing economic and political order. The twentieth century would present novel and more difficult challenges because the arrival of thousands of new settlers from Mexico and the United States significantly altered the fabric of Tejano society. That story would be played out in the era of land development that initiated another boom in the region in the early decades of the twentieth century.

The evidence for other parts of the Southwest is conclusive as to the erosion of significant Hispanic landholdings during the second half of the nineteenth century, but the manner and pace also varied from place to place. The process of land loss in New Mexico resembled that of the Lower Valley in that it was protracted, but it differed in that it was perhaps still more complicated due to the variety of land grants (such as communal grants and grants to Indian pueblos), conflicting claims, and the slowness of the adjudicatory process. The experiences of northern *californios* and Hispanic Arizonans differ from those of the Lower Valley Tejanos and the New Mexicans in that land loss was rapid. The available evidence, however, points to strong similarities between northern California and the experience that befell Tejanos in the San Antonio-Goliad, Victoria, and Nacogdoches districts. It is true that southern *californios* persisted as landholders a generation or so longer than their counterparts in northern California, who were rapidly besieged by Anglo settlers, but they too lost ground by the 1870s. This, of course, preceded the historical experience of *rancheros* in the Lower Valley, for it was not until the 1880s and 1890s that Anglo ranchers and merchant-speculators rapidly enlarged their holdings vis-à-vis the Tejanos. Arizona's experience was different because *rancheros* were so few in number that they basically gave up the struggle to hold onto the land in view of the worsening Indian problem. One key factor in both New Mexico and the Lower Valley of Texas that delayed the rapid erosion of land is the fact that in both regions Hispanics maintained majority populations, and thus there were fewer pressures from newcomers. Also, in both regions economic exploitation by railroad, mining, or industrial concerns was minimal until late in the nineteenth century. In the case of New Mexico and the Lower Valley, land was initially attractive only to small groups of Anglo or European entrepreneurs.

One aspect of Tejano land tenure that is critical to understanding the land-loss issue is land-grant adjudication. Contrary to popular belief and Tejano myth, the state of Texas adjudicated and validated Spanish and Mexican land grants in the Lower Valley more equitably and quickly than the federal government's agencies and courts, which had jurisdiction over Arizona, California, and New Mexico. In addition, it is fundamental to understand that what happened to Mexican landholders after adjudication was of greater significance in determining whether Tejanos as well as other *mejicanos* in the Southwest lost wealth and status in the new order. For once the land grants had been confirmed by the legislature or the courts, competition for the best lands intensified. Due to changing social, economic, and political conditions, Tejano land tenure could not remain at the initial high levels experienced during the early period of incorporation into the United States. Land loss proceeded haphazardly until the 1880s, when Tejanos lost control of their lands in a rapid fashion. As this study shows, it is the period between 1885 and 1900 in which most Tejanos became minority landholders in their own land.

Despite the lack of a frontier in the Turnerian sense of free land, early immigrants from Mexico to the Lower Valley had the best chances of achieving economic mobility. This was the case because ranching proved to be a viable industry in the period of recovery (1848–65) and especially during the boom years (1865–85), one in which they could accumulate capital to invest in the new land. The situation was different for later *mejicano* immigrants—those of the late 1880s and 1890s—who came with no money and at a time when ranching was declining. For many of them, the *ranchos* and towns of the region served merely as way stations. As sojourners, they stayed for a while until opportunities called them farther north. Moreover, town development and the farming bonanza of the early twentieth century could not absorb all of the new Mexican immigrants, many of whom were unskilled.[16] De León and Stewart have documented widespread geographical mobility among the Mexicans in Texas, but their data failed to pick up occupational mobility. Research that addresses the issue of economic mobility by using other methodologies is needed because a purely quantitative approach tends to see people as aggregate numbers instead of as individuals with particular histories.

This history of the Lower Valley provides a useful model for understanding the process of change that took place in a critical region of the Southwest. It is through regional histories such as this one that we can best ascertain what dynamics were at work in producing pluralistic societies that were more complex than most observers are willing to acknowledge. Historical studies of ethnic and national minorities, such as the Mexican Americans, are necessary in order to write a more balanced view of the origins and persistence of diversity in American society. It is important to look at the contributions of Mexicans and their descendants in the Southwest and to see how they adjusted to a changing society. In the Lower Valley of Texas, as elsewhere in the borderlands, competition for natural resources intensified, particularly in districts that held promise of becoming valuable for immediate exploitation or for speculation in the near future. By the last decades of the nineteenth century, a small number of risky large-scale irrigated farming ventures had made their debut in delta lands in Cameron County. More importantly, Tejano–Anglo accommodation and competition gave way to conflict as vast market changes occurred in the 1880s and 1890s. Occasionally, aggressive Anglo land acquisition, as in the cases of King and Kenedy in south Texas and Thomas Benton Catron in New Mexico, bred antagonisms and conflicts that can only be understood through a historical perspective. Hopefully, an appreciation of Southwest history can help us understand why Mexicans often feel like "foreigners in their native land" and hold on to a legacy of bitterness and suspicion of newcomers. By 1885—earlier in different parts of the American Southwest—Mexicans in the Lower Valley were a minority landholding group whose future well-being hung in the balance. Only the coming changes would determine whether they were to remain a second-class people in an emerging society that was becoming increasingly complex as the state of Texas was about to enter its first stage of modernization at the turn of the new century.

APPENDIX ONE

DEFINITION OF TERMS

For the Spanish and Mexican periods, it was relatively simple to identify the population. During the Spanish era, the populace was enumerated and often described by their racial and ethnic background. Spanish supposedly meant "white," but not necessarily born in Spain. However, as used here Spanish settlers encompassed a wide array of ethnic and even multiracial people, as in the case of *mestizos*—those of Spanish-Indian descent—unless the context requires reference to a specific racial or ethnic group. After Mexico's independence in 1821, the term *Mexican* was readily used by the people of the Río Grande border region. This identity reflected their new nationality. Newcomers to this frontier, among them citizens of the United States and Europeans, saw themselves as different and separate from the Mexicans. They rarely gave up their citizenship, but lived on the border as resident aliens with approval of the state governments.

After 1848, Mexicans in Texas (including the newly annexed Trans-Nueces region) called themselves *mejicanos*, or Mexicans. However, the term *Tejano* became a term of self-identity late in the nineteenth century. I have used these terms interchangeably throughout the book. All of those with Spanish surnames were identified as Mexican if born in Texas of Mexican-born parents or if born in Mexico of Mexican-born parents. Needless to say, all persons with Spanish surnames were *not* Mexican in origin; some of the newcomers were persons born in Spain. These were tabulated as Europeans, as were all others born in Europe.

As for the rest of the population of the border region, the manuscript censuses of the United States provided help in distinguishing racial and ethnic origin. Generally, the researcher resorted to the parents' place of origin in cases in which a person's ethnicity was not clear. Mulattoes, a very small group in the population, were grouped with the black population. The term *blend* was used to identify those persons who had Anglo or European and Mexican ancestry. This population group arose as a result of the Anglo and European newcomers who moved to the border as single men and married local Mexican women. Despite this designation, in all probability these persons identified with one or the other parent's ethnicity and culture on the basis of individual choice. However, among some of the European—*mejicano* settlers, it was evidently easier to Hispanicize. Perhaps it was a common European-based culture and/or religion that facilitated this process. Again, it is impossible to quantify this social process, but its lasting legacy is real. Today, these individuals see themselves as Hispanic.

APPENDIX TWO

A NOTE ON SOURCES

The manuscript and archival materials consisted of sources that were basic to the quantitative and qualitative data used in writing this study. The three most important manuscript sources of data for the quantitative part of the book were the U.S. Census of Population, the non-population censuses (or agricultural census), and tax rolls of the various counties of the Lower Río Grande Valley. Population manuscripts used here included the Webb, Cameron, and Starr County census of 1850, which covered the entire Lower Valley, and censuses for Hidalgo County for 1860, 1870, 1880, and 1900. There is no manuscript for 1890 due to the loss of U.S. archival materials in a fire. However, a total is available and was used wherever appropriate. The agricultural censuses used here are for the years 1860, 1870, and 1880. As noted in the text, I was able to use data reported complete for the individual counties. Unfortunately, not all of the core counties in south Texas have complete returns. Still, the data for those counties that are complete yielded sufficient totals on stockraising, and I used these to show the value of Tejano ranching and its domination in the region during this period. Supplementary published data consisting of other official reports on livestock production were also utilized. Bills of sale that reported livestock transactions in Hidalgo and Webb counties were tabulated and analyzed in order to assess Tejano ranching and marketing practices. Records of brands and ear marks were also studied in order to determine the changing nature of the livestock industry in Texas.

There were some insignificant deficiencies in the census data. The 1850 census was not demarcated by clear geographic boundaries other than for

Brownsville and Laredo. Thereafter, the census was collected by counties, and the data used represent not a sample but the total population.

A few other problems were encountered in the census materials. The most common were misspelled names and different ages for the same person in later censuses. These shortcomings in the manuscripts made it necessary to "clean" the data. Because the data base consisted of several decennial censuses, most of the inaccuracies and inconsistencies were corrected, especially if a person was enumerated more than once. The most important corrections were made with regard to the spelling of names and ethnic identity. Standard lists of correct spellings and ethnic identity were kept and used throughout. Also, a few individual entries were incomplete as to one or more pieces of data, such as occupation or parents' place of birth. Because these incomplete entries were less than 1 or 2 percent, the overall totals are accurate. Finally, it is probable that the population was undercounted by 5 to 10 percent, but it is impossible to precisely determine this phenomena. The only year in which the census specifically noted the absence of some of the population was 1860. This was due to Juan N. Cortina's uprising in the Lower Valley. About 15 percent of the households were listed as being vacant. Due to the predominance of a ranching economy, it is unlikely that socioeconomic characteristics would have been different than those which typified the enumerated population. The total census data base consisted of nearly ten thousand cases.

The tax rolls were generally complete as to individual entries, except for 1865, although that year's total is complete because it is given in the county tax assessor's summary sheets, which were customarily reported to the state throughout the nineteenth century. As noted previously, tax data were compiled in five-year intervals in order to assess change over time. For the purposes of this study, any landholder holding fifty or more acres was included. This amount of land was chosen arbitrarily, but it is a reasonable lower unit of landholding in view of the fact that Hidalgo County was a ranching society. Toward the end of the nineteenth century, those individuals who owned small acreages tended to own more than one tract, so they seldom owned less than fifty acres of land. Also excluded from the study were railroad lands, which accounted for less than 10 percent of the land in the county. These were obtained by the railroads in the 1880s and sold late in the nineteenth century. Obviously, they were not included in the lands encompassed in the Spanish and Mexican land grants, which are the basis of this study. A total of sixty-five hundred cases comprised the tax data base.

The tax data also presented several problems, including misspelled names and incomplete and inaccurate descriptions of the land grant where the land was located. These problems were corrected in most cases by resorting to other years for comparison. In addition, the manuscript census data helped to resolve problems related to the ethnicity of individuals for purposes of identification.

The study's narrative of Tejano social and economic life benefited from the use of several qualitative materials. These included Tejano wills and testaments, the *protocolos* of Nuevo León, a few interviews with *rancheros* and their descendants, and genealogy histories. No doubt there is considerably more material of this nature available in public and private holdings, and more research can be undertaken on the topic of Tejano social history. However, for this study I relied on case studies of individuals and families, using those sources that were most accessible to me at the present time. I believe that further research would agree with my findings on the nature of Hispanic society.

I have also used the term *Hispanic* to refer to the universal history and culture of the peoples of Spanish, Mexican, and Tejano descent. It is presently used in the Lower Valley, but it was not used in the nineteenth century.

APPENDIX THREE

LIVESTOCK TRANSACTIONS RECORDED IN HIDALGO COUNTY, 1874–1899

Year	Buyer(s)	Seller(s)	No. & Kind of Stock	Month
1874	Ramón Reyna	8 Tejanos	43 horses	August-October
	Félix Cárdenas	4 Tejanos	20 horses	August, September
	Félix Cárdenas	—	47 horses, inspected	September
	Blas Cavazos	4 Tejanos	43 horses	October
	Blas Cavazos	—	4 horses, inspected	September
	Vicente Cárdenas	7 Tejanos	55 cattle	November
	John E. Nix	7 Tejanos	51 cattle, 4 horses	November
	Salvador Cárdenas	1 Tejano	1 mare	September
	Salvador Cárdenas		26 horses, inspected	September
	Macedonio Vela	3 Tejanos	22 cattle	November
	Julia Teblier	1 Tejano	12 mares	November
1875	J. N. Guerra	5 Tejanos	101 cattle	March
	J. N. Guerra	—	55 cattle, inspected	March
	Gaspar Chapa	3 Tejanos	10 cattle	March
	Tomás Gómez	7 Tejanos	91 cattle	March
	Tomás Gómez	—	34 cattle, inspected	March
	John B. Bourbois, agent	—	30 cattle, inspected	July
	Blas M. Cavazos Cárdenas	5 Tejanos	163 mares & horses	July
1876	John McAllen	2 Anglos	"all our cattle"	April
	Antonio Garza	—	17 cattle, inspected	December
	Francisco Anzaldúa	—	30 cattle, inspected	December
1877	Antonio Garza	—	8 cattle, inspected	February

Year	Buyer(s)	Seller(s)	No. & Kind of Stock	Month
1878	Crisóforo Lozano	5 Tejanos	41 horses	March
	John Young	John McAllen	2,000 steers, 400 cows, 75 horses	March
	Guadalupe Longoria	14 Tejanos	58 horses	April
	Francisco Anzaldua	—	17 horses, inspected	May
	Jacinto López	—	44 cattle, inspected	May or June
	José Estapa & Luis Hernández	—	26 horses	
	Tomás Garza	—	20 horses, inspected	June
	Silver Tiblier	2 Tejanos	18 horses	December
1879	John B. Young	John McAllen	2,000 cattle	March
	Manuel Alemán	Luis Alemán	"brand, mark, and animals"	March
	Prájedes Garza & Co.	2 Tejanos John B. Bourbois	56 horses & cattle	March
	John Young	Píoquinto Olivares	334 horses & cattle	March
	John Young	Estate of Jacinto Olivares	not given	March
	G. W. Johnston	Luis Garza	25–35 stock & 100 sheep & goats	June
	Evaristo Domínguez	Ramón Munguía	all of his stock	October
	R. R. Savage	17 Tejanos	135 steers	December
	Fernando G. González	—	199 steers, inspected	December
	Jorge Cavazos	—	14 steers, inspected	December
	Vicente Cárdenas	—	22 steers & cows	December
	Mateo & Dolores Solis	—	26 horses	December
1880	John Tiblier	M. Vela	35 horses	January
	R. R. Savage	3 Tejanos	38 horses	January
	R. R. Savage	18 Tejanos	240 steers	January
	Vicente Cárdenas	6 Tejanos	433 horses, mares & mules	February
	Antonio Hinojosa		15 horses, inspected	February
	Antonio Hinojosa	3 Tejanos	18 horses	February
	Mateo Solis		7 horses	February
	Dolores Solis	Silverio Solis	7 horses	February
	Dolores Solis	—	17 horses, inspected	February
	Fernando G. González	—	88 steers, inspected	January
	J. Angel García	—	71 horses, mares inspected	February
	J. María Guzmán	—	10 horses, inspected	February

Year	Buyer(s)	Seller(s)	No. & Kind of Stock	Month
	Felix Teblier	2 Tejanos	52 horses, mules	February
	Fructuoso García	4 Tejanos	17 horses	February
	John B. Young	John McAllen	2400	March
	Ysabel Cantú	3 Tejanos	34 cattle	March
	Francisco Cantú & Co.	2 Tejanos	31 cattle, inspected	April
	Julio Guzmán	—	20 cattle, inspected	April
	Faustino Villarreal	4 Tejanos	59 cows, steers	April
	Faustino Villarreal	?	(?) stock	April
	Felix Teblier	3 Tejanos	31 horses	May
	Faustino Villarreal	2 Tejanos	48 beeves	May
	Faustino Villarreal	—	40 cattle, inspected	May
	Faustino Villarreal	6 Tejanos	24 cattle	May
	Faustino Villarreal	T. M. Rhodes	43 cows, steers	May
	F. Oliver	8 Tejanos	27 horses	June
	F. Oliver	2 Tejanos	6 horses	June
	Vidal G. Cantú	8 Tejanos	31 horses	June
	Juan Cavazos	5 Tejanos	18 cattle	June
	Juan Cavazos	—	27 cattle, inspected	June
	Geo. Willman	2 Tejanos	11 horses, mules	July
	H. M. Field	not given	21 cattle	July
	Guadalupe Moya	H. M. Field	20 cattle	July
	Guadalupe Moya	2 Tejanos	15 cows	July
	Feliciano Treviño	4 Tejanos	20 horses	August
	Feliciano Treviño	—	29 horses, inspected	August
	Jesús María Guerra	—	84 horses, imported	October
	Manuel Cantú Garza	—	35 steers, cows imported	November
	José María Ballí	4 Tejanos	25 cattle	November
1881	Francisco Anzaldúa	15 Tejanos	35 steers	February
	Encarnación Luna	Agustín García	25 horses	February
	Encarnación Luna	—	9 horse stock, inspected	February
	José María Ballí	2 Tejanos	8 cows	February
	Jacinto Zamora	—	24 horse stock, inspected	March
	Epimenio Cantú	—	9 horse stock, inspected	March
	Louis Rutledge	Ma. E. Anaya de la Garza	all cattle & horse stock	April
	Inocencio Uresti	—	27 horse stock	April
	Salvador Barrientes	Ambrosio Argüelles & Bro.	9 horse stock	April

Year	Buyer(s)	Seller(s)	No. & Kind of Stock	Month
	Lucas Cantú	—	22 horse stock, inspected	April
	Francisco de Abrigo	—	51 horse stock, inspected	April
	Yndalecio González	5 Tejanos	17 cattle	Apr. & June
	J. N. Cisneros	—	22 horses, imported, inspected	August
	Manuel Cantú	—	37 horse stock, inspected	August
	Robert Rutledge	—	8 horses, inspected	August
	F. A. Goodbody	Estate of T. J. Handy	100 horse stock	September
	Miguel Lozano	—	11 horse stock, inspected	September
	Miguel Lozano	—	3 horses, imported, inspected	September
1882	Antonio Orta	Gregoria Rodríguez de Orta	40 horse stock, sheep, goats	December
1883	James King	2 Tejanos	13 horses	February
	James King	Manuel Ballí	35 horses & mules	February
	Oliver Jones	various Tejanos & others	48 horse stock	February
	Theo Marks	A. Argüelles & Juan B. Zolezzi	26 cattle	March
	Desiderio Garza	2 Tejanos	12 horses	March
	Pantaleón Villarreal, Agent	various owners	30 horses, some imported	March
	L. E. Smithwick	various Tejanos	64 horse stock	March
	L. E. Smithwick	—	4 horses, inspected	March
	Manuel Ballí	various Tejanos	7 cattle	April
	Manuel Ballí	Salvador Cavazos, Sr. Salvador Cavazos, Jr.	55 cattle	April
	Manuel Ballí	Dionicio Muñoz	3 cattle	April
	Kenedy Pasture Co.	Albert Dean	64 cattle	April
	Oliver Jones	various Tejanos & others	54 horse stock	April
	Albert Dean	Louis Rutledge & A. McHaney	30 cows, some with calves	May
	Antonio Garza	E. Domínguez	62 horse stock	June
	John J. Dix	Francisco Anzaldúa	117 cattle	July

Year	Buyer(s)	Seller(s)	No. & Kind of Stock	Month
	John J. Dix	Albert Dean	31 cattle	July
	Oliver Jones	various Tejanos	3 horse stock	July
	Cornelius Stillman	Salvador C. Cárdenas & wife	all cattle & horses	July
	Cornelius Stillman	Félix Cárdenas & Ma. de Jesús Cárdenas de Guerra	all cattle & horse stock	July
	Oliver Jones	various Tejanos	25 horses	Auguse
1885	Gabriel Valle Recio	A. Villarreal López	all cattle & horse stock	July
	Charles Schunior	Juan C. Buentello & A. V. López	horse stock	October
1887	H. M. Field	Antonio Olivares	2,400 sheep & 700 goats, a chattel mortgage	January
1888	J. L. Dougherty	Adelaida López	all her stock	March
	Adelaida López	J. L. Dougherty	all his stock	April
	H. M. Field	Antonio Olivares	1,700 sheep, 2,100 goats	August
	Bernardina L. Schunior	Charles Schunior	all of his stock	end of 1888
1890	Charlotte M. Sidbury	A. P. Rachal	730 female cattle	September
	A. Bollack	Thomas January	20 mares, 12 saddle horses, 30 cattle	December
1896	W. F. Sprague	Marcos Cantú	all cattle & horse stock	February
1897	D. Sullivan & Co.	D. K. Fant	2,758 cattle	June
	Juan Hinojosa	Lino Hinojosa	c. 100 cattle, 60 horses, 4 mules	July
1898	W. F. Sprague	Miguel Fernández	all cattle & horse stock	January
	Francisca F. de Muñoz	Dionicio Muñoz	all animals brand & all stock	April
	Patricio Pérez Salinas	Patricio Pérez	brand, ear mark, & all animals	October
1899	W. F. Sprague	Eugenie R. Raphael	all stock	December

Source: Hidalgo County, Texas, *Bill of Sale, Book "C,"* 1874–1881; Hidalgo County, *Bill of Sale,* 1881–1913.

APPENDIX FOUR

LIVESTOCK TRANSACTIONS IN WEBB COUNTY, TEXAS, 1876–1890

Year	Buyer(s)	Seller(s)	No. & Kind of Stock	Month
1876	Gillespie Reed & Co.	Nicolás Sánchez	1,317 cattle	May
	Santiago Sánchez	Sánchez & Salinas	983 cattle	May
	W. H. McGrier	Bernardo Mendiola	130 cattle	July
	William Wangle	various Tejanos, including Luis Guerra whose share was 107 head	282 beeves	November
	William Wangle	9 Tejanos & Peter Steffian	145 cattle	December
1877	Waugh & Stephenson	7 Tejanos	128 beef cattle	January
	M. B. Stephenson	Luis, José María, & Juan Guerra; Hilario Busto; Francisco Peña, & López	231 beeves	January
	Waugh & Stephenson	Justo Guerra, Eluterio Camacho, and 2 other Tejanos	189 cattle	March
	Waugh & Stephenson	—	774 cattle, inspected	April
	Waugh & Stephenson	Bartolo García	781 cattle	April
	Waugh & Stephenson	Rosendo García, Evaristo López and 22 others	1,241 cattle	May
	Waugh & Stephenson	4 Tejanos	263 cattle	July
	Waugh & Stephenson	2 Tejanos	35 cattle	July

Year	Buyer(s)	Seller(s)	No. & Kind of Stock	Month
	Waugh & Stephenson	9 Tejanos	216 cattle	July
	Waugh & Stephenson	3 Tejanos	88 cattle	July
	Waugh & Stephenson	9 Tejanos	162 cattle	July
	Halff & Bishop	Florencio Garza	26 cattle	August
	Halff & Bishop	Meyer M. Levy	1,265 cattle	August
	Waugh & Stephenson	13 Tejanos	433 cattle	September
	I. F. Camp	Juan Ortiz	849 cattle	September
	I. F. Camp	Eulalio Benavides	594 cattle	September
	I. F. Camp	Rosendo García	502 cattle	September
	Waugh & Stephenson	8 Tejanos	1,587	October
	C. R. S. Ragdale	7 ranchers from Lampazos, Nuevo León	344 steers	October
	Waugh & Stephenson	7 Tejanos	894 cattle	November
	G. F. Hindes & Oden	Martín González	699 cattle	November
	G. F. Hindes & Oden	5 Tejanos	802 cattle	November
	G. F. Hindes & Oden	Rosendo García	623 cattle	November
1878	Waugh & Stephenson	8 Tejanos	128 cattle	December
	C. M. McDaniel	José María González	374 steers	December
	Herderley & Smith	Darío González	989 cattle	April
	J. D. Smith	—	322 cattle imported, inspected	April
	J. D. Smith	Luis R. Ortiz	59 cattle	April
	Waugh & Stephenson	Martín Ramón	75 cattle	October
	Waugh & Stephenson	8 Tejanos	761 cattle	October
1879	Waugh & Stephenson	Florencio Garza	142 cattle	February
	Waugh & Stephenson	5 Tejanos	165 cattle	February
	W. K. Adams	Meyer M. Levy	all horse stock	October
	Waugh & Stephenson	4 Tejanos	25 cattle	December
	Waugh & Stephenson	5 Tejanos	24 cattle	December
	W. A. Waugh	Francisco Pérez Treviño	87 cattle	December
	W. A. Waugh	Jesús Martínez	63 cattle	December
	W. A. Waugh	5 Tejanos	256 cattle	December
	W. A. Waugh	Manuel Vela	142 cattle	December
1880	W. A. Waugh	Darío Benavides, Desiderio García	97 cattle	January
	W. A. Waugh	Cesario García Benavides, Cecilio Villarreal & 1 other Tejano unnamed	267 cattle	February

Year	Buyer(s)	Seller(s)	No. & Kind of Stock	Month
	W. A. Waugh	5 Tejanos, with Cecilio Villarreal owning 95 head of stock	192 cattle	February
	Louis Shely	*rancheros* from Mexico	2,130 cattle	February
	W. A. Waugh	9 Tejanos	667 cattle	March
	P. R. Fakes & Co.	21 Tejanos	519 cattle	August
	Cleofas A. Stewart	—	228 cattle inspected	October
	Lytle & Co.	Cleofas A. Stewart	228 cattle	October
	G. F. Hindes	Bartolo Juárez	7 cattle	November
	Mitchell, Pressnal, & Waugh	Epigenio Martínez & Antonio Peña Vidaurri	92 cattle	November
	Mitchell, Pressnal, & Waugh	Martín Ramón, Marcial Ramos, & Avelino Guajardo	243 cattle	November
	Lytle & Co.	Antonio Peña, agent for Mexican *rancheros*, Nuevo Laredo	243 cattle	November
	Lytle & Co.	Marcelino Peréz, Nuevo Laredo	220 cattle	December
1881	Lytle & Co.	—	885 cattle, inspected	January
	H. Nein	Teodoro Treviño, (Zapata County, Texas)	38 steers	January
	William H. Adams	Merced C. López	all cattle & horses	January
	Mitchell, Pressnal, & Waugh	Juan Manuel Molina	4 horses	January
	Mitchell, Pressnal, & Waugh	4 Tejanos	81 horses & cattle	January
	Mitchell, Pressnal, & Waugh	—	80 head of stock, inspected	January
	W. A. Waugh	3 Tejanos	60 head of stock	February
	H. W. Earnest	—	57 cattle, imported, inspected	February
	W. A. Waugh	Leonides Mendoza	6 head	March
	—	Mexican *rancheros*	310 cows, heifers, & 32 calves	March (?)
	Lytle & Co.	Don Tomás Rodríguez, Cuidad Guerrero	73 steers	March

Year	Buyer(s)	Seller(s)	No. & Kind of Stock	Month
	José María Treviño	5 Mexican *rancheros* from Vallecillo	173 cattle	March
	Lytle & Co.	—	1,038 inspected	March
	W. A. Waugh	Lucas Villarreal, Lampazos, Nuevo León	1,692 cattle	February
	A. L. Johnston	M. Santos García	32 cattle	March

Source: Webb County, Texas, *Marks and Brands, Miscellaneous Record*, vol. 1, American History Center, University of Texas, Austin, Box 4K559.

NOTES

INTRODUCTION

1. Israel Cavazos Garza, *Breve historia de Nuevo León*, (Mexico City, 1994), 98–99, 101. I am using Lower Valley and south Texas interchangeably to mean the lands from the Río Grande to the Nueces River, but it should be understood that up to 1848 the Lower Valley included the original towns on the south side of the Río Grande. Chronologically, the first settlers were the Spanish, who after 1821 renamed themselves Mexican. These Mexican or *mejicano* settlers, in turn, became Tejano following the annexation of the Lower Valley after 1848. I employ the term *Hispanic* to refer to the general character of all of these settlers. *Anglo* refers to the citizens of the United States who began arriving in the region in small numbers in the 1820s. See Appendix 1 for a fuller definition of these terms.

2. These statements constitute responses to questions made by the royal inspector Don José Tienda de Cuervo to the town founders and local missionaries. Secretaría de relaciones exteriores, *Estado general de las fundaciones hechas por d. José de Escandón en la Colonia del Nuevo Santander costa del Seno Mexicano*, 2 vols. (Mexico City, 1929), 1:383, 394–95. There are very few early monographs on Nuevo Santander. Among the best recent syntheses of the colony are Juan Fidel Zorrilla, *El poder colonial en Nuevo Santander* (Mexico City, 1976); Zorrilla, *Estudio de la legislación en Tamaulipas*, 2d ed. (C. Victoria, Tamaulipas, 1980). Zorrilla, "Nuevo Santander and the Integration of the Mexican Northeast," trans. Gregory Knapp (paper presented at the Cultural Adaptation at the Edge of the Spanish Empire Symposium, University of Texas, Austin, May 1990; copy in my possession); Oakah L. Jones, Jr., *Los Paisanos: Spanish Settlers on the Northern Frontier of New Spain* (Norman, Okla., 1979), chap. 3, 65–78. Also, see Jesús Franco Carrasco, *El Nuevo Santander y su arquitectura* 2 vols. (Mexico City, 1991), esp. vol. 1, pt. 1, 16–180.

3. Will and Testament of Juan N. Cavazos, File no. 5, County Clerk, Cameron County, Brownsville, Tex. Cavazos wrote his will at Rancho del Tanque de Carricitos on Aug. 4, 1876.

4. My long-view approach to the history of the Lower Valley resembles that of Lisbeth Haas, *Conquests and Historical Identities in California, 1769–1936* (Berkeley, 1995). On the boundaries of Nuevo Santander, see Peter Gerhard, *The Northern Frontier of New Spain* (Princeton, 1982), 358. Shortly after Mexico's independence, Mexican federalists had sought to link Tamaulipas with several other political units, including Texas, to form one large state

in northeast Mexico. This idea was turned down, resulting in the creation of individual states. David J. Weber, *The Mexican Frontier, 1821–1846* (Albuquerque, 1983), 22, 24. On the issue of defining the West and its history, see Clyde A. Milner II, Anne M. Butler, and David Rich Lewis, eds., *Major Problems in the History of the American West,* 2d ed. (Boston, 1997), chap. 1, 1–41.

5. On town settlements in the borderlands, see Jones, *Los Paisanos*; Gilberto M. Hinojosa, *Borderlands Town in Transition: Laredo, 1755–1870* (College Station, Tex., 1983); and Gilberto R. Cruz, *Let There Be Towns: Spanish Municipal Origins in the American Southwest, 1610–1810* (College Station, Tex., 1988). Two new studies for the colonial period have appeared recently: Jesús F. de la Teja, *San Antonio de Béxar: A Community on New Spain's Northern Frontier* (Albuquerque, 1995); and Cheryl English Martin, *Governance and Society in Colonial Mexico: Chihuahua in the Eighteenth Century* (Stanford, 1996).

6. Upriver from Laredo, on the south side of the Río Grande, there was an important presidio and mission complex called Río Grande. It dated to 1701, but was in the jurisdiction of Coahuila.

7. Political rivalry between a Lower Valley family, the Gutiérrez de Lara family of Revilla, and the Fernández family of Aguayo at the beginning of the state government resulted in the consolidation of power in the Fernández family. Their hometown was renamed Ciudad Victoria and made state capital in 1826. Juan Fidel Zorrilla, *Origen del gobierno federal en Tamaulipas* (C. Victoria, 1978), 18, 22–23, 25.

8. The first to address the resiliency of *mejicanos* in nineteenth-century Texas was Arnoldo de León, in *The Tejano Community, 1836–1900* (Albuquerque, 1982). On the origin of the word *Tejano,* see Adán Benavides, *The New Handbook of Texas,* 6 vols. (Austin, 1996), 6:237.

9. Frank C. Pierce, *A Brief History of the Lower Rio Grande Valley* (Menasha, Wisc., 1917); Walter Prescott Webb, *The Great Plains* (Boston, 1931), and *The Texas Rangers* (Cambridge, 1935); T. R. Fehrenbach, *Lone Star: A History of Texas and the Texans* (New York, 1983), chaps. 10–15, 25–29, 31–32.

10. For a similar conceptualization of an Anglo pioneer history based on "a shared historical perception that is based on what is emotionally believed whether it is factually accurate or not," see Clyde A. Milner II, "The Shared Memory of Pioneers," in *Major Problems in the History of the American West,* ed. Clyde A. Milner II (Lexington, Mass., 1989), 454–64. On the notion that King and Kenedy were pioneer builders who brought civilization to the Lower Valley, see L. E. Daniell, *Personnel of the Texas State Government with Sketches of Representative Men of Texas* (San Antonio, 1892), 642–50. This thesis is fully developed in Tom Lea, *The King Ranch,* 2 vols. (Boston, 1957). Also, see Stephen B. Oates, ed., *Rip Ford's Texas* (Austin, 1963). A restatement of this interpretation is in Bruce S. Cheeseman, " 'Not to let a foot of dear old Santa Gertrudis get away' " (paper presented at the Rio Bravo Association, San Antonio, Spring 1996; copy in my possession). Cheeseman was archivist-historian of the King ranch to 1996.

11. Maude T. Gilliland, *Rincón: A Story of Life on a South Texas Ranch at the Turn of the Century* (Brownsville, Tex., 1964), 2, 7, 54. But see Dale Lasater, *Ed. C. Lasater and the Development of the South Texas* (College Station, Tex., 1985).

12. Ada Morehead Holland, *Brush Country Woman* (College Station, Tex., 1992), 15–16.

13. J. Lee and Lillian J. Stambaugh, *The Lower Rio Grande Valley of Texas* (Austin, 1974). Also, see Dorothy Lee Pope, *Rainbow Era on the Rio Grande* (Brownsville, Tex., 1971).

14. Miriam Chatelle, *For We Love Our Valley Home* (San Antonio, 1948), 19–20.

15. Emilia Schunior Ramírez, *Ranch Life in Hidalgo County after 1850* (Edinburg, Tex., 1971), pt. 1, n.p. Tejano *ranchero* stories of their pioneer efforts can be found in Texas Department of Agriculture, *Texas Family Land Heritage Registry*, 12 vols. (Austin, 1974–85), and in Frances W. Isbell, ed., *Hidalgo County Ranch Histories* (Edinburg, Tex., 1994).

16. Quoted in David Montejano, *Anglos and Mexicans in the Making of Texas* (Austin, 1987), 70.

17. Interview with Leo J. Leo by Dr. Hubert J. Miller, Sept. 4, 1980. Transcript and tape located at Lower Rio Grande Valley Historical Collection, University of Texas at Pan American, Edinburg, Tex. (hereafter cited as Special Collections, Pan American).

18. Quoted in Roberto M. Villarreal, "The Mexican-American Vaqueros of the Kenedy Ranch: A Social History" (Master's thesis, Texas A & I University, Kingsville, 1972), 16–19. I collected this *refrán* from Erasmo García, who was born on the Los Garzas ranch in 1914 in Starr County, Texas, where his father and grandfather owned a *rancho* of about three thousand acres.

19. For a similar interpretation, see the argument made by the Californios in Leonard Pitt, *The Decline of the Californios: A Social History of the Spanish-speaking Californios, 1846–1890* (Berkeley, 1966).

20. Ibid.

21. Victor Westphall, *Mercedes Reales: Hispanic Land Grants of the Upper Rio Grande Region* (Albuquerque, 1983); Roxanne Dunbar Ortiz, *Roots of Resistance: Land Tenure in New Mexico, 1680–1980* (Los Angeles, 1982).

22. Carey McWilliams, *North from Mexico: The Spanish-Speaking People of the United States* (Philadelphia, 1949; repr., New York, 1968).

23. Rodolfo F. Acuña, *Occupied America: The Chicano's Struggle toward Liberation* (San Francisco, 1972).

24. David J. Weber, ed., *Foreigners in Their Native Land: Historical Roots of the Mexican Americans* (Albuquerque, 1973).

25. Terry G. Jordan, *North American Cattle-Ranching Frontiers: Origins, Diffusion, and Differentiation* (Albuquerque, 1993).

26. The idea of a Hispanic homeland in the Southwest was first introduced by Richard L. Nostrand, "The Hispano Homeland in 1900," *Annals, Association of American Geographers* 70 (September 1980): 382–96. New Mexico's Hispanic homeland has attracted the most study. See Alvar W. Carlson, *The Spanish-American Homeland: Four Centuries in New Mexico's Río Arriba* (Baltimore, 1990); Frances Leon Swadesh, *Los Primeros Pobladores: Hispanic Americans of the Ute Frontier* (Notre Dame, 1974).

27. Sense of place is an important theme in Texas history, but one that most journalists and social scientists rarely associate with *mejicanos* of the Lower Valley. Consequently, the state's history is distorted with the Anglos claiming "ownership" rights to Texas without

regard to the contributions of others. For a recent statement of a Hispanic "sense of place" in the Lower Valley by a native-born writer, see Rolando Hinojosa, "A Sense of Place," *Texas Journal of Ideas, History, and Culture* 17, no. 1 (Fall/Winter 1994), 18–21.

28. Garry Mauro, Commissioner of the General Land Office, comp., *Guide to Spanish and Mexican Land Grants* (Austin, 1980).

29. Joseph Milton Nance, *After San Jacinto: The Texas–Mexico Frontier, 1836–1841* (Austin, 1963), 3–9; Hinojosa, *Borderlands Town*, 93, 102–3; David Montejano, *Anglos and Mexicans*, 18–19.

30. H. P. Gammel, *The Laws of Texas, 1822–1897*, 10 vols. (Austin, 1895), 2:18; ibid., 3:24, 26–27; ibid., 4:910–11.

31. Montejano, *Anglos and Mexicans*, chap. 6, 129–55.

32. *U.S. Census of Population*, 1850, Lower Rio Grande Valley and Nueces County (manuscript on microfilm, Special Collections, Pan American); *U.S. Census of Population*, 1900.

33. Alfonso Ramírez, comp., *Four Generations of Velas* (Edinburg, Tex., 1986), n.p.

CHAPTER 1

1. John Francis Bannon, *The Spanish Borderlands Frontier* (New York, 1970), 8–21, 25–27, 28–42, 100–102; "Nuevo Santander in 1795: A Provincial Inspection by Felix Calleja," ed. and trans. David M. Vigness, *Southwestern Historical Quarterly* 75 (April 1972): 461.

2. "Nuevo Santander in 1795," 486–87; Hinojosa, *Borderlands Town*, 3; Jones, *Los Paisanos*, 65.

3. Israel Cavazos Garza, *Cedulario autobiográfico de pobladores y conquistadores de Nuevo León* (Monterrey, Nuevo León, 1964), 12, 49–50.

4. Vidal Efren Covián Martínez, *Historia de la ganadería en Tamaulipas* (C. Victoria, Tamaulipas, 1987), 10–16. Hubert J. Miller, *José de Escandón: Colonizer of Nuevo Santander* (Edinburg, Tex., 1980), 3–4.

5. Zorrilla, *El Poder Colonial*, 26.

6. Gerhard, *Northern Frontier*, 351–52. This *alcaldía* was under Escandón's jurisdiction for a while in the 1750s, and eventually the valley of San Antonio de los Llanos was transferred to Nuevo Santander's control.

7. John Tutino, *From Insurrection to Revolution in Mexico: Social Bases of Agrarian Violence, 1750–1940* (Princeton, 1986), 196–201. Tutino argues that as arid lands in San Luis Potosí and other northern borderlands became productive with a shift to ranching activities to replace livestock and its by-products produced in the Bajío, and because those lands were poorly populated, estate dependents were able to obtain permanent employment and were guaranteed corn rations, and thus the security essential for social stability. For these and other reasons, estate workers remained loyal to the Spanish during the Hidalgo Revolt.

8. Covián Martínez, *Historia de la ganadería*, 16.

9. Gerhard, *Northern Frontier*, 360. French expansion in the Gulf of Mexico during the last quarter of the seventeenth century led the Spanish to occupy several sites in the area and prompted the first occupation of Texas in 1690. This proved to be temporary once French threats dissipated after Robert Cavelier, sieur de La Salle, failed in his attempt to establish a

colony in Texas. Renewal of French activities in the 1710s in Louisiana forced the Spanish to permanently settle Texas in 1716. Bannon, *Spanish Borderlands Frontier*, 92–97, 108–23, 139; Cruz, *Let There Be Towns*, 81; Miller, *José de Escandón*, 6.

10. Gerhard, *Northern Frontier*, 358.

11. Ibid.

12. Marshall C. Johnston, "Past and Present Grasslands of Southern Texas and Northeastern Mexico," *Ecology* 44, no. 3 (Summer 1963): 456–66; Robert C. West, "The Natural Regions of Middle America," in *Handbook of Middle American Indians*, gen. ed. Robert Wauchope, *Natural Environment and Early Cultures*, ed. Robert C. West (Austin, 1964), 1:370; A. Joachim McGraw, "Old Padres, Mustang Trails, and the Apaches of Minnow Hill: Historiography of the Ancestral Landscape" (paper presented at the Ninety-Seventh Annual Meeting of the Texas State Historical Association, Houston, March 4, 1993, copy in my possession), 7–8.

13. Jorge L. Tamayo and Robert C. West, "The Hydrography of Middle America," in *Handbook of Middle American Indians, Natural Environment and Early Cultures*, 1:89.

14. McGraw, "Old Padres, Mustang Trails, and the Apaches of Minnow Hill," 7.

15. Johnston, "Past and Present Grasslands of Southern Texas and Northeastern Mexico," 456–66; Allan A. Stovall, *Breaks of the Balcones: A Regional History*, ed. Wanda Pope and Allan Stovall (privately printed by author, Barksdale, Tex., 1967), 108–9. Stovall notes that the first permanent resident in the upper Nueces was a Sánchez family in 1867, but gives no further details.

16. Gerhard, *Northern Frontier*, 358.

17. Carlos E. Castañeda, *Our Catholic Heritage in Texas*, 7 vols., (Austin, 1938), 3:147.

18. Florence Johnson Scott, *Historical Heritage of the Lower Rio Grande Valley* (San Antonio, 1937), 66–67.

19. "Nuevo Santander in 1795," 470–73.

20. Tamayo and West, "Hydrography of Middle America," 89–90.

21. "Nuevo Santander in 1795," 472.

22. Edmund J. Davis, "Description of South-Western Texas," *The Texas Almanac* (Galveston, 1868), 114–15; Wallace Hawkins, *El Sal del Rey* (Austin, 1947).

23. Agustín López de la Cámara Alta, *Descripción general de la nueva Colonia de Santander*, comp. Gabriel Saldívar, Archivo de la historia de Tamaulipas, vol. 5 (C. Victoria, Tamaulipas, 1946); "Nuevo Santander in 1795," 461, 470–71, 473; and José Miguel Ramos Arizpe, *Report that Dr. Miguel Ramos de Arizpe Presents to the August Congress on the Natural, Political, and Civil Condition of the Provinces of Coahuila, Nuevo León, Nuevo Santander, and Texas*, trans. Nettie Lee Benson (New York, 1950), 4–5. A native of San Nicolás, Coahuila, Ramos Arizpe was educated as a priest and lawyer. As a priest, he served at Saltillo, Monterrey, and several frontier towns in Nuevo Santander. He presented his report to the Cortes of Cádiz on November 7, 1811. Although he was official delegate only of Coahuila, he spoke for all four provinces. He served two terms at the Cortes, from 1811 to 1814 and from 1820 to 1821. In the intervening years, he was imprisoned in Spain by Ferdinand VII because Ramos Arizpe condemned monarchial despotism. Nettie Lee Benson, introduction to Ramos Arizpe, *Report*, vii–x. Also, see West, "Natural Regions of Middle America," 370; Gerhard, *Northern Frontier*, 358.

24. Cámara Alta, *Descripción general*, 121, 124.

25. Juan Fernando de Palacios, *Informe de la general visita practicada en 1768 y 1769*, comp. Gabriel Saldívar, Archivo de la historia de Tamaulipas (C. Victoria, Tamaulipas, 1946), 7:33.

26. Gerhard, *Northern Frontier*, 358.

27. Cámara Alta, *Descripción general*, 118–19.

28. Nicolás de Lafora, *Relación del viaje que hiso a los presidios internos situados en la frontera de la America Septentrional perteneciente al rey de España*, anno. Vito Alessio Robles (Mexico City, 1939), 12, 229.

29. Castañeda, *Our Catholic Heritage*, 3:159.

30. Dan E. Kilgore, *Nueces County, Texas, 1750–800: A Bicentennial Memoir* (Corpus Christi, 1975), 6.

31. Cámara Alta, *Descripción general*, 119–20.

32. Tamayo and West, "Hydrography of Middle America," 89–90.

33. West, "Natural Regions of Middle America," 370.

34. Gerhard, *Northern Frontier*, 358–60. On Coahuiltecans, see W. W. Mewcomb, Jr., *The Indians of Texas* (Austin, 1961), chap. 2; on the Lipans and the Comanches of early nineteenth-century Texas, see Jean Louis Berlandier, *The Indians of Texas in 1830*, ed. John C. Ewers (Washington, D.C., 1969).

35. Manuel de Escandón, "Dictamen del Conde de Sierra Gorda sobre nuevo método de gobierno de las misiones," in *Estado de la misiones, 1753–1790*, comp. and ed. Gabriel Saldívar, Archivo de la Historia de Tamaulipas (C. Victoria, 1946), 4:70, 73.

36. Isidro Vizcaya Canales, *La invasión de los indios bárbaros al noreste de Mexico en los años de 1840 y 1841*, no. 7, History Series (Monterrey, Mexico: Instituto Tecnológico y de Estudios Superiores de Monterrey, 1968), 22–23.

37. Escandón, "Dictamen," 70–71.

38. Gerhard, *Northern Frontier*, 360.

39. "Nuevo Santander in 1795," 462–64, 487–504. Calleja reported that the Comanches harassed the Lipan Apaches, who by 1750 "appeared on the edges of Texas from the interior—from the hills of San Saba—in a number exceeding 2,000" and "were admitted in peace, and permitted to locate on the Medina River . . . in the year of '51, the Lipans transferred to a point between the Nueces river and the Río Grande." Also, see Cruz, *Let There Be Towns*, 90.

40. Ernest Wallace, *Ranald S. Mackenzie on the Texas Frontier* (Lubbock, Tex., 1964; repr., College Station, 1993), chaps. 2, 6, and 10. Much of the raiding in the third quarter of the nineteenth century involved the so-called Mexican Kickapoos, but Lipans were still a menace. These Indians operated from bases in Coahuila.

CHAPTER 2

1. Fray Vicente de Santa María, *Relación histórica de la colonia del Nuevo Santander* (Mexico City, 1973), 170–75; Miller, *José de Escandón*, 6–7; Zorrilla, *El Poder Colonial*, 24–25, 62–68. Don Antonio Ladrón de Guevara, *Noticias de los poblados de que se componen el*

Nuevo Reino de León, Provincia de Coahuila, Nueva-Extremadura, y la de Texas, ed. Andrés Montemayor Hernández (1739; repr. Monterrey, 1969), xix.

2. Santa María, *Relación histórica,* 171–74; Guevara, *Noticias de los poblados,* xvii–xviii.

3. Santa María, *Relación histórica,* 171–73; Guevara, *Noticias de los poblados,* xix. The viceregal accounts in this chapter are found in Ernesto de la Torre Villar, ed., *Instrucciones y memorias de los virreyes novohispanos,* comp. Ramiro Navarro de Anda, 2 vols. (Mexico City, 1991), 2:838–39.

4. Santa María, *Relación histórica,* 173–75; the viceroy reported that Escandón made "four general *entradas*. . . " Torre Villar, *Instrucciones,* 2:838–39; Guevara, *Noticias de los poblados,* xix–xx.

5. Santa María, *Relación histórica,* 187–88; Torre Villar, *Instrucciones,* 2:839–40; Guevara, *Noticias de los poblados,* xxi; Bannon, *Spanish Borderlands Frontier,* 139–40; Miller, *José de Escandón,* 7, 9. Although not selected as colonizer, Guevara was an important collaborator of Escandón, serving as acting governor in June 1749, when the latter took a leave of absence.

6. Santa María, *Relación histórica,* 181–82; Zorrilla, *El Poder Colonial,* 76–79; María del Carmen Velázquez, *Establecimiento y pérdida del Septentrión de Nueva España,* (Mexico City, 1974), 139.

7. Zorrilla asserts that Escandón did not make much as a military officer, but inherited wealth from his two wives, who both came from prominent colonial families of Querétaro. Zorilla, *El Poder Colonial,* 80–81.

8. Miller, *José de Escandón,* 9, 11; Cruz, *Let There Be Towns,* 86.

9. Miller, *José de Escandón,* 9, 11, 13.

10. Ibid., 12–13.

11. Torre Villar, *Instrucciones,* 2:840; Miller, *José de Escandón,* 13–14.

12. Miller, *José de Escandón,* 14; Cruz, *Let There Be Towns,* 86–87.

13. *Estado General,* 1:19; Miller, *José de Escandón,* 14, 16; Cruz, *Let There Be Towns,* 87. According to Calleja, it was not until the Palacios *visita* of 1767 that half *cabildos* were established in the towns of the colony. "Nuevo Santander in 1795," 487. Zorrilla notes that under this arrangement the *cabildo* consisted of one *justicia mayor,* or chief justice; two *regidores,* or aldermen; and one *procurador,* or attorney. In 1794 the towns were again placed under a military administration, as had been done during José de Escandón's governorship. Zorilla, *Estudio de la legislación,* 11–12.

14. On the settlements of the Lower Valley towns, see *Estado General,* 1:31–34; "Visita General del Nuevo Reino de León por el Gobernador Don Pedro de Barrio Junco y Espriella en 1754," *Actas* 10 (October–December 1979): 8, 13–15; Miller, *José de Escandón,* 18, 21–22, 24; Cruz, *Let There Be Towns,* 87–89. Scott, *Historical Heritage.* On Carlos Cantú's visit to the Reynosa area, see Castañeda, *Our Catholic Heritage,* 3:162. This early visit is probably the one Monterrey troops made during Escandón's 1747 *entrada.* On Cantú's failure to locate the previously visited site, see Jesús Franco Carrasco, *El Nuevo Santander,* 1:86. On the Vicente Guerra family, see Israel Cavazos Garza, *Catálogo y síntesis de los protocolos del Archivo Municipal de Monterrey, 1726–1756,* no. 2051 (Monterrey, 1986), 166–67; and "Guerra Cañamar Family," in *Su Vida y Su Espíritu: Webb County Family Histories* (Laredo, 1982), 1:43–44. For a brief biography of Camargo's founder, see Clotilde P. García, *Captain Blas*

María de la Garza Falcón (Austin, 1984), 21–26. On the origins of the families already living in the vicinity of Mier prior to its founding, see Octavio Herrera Pérez, *Anales y testimonios del Cántaro* (C. Victoria, Tamaulipas, 1986), 99–101.

15. *Estado General*, 1:35–36; Miller, *José de Escandón*, 22; Cruz, *Let There Be Towns*, 90–92. The Texas courts eventually set the grant's acreage at 276,350 acres. See Mauro, comp., *Guide to Land Grants*, item no. 20. On the number of settlers at Dolores, see Rogelia O. García, *Dolores, Revilla, and Laredo* (Austin, 1970), 4–5.

16. *Estado General*, 1:36–37; Cavazos Garza, *Catálogo y síntesis*, no. 2150, 165; Miller, *José de Escandón*, 24; Cruz, *Let There Be Towns*, 93. Also, see Oralia Barrientos, "Don Tomás Sánchez," in *Su Vida y Su Espíritu*, 1:iii. On Vásquez Borrego's adjudication of the town site and resources to its founder, see Velázquez, *Establecimiento y pérdida*, 139 n. 14, 162–63.

17. Israel Cavazos Garza, *Cedulario autobiográfico de Nuevo León* (Monterrey, 1964), 12, no. 161, 161a, 113—14. On the genealogy of Captain Marcos Alonso Garza y del Arcón, see Raul J. Guerra, Jr., Nadine M. Vásquez, and Baldomero Vela, Jr., *Index to the Marriage Investigations of the Diocese of Guadalajara: Provinces of Coahuila, Nuevo León, Nuevo Santander, Texas, 1653–1750* (privately published, 1989), 327, chart 4. On the conflicts between the Sánchez Navarros and the de la Garza Falcones in Coahuila, see Charles H. Harris, *A Mexican Family Empire: The Latifundio of the Sánchez Navarros, 1765–1867* (Austin, 1975).

18. Cavazos Garza, *Cedulario autobiográfico de Nuevo León*, no. 187, 125; Cavazos Garza, *Catálogo* y síntesis, 166–67.

19. On the Cantús' early history, see Cavazos Garza, *Cedulario autobiográfico de Nuevo León*, 8, 12, no. 53, 49–51, no. 383, 209–10, no. 388, 211–12; Eugenio del Hoyo, *Historia del Nuevo Reino de León, 1577–1723*, 2 vols. (Monterrey, 1972), 2:452, 459–61; and Carl Laurence Duaine, *With All Arms: A Study of a Kindred Group* (Edinburg, Tex., 1987), 175, 193, 206, 234. On the Cantús genealogy, see Guerra et al., *Index to the Marriage Investigations*, 327, chart 3, and 330, chart 7.

20. While Carlos Cantú is credited with the first documented case of building a *trapiche*, it appears that since sugar cane was first introduced into Nuevo León about 1616 sugar mills may have existed earlier than 1692. See del Hoyo, *Historia del Nuevo Reino*, 1:324–25. On the persistence of the Cantús in the eighteenth century, see Cavazos Garza, *Catálago y síntesis*, no. 2470, 90, no. 2559, 119.

21. *Estado General*, 1:38–47. Torre Villar, *Instrucciones*, 2:827, 841. Also see Miller, *José de Escandón*, 24–25.

22. *Estado General*, 1:39; Miller, *José de Escandón*, 25.

23. Miller, *José de Escandón*, 33.

24. Ibid., 33–34.

25. *General Visit to the Villa de Reynosa*, 1767; hereafter referred to as *Visita general*, Reynosa. But see Cruz, *Let There Be Towns*, 96–104, for a brief history of the 1767 *visita* of Laredo and the formation of its first *cabildo*. In Laredo, eighty-nine *porciones* were marked off, but only sixty-four were assigned to settlers. It was expected that new settlers would take up the vacant tracts.

26. Fidel de Lejarza, *Conquista espiritual del Nuevo Santander*, Biblioteca missionalia hispanica, no. 4 (Madrid, 1947), 113, 119.

27. Cámara Alta, *Descripción general*, 113.

28. *Visita general*, Reynosa.

29. Ibid.

30. Miller, *José de Escandón*, 36.

31. Torre Villar, *Instrucciones*, 2:999; Carrasco, *El Nuevo Santander*, 1:108 n. 19.

32. Officially, a hacienda contained five *sitios* of land. Sandra L. Myres, *The Ranch in Spanish Texas* (El Paso, 1969), 22.

33. Miller, José de Escandón, 35.

34. "Nuevo Santander in 1795," 474–75; Carrasco, *El Nuevo Santander*, 1:112; Juan Fidel Zorrilla, "Nuevo Santander and the Integration of the Mexican Northeast," 4.

35. Fernando Navarro y Noriega, *Catálogo de los curatos y misiones de la Nueva España* (Mexico City, 1813; repr., 1943), 62 and unnumbered table between 68 and 69; Jones, *Los Paisanos*, 240. The census of 1816, which counted only persons between the ages of seven and fifty, found a total of 56,715 persons in the colony.

36. Zorrilla, *El Poder Colonial*, 285–86. Zorrilla, "Nuevo Santander," 4, 16. Ramos Arizpe, *Report*, 14, claimed in his report to the Cortes that in 1812 Nuevo Santander had more than sixty thousand inhabitants.

37. For a study of population trends in the late colonial period, see Nicolás Sánchez-Albórnoz, *The Population of Latin America* (Berkeley, 1974).

38. Cámara Alta, *Descripción general*, 118.

39. The annual growth rate of the population in the *villas del norte* from 1757 to 1821 was 3.2 percent, which is considered to be high even by today's standard. The state average for this period was also 3.2 percent. Carrasco, *El Nuevo Santander*, 1:112–14, 118–19, 121, and tables 23, 24, 25, 120, 123. The port of Matamoros was opened on November 11, 1820; its harbors were on the north side of the Río Grande at Punta Isabel and the island of Brazos Santiago, a few miles upriver from Matamoros. Eliseo Paredes Manzano, *Homenaje a los fundadores de la heroíca, leal e invicta Matamoros en el sesquicentario de su nuevo nombre* (H. Matamoros, Tamaulipas, Mexico, 1976), 86.

40. On Laredo's demographic history, see Hinojosa, *Borderlands Town*, 32–38.

41. *Estado General*, 2:7; "Visita General del Nuevo Reino," 8, 13–15; Carrasco, *El Nuevo Santander*, 94 and 95, table 14. Israel Cavazos Garza, "Estado de Nuevo León," *Enciclopedia de México* (Mexico City, 1976), 9:307, 426; Jones, *Los Paisanos*, 66–67, 70, 247.

42. Cámara Alta, *Descripción general*, 121, 123, 125–26.

43. Palacio, *Informe*, 118, 123, 125–26.

44. "Nuevo Santander in 1795," 476. On the value of Laredo dwellings, see J. B. Wilkinson, *Laredo and the Rio Grande Frontier* (Austin, 1975), 94.

45. On Escandón's policy of requiring the settlers to build a home in the towns, see Paredes Manzano, *Homenaje*, 37–38. These examples of *pobladores* who occupied *ranchos* are taken from the *Visita general* of Reynosa.

46. Jones, *Los Paisanos*, 65. Historians have seldom noted the impact of Indian raids on the older frontier communities as a motive for settlement in the more-secured towns founded by Escandón. But see Hortencia Camacho Cervantes, *Fundaciones y asentamientos en Nuevo León siglos xviii y xix: cuatro villas en el norte* (Zuazua, Nuevo León, 1991), 158.

47. Guerra et al., *Index to the Marriage Investigations*, introduction, esp. x, and 318 nn. 17 and 19.

48. One scholar asserts that the strict rules under which "social hierarchy was strongly correlated with racial origins . . . may fit 'rich' societies like those of Mexico and Peru," but not the borderlands. Alicia Viduarreta Tjarks, "Comparative Demographic of Texas, 1777–1793," in *New Spain's Far Northern Frontier: Essays on Spain in the American West, 1540–1821*, ed. David L. Weber (Albuquerque, 1979), 153, 157.

49. That Spanish settlers had to work with their own hands in most cases applies to Coahuila, Nuevo León, and Texas as well as Nuevo Santander. Jones, *Los Paisanos*, 28, 31, 35, 37, 52–54, 63, 71, 78.

50. Paredes Manzano, *Homenaje*, 31–32. Social and labor relations in the *haciendas* of New Spain's northern provinces have not been studied with much depth, except for Charles Harris's work on the Sánchez Navarros. However, conditions in the *haciendas* did produce social conflict between workers and owners. Celso Garza Guajardo, town historian of Sabinas Hidalgo, Nuevo León, has noted: "As is natural, there was always conflict between the townspeople and the *hacendados*, misunderstandings and slights among them . . . sometimes there were tragedies . . . but above all, I think the more common was resentment between peons and *hacendados*, and between tenants and landowners." Apparently, many of the so-called *haciendas* in Nuevo León tended to be small in land area, as the original *mercedes de tierras* as well as purchased lands were constantly being subdivided among the owners or heirs. Sections of *haciendas* were also sold or given as inheritance to family members. All of these factors fostered the proliferation of smaller landholdings commonly called *ranchos*. See Celso Garza Guajardo, *Los barrios de Sabinas Hidalgo: sentimientos de tiempos y espacios*, 2d ed. (Monterrey, Nuevo León, 1990), 13–17.

51. Jones, *Los Paisanos*, 71–72; "Nuevo Santander in 1795," 474–75.

52. In Nuevo León, the practice of sending large sheep herds under the management of overseers began in the early seventeenth century and led to the customary employment of administrators by absentee landowners. See Francois Chevalier, *Land and Society in Colonial Mexico: The Great Hacienda* (Berkeley, 1963), 182–83. For other evidence of this practice in the northern frontier, see John C. Super, "The Agricultural Near North: Querétaro in the Seventeenth Century," in *Provinces of Early Mexico*, ed. Ida Altman and James Lockhart (Los Angeles, 1976), 242; and Ida Altman, "A Family and Region in the Northern Fringe Lands: The Marqueses de Aguayo of Nuevo León and Coahuila," in ibid., 258, 266–68.

53. Kilgore, *Nueces County*, 7; Scott, *Historical Heritage*, 185.

54. Scott, *Historical Heritage*, 41, 91, 184–85; Cavazos Garza, *Catálago y síntesis*, no. 2949.

55. Américo Paredes, *With His Pistol in His Hand: The Ballad of Gregorio Cortez* (Austin, 1959), 9–10. In Laredo, the *alcalde* threatened citizens who left the town for outlying districts or *ranchos* with fines and jail terms unless they resettled in town. Hinojosa, *Borderlands Town*, 11–12.

56. "Nuevo Santander in 1795," 487.

57. Cámara Alta, *Descripción general*, 115, 118–19, 124–25.

58. "Nuevo Santander in 1795," 476 n. 31, 477–78, 485.

59. Ramos Arizpe, *Report*, 16–17.

60. Benjamin Lundy, *A Circular Addressed to Agriculturalists, Manufacturers, Mechanics, &c. on the Subject of Mexican Colonization with a General Statement Respecting Lundy's Grant, in the State of Tamaulipas: Accompanied by a Geographical Description, &c. of that Interesting Portion of the Mexican Republic* (Philadelphia, 1835), 14–15.

61. Paredes Manzano, *Homenaje*, 53.

62. Cervantes, *Fundaciones*, 59–61.

63. Ibid.; Scott, *Historical Heritage*, 86; Mauro, *Guide*, item no. 3.

64. Cavazos Garza, *Catálogo y síntesis*, no. 2598.

65. *The Impossible Dream by the Río Grande: A Documented Chronicle of the Establishment and Annihilation of San José de Palafox*, ed. and trans. Carmen Perry (San Antonio, 1971), 44, 81.

66. Paredes Manzano, *Homenaje*, passim.

67. Gerhard, *Northern Frontier*, 366. The first censuses of each settlement are contained in the *Estado General*, vol. 1; Zorrilla, "Nuevo Santander," 4. For a discussion of these terms of racial and ethnic identity, see Magnus Morner, *Race Mixture in the History of Latin America* (Boston, 1967), esp. chap. 5, 53–74.

68. On Laredo's population, see Hinojosa, *Borderlands Town*, 17–20, 99.

69. Paredes Manzano, *Homenaje*, 58. Hinojosa, *Borderlands Town*, 18, 42. For a good example of what occurred after Mexican independence, take the case of the separate Tlaxcalan Indian communities of the Coahuilan and Nuevo Leonese frontier. In spite of their strong pleas for the continued recognition of their racial identity and status, the new Mexican rulers denied them the right to maintain their unique identity, in the hope of forging a new nation. See David Bergen Adams, "The Tlaxcalan Colonies of Spanish Coahuila and Nuevo León: An Aspect of Settlement of Northern Mexico" (Ph.D. diss., University of Texas at Austin, 1971), 294–95.

70. Hinojosa, *Borderlands Town*, 101; Gerhard, *Northern Frontier*, 27; Jones, *Los Paisanos*, 10; Paredes, *With His Pistol*, 10–11.

71. Hinojosa, *Borderlands Town*, 18–19, 100–1.

72. "Nuevo Santander in 1795," 487.

73. Torre Villar, *Instrucciones*, 2:1157.

74. Bourbon reforms that affected frontier military defense policy are discussed in a number of sources. See Vásquez, *Establecimiento y pérdida*, chap. 5; Sidney B. Brinckerhoff and Odie B. Faulk, *Lancers for the King: A Study of the Frontier Military System of Northern New Spain, with a Translation of the Royal Regulations of 1772* (Phoenix, 1965), esp. part 4, 81–95; Max L. Moorhead, *The Presidio: Bastion of the Spanish Borderlands* (Norman, 1975). Exposed new frontier settlements in northern New Spain, which were founded for the purpose of serving as a bulwark against hostile Indians, failed during this period. One such town was N. S. de la Candelaria de Azanza on the Río Grande in 1798. Torre Villar, *Instrucciones*, 2:1368; Cervantes, *Fundaciones*, 51–58, 77.

75. Torre Villar, *Instrucciones*, 2:1158.

76. Ibid., and chart following 1298.

77. "Nuevo Santander in 1795," 504.

78. Torre Villar, *Instrucciones,* 2:1427.

79. Ibid., 1368.

80. Ibid., 1427–28.

81. Ibid., 1400.

82. Vásquez, *Establecimiento y pérdida,* 191–93.

83. David J. Weber, *The Mexican Frontier, 1821–1846: The American Southwest under Mexico* (Albuquerque, 1982), chaps. 5 and 6.

84. Gerhard, *Northern Frontier,* 24–26, table B, 365, table II, and 358–60, 365–66. But see Martín Salinas, *Indians of the Rio Grande Delta: Their Role in the History of Southern Texas and Northeastern Mexico* (Austin, 1990), 138–41. For the mid-eighteenth century, Salinas gives an estimate of fifteen thousand Indians in the Río Grande delta alone, based on two contemporary Spanish reports, including one by José de Escandón. Gerhard's estimate for the entire territory is slightly under fifteen thousand. While the correct number will never be known, Salinas's estimate appears too high in few of the relatively small number of Indian families in missions at midcentury, given the natives' favorable disposition toward missionary activity in the Lower Valley.

85. del Hoyo, *Historia del Nuevo Reino,* 354–60, 441—48.

86. Paredes Manzano, *Homenaje,* 27. On the Spanish campaigns against the natives in Nuevo Santander, see Zorrilla, *El Poder Colonial,* 109–10, 220–23. Zorrilla argues that José de Escandón failed to pacify the Indians and that Spanish injustice and lack of understanding of the Indians caused the uprisings in the 1770s. Zorrilla admits, however, that in the late colonial period the Indians in Texas had become a greater problem as larger numbers migrated into the frontier lands in northern New Spain. He recognized that such a situation made it difficult for Governor Escandón to formulate a workable policy. For a discussion of these Indian problems as they affected Texas and Nuevo Santander, see also Elizabeth A. H. John, *Storms Brewed in Other Men's Worlds* (College Station, Tex., 1975), 287–88, 301, 502, 504, 636, 653, 700, 755, 764–65.

87. Vásquez, *Establecimiento y pérdida,* 175.

88. Gerhard, *Northern Frontier,* 366.

89. *Visita a la Colonia del Nuevo Santander, hecha por el Licenciado Don Lino Nepomuceno Gómez el año de 1770* (Mexico City, 1942), 56–61; hereafter cited as Gómez, *Visita.* Also, see Carrasco, *El Nuevo Santander,* 1:152, table 30.

90. Fernando Ocaranza, *Crónica de las Provincias Internas de Nueva España* (Mexico City, 1939), 223–33; "Nuevo Santander in 1795," 493. The Franciscans made a number of charges against Escandón, who was recalled from office by the viceroy in 1766 and subsequently investigated. Basically, the missionaries charged that Escandón was more interested in founding Spanish towns than missions. The conflict broke out at the very beginning of the colonization venture and led the missionaries to leave the missions in 1766. Zorrilla argues that the charges made by the Franciscans in 1765 were mainly "to justify their abandonment of the missions." Escandón died on September 10, 1770, prior to the conclusion of an extensive viceregal investigation. On the basis of the findings of that investigation, King Charles III vindicated Escandón and his son, Manuel Ignacio de Escandón, was designated governor in 1780. Zorrilla, *El Poder Colonial,* 30–31, 43–44, 102–13, 135–36, 143–45, 218–19.

91. Gómez, *Visita*, 61; Ocaranza, *Crónica*, 233; Carrasco, *El Nuevo Santander*, 1:160, table 31.

92. "Nuevo Santander in 1795," 474–75.

93. On the number of natives in 1810, see Ramos Arizpe, *Report*, 14. Also, see Navarro y Noriega, *Catálogo de los curatos*, 48; and Carrasco, *El Nuevo Santander*, 1:163–65.

94. Angel Sepúlveda Brown and Gloria Villa Cadena, *San Agustín Parish of Laredo: Marriage Book I, 1790–1857* (Saltillo, 1989), entry nos. 14–16, 19–20, and 236, pp. 50–51, 103.

95. Jean Louis Berlandier, *Journey to Mexico during the years 1826–1834*, trans. Sheila M. Ohlendorf, Josette M. Bigelow, and Mary M. Standifer, 2 vols. (Austin, 1980), 2:428–30. It is not clear why Berlandier mentions missions as existing as late as the early 1830s, although it is clear that secularization of the missions had begun earlier in the 1810s and that by 1840 there was no Franciscan missionary activity in Tamaulipas. Carrasco, *El Nuevo Santander*, 1:163. For a brief discussion of the *mestizaje* prior to the founding of Nuevo Santander, see Hinojosa, *Borderlands Town*, 18.

96. "Representación de la Nación de los Indios Garza de la Villa de Mier, al gobernador del estado, 1832," in *Tamaulipas: textos de su historia, 1810–1921*, 2 vols., ed. Juan Fidel Zorrilla and Octavio Herrera Pérez (Ciudad Victoria, Instituto de Investigaciones, Dr. José María Luis Mora, 1990), 1:182–84.

97. Paredes Manzano, *Homenaje*, 52–53; Scott, *Historical Heritage*, 99–107; Florence Johnson Scott, *Royal Land Grants North of the Rio Grande, 1777–1821: Early History of Large Land Grants Made by Spain* (Rio Grande City, 1969), 24–25, 30–31.

98. Scott, *Royal Land Grants*, 36, 40–41, 44, 49–51.

99. *Abstract of Title to 200 Acres of Land, Part of Partition Share No. 1 of Espíritu Santo Grant in Cameron County, Texas* (Brownsville, Tex., n.d.), 2–7.

100. For the history of the Farías grants, I relied on the Francis William Seabury Papers, Center for American History, Barker Library, University of Texas, Austin, Box 2G166; hereafter cited as Seabury Papers. Very brief notes are also found in Mauro, *Guide*, items nos. 67, 69, and 71.

101. Mauro, *Guide*, item 308.

102. For a brief account of the Rincón del Oso grant, see ibid., item 330; and Clotilde P. García, *Captain Enrique Villarreal and Rincón del Oso Grant* (Corpus Christi, 1986), 5–6, 21, 27–28.

103. Berlandier, *Journey to Mexico*, 2:432, 438.

104. On the population of Tamulipas in 1840, see Zorrilla, "Nuevo Santander," 17. Also, see Nance, *After San Jacinto*, 4–5. On Anglo settlements in Texas and Mexican reaction to immigration from the United States, see Weber, *Mexican Frontier*, chap. 9, 158–78.

105. *Abstract of Title to Antonio Rivas Grant* (San Antonio, n.d.), 4–5; copy in Evans Library, Special Collections, Texas A & M University. For other examples of forfeited lands in south Texas, see Mauro, *Guide*, items 89, 90, and 162.

106. On Guerra Chapa, see Seabury Papers, Box 2G168; Mauro, *Guide*, items 30, 31, 35, 37, 79, 235, 293, 298, and 353. On the Treviño claims, see idem., item 301.

107. Cavazos Garza, *Catálogo y síntesis*, no. 2718.

108. Seabury Papers, Box 2G168.

109. Cavazos Garza, *Catálogo y síntesis*, no. 2307.

110. Ibid., no. 2523.

111. Ibid., no. 2686.

112. Mercurio Martínez Papers, University Archives, Texas A & M University, Box 27, folders 13, 15, and 16; hereafter cited as Martínez Papers.

113. Mauro, *Guide*, item 96.

114. Ibid., item 127.

CHAPTER 3

1. Cámaras Alta, *Descripción general*, 115, 118–19, 124–25.

2. Palacios, *Informe*, 29–33. Other reforms included severe cutbacks in the size of the regular troops and elimination of crown subsidies to resident missionary clergy who served the townspeople. Zorrilla, *El Poder Colonial*, 181–82. Miners in Nuevo Santander were also subjected to the king's customary one-fifth share, or *quinto*, beginning in 1768.

3. "Nuevo Santander in 1795," 472, 477. Ochoa's account of the administration of Sal del Rey is found in Interrogatories to Pacífico Ochoa, *State v. Salvador Cárdenas*, Nov. 13, 1872; copy in the Archives, Hidalgo County Historical Museum, Edinburg, Tex.

4. Zorrilla, *El Poder Colonial*, 36–39; 42; Cruz, *Let There Be Towns*, 95.

5. Ramos Arizpe, *Report*, 22.

6. Torre Villar, *Instrucciones*, 2:842; "Nuevo Santander in 1795," 479, 481–82; Stanley C. Green, *The Mexican Republic: The First Decade, 1823–1832* (Pittsburgh, 1987), 133.

7. "Nuevo Santander in 1795," 478–83. Escandón's account of the use of his *goleta* is found in *Estado general*, 2:55.

8. Jackie R. Booker, *Veracruz Merchants, 1770–1829: A Mercantile Elite in Late Bourbon and Early Independent Mexico*, Dellplain Latin American Studies, no. 29 (Boulder, 1993), 132.

9. Guillermo Tardiff, *Historia general del comercio exterior mexicano*, 2 vols. (Mexico City, 1968), 1:143; Tampico received a maritime administration agency in 1827. Ibid., 278; Zorrilla, *El Poder Colonial*, 91–96.

10. Green, *Mexican Republic*, 134.

11. Leroy P. Graf, "The Economic History of the Lower Río Grande Valley, 1820–1875," 2 vols. (Ph.D. diss., Harvard University, 1942) 1:4–5, 20, 26–36, 51–55; Hinojosa, *Borderlands Town*, 64. Berlandier, *Journey to Mexico*, 438.

12. Green, *Mexican Republic*, 137.

13. J. J. Linn, *Reminiscences of Fifty Years in Texas* (New York, 1883), 10–11, 15–16; Noah Smithwick, *The Evolution of a State, or Recollections of Old Texas Days*, comp. Nanna Smithwick Donaldson (1900; repr., Austin, 1990), 29.

14. Chauncey Devereux Stillman, *Charles Stillman, 1810–1875* (New York, 1956), 4–8.

15. Tardiff, *Historia general del comercio*, 1:292, 299, 320. The official values exclude contraband traffic, which is difficult to estimate reliably. Tardiff noted its inception along the coast of Veracruz, at Tuxpán and at the Pánuco River, and he dates this traffic to 1811. Ibid., 143. It is unclear when the *contrabandistas* began operating in the Matamoros district, but

they obviously introduced goods at about the same time the port was officially opened, if not earlier. The illegal entry of goods was a growing problem in the northeastern Mexican states.

16. Green, *Mexican Republic*, 134.

17. Tardiff, *Historia general del comercio*, 1:449.

18. Ibid., 401, 447, 458, 484–85, 502–3, 542–43.

19. Ibid., 449.

20. "Iniciativa del Congreso Tamaulipeco a las cámaras de la unión, para impedir el cierre del puerto de Matamoros al comercio extranjero," in Zorrilla, Miro Fláquer, and Herrera Pérez, *Tamaulipas: su historia*, 1:210–14. It is also found in *Atalaya* 2, no. 36 (September 2, 1835).

21. Juan N. de la Garza y Evía, Gobernador del departamento de Nuevo León, Monterrey, Aug. 4, 1836, circular, DeGolyer Library, Southern Methodist University, Dallas, Tex., 1.

22. Hinojosa, *Borderlands Town*, 47–51. For an incisive look at the Texas Revolt of 1835, see Weber, *Mexican Frontier*, 242–55; also, see Westphall, *Mercedes Reales*, 67–72.

23. Berlandier, *Journey to Mexico*, 2:438; Nance, *After San Jacinto*, 75–82, 100–110; on the decline of Mexico's foreign trade, see Tardiff, *Historia general del comercio*, 1:458.

24. *Valley of the Río Grande; Its Soil, Productions, Climate* (New York, 1847), 20.

25. Tardiff, *Historia general del comercio*, 1:175–76.

26. Lundy, *Circular*, 12.

27. Berlandier, *Journey to Mexico*, 1:262 and 2:426, 428, 430–31, 434, 441, 444–45; Graf, "Economic History," 1:46; Lt. W. H. Chatfield, comp., *The Twin Cities of the Border: Brownsville, Texas and Matamoros, Mexico* (New Orleans, 1893; repr., Harlingen, Tex., 1959), 12; Margaret Harrison Smith, "The Lower Rio Grande Region in Tamaulipas, Mexico" (Ph.D. diss., University of Texas at Austin, 1961), 149.

28. Green, *Mexican Republic*, 115.

29. Lundy, *Circular*, 12.

30. On the desire of the Indians along the Río Grande to be settled in missions, see *Estado general*, 1:375, 383–84, 394–95, 411, 413, 415–16, 427–28, 431, 435–37, 442, 448, and 2:109, 113–14, 116–17, 120; Gómez, *Visita*, 33, 56–62; Don Vicente González de Santianes, *La república de indios de Don Vicente González de Santianes*, ed. Jesús Franco Carrasco (C. Victoria, Tamaulipas, 1983), 41; "Nuevo Santander in 1795," 488; Cruz, *Let There Be Towns*, 87–95; Jones, *Los Paisanos*, 70–72; Scott, *Historical Heritage of the Lower Río Grande*, 28–29, 31–32, 40–41, 97, 99–102.

31. Jones, *Los Paisanos*, 67; Miller, *José de Escandón*, 31; Zorrilla, *El Poder Colonial*, 36, 42–43, 50, 54; Carrasco, *El Nuevo Santander*, 1:43.

32. *Estado general*, 2:48, 54, 59, 64, 71, 77.

33. "Nuevo Santander in 1795," 470, 475.

34. Ibid., 483.

35. *Estado general*, 2:55, 113; Zorrilla, *El Poder Colonial*, 183. On the customs and regulations related to the livestock industry, see Matamoros Archives, vol. 9 (1824) and vol. 24 (1837) (photocopies, Center for American History, University of Texas at Austin); and Zorrilla, "Nuevo Santander," 5–6.

36. "Nuevo Santander in 1795," 473, 477.

37. Ibid., 476, 481.

38. John, *Storms Brewed*, 482. Jack D. L. Holmes, "De México a Nueva Orleans en 1801: el diario inédito de Fortier y St. Maxent," *Historia Mexicana* 61 (1966), 48–70.

39. Ramos Arizpe, *Report*, 1, 20–23. By "exterior," Ramos Arizpe meant outside the provinces of Coahuila, Texas, Nuevo León, and Nuevo Santander. In order to deal more effectively with problems specific to the northern frontier, Spain, under Charles III, initiated economic and administrative reforms that led to the reorganization of the frontier provinces, including Nuevo Santander. In 1776 the northern provinces were removed from the jurisdiction of the viceroy and made part of a separate administrative unit, the Comandancia General de las Provincias Internas. Texas, Nuevo Santander, Nuevo León, and Coahuila made up the eastern division at the time of Ramos Arizpe's report to the Spanish Cortes. Bannon, *Spanish Borderlands Frontier*, 167–89; Weber, *Mexican Frontier*, xix–xx.

40. Virginia H. Taylor, ed., *The Letters of Antonio Martinez: Last Spanish Governor of Texas, 1817–1822* (Austin, 1957), 77, 82.

41. García, *Dolores, Revilla, and Laredo*, 20.

42. Will of Don José Domingo González, Laredo, June 6, 1819, in Martínez Papers, Box 32–11.

43. On *ranchos* and livestock in the Matamoros district, see Matamoros Archives, Box 2Q269 and 2Q267. Also, see Smith, "Lower Rio Grande Region," 149. The figure on livestock in 1835 is taken from Paredes, *With His Pistol*, 9 n. 2, citing Cecil Bernard Smith, "Diplomatic Relations between the United States and Mexico" (Master's thesis, University of Texas, 1928), 5.

44. On Texan—Mexican problems in the Trans-Nueces, see Nance, *After San Jacinto*, esp. chaps. 2–4, 10–82.

45. Rafael de Alba, *La República Mexicana, Tamaulipas: reseña geográfica y estadística* (Paris, 1910), 57; Zorrilla, *Estudio de la legislación*, 138 n. 2.

46. Berlandier quote in de Alba, *La República Mexicana*, 64.

47. Tardiff, *Historia general del comercio*, 1:224. José Rafael Gonzales, "Report on the State of Coahuila y Tejas," ed. Andrés Tijerina and David T. Weber, *Southwestern Historical Quarterly* 100, no. 2 (October 1996), 200. Some of the ships that left the port of Matamoros carried mules to New Orleans and other places as far as Connecticut. Matamoros Consular Reports (microfilm, Texas A & M University, Evans Library).

48. Lundy, *Circular*, 9, 11–12.

49. David Woodman, Jr., *Guide to Texas Emigrants* (Boston, 1835; repr., 1974), 61.

50. *Texas in 1840, or the Emigrants Guide to the New Republic* (New York, 1973), 135.

51. Edward Dougherty, *The Rio Grande Valley: A Lecture Delivered before the Lone Star Literary Association of Brownsville, Texas, May 29, 1867* (Brownsville, 1867; repr., Brownsville, 1955), 19, 22.

52. Joseph G. McCoy, *Historic Sketches of the Cattle Trade of the West and Southwest* (Glendale, Cal., 1940; repr., Lincoln, 1985), 22–40.

53. Joseph Dorst Patch, *The Concentration of General Zachary Taylor's Army at Corpus Christi, Texas* (Corpus Christi, 1962), 12–14.

54. K. Jack Bauer, *The Mexican War, 1846–1848* (New York, 1974), 35, 37.

55. Zorrilla, *El poder colonial*, 46–48.

56. Zorrilla, "Nuevo Santander," 6.

57. Zorrilla, *El poder colonial*, 49–51, 53–54. According to Zorrilla, some of these older *haciendas* owned massive herds of sheep that numbered in the hundreds of thousands.

58. Cavazos Garza, *Catálogo y síntesis*, no. 2949.

59. *Visita General*, Reynosa, 20; Mauro, *Guide*, entry no. 24; Max Dreyer, "San Juan de Carricitos Land Grant as Given to José Narciso Cavazos," *Las Porciones Genealogical Society Journal* (Edinburg, Tex,) 2, no. 1 (Spring 1987): 77; Carroll Norquest, Jr., "Will and Testament of José Narciso Cavazos," ibid.: 76–82.

60. Scott, *Royal Land Grants*, 60–61.

61. Will and Testament of José María Ballí, 1788, Reynosa Archives; Will and Testament of Rosa María de Hinojosa de Ballí, 1798, Reynosa Archives. On Padre Ballí, see Scott, *Royal Land Grants*, 71–72.

62. Jones, *Los Paisanos*, 66–67.

63. Ibid.

64. Will of Don José Domingo González, Laredo.

65. Paredes Manzano, *Homenaje*, 24–25, 28–29.

66. Ibid., 29.

67. Will of María Gertrudes de la Garza (transcript), Center for American History, University of Texas, Austin.

68. Will of Antonia Longoria, in Antonio Domínguez Papers, Barker Library, Center for American History, University of Texas, Austin.

69. "Nuevo Santander in 1795," 495–96.

70. Hinojosa, *Borderland Towns*, 50–55; Montejano, *Anglos and Mexicans*, 30.

71. Berlandier, *Journey to Mexico*, 2:442, 444.

72. Hinojosa, *Borderlands Town*, 50–51, 53, 55, 60, 97.

73. David M. Vigness, "Indian Raids on the Lower Rio Grande, 1836–1837," *Southwestern Historical Quarterly* 59 (July 1955): 14–16.

74. Vigness, "Indian Raids," 16–19.

75. Mariano Arista, General en jefe, Ejército del Norte, departamento del Oriente, Saltillo, Dec. 15, 1840, broadside (DeGolyer Library, Southern Methodist University, Dallas). *Semanario político del gobierno de Nuevo León*, vol. 4, no. 45, Nov. 7, 1844, DeGolyer Library.

76. Vigness, "Indian Raids," 22–23; Hinojosa, *Borderlands Town*, 54; Wayne Gard, *The Chisholm Trail* (Norman, 1954), 8–9; Nora Ethel Ramírez, "The Vaquero and Ranching in the Southwestern United States, 1600–1970" (Ph.D. diss., Indiana University, 1979), 50; V. W. Lehmann, *Forgotten Legions: Sheep in the Rio Grande Plains of Texas* (El Paso, 1969), 134; Tom Lea, *The King Ranch*, 2 vols. (Boston, 1957), 1:107–8.

77. Berlandier, *Journey to Mexico*, 2:362–63; 422–23; 542–46, 549, 564, 567; Gard, *Chisholm Trail*, 8–10; Don Worcester, *The Texas Longhorn: Relic of the Past, Asset for the Future* (College Station, 1987), 32–38; Hinojosa, *Borderlands Town*, 49; De León, *Tejano Community*, 55; Ford, *Rip Ford*, 143–44.

78. For the assertion that all cattle were rounded up by 1840, see Lehmann, *Forgotten*

Legions, 134, citing J. H. Brown, *History of Texas from 1685–1892* (St. Louis, 1892), 2:138. On Gussett, see James Cox, comp., *Historical and Biographical Record of the Cattle Industry and the Cattlemen of Texas and Adjacent Territory*, 2 vols. (St Louis, 1895; repr., New York, 1959), 2:592.

79. Gard, *Chisholm Trail*, 12–13.

80. Ibid., 20–22.

81. Berlandier, *Journey to Mexico*, 2:430.

82. Joseph Milton Nance, *Attack and Counter-Attack: The Texas—Mexican Frontier, 1842* (Austin, 1964), 10, 18, 27, 30, 240, 242, 454, 513, 535.

83. *Estado general*, 1:16, 105, 113, 116, 119.

84. The province of Coahuila produced a surplus of excellent wheat that supplied much of northern New Spain, including Texas and Nuevo Santander. Ramos Arizpe, *Report*, 20–21. Also, see Cruz, *Let There Be Towns*, 95; Berlandier, *Journey to Mexico*, 1:262–63 and 2:429, 444.

85. Fray Agustín de Morfi, *Descripción del territorio del Real Presidio de San Juan Bautista* (Mexico City, 1950), 299.

86. Graf, "Economic History," 1:426.

87. Berlandier, *Journey to Mexico*, 2:423, 428, 430.

88. This valley farm is described in Pedro Hernández Carrasco, *Manifesto made public by the empowered representative of the Hacienda which belongs to Mr. Antonio Salinas* (1897), 1; copy in Library of Congress, Washington, D.C.

89. de Alba, *La República Mexicana*, 57.

90. For descriptions of the crops grown in the Lower Valley, see Berlandier, *Journey to Mexico*, 2:438; Juan Fidel Zorrilla, "Tamaulipas," in *Vision historica de la frontera Norte de Mexico*, 3 vols., ed. David Piñera Ramírez (Mexicali, 1987), 2:113. Lists of cotton farmers in Matamoros and Reynosa for 1844 are found in Matamoros Archives, Box 2Q278; *Valley of the Río Grande*, 4, 13; Dougherty, *Río Grande Valley*, 22–27; Graf, "Economic History," 1:426. The quote is found in Frederick A. Wislizenus, *Memoir of a Tour to Northern Mexico, Connected with Col. Doniphan's Expedition, in 1846 and 1847* (U.S. Senate, 30th Cong., 1st sess., Misc. No. 26, 1848; repr., Glorieta, N.M., 1969), 79.

91. Francisco Vital Fernández, *Expediente formado para tratar de la indemnización que solicita el Estado de Tamaulipas con motivo de las pérdidas consiguentes a la cesión de territorio a los Estados Unidos por el tratado de paz, celebrado el 2 de Febrero de 1848 en Guadalupe con las resoluciones dictadas en el caso* (C. Victoria, 1848), 11–13, 15–16. It is not known whether the national government replied to the governor.

92. de Alba, *La República Mexicana*, 30.

93. Ibid.; U.S. Census of Population, 1850, Lower Valley, and Nueces County (manuscript), microfilm copy, Special Collections, University of Texas at Pan American, Edinburg, Texas.

94. Robert J. Rosenbaum, *Mexicano Resistance in the Southwest: "The Sacred Right of Self-Preservation"* (Austin, 1981), 5–7, 36–37; Weber, *Mexican Frontier*, 274; Westphall, *Mercedes Reales*, 74.

95. Reports of the destruction of *ranchos* and villages located inland from the Río Grande

fanned some of the Mexican fears of Americans. See Wislizenus, *Memoir of a Tour*, 78–79; and A. B. Clarke, *Travels in Mexico and California*, ed. Anne M. Perry (College Station, Tex., 1988), 18.

CHAPTER 4

1. The 1920s saw the rise of the so-called Mexican problem. For a brief discussion, see Mario T. García, *Mexican Americans: Leadership, Ideology, and Identity, 1930–1960* (New Haven, 1989), 26–27. Arnoldo De León and Kenneth L. Stewart, *Tejanos and the Numbers Game* (Albuquerque, 1989), 3–4, 91–93.

2. The key critic was Octavio Ignacio Romano V., of Berkeley, who edited *El Grito: A Journal of Contemporary Mexican American Thought.* His most important writings are cited in García, *Mexican Americans*, 308 n. 2. Also, see De León and Stewart, *Tejanos and the Numbers Game*, 4–6.

3. Acuña, *Occupied America*; Mario Barrera, *Race and Class in the Southwest: A Theory of Racial Inequality* (Notre Dame, 1970). Also, see Montejano, *Anglos and Mexicans.*

4. De León, *Tejano Community.*

5. Alex Saragoza, "Recent Chicano Historiography: An Interpretative Essay," *Aztlán* 19 (Spring 1990): 1–77. De León and Stewart, *Tejanos and the Numbers Game*, 93–94.

6. Jay P. Dolan and Gilberto M. Hinojosa, eds., *Mexican Americans and the Catholic Church, 1900–1965* (Notre Dame, 1994), 24.

7. Leobardo F. Estrada, F. Chris García, Reynaldo Flores Macias, and Lionel Maldonado, "Chicanos in the United States: A History of Exploitation and Resistence," in *Latinos and the Political System*, ed. F. Chris García (Notre Dame, 1988), 28–64; and Frank D. Bean and Marta Tienda, *The Hispanic Population of the United States* (New York, 1987), 17–18.

8. De León and Stewart, *Tejanos and the Numbers Game.* For an example of the persistence of the use of the internal colonial theory, see Ronald Takaki, *A Different Mirror: A History of Multicultural America* (Boston, 1993), chap. 7.

9. *De Bow's Journal* 3 (New Orleans, 1853), 326.

10. De León and Stewart, *Tejanos and the Numbers Game*, 16–17.

11. For a concise description and analysis of this intricate pattern of border commerce, see Mario Cerutti and Miguel González Quiroga, "Guerra y comercio en torno al Río Bravo (1855–1867): línea fronteriza, espacio económico común," *Historia Mexicana* 40, no. 2 (1991): 217–97. On the length of the trail drives, see Ramírez, comp., *Four Generations of Velas*, n.p.

12. Brownsville's proximity to the port of Bagdad during the Civil War was a crucial factor in its growth in the 1860s; see James A. Irby, *Backdoor at Bagdad: The Civil War on the Rio Grande*, Southwestern Series, No. 53 (El Paso, 1977).

13. A perusal of the population censuses for the region bears this out. Also, see De León, *Tejano Community*, and De León and Stewart, *Tejanos and the Numbers Game.*

14. For an example of contracts, see *Letter from the Secretary of War communicating in obedience to law, statements showing the contracts made by the bursar of the War Department, on behalf of the United States during the year 1878*, 45th Cong., 3d sess., Senate Exec. Doc. no. 40

(Washington, D.C., 1878), 10–50. Also, see Jerry D. Thompson, *Warm Weather and Bad Whiskey: The 1886 Laredo Election Riot* (El Paso, 1991), 6.

15. "Col. J. K. F. Mansfield's Report of the Inspection of the Department of Texas in 1856," ed. M. L. Crimmens, *Southwestern Historical Quarterly* 43 (1940–41): 133–48. Major W. W. Chapman was acting quartermaster at Corpus Christi. No troops were stationed there, but it supplied several western forts. Major Chapman reported that he had 142 citizens in his employ in April 1856. Ibid., 147.

16. Chatfield, *Twin Cities*, 24.

17. John L. Haynes Papers Center for American History, University of Texas at Austin, Scrapbook, 5, in Box 2J144.

18. Caleb Coker, ed., *The News from Brownsville: Helen Chapman's Letters from the Texas Military Frontier, 1848–1852* (Austin, 1992), 107.

19. Rankin, *Texas in 1850*, 191–92.

20. Coker, *News from Brownsville*, 368. Mrs. Chapman estimated 2,000 persons in Brownsville at the end of 1848. Ibid., 93. The town's 1850 population was 2,500. Ibid., 161.

21. A. W. Spaight, Commissioner, Texas Dept. of Agriculture, Insurance, Statistics and History, *The Resources, Soil and Climate of Texas* (Galveston, 1882), 51.

22. Hinojosa, *Borderlands Town*, 73–74, 119, 123; Thompson, *Warm Weather*, 45–49, 163 n. 52.

23. Coker, *News from Brownsville*, 385.

24. *De Bow's Journal* 18 (1850), 708.

25. Ibid. (1860), 28:460–61.

26. Karen J. Weitze, "National Historic Landmark Nomination for Roma, Texas" (copy at Texas Historical Commission, Austin, 1993).

27. Spaight, *Resources, Soil, and Climate of Texas*, 289–91.

28. Daniel Arreola, "Plaza Towns of South Texas," *Geographical Review* 82, no. 1 (January 1992), 66.

29. Weitze, "National Historical Landmark Nomination," 6.

30. Coker, *News from Brownsville*, 385.

31. Eugenia Reynolds Briscoe, "A Narrative History of Corpus Christi, Texas, 1519–1875" (Ph.D. diss., University of Denver, 1972), 282, 295, 297, 321, 501.

32. Spaight, *Resources of Texas*, 239–41.

33. U.S. Congress, Senate, Joseph Nimmo, Jr., "The Improvement of the Harbor of Galveston," 48th Cong., 1st sess., Misc. Doc. no. 111 (Washington, D.C., 1884), 30.

34. Spaight, *Resources of Texas*, 87–89.

35. *U.S. Census of Population*, 1870, Maverick, Val Verde, La Salle, Uvalde, and Dimmit counties.

36. De León and Stewart, *Tejanos and the Numbers Game*, 24, table 2.3.

37. Ibid., 15, 23–24, 59–60.

38. *U.S. Census of Population*, 1850, Lower Río Grande Valley.

39. Thompson, *Warm Weather*, 16.

40. Virgil N. Lott and Mercurio Martínez, *The Kingdom of Zapata* (San Antonio, 1953), 100.

41. Typescript in Martínez Papers.

42. *Abstract of Title to the Part of the Beamer Syndicate and J. C. McDowell Properties That lie in the "Llano Grande" and "La Blanca" Grants in Hidalgo County* (copy in Hidalgo County Historical Museum, Edinburg, Tex.).

43. Estate of Guillermo Cano, County Clerk, Hidalgo County, Probate File No. 173, Edinburg, Tex.

44. Estate of Ramón Vela, County Clerk, Hidalgo County, Probate File No. 669, Edinburg, Tex.; Ramírez, *Four Generations*, n.p.

45. Except for a Spanish physician, all of the doctors enumerated in censuses for Hidalgo County from 1860 to 1900 were Anglos. U.S. Census of Population, 1860, 1870, 1880, 1900, Hidalgo County.

46. Anna Marietta Kelsey, *Through the Years: Reminiscences of Pioneer Days on the Texas Border* (San Antonio, 1952), 64.

47. De León, *Tejano Community*, 149–51.

48. Coker, *News from Brownsville*, 100–1, 115–26.

49. *U.S. Census of Population*, 1860, 1870, 1880, 1900, Hidalgo County, 1860, 1870, 1880, 1900; U.S. Congress, House, *Troubles on [the] Texas Frontier*, 36th Cong., 1st sess., Exec. Doc. No. 81, p. 13.

50. See John Mack Faragher, "Open-Country Community: Sugar Creek, Illinois, 1820–1850," in *The Countryside in the Age of Capitalist Transformation: Essays in the History of Rural America*, ed. Steven Hahn and Jonathan Prude (Chapel Hill, 1985), 233–58.

51. Estate of Ramón Vela, Hidalgo County, Probate File No. 669; Ramírez, *Four Generations.*

52. Ramírez, *Four Generations.*

53. *U.S. Census of Population*, 1850, Lower Río Grande Valley; María Concepción Garza de Ramírez and María del Carmen Garza, interviews, Edinburg, Tex., Nov. 21, 1994.

54. Anna M. Champion, Margarito Hinojosa Sr., File No. 94.30, (typescript in Hidalgo County Historical Museum, Edinburg, Tex.).

55. *McAllen Monitor* (McAllen, Tex.), Sept. 29, 1991, 17a, 24a.

56. U.S. Congress, House, *Memorial of [Col.] M. R. Jefferds, Galveston, Texas, to Accompany H.R. Bill 2067*, 45th Cong., 2d sess., Misc. Doc. no. 46 (Washington, D.C., 1875), appendix 6, n.p.

57. U.S. Department of State, *Proceedings of the International Water Boundary Commission, United States and Mexico, Treaties of 1884 and 1889: Equitable Distribution of the Waters of the Río Grande*, 2 vols. (Washington, D.C., 1903), 1:174.

58. The Merchants Association of New York, *The Natural Resources and Economic Conditions of the State of Texas* (New York, 1901), 56.

59. Emilia Schunior Ramírez, *Ranch Life in Hidalgo County.*

60. Weitze, "Roma, Texas," 6.

61. Hinojosa, *Borderlands Town*, 80, 120.

62. U.S. Congress, House, Moses R. Jefferds, "Mexican Commerce Can Only Be Controlled by Railroads: Camargo, the Military and Commercial Key to Mexico," 45th Cong., 2d sess., Misc. Doc. no. 46 (Washington, D.C., 1875), n.p.

63. Bruce S. Cheeseman, "Richard King: Pioneering Market Capitalism on the Frontier," in *Ranching in South Texas: A Symposium*, ed. Joe S. Graham (Texas A & M University, Kingsville, 1994), 89.

64. *U.S. Census of Population*, 1850, Lower Río Grande Valley.

65. *U.S. Census of Population*, 1880, Cameron County.

66. Briscoe, "Narrative History of Corpus Christi," 253–54.

67. Guadalupe San Miguel, "Endless Pursuits: The Chicano Educational Experience in Corpus Christi, Texas, 1880–1960" (Ph.D. diss., Stanford University, 1978), 30.

68. Hinojosa, *Borderlands Town*, 102–3.

69. But see De León and Stewart, *Tejanos and the Numbers Game*, 19–20. They argue that Anglo migration to south, central, and west Texas stopped in the 1860s due to the Civil War, whereas Mexican immigration increased after that time.

70. The best social history of the Mexican American family is Richard Griswold del Castillo, *La Familia: Chicano Families in the Urban Southwest, 1848 to the Present* (Notre Dame, Ind., 1984). Also, see Silvia M. Arrom, *The Women of Mexico City, 1790–1857* (Stanford, 1985), chaps. 1–2.

71. On affection for relatives, see Baldomero Vela, introduction in Ramírez, *Four Generations*, n.p.; and Erasmo García, interview. Also, see Swadesh, *Los Primeros Pobladores*, 175–77, for differences in the matter of addressing relatives among Hispanos in New Mexico.

72. Hinojosa, *Borderlands Town*, 128, table 13.

73. De León and Stewart, *Tejanos and the Numbers Game*, 51, table 4.1.

74. For a discussion of Mexican American patriarchy, see Griswold del Castillo, *La Familia*, chap. 3. The prohibition against marrying outside one's social class encouraged the perpetuation of Hispanic patriarchy. See Charlotte Whaley, *Nina Otero-Warren of Santa Fe* (Albuquerque, 1994), 10–27. For the colonial and Mexican origins of patriarchy, see Arrom, *Women of Mexico City*, 76–78.

75. Ramírez, *Ranch Life in Hidalgo County after 1850.*

76. *De Bow's Journal* 18 (1850), 709.

77. *U.S. Census of Population*, 1850, Lower Río Grande Valley.

78. County Clerk, Hidalgo County, *Deed Record "A"*, Edinburg, Tex., 20.

79. County Clerk, Hidalgo County, *Marriage Records*, vols. A, B, and 1, Edinburg, Tex.

80. Erasmo García, interview.

81. Heath Dillard, *Daughters of the Reconquest: Women in Castilian Town Society, 1100–1300* (New York, 1984), 44–45, and chap. 4; Will of Juan Anaya, Hidalgo County, Tex., Probate Records, Minutes, Book A, 143–44; Estate of Martín Hinojosa del Toro, Probate File No. 53, Hidalgo County, Edinburg, Tex.

82. *U.S. Census of Population*, 1850, Lower Río Grande Valley.

83. Will of Fernando Uribe, Box 30–8, Martínez Papers.

84. Estate of Ramón Chapa, Probate File no. 669, Hidalgo County, Edinburg, Tex.

85. Box 30–10, Martínez Papers.

86. Ramírez, *Four Generations.*

87. J. T. Canales, *The Recollections of a Neighbor of Mrs. H. King* May, 1956 (typescript, King Ranch Archives, Kingsville, Tex.).

88. Ramírez, *Four Generations.*

89. Lott and Martínez, *Kingdom of Zapata*, 25.

90. Hidalgo County, *Probate Records*, Minutes, Book B, 523–27. Will of Victoria Ballí.

91. Hidalgo County, *Probate Records*, Minutes, Book A, 159, Will of Sotero Alvarez.

92. "Toluca Ranch," in Texas Dept. of Agriculture, *Family Land Heritage Program* (1980), 6:40–42.

93. Thomas, "Passing the Light."

94. Mary Ann Casstevens, "Randado," in Graham, *Ranching in South Texas*, 46.

95. County Clerk, Cameron County, *Patents, Affidavits, Plats and Surveys, Dedications, Grants, Charters, Judgments*, Brownsville, Tex., 75—88.

96. Kelsey, *Through the Years*, 30–31.

97. County Clerk, Hidalgo County, *Commissioners' Court Minutes*, Apr. 1, 1857, 55.

98. Affidavit of Jesús Treviño, Probate Record, Minutes, Book B, County Clerk, Hidalgo County, Edinburg, Tex., 551.

99. Guardianship of the Estate of the Person of Antonia García Cano, File No. 126, County Clerk, Hidalgo County, Edinburg, Tex.

100. Kelsey, *Through the Years*, 24.

101. Application for Guardianship of the Estate of Juan Garza Treviño, File No. 146, County Clerk, Hidalgo County, Edinburg, Tex.

102. Esteban García, interview with Dr. Hubert J. Miller (Special Collections Library, University of Texas at Pan American, Edinburg, Tex.), Jan. 19, 1978. Even as Tejanos were uprooted from their small holdings in the late nineteenth and early twentieth centuries, and as their numbers increased through immigration from northeast Mexico, their ethnic identity, based on a shared culture, remained a source of strength in confronting the new social and economic order. This has been shown in a comparative study of Czech farmers and Mexican laborers in Nueces County. See Josef J. Barton, "Land, Labor, and Community in Nueces: Czech Farmers and Mexican Laborers in South Texas, 1880—1930," in *Ethnicity on the Great Plains*, ed. Frederick C. Luebke (Lincoln, 1980), 190–209.

103. Ramírez, *Ranch Life in Hidalgo County after 1850.*

104. Garza de Ramírez, interview.

105. Vela, introduction, in Ramírez, *Four Generations.*

106. For an example of the role that family alliances played in land acquisition in the case of Hipólito García, a large and successful *ranchero*, see Casstevens, "Randado," 44–47. Also, see Griswold del Castillo, *La Familia*, 40.

107. On social and economic activities held in plazas, see Arreola, "Plaza Towns of South Texas," 56–73.

108. Domenech, *Missionary Adventures*, 254.

109. The diverse cultural traditions of the colonial settlers in the region were first noted by José de Escandón, *Informe de Don José de Escandón al virrey de la Nueva España sobre los primeros actos culturales en la provincia de Nuevo Santander, 1760* (Mexico, 1943); copy in the Benson Library, Austin, Tex. Also see Américo Paredes, *A Texas-Mexican Cancionero: Folksongs of the Lower Border* (Urbana, Ill., 1976), esp. the introduction, xviii–xxiv. Some *corridos* and other compositions can be found in the Martínez Papers.

110. Kelsey, *Through the Years*, 63.

111. Biography of M. Martínez, Box 30–10, in Martínez Papers.

112. Erasmo García, interview.

113. Ibid.; Garza de Ramírez, interview; Ramírez, *Ranch Life in Hidalgo County after 1850.*

114. Esteban García, interview; Erasmo García, interview.

115. Paredes, *Texas-Mexican Cancionero*, introduction and 113; Kelsey, *Through the Years*, 121.

116. Garza de Ramírez, interview.

117. Erasmo García, interview.

118. Ramírez, *Ranch Life in Hidalgo County after 1850.*

119. Erasmo García, interview.

120. Ramírez, *Ranch Life in Hidalgo County after 1850.*

121. The standard Oblate history is found in Bernard Doyon, O.M.I., *The Cavalry of Christ on the Rio Grande* (Milwaukee, 1956). Also, see James Talmadge Moore, *Through Fire and Flood: The Catholic Church in Frontier Texas, 1836–1900* (College Station, Tex., 1992); and Robert E. Wright, O.M.I., "Popular and Official Religiosity: A Theoretical Analysis and a Case Study of Laredo-Nuevo Laredo, 1755–1857" (Ph.D. diss., University of California, Berkeley, May 1992).

122. Moore, *Through Fire and Flood*, 92, 192.

123. Sister E. Vela, in Ramírez, *Four Generations.*

124. Edward Kennedy, O.M.I., *A Parish Remembers: Fifty Years of Oblate Endeavor in the Valley of the Río Grande* (Mercedes, Tex., 1959), 1–2, 41–42.; Briscoe, "Narrative History of Corpus Christi," 293–94; Moore, *Through Fire and Flood*, 192. Some of the religious women taught in the public schools of the region into the twentieth century. For example, in Mercedes they served from 1909 to 1915. Kennedy, *Parish Remembers*, 36–37.

125. José Roberto Juárez, "Los Padres Rancheristas: The Nineteenth Century Struggle for Mexican American Catholicism in South Texas," in Graham, *Ranching in South Texas*, 15–43.

126. Hinojosa, *Borderlands Town*, 88–89.

127. Pierre F. Parisot, *The Reminiscences of a Texas Missionary* (San Antonio, 1899), 74, 90–91, 127; Pierre F. Parisot and C. F. Smith, *History of the Catholic Church in the Diocese of San Antonio* (San Antonio, 1897); Doyon, *Cavalry of Christ*, 129, 132–35; Moore, *Through Fire and Flood*, 184–94.

128. Kennedy, *Parish Remembers*, 7–8; Mary Ann Casstevens, "Randado: The Built Environment of a Texas-Mexican Ranch," in *Hecho en Tejas*, ed. Joe S. Graham (Denton, Tex., 1991), 314–17.

129. For an example of the continuing creation of religious icons, see Cynthia L. Vidaurri, "Texas-Mexican Religious Folk Art in Robstown, Texas," in Graham, *Hecho en Tejas*, 222–49.

130. Kennedy, *Parish Remembers*, 38; Casstevens, "Randado: The Built Environment," 316. Personal observation, Nov. 21, 1994.

131. Dolan and Hinojosa, *Mexican Americans and the Catholic Church*, 21–23; Juárez, "Los Padres Rancheristas," 33–34. As of 1911, the Catholic church in south Texas had seventy-five

chapels and churches, two hospitals, one orphanage, and one college. It also operated nine parochial schools and five academies for girls. And there were thirty-two clerics, of whom one-third were Spanish. Ibid., 31.

132. Coker, *News from Brownsville*, 175 nn. 28 and 29.

133. Melinda Rankin, *Twenty Years among the Mexicans, a Narrative of Missionary Labor* (Cincinnati, 1875), 33, 51.

134. Coker, *News from Brownsville*, 172, 180.

135. De León, *Tejano Community*, 152.

136. Samuel A. Purdie, *Memories of Angela Aguilar de Mascorro; and Sketches of the Friends' Mexican Mission* (Chicago, 1885), 21–26.

137. Weber, *Foreigners in Their Native Land*, 209, 212–16, 220, asserts that this process of adaptation to U.S. institutions was more relevant in New Mexico. But see De León, *Tejano Community*, chap. 2 and 187–94; and Guadalupe San Miguel, *"Let All of Them Take Heed": Mexican Americans and the Campaign for Educational Equality in Texas, 1910–1981* (Austin, 1987), 8–13.

138. Voter Register of 1867–1869. Film B/3774, in Evans Library, Texas A & M University.

139. For Tejano politics in the pre–Civil War era, see Walter L. Buenger, *Secession and the Union in Texas* (Austin, 1984), 88. Also, see Hinojosa, *Borderlands Town*, 72–73. For the best overall history of the role of Tejano *rancheros* in American politics, see Evan Anders, *Boss Rule in South Texas: The Progressive Era* (Austin, 1982), especially chap. 1. What I am arguing here is that Tejanos in south Texas acted in a practical way in politics because they had sufficient numerical strength to participate in government and therefore protect their property interests. Anders' assertion that Tejanos represented a mass of "corralled or controlled" voters must be qualified. But see García, *Mexican Americans*, 14, who characterizes nineteenth-century Hispanics as accommodationist or rebels.

140. Calderón, "Mexican Politics in the American Era, 1846–1900."

141. Hinojosa, *Borderlands Town*, 82. 88, 103–5.

142. Calderón, "Mexican Politics."

143. Election and other court records, especially those of county commissioners, often include the same person holding office or participating in one way or another in elections, trials, and other proceedings. See for example, Elections Administrator, Cameron County, *Record of Elections*, Book A, 1873–92, and Book B, 1892–1928, Brownsville, Tex.

144. Cameron County file, 100–377, Hidalgo County file, 100–414, Duval County file, 100–392, Nueces County file, 100–441, Texas State Library, Austin.

145. Hinojosa, *Borderlands Town*, 117; De León, *Tejano Community*, 101–4.

146. Spaight, *Resources of Texas*, 146–47.

147. Hinojosa, *Borderlands Town*, 36–37; Paredes Manzano, *Homenaje*, 49.

148. Ramírez, *Ranch Life in Hidalgo County after 1850*; Champion, Margarito Hinojosa Sr., File no. 94.30.

149. Briscoe, "Narrative History of Corpus Christi," 292–93.

150. Hidalgo County, *Commissioners' Court Minutes*, May 19, 1856, July 2, 1856.

151. Hinojosa, *Borderlands Town*, 88–89.

152. Kingsbury Papers, Center for American History, Austin, Tex.

153. Lott and Martínez, *Kingdom of Zapata*, 67.

154. San Miguel, *"Let All of Them Take Heed"*, 11–12.

155. De León, *Tejano Community*, 188, 191–92.

156. Swadesh, *Los Primeros Pobladores*, 199.

157. Sarah Deutsch, "Landscape of Enclaves: Race Relations in the West," in *Under an Open Sky: Rethinking America's Western Past*, ed. William Cronon, George Miles, and Jay Gitlin (New York, 1992), 113.

158. Hidalgo County, *Probate Minutes*, Book A, 132–43 and 143–49.

159. John C. Rayburn and Virginia Kemp Rayburn, eds., *Century of Conflict, 1821–1913: Incidents in the Lives of William Neale and William A. Neale, Early Settlers in South Texas* (Waco, 1966), 68, 102.

160. Rankin, *Twenty Years*, 80–81.

161. Coker, *News from Brownsville*, 110 n. 14; Chauncey Devereux Stillman, *Charles Stillman, 1810–1875* (New York, 1956), 11.

162. For a study of intermarriage that asserts it promoted Hispanic—Anglo accommodation, see Rebecca Mcdowell Craver, *The Impact of Intimacy: Mexican—Anglo Intermarriage in New Mexico, 1821–1846*, in *Southwestern Studies* 66 (El Paso, 1982). *U.S. Census of Population, 1850*, Lower Río Grande Valley; Paredes Manzano, *Homenaje*, 86–87.

163. Hidalgo County Clerk, *Marriage Record*, vols. A, B, C, D, Edinburg, Tex.

164. Hidalgo County Clerk, *Marriage Record*, vol. 2, Edinburg, Tex.

165. Hidalgo County, *Probate Minutes*, Book A, Edinburg, Tex., 176–78 and 192–93.

166. Ibid., 213–16 and 241–42.

167. Estate of Gregorio Chapa Zamora, Probate File no. 62, Hidalgo County, Edinburg, Tex.

168. Canales, *Recollections of a Neighbor*.

169. Martín Alvarado, *Recollections*, n.d. (typescript, in King Ranch Archives, Kingsville, Tex.).

170. Mary Eloise de Garmo, *Pathfinders of Texas, 1836–1846: Being the Stories of Pioneer Families that Builded Well For Nueces County and Corpus Christi* (Austin, 1951), 120.

171. Ibid., 177.

172. Paul S. Taylor, *An American-Mexican Frontier: Nueces County, Texas* (Chapel Hill, 1934), 52–58. In much of the general literature, there is a depiction of conflict as an all-consuming process in which significant activities of the settlers are overlooked. For an example of this kind of historical writing, see Pierce, *Texas' Last Frontier*.

173. Deutsch, "Landscape of Enclaves," 110–31.

174. Weber, *Foreigners in Their Native Land*, 52–53, 59–61.

175. Coker, *News from Brownsville*, 328–30.

176. Rankin, *Twenty Years*, 51.

177. Anglos in Corpus Christi controlled the sale of black slaves obtained in the New Orleans to merchants who lived in the Lower Río Grande Valley. Briscoe, "Narrative History of Corpus Christi," 253.

178. Emory, *U.S.-Mexico Boundary*, vol. 1, pt. 1, 69.

179. Coker, *News from Brownsville*, 331; Taylor, *American-Mexican Frontier*, 58–59 n. 26.

180. *De Bow's Journal* 18 (1850), 709.

181. Domenech, *Missionary Adventures*, 254.

182. Clarke, *Travels in Mexico and California*, 8.

183. "Diary of C. C. Cox," *Southwestern Historical Quarterly* (October 1925), 131.

184. *John McAllen vs. Thaddeus M. Rhodes*, 65 Texas, 348–54.

185. G. D. Kingsbury to his sister, Aug. 16, 1858, Kingsbury Papers, Center for American History, University of Texas at Austin.

186. Coker, *News from Brownsville*, 330.

187. County Clerk, Hidalgo County, *Minutes of the District and County Courts*, vol. A, 1853–1886, Edinburg, Tex.

188. *U.S. Census of Agricultural Production*, 1880, manuscript, roll no. 44.

189. Hinojosa, *Borderlands Town*, 73.

190. Hidalgo County Clerk, *Court Minutes*, Book B.

191. Hidalgo County, *Commissioners' Court Minutes*, Aug. 19, 1861.

192. Hidalgo County, *Commissioners' Court Minutes.*

193. Mario T. García, "Porfirian Diplomacy and the Administration of Justice in Texas, 1877–1900," *Aztlán* 16, nos. 1–2 (1987), 1–25.

194. James B. Wells Papers, Center for American History, University of Texas at Austin, Box 2H222.

195. Martínez Papers, Box 32–2.

196. Hidalgo County Clerk, *Minutes of the District and County Courts*, vol. A., 1853–86, 175.

197. *The Sentinel* (Hidalgo, Tex.), Aug. 6, 1899, extract of article in Hidalgo County Historical Museum.

198. For the classic statement of these cowboy activities, see "Stock-Raising," *Texas Almanac for 1861* (Galveston, Tex., 1860), 148–49.

199. *Letters Received by the Office of the Adjutant General*, Main Series, 1881–1889, microcopy no. 689, National Archives, file 4389.

200. *De Bow's Journal* 18 (1850), 708.

201. Crummins, "Mansfield's Report of the Inspection of Texas in 1856," 128.

202. Mario Cerutti, "Monterrey and Its Ambito Regional, 1850–1910: Historical Context and Methodological Recommendations," in *Mexico's Regions: Comparative History and Development*, ed. Eric Van Young (San Diego, 1992), 150–52, 156.

203. See the testimony of witnesses to these raids on American-owned herds, in *United States of America on behalf of Robert J. Kleberg, Sr., et al., Richard King v. United Mexican States* (Washington, D.C., 1923), 51–61.

204. de Garmo, *Pathfinders of Texas*, 270.

205. Domenech, *Missionary Adventures*, 176, 228, 233–34, 240–41.

206. *De Bow's Journal* 18 (1850), 710.

207. Coker, *News from Brownsville*, 161, 178. 373–76, 390.

208. Hidalgo County, *Commissioners' Court Minutes*, Apr. 29, 1854.

209. Spaight, *Resources of Texas*, 50.

CHAPTER 5

1. Until 1911, Texas courts ruled that the treaty did not apply to lands in Texas because Texas had been a republic and then, prior to the signing of the treaty, a state. Richard Griswold del Castillo, *The Treaty of Guadalupe Hidalgo: A Legacy of Conflict* (Norman, 1990), 81–86. Also, see Galen D. Greaser and Jesús F. de la Teja, "Quieting Title to Spanish and Mexican Land Grants in the Trans-Nueces: The Bourland and Miller Commission, 1850–1852," *Southwestern Historical Quarterly* 95 (April 1992): 463–64. On Anglo–Hispanic conflict over land rights throughout the Southwest, see Weber, *Foreigners in Their Native Land*, 140–56; Westphall, *Mercedes Reales*, 74–76.

2. On conflict between Hispanics and Anglo newcomers, see Frank H. Dugan, "The 1850 Affair of the Brownsville Separatists," *Southwestern Historical Quarterly* 61 (October 1957), 271 n. 4, 273, 276, 282; and Robert J. Rosenbaum, *Mexicano Resistance in the Southwest: "The Sacred Right of Self-Preservation"* (Austin, 1981), 41; Montejano, *Anglos and Mexicans*, chap. 3, 50–74.

3. Hinojosa, *Borderlands Town*, 54–59.

4. Dugan, "1850 Affair of the Brownsville Separatists," 273–74. Garland was judge of Cameron County in 1853–54. He had previously served in the U.S. Congress and Louisiana Supreme Court. Ibid., 285 n. 28; Coker, News from Brownsville, 343. Mrs. Chapman was the wife of Major William W. Chapman, the first quartermaster at Fort Brown. She claimed that Garland was a fugitive from the law in Louisiana, where he had committed a forgery. Ibid., 93.

5. Dugan, "1850 Affair of the Brownsville Separatists," 273–75; *Cavazos v. Treviño*, 35 Texas, 135; Mauro, *Guide*, item 137.

6. Acuña, *Occupied America*, 43–44. García also felt beleaguered by squatters who claimed to have received title to *labor* rights from the government of Matamoros. The Bourland Commission, in 1850, rejected outright the petitions of numerous individuals for these *labores*. Texas General Land Office, *Bourland-Miller Commission Report* (Austin, 1851), n.p.

7. The conflicts generated over title to the Espíritu Santo grant led Juan N. Cortina, a Cavazos descendant, to launch a rebellion against what he called Anglo usurpers in 1859. Charles W. Goldfinch, "Juan N. Cortina, 1824–1892: A Re-Appraisal" (Master's thesis, University of Chicago, 1949), 35–41.

8. Dugan, "1850 Affair of the Brownsville Separatists," 273. On the defrauding of Nueces County Hispanic landholders and land purchases at tax sales, at "ridiculously low prices," see Taylor, *American-Mexican Frontier*, 9–14, 179–80, 182–83; and Briscoe, "Narrative History of Corpus Christi," 269–70.

9. Scott, *Royal Land Grants*, 64. Greaser and de la Teja, "Quieting Title," 447–49. Tamaulipas' colonization law of Dec. 15, 1826, allowed Anglos and Europeans to acquire land grants in its territory. One or two *empresario* contracts were awarded, but colonization efforts failed. See Secretary of State, *Laws and Decrees of the State of Coahuila and Texas in Spanish and English to which is added the Constitution of said State—Also—the Colonization Law of the State of Tamaulipas and Naturalization Law of the General Congress*, trans. J. P. Kimball, M.D. (Houston, 1839), 348. Previous to adjudication, less than a handful of

newcomers, such as John Young at Brownsville and H. L. Kinney of Corpus Christi, had acquired *derechos* and/or deeds to land grants. On Young's claims, see Mauro, *Guide*, items 185, 254, 308, 332; and on Kinney's, see ibid., item 330.

10. Greaser and de la Teja, "Quieting Title," 448–49. Smyth (1803–1866) was a North Carolina native who settled in Nacogdoches, Texas, in 1830. He was a teacher, surveyor, and elected official. He served as commissioner of the General Land Office from March 10, 1848, to March 1, 1857. Walter Prescott Webb, H. Bailey Carroll, and Eldon Stephen Branda, eds., *The Handbook of Texas*, 3 vols. (Austin, 1952; repr., Ann Arbor, 1976), 2:629.

11. Greaser and de la Teja, "Quieting Title," 450–52. Virginia-born Peter Hansborough Bell (1812–1898) came to Texas to fight for its independence. A soldier, Texas Ranger, and officer in the Mexican War, he was elected governor of Texas in 1849 and 1851. He also served in the U.S. Congress from 1853 to 1857. Later, he was a colonel in the Confederate Army. Webb et al., *Handbook of Texas*, 1:141.

12. Dugan, "1850 Affair of the Brownsville Separatists," 270–72, 276–77, 280–82; Greaser and de la Teja, "Quieting Title," 450–51.

13. Dugan, "1850 Affair of the Brownsville Separatists," 277–80; Greaser and de la Teja, "Quieting Title," 452.

14. Dugan, "1850 Affair of the Brownsville Separatists," 282–84. Judge Israel B. Bigelow, an ex-military contractor, was the first chief justice of Cameron County and state senator from 1851 to 1853. Mrs. Chapman wrote that Bigelow had started out as a carpenter, a trade he did not know; then he owned a grog shop in Matamoros, joined an expedition, and afterward "went to practicing law." He liked quarrels and frequently engaged in physical fights. Coker, *News from Brownsville*, 95–98, 112, 160, 182, 194, 292, 376. Milo Kearney, "De La Garzas, Ballís, and the Political History of the Region that Would Later Become Cameron County," in *More Studies in Brownsville History*, ed. Milo Kearney (Brownsville, 1989), 53–54.

15. Greaser and de la Teja, "Quieting Title," 453–54.

16. Dugan, "1850 Affair of the Brownsville Separatists," 285–87.

17. Greaser and de la Teja, "Quieting Title," 455–56.

18. H. P. Gammel, comp., *Laws of Texas*, General Laws, vol. 3, pt. 1, 582–87; Greaser and de la Teja, "Quieting Title," 454. Kentuckian William H. Bourland (1811–1865?) came to Texas in 1840. He served in two congresses of the Republic of Texas and in three state legislatures. He also served as a major in the Mexican War. Webb et al., *Handbook of Texas*, 1:196. James B. Miller, a native of Kentucky, moved to Texas in 1829 and settled at San Felipe de Austin, where he practiced medicine. Active in politics and a friend of Austin, he served in various offices. Ibid., 2:195. A well-known practicing attorney and judge who traveled the circuit in Texas, Robert Jones Rivers (1807–1854) was born in Virginia, migrated to Tennessee in the 1840s, and then to Texas in the late 1840s. Ibid., 2:480.

19. Gammel, *Laws of Texas*, Third Legislature, 2d sess., vol. 2, pt. 2, 798; Greaser and de la Teja, "Quieting Title," 455–56.

20. Greaser and de la Teja, "Quieting Title," 456–57.

21. Ibid., 457.

22. The tracts are listed in Gammel, *Laws of Texas*, vol. 4, pt. 1, 941–49; Greaser and de la

Teja, "Quieting Title," 459. On three of the applications, Young claimed sole ownership. On the other two, he claimed co-ownership with Mexican landholders. Mauro, *Guide*, items 27, 185, 254, 308, and 332.

23. Montejano, in *Anglos and Mexicans*, 34–38, asserts that this resolution of conflict was part of the peace structure in which Tejano elites accommodated Anglo merchants. At best, however, this must have been a gradual process, and it affected limited numbers of Tejano landholders, since not all merchants married Tejano landholders' daughters and in some places there were few Anglo or European merchants. The dynamics involved in this process are not fully explored by Montejano. For a view of its complexity, a process involving very few newcomers in Laredo, see Hinojosa, *Borderlands Town*, 102–5, 118.

24. Mauro, *Guide*, items 8 and 349.

25. Ibid., passim; Greaser and de la Teja, "Quieting Title," 460–61.

26. Mauro, *Guide*, passim.

27. Ibid., item 6.

28. Peter H. Bell, Governor, *Message of the Governor Transmitting the Report of the Commissioners to Investigate Land Titles West of the Nueces* (Austin, 1851), 42.

29. *The State of Texas v. A. A. Rodríguez et al.*, Judgement File, San Patricio, 1–738 (Austin, General Land Office).

30. Mauro, *Guide*, item 361.

31. *The State of Texas v. William F. Sprague et al.*, Cause No. 18,380, Judgement File, San Patricio, 1–386 (Austin, General Land Office).

32. Mauro, *Guide*, passim.

33. Greaser and de la Teja, "Quieting Title," 462–63.

34. Mauro, *Guide*, item 7.

35. Ibid., item 253.

36. Ibid., item 46.

37. Ibid., items 37, 55, 135, 141, 216, 219, 275, 286, 290, 306, 334. On H.B. No. 496, see *General Laws of the State of Texas*, 37th Legislature, reg. sess., Jan. 11, 1921. The bill passed in the House by a vote of 99 to 0 and in the Senate by a vote of 26 to 0.

38. Mauro, *Guide*, items 281, 327.

39. Ibid., items 33, 57.

40. Francisco de la Teja, General Land Office, personal communication, July 7, 1990; Greaser and de la Teja, "Quieting Title," 462, note under graph.

41. Dugan, "1850 Affair of the Brownsville Separatists," 281–82; Hinojosa, *Borderlands Town*, 21; Mauro, *Guide*, item 194; Hidalgo County, *Tax Rolls*, 1865.

CHAPTER 6

1. Outside of Corpus Christi and Brownsville, there were few Anglo and European settlers. Laredo had only seven Anglo households in 1850. Hinojosa, *Borderlands Town*, 61.

2. Hinojosa, *Borderlands Town*, 82–83; Jerry Thompson, *Mexican Texans in the Union Army* (El Paso, 1986), vii–ix.

3. Mauro, *Guide*, item 308; *U.S. Census of Population*, 1860, Hidalgo County. On Webber's purchase, see *Abstract of Title to Lands in the Agostadero del Gato Grant* (copy of abstract, Hidalgo and Starr Counties Abstract Company, Edinburg, Tex.). These white southerners had come to the Río Grande frontier to escape ostracism. The earliest arrived prior to 1860. Irby, *Backdoor at Bagdad*, 34, 64 n. 155.

4. Mauro, *Guide*, item 19.

5. Hidalgo County, *Tax Rolls*, 1852, 1865.

6. Seabury Papers, Box 2G168, 1–4. I do not mean to say that the settlers never conducted proper legal transactions on property matters. Their wills often indicate that documents of land purchases and sales and other contracts were to be found in their files, located in trunks and other deposit boxes. One of the first formal partitions involved the Llano Grande grant, which was partitioned into eight shares in early 1848. See *Abstract of Title to the Part of the Beamer and McDowell Properties in the "Llano Grande"*.

7. Scott, *Royal Land Grants*, 65. John Young and the McAllens acquired the bulk of the Santa Anita grant over a period covering three decades, purchasing undivided interests from the Domínguez family members who were the heirs to the grant and other Domínguez grantees. *Abstract of Title to the Lands in the Santa Anita Grant* (copy of abstract, Hidalgo and Starr Counties Abstract Company, Edinburg, Tex.).

8. *U.S. Census of Population*, 1900, Hidalgo County; Hidalgo County, *Tax Rolls*, 1895, 1900.

9. *U.S. Census of Population*, 1860, 1870, 1880, Hidalgo County; Hidalgo County, *Tax Rolls*, 1852, 1860, 1875, 1880, 1885.

10. Scott, *Royal Land Grants*, 66–67.

11. *U.S. Census of Population*, 1870, 1880, Hidalgo County; Hidalgo County, *Tax Rolls*, 1870, 1875, 1880.

12. Hidalgo County, *Tax Rolls*, 1870, 1880, 1885, 1896, 1900.

13. Ibid., 1865, 1870, 1880, 1885, 1896; Ramírez, *Four Generations*.

14. Hidalgo County, *Tax Rolls*, 1895, 1896.

15. Hidalgo County, *Probate Records*, Guardianship of the Person and Estate of Máxima Longoria de Ochoa, File no. 23.

16. Ibid., 1896.

17. Seabury Papers, Box 2G168, 6–7.

18. Hidalgo County, *Probate Records*, Guardianship of the Estate of the Minors, Moisés, Vicente, Sara, Virginia Cárdenas, File no. 40.

19. Hidalgo County, *Tax Rolls*, 1885, 1890, 1900.

20. Ibid., 1900.

21. Ibid., 1890, 1895, 1900.

22. Wells Papers, Box 2H203. For a very large foreclosure by a broker of Tejano lands, see *The Scottish American Mortgage Company, Limited v. Alejandro González and Estéfana Cadena de González, Albino Canales and Mauricio González*, Wells Papers, Box 2H203. This lawsuit involved a foreclosure of a twenty-two-thousand-dollar loan, for which the security consisted of fifty-three tracts of land of 640 acres each (fifty-three square miles of land).

These were lands purchased by the Tejanos from railroad surveys. The broker turned around and sold the land to Mrs. King under very favorable loan conditions. For two examples of rancher mortgages, see Mortgage with Power of Sale, Jesús Villarreal to Mrs. H. M. King; and Warranty Deed, Tomás Treviño and Mary E. Treviño, wife, to Mrs. H. M. King.

23. Seabury Papers, Box 2G168.

24. Ibid., Box 2G175.

25. Hidalgo County, *Probate Records*, Estate of Gregorio Chapa Zamora, Deceased, File Nos. 58 and 62.

26. Hidalgo County, *Tax Rolls*, 1865, 1870, 1875, 1880, 1885.

27. Ibid., 1885, 1890. On Basilio Pérez, see Seabury Papers, Box 2G168.

28. Joe Robert Baulch, "James B. Wells: South Texas Economic and Political Leader" (Ph.D. diss., Texas Tech University, 1974), 57–58.

29. Patricia Nelson Limerick, *The Legacy of Conquest: The Unbroken Past of the American West* (New York, 1988), 235–40.

30. Hidalgo County Commissioners' Court, *Minutes, Book A*, May 16, 1854, 21.

31. Ibid., May 14, 1877, 131; and May 6, 1878, 149–50. The deed to T. M. Rhodes is found in Hidalgo County, *Deed Records, Book C*, Feb. 15, 1877, 63.

32. Seabury Papers, Box 2G168.

33. For a good example of property disputes that escalated into armed threats, confrontations, and law suits, see the actions of Doña Eulalia Tijerina of Cameron County, in Wells Papers, Box 2H203, Letter from John G. Kenedy to James B. Wells, Feb. 20, 1888; *E. T[ijerina] de Cisneros v. The Kenedy Pasture Company*, No. 1513, District Court, Cameron County, Texas, April Term, 1888; Decree of the District Court, May 30, 1890. Montejano relies on the *vaqueros*' oral tradition in his discussion of this case. Whereas the *vaqueros* saw the conflict as one over access to a lake, the court records reveal that Mrs. Tijerina was claiming that the Kenedys interfered with her entry into and out of her *rancho*. The court agreed with her claim. See Montejano, *Anglos and Mexicans*, 52.

34. Moving fences to take in a neighbor's land persisted into the early decades of the twentieth century. The effects of those actions were detrimental to *rancheros* whose landholdings were not very extensive or who could not stop a trespasser in court. Montejano mentions this problem, but he offers no evidence on its occurrence in south Texas. Montejano, *Anglos and Mexicans*, 53. Also, see Roberto M. Villarreal, "The Mexican-American Vaqueros of the Kenedy Ranch; A Social History" (Master's thesis, Texas A & I University, 1972), 18–19. For an example of Anglos driving out *rancheros* by force, see the petition drawn up by Francis W. Seabury for the Plaintiff in *Rosendo Martínez v. Reuben Holbien and G. R. Adams*. Seabury Papers, Box 2G176. This incident allegedly occurred in Starr County in 1907.

35. For example, in neighboring Cameron County, Tamaulipas-born Francisco Yturria, an old associate of King and Kenedy, was a well-known and wealthy merchant, private banker, and landowner. His economic base made it possible for him to persist as an elite *ranchero*. In 1900, he owned seventy thousand acres of land in the county and grazed six thousand head of cattle as well as other livestock. Cameron County, *Tax Roll*, 1900. Most old Tejano *rancheros* and Mexican immigrants who persisted, however, generally did not have such extensive landholdings and livestock as Yturria.

36. Ramón V. Vela, interview, Edinburg, Tex., Mar. 9, 1981; *Edinburg Valley Review*, Dec. 12, 1924, l; J. L. Allhands, *Railroad to the Rio* (Salado, Tex., 1960), 132.

37. I have cited the appropriate sources evaluated here in the Introduction.

CHAPTER 7

1. Graf, "Economic History," 1:26–27, 48–49; Oscar J. Martínez, *Border Boom Town: Ciudad Juárez since 1848*, (Austin, 1975), 10–15; Hinojosa, *Borderland Town*, 64–65.

2. Graf, "Economic History," 1:xi, argues that the importance of the Lower Valley was its strategic commercial position, because the Río Grande was a funnel to lucrative trade markets in Mexico. Montejano, *Anglos and Mexicans*, 15–21, 41–43, sees economic penetration and development as the main themes in the "making of Texas."

3. Hinojosa, *Borderlands Town*, 65, 102; Arnoldo De León and Kenneth L. Stewart, "Lost Dreams and Found Fortunes: Mexican and Anglo Immigrants in South Texas, 1850–1900," *Western Historical Quarterly* 14 (July 1983), 295–96.

4. Nueces County, *Probate Minutes, "B," 1854–56*, 1.

5. *Texas Almanac, 1860*, 125–26.

6. John Zirvas Leyendecker Papers, Center for American History, University of Texas at Austin, Box 2M316.

7. Estate of Mary Cook, Nueces County, *Probate Minutes, "B," 1854–56*, 4; Estate of William Ward, Nueces County, *Probate Minutes, "B," 1854–56*, 60; and Estate of Gideon K. Lewis, Nueces County, *Probate Minutes, "B," 1854–56*, 69–70.

8. Estate of Gideon K. Lewis, Nueces County, *Probate Minutes, "B," 1854–56*, 69–70.

9. *Rancho Santa Gertrudis, Account Book, 1854*, King Ranch Archives, Kingsville, Tex.

10. John L. Haynes to John Hemphill, U.S. Senator, and A. J. Hamilton, U.S. Representative, Oct. 1, 1859, Haynes Papers, Box 2J144. On the movement of Mexican-owned herds to the south side of the river, see statement of E. H. Winfield, Assistant Marshall, *U.S. Census of Population*, 1850, Cameron, Starr, and Webb counties, manuscript.

11. *U.S. Non-Population Census, 1860*, Cameron and Hidalgo counties, manuscript.

12. Starr County, *Tax Rolls, 1860*, manuscript, Texas State Library, Austin.

13. Cameron County, *Brands "B," 1852–1870*. Volume A, which evidently covered the first four years of registrations (1848–52), is missing.

14. Starr County, *Record of Marks and Brands*, vol. 1, Special Collections, University of Texas at Pan American, Edinburg, Tex.

15. Webb County, *Marks and Brands*, vol. 1, Box 4L173, Center for American History, University of Texas at Austin. Similar registrations exist for Nueces County. *Book "A," A Record of Bonds, Etc., and Marriage Licences, 1846–1854*, is the first volume that contains, among other things, stock marks and brands of both Tejanos and Anglos. A second book, *Brands, "B," 1854–1869*, includes 194 pages of stock marks and brands, yeilding about eight hundred individual registrations by Tejanos as well as Anglos. Nueces County, *Book "A," A Record of Bonds, Etc., and Marriage Licences, 1846–1854*, and *Brands, Book "B," 1854–1869*.

16. Hidalgo County, *Marks and Brands, 1866–1873*; and ibid., *Marks and Brands, Book "B," 1873–1877*. Border *rancheros* had originally registered their brands in the river *villas* that

had jurisdiction over their districts. A U.S. official compiled a detailed list of these registrations. See U.S. Treasury Department, *Book 1041*, copy in Special Collections, Texas A & M University, College Station, Box 9, Western W9; also, see stockraisers lists for Reynosa in Reynosa Archives Special Collections, University of Texas at Pan American, Edinburg, Tex. And see Ray August, "Cowboys v. Rancheros: The Origins of Western American Livestock Law," *Southwestern Historical Quarterly* 96, no. 4 (April 1993), 457–88.

17. Cameron County, *Brand Record, Vol. B, 1852–1865.*

18. Ibid.

19. Webb County, *Marks and Brands*, vol. 1.

20. Webb County, *Marks and Brands*, vol. 2.

21. Livestock contracts, King Ranch Archives.

22. Hidalgo County, *Marks and Brands, Book B, 1873–1877.*

23. Cameron County, *Brands "B," 1852–1870.*

24. Webb County, *Marks and Brands*, vol. 2.

25. Hidalgo County, *Marks and Brands, Book B, 1873–1877.*

26. Gammel, *Laws of Texas*, 8:39.

27. Cameron County, *Brands "B," 1852–1870.*

28. Starr County, *Record of Marks and Brands*, vol. 1.

29. Hidalgo County, *Marks and Brands, 1866–1873.*

30. Webb County, *Marks and Brands*, vol. 1.

31. Starr County, *Record of Marks and Brands*, vol. 1.

32. There is a considerable historiography on "cattle kings," some on individual ranchers as well as books of a general nature. See Lea, *King Ranch*, both vols.; Robert Moorman Denhardt, *The King Ranch Quarter Horses: And Something of the Ranch and the Men that Bred Them* (Norman, 1970). Also, see Lewis Atherton, *The Cattle Kings* (Bloomington, 1961); Cox, *Historical and Biographical Record*, vol. 2.

33. Graf, "Economic History," 2:467–68.

34. Chatfield, *Twin Cities*, 40.

35. See, for example, *U.S. Census of Population*, 1860, 1870, 1880, and 1900, Hidalgo County, manuscript; and Hidalgo County, *Tax Rolls*, 1852–1900 inclusive.

36. *U.S. Non-Population Census, 1860*, Cameron and Nueces counties, manuscript.

37. *U.S. Non-Population Census, 1860*, Starr County, manuscript.

38. Ibid. For a brief history of the San Salvador del Tule grant, see Scott, *Royal Land Grants*, 49–56.

39. Estate of Miguel Ramírez García, File no. 237, Probate Records, Nueces County.

40. Abstract of Title to El Pasadizo, King Ranch Archives.

41. Zapata County, *Tax Rolls*, 1858, 1860, 1867, 1888–90.

42. Octavio Escobar Valadez, *Datos Biográficos de José María Valadez* (typescript copy in author's possession, courtesy of Laura Lamar García, Harlingen, Tex.), Dec. 12, 1947; *U.S. Non-Population Census*, 1870 and 1880, Nueces County, manuscript.

43. See statement of census marshal at the end of his enumeration in *U.S. Population Census*, Cameron, Starr, and Webb counties, 1850, manuscript.

44. *U.S. Non-Population Census*, Cameron County, 1860 and 1870, manuscript.

45. U.S. Congress, House, *Troubles on [the] Texas Frontier*, 36th Cong., 1st sess., Ex. Doc. no. 81 (Washington, D.C., 1860), 2–14; U.S. Congress, House, *Difficulties on the Southwestern Frontier*, 36th Cong., 1st sess., Ex. Doc. no. 52 (Washington, D.C., 1860), 70–82. The quote can be found in Weber, *Foreigners in Their Native Land*, 231–34.

46. Isidro Vizcaya Canales, *Los orígenes de la industrialización de Monterrey: una historia económica y social desde la caída del segundo imperio hasta el fin de la revolucion, 1867–1920* (Monterrey, Mexico, 1971), xiii–xiv.

47. Thompson, *Mexican Texans in the Union Army*, 37.

48. Robert L. Kerby, *Kirby Smith's Confederacy: The Trans-Mississippi South, 1863–1865* (New York, 1972), 77, 193, 385.

49. Partly in response to Cortina's disruption of normal economic and political relations with the United States, Mexican president Sebastian Lerdo de Tejada placed Cortina under arrest in February 1872. In May of 1876, Cortina escaped and made his way to the border, where he joined Porfirio Díaz, who was facing serious problems in maintaining peace along the border and who apparently doubted Cortina's loyalty to him. When Cortina faced execution by his enemies in Tamaulipas, who had arrested him again in early 1877, Díaz intervened and placed Cortina under house arrest in Mexico City, where he died in 1892. Michael G. Webster, "Texan Manifest Destiny and the Mexican Border Conflict" (Ph.D. diss., Indiana University, 1972), 17–21, 67–74, 79–89, 139–40, 143–44, 171, 178–79.

50. William Lee Richter, "The Army in Texas during Reconstruction" (Ph.D. diss., Louisiana State University, 1970), 168.

51. J. Nimmo Jr., *Letter from the Secretary of the Treasury Transmitting a Report from the Chief of the Bureau of Statistics in Response to a Resolution of the House Calling for Information in Regard to the Range and Ranch Cattle Traffic in the United States and Territories*, in U.S. Congress, House, Exec. Doc. No. 267, 1885, 11–12, 32, 74, 108–9; Cox, *Historical and Biographical Record*, 1:87; Hinojosa, *Borderlands Town*, 115–17; Lasater, *Falfurrias*, 23–24; Lehmann, *Forgotten Legions*, passim.

52. Hidalgo County, *Tax Rolls*, 1900.

53. Lehmann, *Forgotten Legions*, 23–33.

54. Graf, "Economic History," 2:438, 451; Chatfield, *Twin Cities*, 12, 37, 40–42; Cox, *Historical and Biographical Record*, 2:589–90; ibid., 1:15, 34–35; Nora Ethel Ramírez, "The Vaquero and Ranching in the Southwestern United States," (Ph.D. diss., Indiana University, 1979), 102. Also, see Walter Prescott Webb, *The Great Plains* (New York, 1931), 209–10.

55. For a thorough study of the Mexican *vaquero* in the Southwest, see Ramírez, "Vaquero and Ranching," 58–101. Also, see Webb, *Great Plains*, 210–11; Richard W. Slatta, *The Cowboy Encyclopedia* (Santa Barbara, Calif., 1994), 382–83.

56. Paredes, *With His Pistol*, 11.

57. Lea, *King Ranch*, 1:118–20, 123; Ramírez, "Vaquero and Ranching," 252.

58. Ramírez, "Vaquero and Ranching," 252.

59. Slatta, *Cowboy Encyclopedia*, 85–86. Among these, one must include cooks, household servants, masons, brickmakers, saddlemakers, carpenters, mechanics, silversmiths, teamsters, schoolteachers, and *caporales*, or foremen and administrators. For a detailed description of the variety of workers, men and women, found in a very large ranch and the apparent

ease with which they found employment and left, see Andrew Herbert Young, "Life and Labor on the King Ranch: 1853–1900" (Master's thesis, Texas A & M at Kingsville, 1992), chaps. 2–4.

60. Roberto Vela, "Memories of Laguna Seca," ed. and trans. Antonio H. Vela and Carlos F. Vela (typescript, copy in Special Collections, University of Texas at Pan American, 1978), 21–22, 24. Permanent cowboys developed a quasi-familial relationship to the *ranchero*, whereas seasonal workers were considered hired help. Slatta, *Cowboys of the Americas*, 93.

61. Ramírez, *Ranch Life in Hidalgo County after 1850*, sec. 5.

62. Joe Stanley Graham, *El Rancho in South Texas: Continuity and Change from 1750* (Denton, 1994), 25–26.

63. Ramírez, *Ranch Life in Hidalgo County after 1850*, sec. 1.

64. Since there are no careful studies of *vaquero* mobility, I base my assertion on a perusal of census data for *ranchos* in south Texas and the description of their employment found in the probate records of *rancheros*.

65. Commissioner of Patents, 1852, 340.

66. Young, "Life and Labor on the King Ranch," 29–33.

67. Spaight, *Resources of Texas*, 85–86; but see Slatta, who says eight to twelve dollars and quotes the Texas rate as twenty dollars in 1872, in *Cowboy Encyclopedia*, 384, 393.

68. Estate of Antonio Cantú Sánchez, file no. 72, Hidalgo County; Guardianship of Pedro Garza, file no. 61, Hidalgo County; and Estate of Julio Guzmán, Sr., file no. 79, Hidalgo County.

69. Roberto Vela, "Memories of Laguna Seca," 22.

70. Young, "Life and Labor on the King Ranch," 42–45. This drive started in the first days of March and the herd arrived in Abilene, Kansas, on Apr. 4, 1875.

71. Spaight, *Resources of Texas*, 146–47

72. Slatta, *Cowboy Encyclopedia*, 103.

73. *U.S. Census of Population*, Dimmit County, 1880, manuscript.

74. Texas, upon entering the Union in 1845, retained control over its immense public lands, which made it possible for the state to make use of them for economic development projects. Where public land was available, ranchers frequently obtained it at relatively reasonable prices. See Thomas Lloyd Miller, *The Public Lands of Texas, 1519–1970* (Norman, 1971).

75. Lehmann, *Forgotten Legions*, 29, 35; Ramírez, "Vaquero and Ranching," 39–41, 50–52.

76. Francis J. Parker to Horatio Hale, in the William G. Hale Papers, Center for American History, University of Texas at Austin, June 10, 1876.

77. Fant's lease fee is contained in Box 14, Santa Rosa Ranch Papers, Special Collections Library, Texas A & M University, College Station. Tejanos also made other arrangements with stockmen who had no land of their own or who needed pasture for their stock. For example, Abundio Garza charged the estate of Gregorio Chapa "25 cents [*mejicanos*] per month for each head of beef" that Chapa "placed in my pasture" in 1894 and 1895. See Estate of Gregorio Chapa, Deceased, No. 62, Hidalgo County. On Lasater's purchase price of land purchased from Tejanos, see Lasater, *Falfurrias*, 33–36, 42–45.

78. Hidalgo County, *Tax Rolls*, 1900; Cameron County, *Tax Rolls*, 1900. Montejano, *Anglos and Mexicans*, 68–69.

79. Gene M. Gressley, *Bankers and Cattlemen* (New York, 1966), 192–94.

80. Anders, *Boss Rule in South Texas*, 7–8, 46–48, 153–154, 168. Many of these tax practices continued to benefit ranchers after 1900. On the letter from Kleberg to Wells, see Wells Papers, Box 2H203, July 26, 1897.

81. Nimmo, *Letter from the Secretary of the Treasury*, 26, 32. According to Nimmo, it took ten years to stock the arid West with Texas cattle. See J. Nimmo, Jr., "Uncle Sam's Farm: The Reclamation of the Arid Region of the United States by Means of Irrigation," in *Frank Leslie's Illustrated Newspaper*, Nov. 16, 23, and 30, 1889, and Dec. 7, 1889, 12. Also, see Lehmann, *Forgotten Legions*, 47–48.

82. *U.S. Census of 1880*, Cotton Production, 33.

83. Lehmann, *Forgotten Legions*, 48.

84. *U.S. Census of 1880*, Cotton Production, 33–34; Lehmann, *Forgotten Legions*, 43, 45.

85. James C. Nagle, *Irrigation in Texas* (Washington D.C.: U.S. Dept. of Agriculture, 1910), 9.

86. E. J. Davis, "Description of South-Western Texas," *Texas Almanac, 1868*, 112.

87. Lehmann, *Forgotten Legions*, 43–45, 90–96; De León, *Tejano Community*, 84; Lea, *King Ranch*, 2:502–5. Sheep could go without water longer than cattle, but sheep were not saved from the ravages of droughts.

88. U.S. Congress, House, *Letter from the Secretary of State Transmitting to the Speaker of the House Reports from the Consuls of the United State on Cattle and Dairy Farming*, 49th Cong., 1st sess., Ex. Doc. no. 51 (Washington, D.C., 1887), 576–96.

89. Matías Romero, *Geographical and Statistical Notes on Mexico* (New York and London, 1898), 56–57.

90. Ezra A. Carmen, H. A. Heath, and John Minro, "Special Report on the History and Present Condition of the Sheep Industry in the United States," U.S.D.A., Bureau of Animal Industry, (Washington, D.C., 1892), 897–98; henceforth cited as "Special Report."

91. Gilbert, in "Texas and Her Prospects," in *DeBow's Journal* 16 (1848), 474, 476.

92. John L. Hayes, "Sheep Husbandry in the South," in *Message from the President of the United States Communicating in Answer to a Senate Resolution of June 17, 1878*, 45th Cong., 3d sess., Senate Exec. Doc. No. 15, 35, 41. In regard to ranchers' concerns about harmful grasses and disease, see statement of H. Chamberlain of Nueces County in ibid., 52. Also, see "Special Report", 896, 907, 910.

93. Erasmo García, interview.

94. Commissioner of Patents, 1852, 340. For a detailed description of these natural and human assets essential for the sheep industry, see especially the statement of Mr. F. W. Shaeffer of San Diego, Tex., in Hayes, "Sheep Husbandry in the South," 99–104.

95. Ibid., 52, 102, 103.

96. "Special Report," 910.

97. Gilbert, in "Texas and Her Prospects," 474, 476.

98. Commissioner of Patents (1852), 32d Cong., 1st sess., House Exec. Doc. No. 102.

99. "Special Report," 897.

100. Ibid., 907.

101. Hayes, "Sheep Husbandry in the South," 1–2, 6, 17, 19, 31.

102. "Special Report," 910.

103. Hayes, "Sheep Husbandry in the South," 106, 108–10; "Special Report," 910.

104. De León, *Tejano Community*, 79–86.

105. Worcester, *Texas Longhorn*, chaps. 1 and 2, 3–46.

106. John E. Rouse, *The Criollo: Spanish Cattle in the Americas* (Norman, 1977), 86–88, 191–96.

107. According to Nimmo, the quality of the range beef was improved considerably by crossing "native" and Texas cows with graded or full-blooded imported stock. Nimmo, "Uncle Sam's Farm," 12. Also, see Worcester, *Texas Longhorn*, 65–72.

108. Montejano, *Anglos and Mexicans*, 66–67; Cox, *Historical and Biographical Record*, 1:87, 103, 139; Gressley, *Bankers and Cattlemen*, 108–11.

109. Chatfield, *Twin Cities*, 2. It is difficult to know precisely what share of cattle production was produced in south Texas, but it must have been considerable in view of the fact that its national value in 1884 was placed at 40 million dollars by a well-respected government authority on the livestock traffic of the West. See J. Nimmo, Jr., "The American Cow-boy," *Harpers Magazine* (November 1886), 883.

110. Hayes, "Sheep Husbandry in the South," 105.

111. Chatfield, *Twin Cities*, 38.

112. John Ashton, "Livestock Industry of South Texas" (WPA Writers Project, 1936), 20–21, in Center for American History, University of Texas at Austin. See also Lehmann, *Forgotten Legions*, 40.

113. Lasater, *Falfurrias*, 24.

114. J. B. Wilkinson, *Laredo and the Río Grande Frontier* (Austin, 1975), 327. Joseph H. Vale Papers, Center for American History, Austin, Tex., Box 2h116.

115. Marvin Hunter, ed., *The Trail Drivers of Texas*, 2d ed. (Nashville, 1925), 24, 55–56.

116. On the marketing of livestock, see Ashton, "Livestock Industry," 21; De León, *Tejano Community*, 79–82; Lehmann, *Forgotten Legions*, 31–32, 70–72, 77.

117. *U.S. Non-Population Census*, 1870, Cameron County, manuscript.

118. *U.S. Non-Population Census*, 1870, Hidalgo County, manuscript.

119. *U.S. Non-Population Census*, 1870, Duval County, manuscript.

120. *U.S. Non-Population Census*, 1870, Nueces County, manuscript.

121. *U.S. Non-Population Census*, 1870, Webb County, manuscript.

122. These records of livestock sales are based on laws that were adopted shortly after the Civil War. In 1867, Texas law required that upon the sale, alienation, or transfer of livestock, a written conveyance specifying the number of animals, marks, and brands must accompany such a transaction and, upon the completion of the transaction, the purchaser was to provide a bill of sale to the county clerk's office, to be properly recorded in a book kept by the clerk for that purpose. Such a sale would then be noted on the record of the original marks and brands in the name of the purchaser. In addition to the above provisions, an 1871 statutory provision required an inspector or his deputy to inspect the animals before they

left the county. In 1874, a new law required that the signing of the transaction between the vendor and vendee was to take place under the supervision of "some officer authorized to authenticate instruments for record in this State [Texas]." Gammel, *Laws of Texas,* 5:1141; ibid., 6:1017; and the quotation is from ibid., 8:38.

123. Hidalgo County, *Tax Rolls,* 1852, 1855, 1865.

124. Hidalgo County, *Tax Rolls,* 1865; Scott, *Royal Land Grants,* 64.

125. Hidalgo County, *Tax Rolls,* 1852, 1855, 1865.

126. Hidalgo County, *Marks and Brands, Book "B," 1866–1873.*

127. Hidalgo County, *Marks and Brands, 1873–1877.*

128. Hidalgo County, *Probate Minutes,* Book "A," 113–16; Hidalgo County, *Tax Rolls,* 1870, 1875, 1880, 1885.

129. Lehmann, *Forgotten Legions,* 36–37, 164, 169, 171, 178–79.

130. "Leo J. Leo to Speak on Dougherty Era," *Edinburg Daily Review,* Sept. 14, 1980, 1. Dougherty, who was Irish, came to the Lower Valley with Gen. Zachary Taylor in 1846. He stayed and became a district judge. His ranch, Zacatal, was located on the southeastern corner of Hidalgo County.

131. Chatfield, *Twin Cities,* 7.

132. Lasater, *Falfurrias,* 25–26, 33–36; Lehmann, *Forgotten Legions,* 29, 54, 87, 90, 110, 164. Prior to the Civil War, Texas wool sold for twenty cents per pound. J. de Cordova, *Texas: Her Resources and Her Public Men* (Philadelphia, 1858; repr., Waco, 1969), 55.

133. Scott, *Royal Land Grants,* 64; Hidalgo County, *Tax Rolls,* 1852.

134. Scott, *Royal Land Grants,* 65; John McAllen to Gilbert D. Kingsburg, Jan. 31 and Nov. 4, 1869, and Nov. 24, 1870, Kingsbury Papers.

135. *U.S. Census of Population,* 1880, Hidalgo County, manuscript.

136. These Anglos were a mixed community of people. The men were married to mostly black or mulattoes. Some of their children married Mexicans. *U.S Census of Population,* 1860, 1870, 1880, 1900, Hidalgo County.

137. Ibid.

138. Hidalgo County, *Tax Rolls,* 1870, 1875, 1880, 1885, 1890, 1895, 1900.

139. Thaddeus M. Rhodes to H. M. Fields, Feb. 11 and 19, 1898. H. M. Fields Papers, Center For American History, University of Texas at Austin.

CHAPTER 8

1. Hidalgo County, *Tax Rolls,* 1885, 1890, 1895, 1900; Jimmy M. Skaggs, *The Cattle-Trailing Industry: Between Supply and Demand, 1866–1890* (Lawrence, Kans., 1973), 3–4, 63–65, 68, 71, 148 n. 27. For evidence of the strong shift to large-scale commercial ranching, see the chattel mortgages of D. R. Fant to D. Sullivan & Co. of San Antonio and those of Chittum & Parr to R. Driscoll of Corpus Christi and to D. Sullivan & Co. For example, on June 5, 1902 Chittum & Parr conveyed 12,500 cattle located on the Santa Rosa ranch in Hidalgo County to D. Sullivan & Co. to secure one note of $194,837.30. The note was due six months from the date of making at 8 percent. Box 14, Santa Rosa Ranch Papers. Special Collections Library, Texas A & M University, College Station.

2. Lasater, *Falfurrias*, 9–10, 15, 19–20, 22, 24–26.

3. Ibid., 28–29, 37–38.

4. Ibid., 39, 46, 49, 51.

5. *U.S. Census of Population*, 1900, Hidalgo County; Hidalgo County, *Tax Rolls*, 1885, 1890, 1895, 1900. Sprague regularly consigned shipments of animal hides, hair, and bones to H. M. Field, for example, on Apr. 28, 1897; Mar. 14, Apr. 7, June 14, Nov. 19, and Dec. 15, 1898, and Jan. 11, 1899. H. M. Field Papers. Also, see William F. Sprague File, Hidalgo County Historical Museum, Edinburg, Tex.

6. Hidalgo County, *Tax Rolls*, 1885, 1890, 1900.

7. Ibid., 1890, 1895, 1900.

8. Ibid.; Chatfield, *Twin Cities*, 12, 20–22, 39.

9. Hidalgo County, *Tax Rolls*, 1890, 1895, 1900.

10. Cameron County, *Tax Rolls*, 1890, 1900.

11. Lea, *King Ranch*, 2:489–90; Lehmann, *Forgotten Legions*, 95–96.

12. Chatfield, *Twin Cities*, 95.

13. N. L. Wood to H. M. Field, Aug. 26 and Nov. 30, 1898, H. M. Field Papers; B. F. Kidder to H. M. Field, July 13, 1899, H. M. Field Papers.

14. Lehmann, *Forgotten Legions*, 86–90; Lea, *King Ranch*, 2:484–85; Lasater, *Falfurrias*, 50.

15. *U.S. Census of Agriculture*, 1890; ibid., 1900.

16. *Corpus Christi Weekly Caller* (hereafter cited as *Caller*), July 21, 1893, 1–3.

17. Department of State, *Proceedings of the International Water and Boundary Commission, United States and Mexico, Treaties of 1884 and 1889: Equitable Distribution of the Waters of the Río Grande*, 2 vols. (Washington, D.C., 1903), 1:174.

18. *Caller*, Apr. 21, 1899, 8–11; N. L. Wood to H. M. Field, Nov. 8, 1898, H. M. Field Papers.

19. D. R. Fant to H. M. Field, Mar. 29, 1899, H. M. Field Papers.

20. Lehmann, *Forgotten Legions*, 90.

21. Chatfield, *Twin Cities*, 40.

22. "Chatones [Ranch] Stock," in H. M. Field, *Letterbook*, Dec. 11, 1893, 461, H. M. Field Papers.

23. L. Ward, in Field, *Letterbook*, Mar. 16, 1895, 692, in ibid.; McAllen to Kingsbury, Nov. 24, 1870, Kingsbury Papers.

24. "D. Villarreal," in Field, *Letterbook*, Feb. 12, 1895, 684, in H. M. Field Papers; Lehmann, *Forgotten Legions*, 29, 54, 87, 90, 110, 164; Lasater, *Falfurrias*, 25–26, 33–36.

25. Rhodes to Field, Dec. 1, 1898, H. M. Field Papers.

26. Fant to Field, Mar. 29, 1899, H. M. Field Papers.

27. Florencio Sáenz to Field, May 29, 1899, H. M. Field Papers.

28. H. P. Drought & Co. Papers, Special Collection Library, University of Texas at San Antonio; Encinal County, *Registry of Chattel Mortgages*, vol. 1 (Special Collections, Pan American); Starr County, *Chattel Mortgages*, Book 1 (Special Collections, Pan American).

29. Lasater, *Falfurrias*, 45–46, 48, 50; Gene M. Gressley, "Broker to the British: Francis Smith and Company," *Southwestern Historical Quarterly* 61 (July 1967): 16–18, 22.

30. *Caller*, Apr. 15, 1892, 1–3, and Aug. 29, 1892, 6–2.

31. Ibid., Sept. 19, 1886, 8–1, 3, 10; Oct. 17, 1886, 4–4;, Oct. 29, 1887, 4–3, 13; and Oct. 20, 1888, 1–6 and 1–4; Nimmo, *Letter from the Secretary of the Treasury*, 105; Ashton, "Livestock Industry," 31–32.

32. *Caller*, May 26, 1893, 3–1; Aug. 26, 1893, 1–3; May 21, 1886, 4–5.

33. Ibid., Oct. 27, 1899, 1–2.

34. Ibid., July 16, 1886, 4–3; July 28, 1888, 1–5; Dec. 22, 1888, 4–3.

35. Estate of Antonio Caño, Hidalgo County, *Probate Minutes*, Book A, 189–91.

36. Estate of Cipriano Hinojosa, June 7, 1878, Hidalgo County, *Probate Minutes*, Book A, 213–16.

37. Estate of John O. Thompson, Feb. 24, 1879, Hidalgo County, *Probate Minutes*, Book A, 246–49.

38. Guadalupe Rivas de Días, Hidalgo County, *Probate Minutes*, Book B, 58.

39. Will of Antonio Cano, June 2, 1876, Hidalgo County, *Probate Minutes*, Book A, 189–90.

40. Félix Cano, Hidalgo County, *Probate Minutes*, Book B, 45–46.

41. Felipe Villanueva Garza, Hidalgo County, *Probate Minutes*, Book B, 408–9.

42. Estate of Antonio Ballí Cavazos, Hidalgo County, Probate File No. 32.

43. Estate of Leandro de la Garza, Hidalgo County, Probate File No. 5; Estate of Josefa Hinojosa, 1855, Hidalgo County, Probate File not numbered. See also Petition of Doña Josefa de Hinojosa and Inventory of the Estate of Leandro de la Garza, Hidalgo County, *Probate Minutes*, Book A, 23–30.

44. Will of Antonio Guerra, Feb. 21, 1875, Hidalgo County, *Probate Minutes*, Book A, 209.

45. Estate of Ignacio de Ochoa, Hidalgo County, Probate File No. 102.

46. Estate of Marcos Guzmán, Hidalgo County, Probate File No. 73.

47. Estate of Mauricia F. de Cano, Hidalgo County, Probate File No. 102.

48. Will of Antonio Cano, June 2, 1876, Hidalgo County, *Probate Minutes*, Book A, 189–90.

49. Estate of Macedonio Vela, Hidalgo County, Probate File No. 213.

50. Estate of Cipriano Hinojosa, Hidalgo County, *Probate Minutes*, Book A, 213–16.

51. Estate of Marcos de Ochoa, Hidalgo County, Probate File No. 21.

52. Estate of Manuela Guzmán de Cantú, Hidalgo County, Probate File No. 15.

53. Estate of A. J. Leo, Hidalgo County, Probate File No. 20.

54. Estate of Felipe Villanueva Garza, Hidalgo County, Probate File No. 26.

55. See petitions of Yreneo Zamora and Tomás Zamora, Hidalgo County, *Probate Minutes*, Book A, 3–5; Petition of Indalecio Domínguez and Inventory of the Estate of Juan José Hinojosa, ibid., 9–14. Estate of José María Mora, Hidalgo County, Probate File No. 25.

56. Estate of Juan Cantú and Guardianship of Gregorio Cantú, Minor, Hidalgo County, Probate File No. 7.

57. Guardianships of the Persons and Estate of Minor Children of Archibald A. Johnston, Hidalgo County, Probate File No. 34.

58. Estate of Juan Cantú and Guardianship of Gregorio Cantú, Minor, Hidalgo County, Probate File No. 7; Estate of Hilario Tijerina, Hidalgo County, Probate File No. 36.

59. Guardianship of the Estate and Person of Manuel Benavides, Hidalgo County, Probate File No. 9.

60. Estate of Minors Moisés, Vicente, Sara, and Virginia Cárdenas, Hidalgo County, Probate File No. 40.

61. Guardianship of the Minors Gregorio Quiroga, Hidalgo County, Probate File No. 49.

62. Estate of L. H. Box, Hidalgo County, Probate File No. 51; Guardianship of the Person and Estate of Box Children, Hidalgo County, Probate File No. 52.

63. Guardianship of the Estate and Person of Crisanta Garza, Hidalgo County, Probate File No. 10.

64. Estate of Minor Children of Manuel Fuentes, Hidalgo County, Probate File No. 2.

65. Guardianship of the Children of Higinia C. de Cano, Hidalgo County, Probate File No. 13; Estate of Higinia C. de Cano, Hidalgo County, Probate File No. 14.

66. Estate of Victoria Ballí, Hidalgo County, Probate File No. 33.

67. Estate of Leonardo Congoria, Hidalgo County, Probate File No. 35.

68. Estate of Ignacio de Ochoa, Hidalgo County Probate File No. 22; Guardianship of Máxima C. de Ochoa, Hidalgo County, Probate File No. 23; Hidalgo County, *Probate Minutes*, Book B, 387–93, 411–12, 414–16, 426–38, 453–54.

69. Estate of Bárbara López de Solís, Hidalgo County, Probate File No. 44 No. 45.

70. Estate of Felicitas Solís Zamora, Hidalgo County, Probate File No. 69 No. 70.

71. Estate of Plácida Cantú de Johnston, Hidalgo County, Probate File No. 16.

72. Inventory of Jacinto Olivares, Hidalgo County, *Probate Minutes*, Book A, 243, 267–69, 272; Book B, 23–26, 35–37.

73. Estate of Juan Camacho, Hidalgo County, Probate File No. 38; Estate of Genoveva Garza, Hidalgo County, Probate File No. 52.

74. Lt. Chatfield, *Twin Cities*, 39–41; Stambaugh and Stambaugh, *Lower Rio Grande*, 182–89.

75. *Eighth and Twelfth Census of the United States, 1860 and 1900.*

76. *Eleventh Census of the United States, 1890.*

77. Lt. Chatfield, *Twin Cities*, 37–38.

78. Starr County, Texas, *Tax Rolls*, 1900; Zapata County, Texas, *Tax Rolls*, 1900.

79. Lt. Chatfield, *Twin Cities*, 43.

80. Ibid., 42; *U.S. Census of Population*, Hidalgo County, 1880.

81. Lt. Chatfield, *Twin Cities*, 41–42; Ramírez, *Ranch Life after 1850*, pt. 2; De León, *Tejano Community*, 100.

82. Lt. Chatfield, *Twin Cities*, 4, 21, 37, 41; *Caller*, May 6, 1892, 6–2; May 20, 1892, 6–2; Apr. 21, 1899, 8–1; *Austin Statesman*, Jan. 22, 1892, 1–4; Apr. 29, 1892, 1–2; Feb. 24, 1894, 1–5.

83. Lt. Chatfield, *Twin Cities*, 5, 26, 37, 40–42.

84. *Seventh, Eighth, Ninth, Tenth, Eleventh, and Twelfth Census of the United States, 1850, 1860, 1870, 1880, 1890, 1900.* Lt. Chatfield, *Twin Cities*, 36.

85. Lt. Chatfield, *Twin Cities*, 22, 36, 40; Anders, *Bosses in South Texas*, 50; and *Brownsville Daily Herald*, Mar. 7, 1904, 1; May 23, 1904, 1.

86. *Twelfth Census of the United States*, 1900.

87. *Eleventh and Twelfth Census of the United States, 1890, 1900.*

88. Lt. Chatfield, *Twin Cities*, 40–41; Stambaugh and Stambaugh, *Lower Rio Grande*, 183–84, 187; and Joseph L. Clark and Elton M. Scott, *The Texas Gulf Coast: Its History and Development*, 2 vols. (New York, 1955), 1:37–38.

89. On Closner's irrigation works, see Clark and Scott, *Gulf Coast*, 38. On Forto and the Longorias, see Stambaugh and Stambaugh, *Lower Rio Grande*, 193. On the Santa María planters, see Ruby Wooldridge, "The Palm Grove-Rabb Plantation," in Kearney, *Studies in Brownsville History*, 257–58. Wooldridge dates the Rabb-Starck plantation as beginning in 1876. Unfortunately, she only provides general information on crop production and related activities.

90. Rhodes to Field, Feb. 19, 1898, Field Papers.

91. Clark and Scott, *Gulf Coast*, 38.

92. On the development of truck farming in parts of south Texas, see De León, *Tejano Community*, 101. On the optimism produced by planned railroad construction, see *Brownsville Daily Herald*, Jan. 10, 1901, 1; ibid., January 14, 1901, 3.

93. Nimmo, *Letter from the Secretary*, 9–11; Nimmo, "The American Cow-boy," *Harpers Magazine* (November 1886), 883.

CHAPTER 9

1. John R. Van Ness, "Hispanic Land Grants: Ecology and Subsistence in the Uplands of Northern New Mexico and Southern Colorado," in *Land, Water, and Culture: New Perspectives on Hispanic Land Grants*, ed. Charles L. Briggs and John R. Van Ness (Albuquerque, 1987), 162–77.

2. Roxanne Dunbar Ortiz, *Roots of Resistance: Land Tenure in New Mexico, 1680–1980* (Los Angeles, 1982), 95–96.

3. Ibid., 103–4; Malcolm Ebright, "New Mexican Land Grants: The Legal Background," in Briggs and Van Ness, *Land, Water, and Culture*, 41.

4. Ortiz, *Roots of Resistance*, 96; Ebright, "New Mexican Land Grants," 46–47.

5. Ortiz, *Roots of Resistance*, 96; Ebright, "New Mexican Land Grants," 37–40, 42–43.

6. Ortiz, *Roots of Resistance*, 95.

7. Westphall, *Mercedes Reales*, 252–54, 258.

8. Ortiz, *Roots of Resistance*, 96–105; Westphall, *Mercedes Reales*, chap. 10, 217–36; González, *Spanish-Americans*, 49–54. There is a strong need for research on the issue of differing legal systems and how they were applied to land grants. See Ebright, *Spanish and Mexican Land Grants and the Law*, introduction, 5–7. This issue demands research beyond the scope of this study. Also, see Malcolm Ebright's newest exposition on this theme in "New Mexican Land Grants," 15–66.

9. Jay J. Wagoner, *Early Arizona: Prehistory to Civil War* (Tempe, 1975), 159, 164–66. Weber, *Mexican Frontier*, 183.

10. Iris H. W. Engstrand, "An Enduring Legacy: California Ranchos in Historical Perspective," in *Spanish and Mexican Land Grants and the Law*, ed. Malcolm Ebright (Manhattan, Kans., 1989), 36.

11. Paul W. Gates, *California Ranchos and Farms, 1846–1862* (Madison, 1967), 6, 9.

12. Ibid., 1–2.

13. Pitt, *Decline of Californios*, 86–94; Paul W. Gates, "Adjudication of Spanish-Mexican Land Claims in California," *The Huntington Library Quarterly* 21, no. 3 (May 1958): 225, 229–30.

14. Gates, "Adjudication of Spanish-Mexican Claims," 215–16, 219–22, 226.

15. Ibid., 230–35.

16. On the Espíritu Santo, see County Clerk, Cameron County, *Deed Records*, vol. 1, 298–323; on the Starr County grants, see Seabury Papers, Box 2G175.

17. Scott, *Historical Heritage*, 121; Scott, *Royal Land Grants*, 37, 57. On land as payment for a legal fee, see deeds from Ramona Dávila to L. R. Wren and R. B. Rentfro in County Clerk, Hidalgo County, *Deed Records*, Vol. "G-H," Oct. 2, 1895. County Clerk, Nueces County, Corpus Christi, Estate of Manuel Ramírez Elizondo, No. 253, Book C, 188–91.

18. Anders, *Boss Rule in South Texas*, 20, 168.

19. Hidalgo County, *Tax Rolls*, 1890, 1893, 1900.

20. Anders, *Boss Rule in South Texas*, 168.

21. Hidalgo County, *Commissioners' Court Minutes*, Feb. 12, 1891, May 15, 1891, Feb. 16, 1898, May 8, 1899, and May 14, 1900. See also Montejano, *Anglos and Mexicans*, 57–58. In Texas, fence-cutting activities peaked in 1883, when livestock prices were high and many cowmen had no access to grass or water for their herds. See Wayne Gard, "The Fence-Cutters," *Southwestern Historical Quarterly* 51 (July 1947): 1–15.

22. Gates, "Adjudication of Spanish-Mexican Claims," 226; Ebright, "New Mexican Land Grants," 37.

23. Gates, "Adjudication of Spanish-Mexican Claims," 229; Engstrand, "Enduring Legacy," 36–39.

24. Mauro, item 244; Martínez Papers, Box 26.

25. Nearly every single history of a major land grant bears this out. See, for example, Clark S. Knowlton, "The Mora Land Grant: A New Mexican Tragedy," in Ebright, *Spanish and Mexican Land Grants*, 59–73.

26. Ebright, "New Mexican Land Grants," 41.

27. Anders, *Boss Rule in South Texas*, 15. Wells Papers, Box 2H224. Raymond had sent a similar contemptible letter regarding other Tejano landholders on Feb. 21, 1897.

EPILOGUE

1. Hass, *Historical Identity in California*, chap. 1, 13–44. Also, see Martin, *Chihuahua in the Eighteenth Century*.

2. Jones, *Los Paisanos*, 70–71; Hass, *Historical Identity in California*, 48–53.

3. Ibid., 70; De la Teja, *San Antonio de Béxar*, esp. chap. 7, 139–56, and 158–60.

4. Arrom, *Women of Mexico City*, 76–78, asserts that social and political stability was the fundamental objective of Spanish government for its New World subjects. Legal principles and social mores regarding patriarchy supported this goal. I believe that further study would show this was applicable to town settlers in regions like the Lower Valley.

5. A brief summary of economic growth in the northeastern part of northern Mexico is in

Pedro Pérez Herrero, "Regional Conformation in Mexico, 1700–1850: Models and Hypotheses," in Van Young, *Mexico's Regions*, 130–31.

6. Weber, *Mexican Frontier*, 280.

7. Montejano, *Anglos and Mexicans*, 79–82.

8. It is likely that the early history of Nuevo León (in the seventeenth century) also reflected a tendency toward large landholdings or haciendas because of the initial desire to obtain settlers at a time when the province was on the verge of complete failure. But more study is needed to clarify the exact nature of land tenure in Nuevo León. See Ida Altman, "A Family and Region in the Northern Fringe Lands: The Marqueses de Aguayo of Nuevo León and Coahuila," in *Provinces of Early Mexico*, 254. The predominance of *ranchos* over *haciendas* in Tamaulipas continued after the war with Mexico. The state governor reported that in 1849 there were 54 *haciendas* and 1,017 ranches. Rosaura Alicia Dávila and Oscar Rivera Saldaña, *Matamoros en la guerra con los Estados Unidos*, Matamoros Collection, no. 2 (Matamoros, Tamp., Mexico, 1996), 61.

9. Hass, *Historical Identity in California*, 62–63, 73–74, 108.

10. Mixed ranching began in the second half of the sixteenth century in central Mexican Bajío, where both cattle and sheep *estancias* were founded, with the latter predominating. Stockmen from the Jilotepec–Huichapan region introduced sheep *haciendas* and cattle into Nuevo León about 1600. Cavazos Garza, *Breve historia de Nuevo León*, chap. 6, 58–69. Also, see Karl W. Butzer and Elisabeth K. Butzer, "The Sixteenth-Century Environment of the Central Mexican Bajío: Archival Reconstruction from Spanish Land Grants," in *Culture, Form, and Place: Essays in Cultural and Historical Geography*, ed. Kent Mathewson, in *Geoscience and Man*, vol. 32 (Baton Rouge, La., 1993), table 1, 94. Jordan, in *North American Cattle-Ranching Frontiers*, 147–56, asserts that Hispanic cattle ranching along the Texas Gulf Coast, from the Lower Valley to Victoria, was influenced by Tamaulipas practices, which arose in the Tampico delta and along the coast of Veracruz. It seems to me that he is partly correct in that the Huasteca contributed some settlers to Escandón's colony, but the contributions of Nuevo León *rancheros* in the Lower Valley were predominant in the development of ranching in south Texas.

11. Hass, *Historical Identity in California*, 64–65.

12. Frederick M. Katz, "Labor Conditions on Haciendas in Porfirian Mexico: Some Trends and Tendencies," *Hispanic American Historical Review* 54, no. 1 (1972): 1–47.

13. Martínez, *Ciudad Juárez since 1848*, 13–21, 25–30.

14. John R. Chávez, *The Lost Land: The Chicano Image of the Southwest* (Albuquerque, 1984).

15. Hass, *Historical Identity in California*, 166–67.

16. County Clerk, Cameron County, Brownsville, Tex., *Record of Alien Owners*, 2 vols.; County Clerk, Hidalgo County, Edinburg, Tex., *Record of Alien Owners*, 3 vols.

INDEX